Middle English Metrical Romances

Middle English Metrical Romances

edited by

Walter Hoyt French

and

Charles Brockway Hale

VOLUME II

NEW YORK

RUSSELL & RUSSELL · INC

1964

FIRST PUBLISHED IN 1930
REISSUED, 1964, BY RUSSELL & RUSSELL, INC.
BY ARRANGEMENT WITH WALTER H. FRENCH
L. C. CATALOG CARD NO: 64—18606

PRINTED IN THE UNITED STATES OF AMERICA

SIR PERCEVAL OF GALLES

SIR PERCEVAL OF GALLES

Few pieces have occasioned so much discussion as this, because it has been taken into consideration by every student of the Grail-legend. But if the author knew the courtly poems on that legend, he broke away from them, and emphasized the spectacular and picturesque elements in his material. He also preserved some primitive features not found in the courtly pieces. Since he only half understood his original material, references to other versions have been given in the hope of making some of the lines clear.

The poem is in the northern dialect of the second half of the fourteenth century. The expression is frequently stumbling and awkward and the grammatical constructions loose. The second parts of compound expressions show frequent ellipsis, especially the omission of relatives. The genitive is often without -s. The scribe often writes s- for sh- (sall, shall); aa- for a- or -o; adds inorganic -e; and uses a superfluous initial h- (habyde).

The text follows Sir Frederick Madden's transcript (now in the Harvard University Library) of the Thornton Manuscript, with corrections from Halliwell's edition.

HERE BYGYNNES THE ROMANCE OFF
SIR PERCYUELL OF GALES

Lef, lythes[1] to me,
Two wordes or thre,
Off one þat was faire and fre
    And fell in his fighte.
His righte name was Percyuell,   5
He was ffosterde in the felle,[2]

---

[1] friends, listen. [2] wilds.

1. On the stanza, see E. Rickert's "Emaré" xviii; cf. also "The Avowing of Arthur."

He dranke water of þe welle:[3]
And ȝitt was he wyghte.
His ffadir was a noble man;
Fro þe tyme þat he began,[4]   10
Miche wirchippe he wan
    When he was made knyghte;
In Kyng Arthures haulle
Beste byluffede[5] of alle:
Percyuell þay gan hym calle,   15
    Whoso redis ryghte.

Who þat righte can rede,
He was doughty of dede,
A styffe body on a stede
    Wapynes to welde;   20
Þarefore Kyng Arthoure
Dide hym mekill honoure:
He gaffe hym his syster Acheflour,
    To haue and to holde
Fro thethyn till his lyues ende,   25
With brode londes to spende;[6]
For he þe knyght wele kende,
    He bytaughte hir to welde;
With grete gyftes to fulfill,
He gaffe his sister hym till—   30
To þe knyght, at þer bothers will,[7]
    With robes in folde.[8]

He gaffe hym robes in folde,
Brode londes in wolde,[9]

---

[3] spring. [4] i.e., began to engage in warfare. [5] beloved. [6] enjoy the revenue of.
[7] with the consent of both of them. [8] in plenty; cf. Sd. 2070. [9] in his possession.

7. In the primitive versions of the story, Perceval's mother seems to have been a water-fairy; thus their life beside a spring is insisted on in this version, from which the fairies have almost disappeared. See A. C. L. Brown's articles in *Modern Philology* xvi ff., "The Grail and the English Sir Percival" (hereafter referred to as Brown).

23. Usually Blanchefleur. Bruce (I.310) thought the form in the text a corruption; viz., [Bl]a[n]chefleur.

Mony mobles vntolde,[10] 35
  His syster to take.
To þe kirke þe knyghte ȝode
For to wedde þat frely fode,[11]
For þe gyftes þat ware gude
  And for hir ownn sake. 40
Sythen, withowtten any bade,[12]
A grete brydale[13] þay made,
For hir sake þat hym hade
  Chosen to hir make;[14]
And after, withowtten any lett, 45
A grete iustyng þer was sett;
Off all þe kempes[15] þat he mett
  Wolde he none forsake.[16]

Wolde he none forsake,
The Rede Knyghte ne þe Blake, 50
Ne none þat wolde to hym take[17]
  With schafte ne with schelde;
He dose als a noble knyghte,
Wele haldes þat he highte;
Faste preues he his myghte: 55
  Deres hym none elde.
Sexty schaftes, i say,
Sir Percyuell brake þat ilke day,
And euer þat riche lady lay
  One walle and byhelde. 60
Þofe þe Rede Knyghte hade sworne,[18]
Oute of his sadill is he borne
And almoste his lyfe forlorne,
  And lygges in the felde.

---

[10] countless furnishings. [11] lovely maid. [12] delay (a tag common in this poem).
[13] wedding festival. [14] mate. [15] warriors. [16] refuse battle. [17] come. [18] i.e.,
sworn the contrary.

46. On the custom of holding tournaments at the wedding of a lord or
the birth of an heir, see W. C. Meller, "The Knight's Life in the Days of
Chivalry," 134.

50. A Red Knight and a Black Knight are two of the villains of the
piece; but possibly this line means merely "knights of all sorts."

There he lygges in the felde— 65
Many men one hym byhelde—
Thurgh his armour and his schelde
   Stoneyde[19] þat tyde.
Þat arghede[20] all þat þer ware,
Bothe þe lesse and þe mare, 70
Þat noble Percyuell so wele dare
   Syche dynttys habyde.
Was þer nowthir more ne lasse
Off all þose þat þer was
Þat durste mete hym one þe grasse, 75
   Agaynes hym to ryde.
Þay gaffe Sir Percyuell þe gree:
Beste worthy was he;
And hamewardeʒ þan rode he,
   And blythe was his bryde. 80

And þofe þe bryde blythe be
Þat Percyuell hase wone þe gree,
ʒete þe Rede Knyghte, es he
   Hurte of his honde;
And þerfore gyffes he a gyfte[21] 85
Þat if he euer couere[22] myghte
Owthir by day or by nyghte,
   In felde for to stonde,
Þat he scholde qwyte hym þat dynt
Þat he of his handes hynte; 90
Sall neuer þis trauell be tynt,[23]
   Ne tolde in þe londe
Þat Percyuell in the felde
Schulde hym schende þus vndire schelde,

---

[19] stunned.   [20] made fearful.   [21] assurance.   [22] recover.   [23] labor be lost; i.e., his effort be in vain.

74. *Was* and *þat* agree with the singular subject of the main clause, not with their real antecedent *þose*.

78. Holthausen emended to *was þat fre*. The text lacks a stressed syllable.

83. MS. *kynghte*.

Bot he scholde agayne it ȝelde,   95
  If þat he were leueande.

Now þan are þay leueande bathe;
Was noȝte þe Rede Knyghte so rathe
For to wayte hym with skathe²⁴
  Er þer þe harmes felle;²⁵   100
Ne befelle þer no stryffe
Till Percyuell had in his lyffe
A son by his ȝonge wyffe,
  Aftir hym to duelle.
When þe child was borne,   105
He made calle it one þe morne
Als his ffadir highte byforne—
  Ȝonge Percyuell.
The knyghte was fayne, a feste made
For a knaue²⁶-childe þat he hade;   110
And sythen, withowtten any bade,
  Offe justyngeȝ þay telle.²⁷

Now of justyngeȝ þay tell:
Þay sayne þat Sir Percyuell,
Þat he will in þe felde duelle,²⁸   115
  Als he hase are done.
A grete justynge was þer sett
Of all þe kempes²⁹ þat þer mett,
For he wolde his son were gette
  In þe same wonne.³⁰   120
Þeroff þe Rede Knyghte was blythe,

---

²⁴ bring violence upon him. ²⁵ before dissension occurred. ²⁶ male. ²⁷ announce.
²⁸ i.e., await all comers. ²⁹ warriors, champions. ³⁰ brought into the same
habit; i.e., would grow up enjoying combat.

95. MS. *it scholde agayne be ȝolden.* Holthausen's emendation.
100. *þer*, abbreviated in the MS., may be a mistake for *þat.*
106. The baptising and christening of infants was never long delayed;
the child was thus enabled at once to enjoy the benefits of the sacrament,
which purged it of original sin. Cf. Gautier, Ch. V. He was also pro-
tected against being carried off by monsters or demons or fairies. Cf.
Hartland's "Science of Fairy Tales," Ch. V.

When he herde of þat justynge kythe,[31]
And graythed hym armour ful swythe,
   And rode thedir riȝte sone.
Agayne Percyuell he rade,   125
With schafte and with schelde brade,[32]
To holde his heste[33] þat he made,
   Of maistres to mone.[34]

Now of maistres to mone,
Percyuell hase wele done,   130
For þe loue of his ȝonge sone,
   One þe firste day.
Ere þe Rede Knyghte was bownn,
Percyuell hase borne downn
Knyght, duke, erle, and baroun,   135
   And vencusede the play.[35]
Right als he hade done þis honour,
So come þe Rede Knyghte to þe stowre;
Bot "Wo worthe wykkyde armour!"
   Percyuell may say;   140
For þer was Sir Percyuell slayne,
And þe Rede Knyghte fayne
(In herte is noȝte for to layne),
   When he went on his way.

When he went on his way,   145
Durste þer no man to hym say,[36]
Nowþer in erneste ne in play,
   To byd hym habyde;
For he had slayne riȝte þare
The beste body at[37] þare ware: 150
Sir Percyuell, with woundeȝ sare,

---

[31] lit., when he heard (it) made known concerning the jousting.   [32] broad.
[33] promise.   [34] call to mind injuries; i.e., his past disgrace.   [35] vanquished in
the sport.   [36] speak.   [37] person that.

139. "A curse on faulty armor!" The references to untrustworthy arms
are numerous. When a sword proved trustworthy, the knight often gave
it a name, and prized it greatly, for his very life might depend on its
durability. Cf. Meller, *op. cit.*, 73 ff.

And stonayed þat tyde.
And þan þay couthe no better rede
Bot put hym in a preuee stede,
Als þat men dose with þe dede—   155
   In erthe for to hyde.
Scho þat was his lady
Mighte be full sary,
Þat lorne hade siche a body:
   Hir aylede no pryde.   160

And now is Percyuell þe wighte
Slayne in batelle and in fyghte,
And þe lady hase gyffen a gyfte,[38]
   Holde if scho may,
Þat scho schall neuer mare wone   165
In stede, with hir ȝonge sone,
Þer dedeȝ of armeȝ schall be done,
   By nyghte ne be daye;
Bot in þe wodde schall he be:
Sall he no thyng see   170
Bot þe leues of the tree
   And þe greues graye;[39]
Schall he nowþer take tent[40]
To justeȝ ne to tournament,
Bot in þe wilde wodde went,[41]   175
   With besteȝ to playe.

With wilde besteȝ for to playe,
Scho tuke hir leue and went hir waye,
Bothe at baron and at raye,[42]
   And went to þe wodde.   180
Byhynde scho leued boure and haulle;
A mayden scho tuke hir withalle,
Þat scho myȝte appon calle
   When þat hir nede stode.

[38] assurance.   [39] grey groves.   [40] i.e., know.   [41] go about.   [42] king.

160. Holthausen suggested [v]aylede, availed; as an idiom, it is much
more common than aylede.

Oþer gudeȝ wolde scho nonne nayte,[43]   185
Bot with hir tuke a tryppe of gayte,[44]
With mylke of þam for to bayte[45]
    To hir lyues fode.[46]
Off all hir lordes faire gere,
Wolde scho noȝte with hir bere   190
Bot a lyttill Scottes spere,
    Agayne hir son ȝode.[47]

And when hir ȝong son ȝode,
Scho bade hym walke in þe wodde,
Tuke hym þe Scottes spere gude,   195
    And gaffe hym in hande.
"Swete modir," sayde he,
"What manere of thyng may þis bee
Þat ȝe nowe hafe taken mee?
    What calle ȝee this wande?"[48]   200
Than byspakke the lady:
"Son," scho sayde, "sekerly,
It is a dart doghty;
    In þe wodde i it fande."
The childe es payed, of his parte,   205
His modir hase gyffen hym þat darte;
Þerwith made he many marte[49]
    In that wodde-lande.

Thus he welke in þe lande,
With hys darte in his hande;   210
Vnder þe wilde wodde-wande[50]

---

[43] use, have.   [44] flock of goats.   [45] feed.   [46] as sustenance for their lives.   [47] in anticipation of (the time when) her son should walk.   [48] staff.   [49] slaughtered animal.   [50] branches.

191. The weapon is obviously a dart, which might be cast at a mark or animal, but was unsuitable for tilting or thrusting. For much material on this and other details of the plot, see R. H. Griffith's "Sir Perceval of Galles" (University of Chicago thesis); he points out (22) that the weapon is elsewhere described as short (478), and suggests that the word in the text is a corruption of this. The word also bears a resemblance to *schot*, cast. Evidently it is a talismanic spear, which alone can accomplish the death of the Red Knight.

He wexe and wele thrafe.[1]
He wolde schote[2] with his spere
Bestes and oþer gere,
As many als he myghte bere;   215
   He was a gude knaue!
Smalle birdes wolde he slo,
Hertys, hyndeȝ also;
Broghte his moder of thoo:
   Thurte hir none craue.[3]   220
So wele he lernede hym to schote,
Þer was no beste þat welke one fote
To fle fro hym was it no bote,
   When þat he wolde hym haue—

Euen when he wolde hym haue.   225
Thus he wexe and wele thraue,
And was reghte a gude knaue
   Within a fewe ȝere.
Fyftene wynter and mare
He duellede in those holtes hare;   230
Nowþer nurture ne lare[4]
   Scho wolde hym none lere.
Till it byfelle, on a day,
Þe lady till hir son gun say,
"Swete childe, i rede þou praye   235
   To Goddeȝ Sone dere,
Þat he wolde helpe the—
Lorde, for his poustee[5]—
A gude man for to bee,
   And longe to duelle here."   240

"Swete moder," sayde he,
"Whatkyns[6] a godd may þat be
Þat ȝe nowe bydd mee
   Þat i schall to pray?"
Then byspakke þe lady euen:[7]   245
"It es þe grete Godd of heuen:

---

[1] throve. [2] strike by casting. [3] she had not to beg for any. [4] manners nor learning. [5] power. [6] what manner of. [7] straightway.

This worlde made he within seuen,
  Appon þe sexte day."
"By grete Godd," sayde he þan,
"And i may mete with þat man,   250
With alle þe crafte þat i kan,
  Reghte so schall i pray!"
There he leuede in a tayte[8]
Bothe his modir and his gayte,[9]
The grete Godd for to layte,[10]   255
  Fynde hym when he may.

And as he welke in holtes hare,
He sawe a gate, as it ware;[11]
With thre knyghtis mett he þare
  Off Arthurs in.[12]   260
One was Ewayne fytz Asoure,
Anoþer was Gawayne with honour,
And Kay, þe bolde baratour,[13]
  And all were of his kyn.
In riche robes þay ryde;   265
The childe hadd no thyng þat tyde
Þat he myȝte in his bones hyde,[14]
  Bot a gaytes skynn.
He was burely[15] of body, and þerto riȝt brade;
One ayther halfe[16] a skynn he hade;   270
The hode[17] was of þe same made,
  Juste to þe chynn.

His hode was juste to his chyn,
Þe flesche halfe[18] tourned within.

---

[8] left with joy, eagerness. [9] goats. [10] seek. [11] it befell that he saw a path.
[12] household. [13] bully. [14] in which to hide his bones. [15] powerful. [16] i.e., back and front. [17] hood. [18] skin side.

247. Seems corrupt. It may have read, *This worlde made in dayes seuen.*
260. MS. *Arthrus.*
264. In this poem, in which the relationships are considerably confused (cf. Loomis, Ch. 27), the mothers of Perceval and Gawain are sisters of Arthur; hence the knights are cousins. Ywain was cousin to Gawain, but not to Perceval; Kay was Arthur's foster brother. But these relationships were altered by medieval writers, and in Malory are not as stated here.

The childes witt was full thyn 275
 When he scholde say oughte.
Þay were clothede all in grene;
Siche hade he neuer sene:
Wele he wened þat thay had bene
 Þe Godd þat he soghte. 280
He said, "Wilke of ʒow alle three
May þe grete Godd bee
Þat my moder tolde mee,
 Þat all þis werlde wroghte?"
Bot þan ansuerde Sir Gawayne 285
Faire and curtaisely agayne,
"Son, so Criste mote me sayne,[19]
 For swilke are we noghte."

Than saide þe fole one þe filde,[20]
Was comen oute of þe woddeʒ wilde, 290
To Gawayne þat was meke and mylde
 And softe of ansuare,
"I sall sla ʒow all three
Bot ʒe smertly now telle mee
Whatkyns thyngeʒ þat ʒe bee, 295
 Sen ʒe no goddes are."
Then ansuerde Sir Kay,
"Who solde we than say
Þat hade[21] slayne vs to-day
 In this holtis hare?" 300
At Kayes wordes wexe he tene:
Bot a grete bukke had bene—

---

[19] bless. [20] fool in the field. [21] would have.

289. In Middle English, "fool" was not so strong a word as to-day;
probably the most satisfactory translation is "fellow."
302. MS. *Bot he a*. *Bukke* may mean "body," "bulk," and *he* = Gawain;
it may mean "stag." Stags appear in legends in various capacities: (1) As
messengers to bring a mortal to a fairy; they are usually killed as the meeting
occurs (see *Am. Jour. Phil.* 37.399). (2) Because they are under an enchantment that they are seeking to dissolve (see *Folklore* 17.435.n.6). In the
French lai of "Tyolet," which closely resembles the first part of "Sir
Perceval," a stag leads the boy to a river, and is disenchanted when his
pursuer kills a roebuck that comes between them. (3) As trophies proving that the hero had arrived at manhood. (Cf. Griffith 33, *PMLA*
32.598.) The second of these possibilities seems to fit best here.

Ne hadd he stonde þam bytwene,—
He hade hym slayne þare.

Bot þan said Gawayn to Kay,   305
"Thi prowde wordes pares[22] ay;
I scholde wyn þis childe with play,[23]
    And þou wolde holde the still.
Swete son," þan said he,
"We are knyghtis all thre;   310
With Kyng Arthoure duelle wee,
    þat houyn es on hyll."[24]
Then said Percyuell þe lyghte,
In gayte-skynnes þat was dyghte,
"Will Kyng Arthoure make me knyghte,   315
    And i come hym till?"
þan saide Sir Gawayne riȝte þare,
"I kane gyffe þe nane ansuare;
Bot to þe Kynge i rede þou ffare,
    To wete his awenn will!"   320

To wete þan þe Kynges will
þare þay houen ȝitt still;
The childe hase taken hym till[25]
    For to wende hame.
And als he welke in þe wodde,   325
He sawe a full faire stode[26]
Offe coltes and of meres[27] gude,
    Bot neuer one was tame;
And sone saide he, "Bi Seyne John,
Swilke thyngeȝ as are ȝone   330
Rade þe knyghtes apone;
    Knewe i thaire name,
Als euer mote i thryffe or thee,
The moste of ȝone[28] þat i see
Smertly schall bere mee   335
    Till i come to my dame."

---

[22] do harm. [23] i.e., by gentle means. [24] who has remained on the hill; i.e., in the open country. [25] set about. [26] stud. [27] mares. [28] largest of (those) yonder.

312. The commoner form is *houande*.

He saide, "When i come to my dame,
And i fynde hir at hame,
Scho will telle [me] þe name
    Off this ilke thynge."   340
The moste mere he þare see
Smertly ouerrynnes[29] he,
And saide, "þou sall bere me
    To-morne to þe Kynge."
Kepes[30] he no sadill-gere,   345
Bot stert vp on the mere:
Hamewarde scho gun hym bere,
    Withowtten faylynge.
The lady was neuer more sore bygone:[31]
Scho wiste neuer whare to wonne,[32]   350
When scho wiste hir ȝonge sonne
    Horse hame brynge.

Scho saw hym horse hame brynge;
Scho wiste wele, by þat thynge,
Þat þe kynde wolde oute sprynge   355
    For thynge þat be moughte.[33]
Þan als sone saide þe lady,
"Þat euer solde i sorowe dry[34]
For loue of þi body,
    Þat i hafe dere boghte!   360
Dere son," saide scho hym to,
"Þou wirkeste th[is]elfe mekill vnroo;[35]
What will þou with þis mere do,
    That þou hase hame broghte?"
Bot the boye was neuer so blythe   365
Als when he herde þe name kythe
Of þe stode-mere stythe:[36]
    Of na thyng þan he roghte.

Now he calles hir a mere,
Als his moder dide ere;   370

---

[29] runs down. [30] pays attention to. [31] overwhelmed. [32] dwell; i.e., knew not what to do. [33] despite anything. [34] suffer. [35] unrest. [36] hardy.

339. *Me* supplied by C.

He wened all oþer horseȝ were
And hade bene callede soo.
"Moder, at ȝonder hill hafe i bene,
Þare hafe i thre knyghtes sene,
And i hafe spoken with þam, i wene,   375
   Wordes in throo;[37]
I haue highte þam all thre
Before þaire Kyng for to be:
Siche on[38] schall he make me
   As is one of tho !"   380
He sware by grete Goddeȝ myȝte,
"I schall holde þat i hafe highte;
Bot-if þe Kyng make me knyghte,
   To-morne i sall hym sloo !"

Bot than byspakke þe lady,   385
Þat for hir son was sary—
Hir thoghte wele þat scho myȝt dy—
   And knelyde one hir knee:
"Sone, þou has takyn thi rede,
To do thiselfe to þe dede !   390
In euerilke a strange stede,
   Doo als i bydde the:
To-morne es forthirmaste[39] ȝole-day,
And þou says þou will away
To make the knyghte, if þou may,   395
   Als þou tolde mee.
Lyttill þou can of nurtoure:
Luke þou be of mesure[40]
Bothe in haulle and in boure,
   And fonde to be fre."[41]   400

Than saide þe lady so brighte,
"There þou meteste with a knyghte,

---

[37] anger. [38] such a one. [39] first. [40] moderate in conduct. [41] try to be well-mannered.

393. Probably Christmas Day itself, although sometimes the Yule season began at the winter solstice. It lasted about twelve days.
397. MS. *nuttoure*.

Do thi hode off, i highte,
  And haylse[42] hym in hy."
"Swete moder," sayd he then,   405
  "I saw neuer ȝit no men;
If i solde a knyghte ken,
  Telles me wharby."
Scho schewede hym þe menevaire[43]—
Scho had robes in payre;[44]—   410
"Sone, þer þou sees this fare[45]
  In thaire hodes lye."
"Bi grete God," sayd he,
Where þat i a knyghte see,
Moder, as ȝe bidd me,   415
  Righte so schall i."

All þat nyȝte till it was day,
The childe by þe modir lay,
Till on þe morne he wolde away,
  For thyng[46] þat myȝte betyde.   420
Brydill hase he righte nane;
Seese he no better wane,[47]
Bot a wythe[48] hase he tane,
  And keuylles[49] his stede.
His moder gaffe hym a ryng,   425
And bad he solde agayne it bryng:
"Sonne, þis sall be oure takynnyng,[50]
  For here i sall þe byde."
He tase þe rynge and þe spere,
Stirttes vp appon þe mere: 430
Fro þe moder þat hym bere,
  Forthe gan he ryde.

---

[42] greet. [43] cloth or fur worn under helmet. [44] sets. [45] thing. [46] despite anything.
[47] means. [48] withy, willow-shoot. [49] bridles, puts a bit on. [50] sign of recognition.

406. In the early versions of the story, Perceval's fairy-mother probably lived in a land of women, to which men did not have access. French poets generally rationalized this detail, because it was so contrary to the social conditions with which they were familiar; but a trace of it is preserved in this line, which contradicts l. 310, etc. See "Degaré" 865.

410. This contradicts 185 ff.; but the expression seems cognate with *in folde* (32).

432. In the MS. the division of a fitte is marked here.

One his way as he gan ryde,
He fande an haulle þer besyde;
He saide, "For oghte þat may betyde,
   Thedir in will i."   435
He went in withowtten lett;
He fande a brade borde sett,
A bryghte fire, wele bett,[1]
   Brynnande þerby.   440
A mawnger[2] þer he fande,
Corne þerin lyggande;
Þerto his mere he bande
   With the withy.
He saide, "My modir bad me   445
Þat i solde of mesure bee;
Halfe þat i here see
   Styll sall it ly."

The corne he pertis[3] in two,
Gaffe his mere þe tone of þoo,   450
And to þe borde gan he goo,
   Certayne that tyde.
He fande a lofe of brede fyne
And a pychere with wyne,
A mese[4] of the kechyne,   455
   A knyfe þer besyde.
The mete þer þat he fande,
He dalte it euen with his hande,
Lefte þe halfe lyggande
   A felawe[5] to byde.   460
Þe toþer halfe ete he;
How myȝte he more of mesure be?

---

[1] kindled.   [2] manger.   [3] divides.   [4] dinner.   [5] i.e., some one else.

433. Griffith (29 and 108) gives a detailed analysis of this episode, which is here so compressed as to be almost unintelligible. Cf. Brown 125, also; he conjectures that in the original form of the story the mother advises Perceval to exchange rings with a damsel, because the mother, a fairy, knows that she can so direct him that he will secure a ring making him invulnerable.

456. A knife was the only utensil given a banqueter.

Faste he fonded to be free,
    Þofe he were of no pryde.[6]

Þofe he were of no pryde,   465
Forthir more gan he glyde
Till a chambir þer besyde,
    Moo sellys[7] to see.
Riche clothes fande he sprede,
A lady slepande on a bedde;   470
He said, "Forsothe, a tokyn to wedde[8]
    Sall þou lefe with mee."
Þer he kyste þat swete thynge;
Of hir fynger he tuke a rynge;
His awenn modir takynnynge[9]   475
    He lefte with þat fre.
He went forthe to his mere,
Tuke with hym his schorte spere,
Lepe on lofte, as he was ere;
    His way rydes he.   480

Now on his way rydes he,
    Moo selles to see;
A knyghte wolde he nedis bee,
    Withowtten any bade.
He come þer þe Kyng was,   485
Seruede of þe firste mese:[10]
To hym was þe maste has[11]
    Þat þe childe hade;
And þare made he no lett
At ȝate, dore, ne wykett,   490
Bot in graythely[12] he gett—
    Syche maistres he made.[13]
At his firste in-comynge,
His mere, withowtten faylynge,

---

[6] tried to be mannerly, though not out of pride. [7] wonders. [8] as a pledge.
[9] mother's token. [10] course. [11] greatest purpose; i.e., fixed intention.
[12] readily. [13] violence he did.

490. For the wicket, cf. Int. III.A.1.
493. Riding a steed into the hall is a common incident in romance.
Cf. Child's notes, II.510; III.508.

Kyste þe forheuede of þe Kynge—   495
 So nerehande he rade!

The Kyng had ferly þaa,
And vp his hande gan he taa
And putt it forthir hym fraa,
 The mouthe of the mere.   500
He saide, "Faire childe and free,
Stonde still besyde mee,
And tell me wythen[14] þat þou bee,
 And what þou will here."
Than saide þe fole of þe filde,   505
"I ame myn awnn modirs childe,
Comen fro þe woddeȝ wylde
 Till Arthure the dere.[15]
ȝisterday saw i knyghtis three:
Siche on sall þou make mee   510
On þis mere byfor the,
 Thi mete or þou schere!"[16]

Bot þan spak Sir Gawayne,
Was þe Kynges trenchepayne,
Said, "Forsothe, is noȝte to layne,   515
 I am one of thaa.
Childe, hafe þou my blyssyng
For þi feres folowynge![17]
Here hase þou fonden þe Kynge
 þat kan þe knyghte maa."   520
Than sayde Percyuell þe free,
"And this Arthure þe Kyng bee,
Luke he a knyghte make mee:
 I rede[18] at it be swaa!"
þofe he vnborely[19] were dyghte,   525
He sware by mekill Goddes myȝte:
"Bot if þe Kyng make me knyghte,
 I sall hym here slaa!"

---

[14] whence. [15] great. [16] cut. [17] following thy fellows. [18] i.e., demand. [19] meanly.

514. Cutter of trenchers. (See Int. III.B.) This was as much an art and duty for the accomplished gentleman as carving.

All þat þer weren, olde and ȝynge,
Hadden ferly[20] of þe Kyng,   530
þat he wolde suffre siche a thyng
    Of þat foull wyghte
On horse houande[21] hym by.
The Kyng byholdeȝ hym on hy;
Than wexe he sone sory   535
    When he sawe þat syghte.
The teres oute of his eghne glade:
Neuer one anoþer habade.[22]
"Allas," he sayde, "þat i was made,
    Be day or by nyghte,   540
One lyue i scholde after hym[23] bee
þat me thynke lyke the:
þou arte so semely to see,
    And þou were wele dighte!"

He saide, "And þou were wele dighte,   545
þou were lyke to a knyghte
þat i louede with all my myghte
    Whills he was one lyue.
So wele wroghte he my will
In all manere of skill,   550
I gaffe my syster hym till,
    For to be his wyfe.
He es moste in my mane:[24]
Fiftene ȝere es it gane,
Sen a theffe hade hym slane   555
    Abowte a littill stryffe![25]
Sythen hafe i euer bene his fo,
For to wayte[26] hym with wo;
Bot i myȝte hym neuer slo,
    His craftes are so ryfe."   560

He sayse, "His craftes are so ryfe,
þer is no man apon lyfe,
With swerde, spere, ne with knyfe
    May stroye[27] hym allan,

---

[20] wonder. [21] staying. [22] one did not wait for another. [23] that I should survive him
(Perceval's father). [24] remembrance. [25] disagreement. [26] afflict. [27] destroy.

Bot if it were Sir Percyuell son,   565
Whoso wiste where he ware done![28]
The bokes says þat he mon
    Venge his fader bane."
The childe thoghte he longe bade
Þat he ne ware a knyghte made,   570
For he wiste neuer þat he hade
    A ffader to be slayne;
The lesse was his menynge.[29]
He saide sone to þe Kynge,
"Sir, late be thi iangleynge![30]   575
    Of this kepe i nane."[31]

He sais, "I kepe not to stande
With thi iangleyn[ge]s to[32] lange;
Make me knyghte with thi hande,
    If it sall be done!"   580
Than þe Kyng hym hendly highte
Þat he schold dub hym to knyghte,
With-thi-þat[33] he wolde doun lighte
    And ete with hym at none.
The Kyng biholdeʒ þe vesage free,   585
And euer more trowed hee
Þat þe childe scholde bee
    Sir Percyuell son:
It ran in the Kynges mode,
His syster Acheflour þe gude—   590
How scho went into þe wodde
    With hym for to wonn.

The childe hadde wonnede in þe wodde:
He knewe noþer euyll ne gude;
The Kynge hymselfe vnderstode   595
    He was a wilde man.

---

[28] put; i.e., is.   [29] grief, moaning.   [30] rambling talk.   [31] to this pay I no heed.
[32] too.   [33] provided.

567. Possibly a relic of an older version in which the son is fated to slay the father's enemy. Cf. Brown, and cf. also the prophetic passages in "King Horn" and "Havelok."

578. MS. *iangleyns*.

So faire he spakke hym withall,
He lyghtes doun in he haulle,
Bonde his mere amonge þam alle,
    And to þe borde wann.   600
Bot are he myghte bygynn
To þe mete for to wynn,
So commes þe Rede Knyghte in
    Emangeȝ[34] þam righte þan,
Prekande one a rede stede;   605
Blode-rede was his wede.
He made þam gammen full gnede,[35]
    With crafteȝ[36] þat he can.

With his craftes gan he calle,
And callede þam recrayhandes[37] all,   610
Kynge, knyghtes within walle,
    At þe bordes þer þay bade.
Full felly þe coupe[38] he fett,
Bifore þe Kynge þat was sett;
Þer was no man þat durste hym lett,   615
    Þofe þat he were ffadde.[39]
The couppe was filled full of wyne;
He dranke of þat þat was þerinn.
All of rede golde fyne
    Was þe couppe made.   620
He tuke it vp in his hande,
Þe coupe that he there fande,
And lefte þam all sittande,
    And fro þam he rade.

---

[34] amongst.   [35] sorry sport.   [36] arts, spells.   [37] traitors, cowards.   [38] fiercely the cup.   [39] bold.

605. The Red Knight seems to be an enchanter. His red armor, etc., are common marks of the supernatural being. Every one is put under a spell that prevents his resisting the knight. Cf. *Rev. Celt.* 22.36.

611. MS. *in with.*

613. Brown and Loomis think the cup very important, in spite of its suppression here. It is some sort of talisman, without which Arthur's realm cannot prosper.

Now fro þam he rade, 625
Als he says þat þis made:[40]
The sorowe þat þe Kynge hade
   Mighte no tonge tell.
"A! dere God," said þe Kyng þan,
"Þat all this wyde werlde wan, 630
Whethir i sall euer hafe þat man
   May make ȝone fende duelle?
Fyve ȝeres hase he þus gane,
And my coupes fro me tane,
And my gude knyghte slayne, 635
   Men calde Sir Percyuell;
Sythen taken hase he three,
And ay awaye will he bee,
Or i may harnayse[41] me
   In felde hym to felle." 640

"Petir!"[42] quod Percyuell þe ȝynge,
"Hym þan wil [i] down dynge
And þe coupe agayne brynge,
   And þou will make me knyghte."
"Als i am trewe kyng," said he, 645
"A knyghte sall i make the,
Forthi þou will brynge mee
   The coupe of golde bryghte."
Vp ryses Sir Arthoure,
Went to a chamboure 650
To feche doun armoure,
   þe childe in to dyghte;
Bot are it was doun caste,[43]

---

[40] i.e., the poet's original.   [41] arm.   [42] by St. Peter!   [43] i.e., taken from the hooks.

633. Campion emended to *fyftene.* The other versions do not help in establishing the right reading; but it seems that the knight takes a cup every fifth year (637); and the poet may have confused this with the fifteen-year period elapsing after the death of Perceval's father. Cf. Griffith 49.n.1.

653. The construction *are . . . ere,* the second correlative being redundant, is fairly common.

Ere was Percyuell paste,
And on his[44] way folowed faste   655
þat he solde with fyghte.

Wi[t]h his foo for to fighte,
None oþergates[45] was he dighte,
Bot in thre gayt-skynnes righte,
    A fole als he ware.   660

He cryed, "How,[46] man on thi mere!
Bryng agayne þe Kynges gere,
Or with my dart i sall þe fere[47]
    And make þe vnfere!"[48]
And after þe Rede Knyghte he rade,   665
Baldely, withowtten bade:
Sayd, "A knyght i sall be made
    For som of thi gere."
He sware by mekill Goddeȝ payne,
"Bot if þou brynge þe coupe agayne,   670
With my dart þou sall be slayne
    And slongen of thi mere."
The knyghte byhaldes hym in throo,[49]
Calde hym fole þat was hys foo,
For he named hym soo—   675
    þe stede þat hym bere.

And for to see hym with syghte,
He putt his vmbrere[1] on highte,
To byhalde how he was dyghte
    þat so till hym spake;   680
He sayde, "Come i to the, appert[2] fole,
I sall caste þe in þe pole,
For all þe heghe days of ȝole,
    Als ane olde sakke."

---

[44] i.e., the Red Knight's. [45] otherwise. [46] stop. [47] terrify. [48] infirm. [49] anger.
[1] visor. [2] impudent.

682. Apparently a common way of disposing of dead wretches was to throw them into marshes and pools; cf. "Havelok" 2110.
683. The Yule-season lasted about twelve days, and during this period all fighting was forbidden. See Brand, on Yule.

Than sayd Percyuell þe free,   685
"Be i fole, or whatte i bee,
Now sone of þat sall wee see
   Whose browes schall blakke."[3]
Of schottyng was þe child slee:[4]
At þe knyghte lete he flee,   690
Smote hym in at þe eghe
   And oute at þe nakke.

For þe dynt þat he tuke,
Oute of sadill he schoke,[5]
Whoso þe sothe will luke,[6]   695
   And þer was he slayne.
He falles down one þe hill;
His stede rynnes whare he will.
Þan saide Percyuell hym till,
   "Þou art a lethir swayne."[7]   700
Then saide þe childe in þat tyde,
"And þou woldeste me here byde,
After þi mere scholde i ryde
   And brynge hir agayne:
Þen myȝte we bothe with myȝte   705
Menskfully[8] togedir fyghte,
Ayther of vs, as he were a knyghte,
   Till tyme þe tone ware slayne."

Now es þe Rede Knyghte slayne,
Lefte dede in the playne;   710
The childe gon his mere mayne[9]
   After þe stede.
Þe stede was swifter þan þe mere,
For he hade no thynge to bere
Bot his sadill and his gere,   715
   Fro hym þofe he ȝede.
The mere was bagged with fole;[10]
   And hirselfe a grete bole;[11]

---

[3] grow pale. [4] the boy was skillful at casting at a mark. [5] tumbled. [6] examine; i.e., in truth. [7] evil knave. [8] honorably; i.e., as befits us. [9] ride. [10] heavy with foal. [11] i.e., swelled.

716. I.e., "Though he was being pursued;" but possibly *þofe*=*þaa*.

For to rynne scho myȝte not thole,[12]
Ne folowe hym no spede.   720
The childe saw þat it was soo,
And till his fete he gan hym too;
The gates þat he scholde goo
Made he full gnede.[13]

The gates made he full gnede   725
In þe waye þer he ȝede;
With strenght tuke he þe stede
And broghte to þe knyghte.
"Me thynke," he sayde, "þou arte fele[14]
Þat þou ne will away stele;   730
Now i houppe þat þou will dele
Strokes appon hyghte.[15]
I hafe broghte to the thi mere
And mekill of thyn oþer gere;
Lepe on hir, as þou was ere,   735
And þou will more fighte !"
The knyghte lay still in þe stede:
What sulde he say, when he was dede?
The childe couthe no better rede,
Bot down gun he lyghte.   740

Now es Percyuell lyghte
To vnspoyle[16] þe Rede Knyghte,
Bot he ne couthe neuer fynd righte
The lacynge of his wede;
He was armede so wele   745
In gude iryn and in stele,
He couthe not gett of[17] a dele,
For nonkyns nede.

---

[12] bear.   [13] stingy; i.e., took no extra steps, ran straight.   [14] trusty.   [15] i.e.,
from on horseback.   [16] despoil.   [17] off.

720. *too,* for *taa;* take, get.
738. Cf. "Ogier de Danemarche" 8474. The dead men on the walls are
addressed by Charlemagne: *Cil sont tot qoi qe nus n'a mot soné: Com
parlera qi ne puet ne ne set?*

He sayd, "My moder bad me,
When my dart solde broken be, 750
Owte of þe iren bren þe tree:[18]
   Now es me fyre gnede."[19]
Now he getis hym flynt,
His fyre-iren[20] he hent,
And þen, withowtten any stynt, 755
   He kyndilt a glede.[21]

Now he kyndils a glede:
Amonge þe buskes[22] he ȝede
And gedirs, full gude spede,
   Wodde, a fyre to make. 760
A grete fyre made he þan,
The Rede Knyghte in to bren,
For he ne couthe nott ken
   His gere off to take.
Be þan was Sir Gawayne dyght, 765
Folowede after þe fyghte
Betwene hym and þe Rede Knyghte,
   For þe childes sake.
He fande þe Rede Knyght lyggand,
Slayne of Percyuell hande, 770
Besyde a fyre brynnande
   Off byrke and of akke.[23]

Þer brent of birke and of ake
Gret brandes and blake.[24]
"What wylt þou with this fyre make?" 775
   Sayd Gawayne hym till.
"Petir!" quod Percyuell then,
"And i myghte hym þus ken,[25]
Out of his iren i wòlde hym bren
   Righte here on this hill." 780
Bot þen sayd Sir Gawayne,
"The Rede Knyghte for þou has slayne,
I sall vnarme hym agayne,
   And þou will holde þe still."

---

[18] burn the wood out of the iron (head).   [19] lacking.   [20] steel, to strike on flint.
[21] fire of coals.   [22] bushes.   [23] birch and oak.   [24] charred.   [25] i.e., get to see.

Þan Sir Gawayn doun lyghte,   785
Vnlacede þe Rede Knyghte;
The childe in his armour dight
    At his awnn will.

When he was dighte in his atire,
He tase þe knyghte bi þe swire,[26]   790
Keste hym reghte in the fyre,
    Þe brandes to balde.[27]
Bot þen said Percyuell on bost,
"Ly still þerin now and roste!
I kepe nothynge of þi coste,[28]   795
    Ne noghte of thi spalde!"[29]
The knyghte lygges þer on brede;[30]
The childe es dighte in his wede,
And lepe vp apon his stede,
    Als hymselfe wolde.   800
He luked doun to his fete,
Saw his gere faire and mete:
"For a knyghte i may be lete[31]
    And myghte be calde."

Then sayd Sir Gawayn hym till,   805
"Goo we faste fro this hill!
Þou hase done what þou will;
    It neghes nere nyghte."
"What! trowes þou," quod Percyuell þe ȝynge,
"Þat i will agayn brynge   810
Vntill Arthoure þe Kynge
    Þe golde þat es bryghte?
Nay, so mote i thryfe or thee,
I am als grete a lorde als he;
To-day ne schall he make me   815
    None oþer gates[32] knyghte.
Take þe coupe in thy hande
And mak þiselfe þe presande,[33]

---

[26] neck. [27] embolden; i.e., replenish. [28] care nothing for your (evil) ways.
[29] shoulder; i.e., strength of arm. [30] sprawling. [31] may pass. [32] in any other
wise. [33] presentation.

For i will forthire into þe lande,
Are i doun lyghte." 820

Nowþer wolde he doun lyghte,
Ne he wolde wende with þe knyght,
Bot rydes forthe all þe nyghte:
So prowde was he than.
Till on þe morne at forthe dayes,[34] 825
He mett a wyche, as men says;
His horse and his harnays
Couthe scho wele ken.
Scho wende þat it hade bene
Þe Rede Knyghte þat scho hade sene, 830
Was wonnt in þose armes to bene,
To gerre þe stede rynne.
In haste scho come hym agayne,
Sayde, "It is not to layne,
Men tolde me þat þou was slayne 835
With Arthours men.

Ther come one of my men:
Till 3onder hill he gan me kenne,[35]
There þou sees þe fyre brene,
And sayde þat þou was thare." 840
Euer satt Percyuell stone-still,
And spakke no thynge hir till
Till scho hade sayde all hir will,
And spakke lesse ne mare.[36]
"At 3ondere hill hafe i bene: 845
Nothynge hafe i there sene
Bot gayte-skynnes, i wene—
Siche ill-farande fare.[37]
Mi sone, and þou ware thare slayne
And thyn armes of drawen, 850

---

[34] late in the morning. [35] show. [36] i.e., neither less nor more. [37] poor stuff.

826. On the witch, see Griffith, Ch. III. By healing him after a disastrous encounter, she prevents the enchanter's enemies from vanquishing him.

I couthe hele the agayne
  Als wele als þou was are."

Than wist Percyuell by thatt,
It seruede hym of somwhatt,[38]
The wylde[39] fyre þat he gatt   855
  When þe knyghte was slayne;
And righte so wolde he, thare
þat þe olde wiche ware.
Oppon his spere he hir bare
  To þe fyre agayne;   860
In ill wrethe[40] and in grete,
He keste þe wiche in þe hete;
He sayde, "Ly still and swete[41]
  Bi þi son, þat lyther[42] swayne!"
Thus he leues thaym twoo,   865
And on his gates gan he goo:
Siche dedis to do moo
  Was þe childe fayne.

Als he come by a wodd-syde,
He sawe ten men ryde;   870
He said, "For oughte þat may betyde,
  To þam will i me."[43]
When þose ten saw hym þare,
þay wende þe Rede Knyghte it ware,
þat wolde þam all forfare,   875
  And faste gan þay flee;
For he was sogates[44] cledde,
Alle belyffe fro hym þay fledde;
And euer þe faster þat þay spedde,
  The swiftlyere sewed[45] hee,   880
Till he was warre of a knyghte,
And of þe menevaire[46] he had syght;
He put vp his vmbrere[47] on hight,
  And said, "Sir, God luke[48] thee!"

---

[38] was of some use. [39] fierce, great. [40] raging anger. [41] sweat. [42] evil.
[43] will I [hie] me. [44] in such wise. [45] followed. [46] helm-lining. [47] visor.
[48] may God be propitious.

The childe sayde, "God luke þe!"   885
The knyght said, "Now wele þe be!
A, lorde Godd, now wele es mee
   Þat euer was i made!"
For by þe vesage hym thoghte
The Rede Knyʒte was it noʒte,   890
Þat hade them all bysoughte;[49]
   And baldely he bade.[50]
It semede wele bi þe syghte
Þat he had slayne þe Rede Knyʒt:
In his armes was he dighte,   895
   And on his stede rade.
"Son," sayde þe knyghte tho,
And thankede þe childe full thro,[1]
"Þou hase slayne þe moste foo
   Þat euer ʒitt i hade."   900

Then sayde Percyuell þe free,
"Wherefore fledde ʒee
Lange are, when ʒe sawe mee
   Come rydande ʒow by?"
Bot þan spake þe olde knyghte,   905
Þat was paste out of myghte
With any man for to fyghte:
   He ansuerde in hy;
He sayde, "Theis children nyne,
All are þay sonnes myne.   910
For ferde or[2] i solde þam tyne,[3]
   Þerfore fledd i.
We wende wele þat it had bene
Þe Rede Knyʒte þat we hade sene;
He walde hafe slayne vs bydene,   915
   Withowtten mercy.

Withowtten any mercy
He wolde hafe slayne vs in hy;

---

[49] searched for. [50] stopped, waited. [1] effusively. [2] fear that. [3] lose.

To my sonnes he hade envy
    Moste of any men. 920
Fiftene ȝeres es it gane
Syn he my brodire hade slane;
Now hadde þe þeefe vndirtane
    To sla vs all then:
He was ferd lesse[4] my sonnes sold hym slo 925
When þay ware eldare and moo,[5]
And þat þay solde take hym for þaire foo
    Where þay myȝte hym ken;
Hade i bene in the stede
Þer he was done to þe dede, 930
I solde neuer hafe etyn brede
    Are i hade sene hym bren."

"Petir!" quod Percyuell, "he es brende:
I haffe spedde better þan i wend
Euer at þe laste ende." 935
    The blythere wexe þe knyghte;
By his haulle þaire gates felle,[6]
And ȝerne he prayed Percyuell
Þat he solde þer with hym duelle
    And be þer all þat nyghte. 940
Full wele he couthe a geste calle;[7]
He broghte þe childe into þe haulle;
So faire he spake hym withalle
    That he es doun lyghte;
His stede es in stable sett 945
And hymselfe to þe haulle fett,
And þan, withowtten any lett,
    To þe mette þay þam dighte.

Mete and drynke was þer dighte,
And men to serue þam full ryghte; 950
Þe childe þat come with þe knyghte,
    Enoghe þer he fande.

---

[4] afraid lest. [5] i.e., larger. [6] way lay. [7] invite a guest.

920. In other versions and similar stories, the sons are under an enchantment which dooms them to fight every day against the enchanter.

At þe mete as þay beste satte,[8]
Come þe portere fro þe ȝate,
Saide a man was þeratte   955
   Of þe Maydenlande;
Saide, "Sir, he prayes the
Off mete and drynke, for charyté;
For a messagere es he
   And may nott lange stande."   960
The knyght badde late hym inn,
"For," he sayde, "it es no synn,
The man þat may þe mete wynn[9]
   To gyffe þe trauellande."

Now þe trauellande man   965
The portere lete in þan;
He haylsede[10] þe knyghte as he can,
   Als he satt on dese.
The knyghte askede hym þare
Whase man þat he ware,   970
And how ferre þat he walde so fare,
   Withowtten any lese.[11]
He saide, "I come fro þe Lady Lufamour,
Þat sendes me to Kyng Arthoure,
And prayes hym, for his honoure,   975
   Hir sorowes for to sesse.[12]
Vp resyn es a sowdane:
Alle hir landes hase he tane;
So byseges he that woman
   That scho may hafe no pese."   980

He sayse þat scho may haue no pese,
The lady, for hir fayrenes,
And for hir mekill reches.
   "He wirkes hir full woo;

---

[8] when the feast was at its height.   [9] i.e., for one who has food.   [10] greeted.
[11] lie. [12] put an end to.

956. Cf. note to 406. On fairy countries inhabited only by women,
see Brown's "Iwain" 30 ff.

He dose hir sorow all hir sythe,[13]　　　　985
And all he slaes doun rythe;[14]
He wolde haue hir to wyfe,
　　And scho will no3te soo.
Now hase þat ilke sowdane
Hir fadir and hir eme[15] slane,　　　　990
And hir brethir[16] ilkane,
　　And is hir moste foo.
So nere he hase hir now soughte[17]
Þat till a castelle es scho broghte,
And fro þe walles will he noghte,　　　　995
　　Ere þat he may hir too.[18]

The sowdane sayse he will hir ta;
The lady will hirselfe sla
Are he, þat es hir maste fa,
　　Solde wedde hir to wyfe.　　　　1000
Now es þe sowdan so wyghte,
Alle he slaes doun ryghte:
Þer may no man with hym fyghte,
　　Bot he were kempe ryfe."[19]
Þan sayde Percyuell, "I þe praye,　　　　1005
Þat þou wolde teche me þe waye
Thedir, als þe gates laye,[20]
　　Withowtten any stryfe;
Mighte i mete with þat sowdan
Þat so dose to þat woman,　　　　1010
Alsone he solde be slane,
　　And i my3te hafe þe lyfe!"[21]

The messangere prayed hym mare[22]
Þat he wolde duell still þare:
"For i will to þe Kynge fare,　　　　1015
　　Myne erande3 for to say."
"For þen mekill sorowe me betyde,
And i lenger here habyde,

_____

[13] time; i.e., days. [14] straight. [15] uncle. [16] (plural). [17] closely has he pursued her. [18] take. [19] renowned warrior. [20] the roads lie. [21] if I may live (to do it). [22] rather.

Bot ryghte now will i ryde,
   Als so faste als i may."   1020
[T]he knyghte herde hym say so;
3erne he prayes hym to too
His nyne sonnes, with hym to goo;
   He nykkes[23] hym with nay.
Bot so faire spekes he   1025
þat he takes of þam three,
In his felawchipe to be—
   The blythere were þay.

þay ware blythe of þer bade,[24]
Busked þam and forthe rade;   1030
Mekill myrthes þay made:
   Bot lyttill it amende.[25]
He was paste bot a while—
The montenance of a myle[26]—
He was bythoghte of a gyle[27]   1035
   Wele werse þan þay wende.
þofe þay ware of þaire fare fayne,
Forthwarde[28] was þaire cheftayne;
Euer he sende one agayne
   At ilke a myle ende,   1040
Vntill þay ware alle gane;
þan he rydes hym allane
Als he ware sprongen of a stane,
   þare naˏman hym kende,

For he walde none sold hym ken.   1045
   Forthe ryde3 he then,

[23] refuses.   [24] these tidings.   [25] did good.   [26] space of a mile.   [27] trick. [28] ahead.

1029. þer for þir, these.
1039. Probably this was done so that the hero could encounter the enemy unaided—the only terms on which success was possible. Cf. Maelduin's troubles in numbering his crew, and the breaking of the charm by foster brothers who insist on accompanying him (*Rev. Celt.* 9.447, 10.50). The precise number is not always known, and the hero must discover it by chance.
1043. Cf. note on "King Horn" 1025.

Amangeȝ vncouthe men
  His maystres[29] to make.
Now hase Percyuell in throo[30]
Spoken with his emes twoo,   1050
Bot neuer one of thoo
  Took his knawlage.[31]
Now in his way es he sett
Þat may hym lede, withowtten lett,
Þare he and þe sowdan sall mete,   1055
  His browes to blake.[32]
Late we Percyuell þe ȝynge
Fare in Goddes blyssynge,
And vntill Arthoure þe Kynge
  Will we agayne take.   1060

The gates agayne we will tane;
The Kyng to care-bedd es gane;
For mournynge es his maste mane:[33]
  He syghes full sore.
His wo es wansome[34] to wreke,   1065
His hert es bownn for to breke,
For he wend neuer to speke
  With Percyuell no more.
Als he was layde for to ly,[35]
Come þe messangere on hy   1070
With lettres fro þe lady,
  And schewes þam righte þare.
Afote myȝte þe Kyng noȝt stande,
Bot rede þam þare lyggande,
And sayde, "Of thyne erande   1075
  Thou hase thyn answare."

---

[29] deeds of valor. [30] haste, a short time. [31] recognised him. [32] make pale.
[33] his greatest lament is mourning (for one dead). [34] wretched; i.e., so great
as to be hard to avenge. [35] was put to bed preparatory to lying ill.

1050. Cf. 23, 922.
1062. The king's illness may be an enchantment. (Cf. Brown 127;
"The Debility of the Ultonian Warriors"; *Romania* 40.628.) The phrase
occurs in the ballad "Sir Cawline."

He sayde, "Þou wote thyne ansuare:
The mane þat es seke and sare,
He may full ill ferre fare
    In felde for to fyghte."   1080
The messangere made his mone:
Saide, "Wo worthe wikkede wone !36
Why ne hade i tournede and gone
    Agayne with the knyghte?"
"What knyghte es þat," said þe Kyng,   1085
"Þat þou mase of thy menynge?
In my londe wot i no lordyng
    Es worthy to be a knyghte."
The messangere ansuerd agayne,
"Wete ȝe, his name es for to layne,   1090
Þe whethir37 i wolde hafe weten fayne
    What þe childe highte.

Thus mekill gatt i of þat knyght:
His dame38 sonne, he said, he hight.
One what maner þat he was dight   1095
    Now i sall ȝow telle:
He was wighte and worthly,39
His body bolde and borely,40
His armour bryghte and blody—
    Hade bene late in batell;   1100
Blode-rede was his stede,
His akton41 and his oþer wede;
His cote of þe same hede42
    Þat till a knyghte felle."
Than comanded þe Kyng   1105
Horse and armes for to brynge:
"If i kan trow thi talkynge,
    That ilke was Percyuell."

---

36 woe befall unwise conduct.   37 although.   38 mother's.   39 fine.   40 goodly.
41 jacket.   42 quality.

1105. The mere mention of Perceval seems enough to dissolve the enchantment.   On the incident, cf. Griffith 82; Wimberly 345.   On the
magic of names, see bibliography and E. Clodd's *Tom Tit Tot* 169.

For þe luffe of Percyuell,
To horse and armes þay felle;   1110
Þay wolde no lengare þer duelle:
    To fare ware þay fayne.
Faste forthe gan þay fare;
Þay were aferde full sare,
Ere þay come whare he ware,   1115
    Þe childe wolde be slayne.
The Kyng tase with hym knyghtis thre:
The ferthe wolde hymselfe be;
Now so faste rydes hee,
    May folowe hym no swayne.   1120
The Kyng es now in his waye;
Lete hym come when he maye!
And i will forthir in my playe[43]
    To Percyuell agayne.

Go we to Percyuell agayne!   1125
The childe paste oute on þe playne,
Ouer more[44] and mountayne,
    To þe Maydenlande;
Till agayne þe euen-tyde,
Bolde bodys[45] sawe he byde,   1130
Pauelouns[46] mekill and vnryde[47]
    Aboute a cyté stonde.
On huntyng was þe sowdane;
He lefte men many ane:
Twenty score þat wele kan,   1135
    Be þe 3ates 3emande—
Ell[even] score one the nyghte,
And ten one þe daye-lighte,
Wele armyde at alle righte,[48]
    With wapyns in hande.   1140

---

[43] performance, narration.   [44] moor.   [45] fellows.   [46] tents, temporary shelters.
[47] ugly.   [48] particulars.

1127. The fairy world always has barriers. Cf. the dangerous pass in
"Iwain;" the ford in "Eger;" the island in "Launfal;" the cave in "Orfeo."

With þaire wapyns in þaire hande,
There will þay fight þer þay stande,
Sittande and lyggande,
 Elleuen score of men.
In he rydes one a rase,[49]   1145
Or þat he wiste where he was,
Into þe thikkeste of þe prese
 Amanges þam thanne.
And vp stirt one þat was bolde,
Bygane his brydill to holde,   1150
And askede whedire[50] þat he wolde
 Make his horse to rynne.
He said, "I ame hedir come
For to see a sowdane;
In faythe, righte sone he sall be slane,   1155
 And i myghte hym ken.

If i hym oghte ken may,
To-morne, when it es lighte daye,
Then sall we togedir playe
 With wapyns vnryde."   1160
They herde þat he had vndirtane
For to sle þaire sowdane;
Thay felle aboute hym, euerilkane,
 To make þat bolde[1] habyde.
The childe sawe þat he was fade,[2]   1165
Þe body þat his bridill hade:
Euen ouer hym he rade,
 In gate þere bisyde.
He stayred[3] about hym with his spere;
Many thurgh gane he bere:[4]   1170
Þer was none þat myȝt hym dere,
 Perceuell, þat tyde.

Tide in townne who will telle,[5]
Folkes vndir his fete felle;

---

[49] rush.   [50] whither.   [1] brave (knight).   [2] determined.   [3] thrust.   [4] strike.
[5] whoever would tell in town (i.e., anywhere) the course of events (would say), etc.

The bolde body Perceuelle,   1175
 He sped, þam to spill.
Hym thoghte no spede at his spere:
Many thurgh gane he bere,
Fonde folke in the here,[6]
 Feghtyng to fill.[7]   1180
Fro that it was mydnyghte
Till it was euen[8] at daye-lighte,
Were þay neuer so wilde ne wighte,
 He wroghte at his will.
Thus he dalt with his brande,[9]   1185
There was none þat myght hym stande
Halfe a dynt of his hande
 þat he stroke till.[10]

Now he strykes for þe nonys,
Made þe Sarazenes hede-bones   1190
Hoppe als dose hayle-stones
 Abowtte one þe gres;[11]
Thus he dalt þam on rawe[12]
Till þe daye gun dawe:[13]
He layd þaire lyues full law,   1195
 Als many als there was.
When he hade slayne so many men,
He was so wery by then,
I tell ȝow for certen,
 He roghte wele þe lesse   1200
Awþer of lyfe or of dede,
To medis þat he were[14] in a stede
þar he myghte riste hym in thede[15]
 A stownde in sekirnes.[16]

Now fonde he no sekirnes,   1205
 Bot vnder þe walle þer he was,
A faire place he hym chese,
 And down there he lighte.

---

[6] foolish folk of the enemy.   [7] to (his own) fill.   [8] just.   [9] dealt (blows) with his sword.   [10] upon.   [11] grass.   [12] in turn.   [13] dawn.   [14] if only he could be in the midst of.   [15] people; i.e., there.   [16] security.

He laide hym doun in þat tyde;
His stede stode hym besyde: 1210
The fole was fayne for to byde—
    Was wery for þe fyght.
Till one þe morne þat it was day,
The wayte[17] appon þe walle lay:
He sawe an vggly play[18]   1215
    In þe place dighte;
ȝitt was þer more ferly:[19]
Ther was no qwyk man left þerby;
Thay called vp þe lady
    For to see þat sighte.   1220

Now commes þe lady to þat sight,
The Lady Lufamour, þe bright;
Scho clambe vp to þe walle on hight
    Full faste scho behelde;
Hedes and helmys þer was   1225
(I tell ȝow withowtten lese),
Many layde one þe gresse,
    And many brode schelde.
Grete ferly thaym thoghte
Who þat wondir[20] had wroghte,   1230
That had þam to dede broghte,
    That folke in the felde,
And wold come none innermare[21]
For to kythe what he ware,
And[22] wist þe lady was þare,   1235
    Thaire warysoune[23] to ȝelde.

Scho wold þaire warysone ȝelde:
Full faste forthe þay bihelde
If þay myghte fynde in þe felde

---

[17] sentinel, watcher.   [18] performance; i.e., sight.   [19] marvel.   [20] destruction.
[21] no further within (the castle).   [22] even though he.   [23] reward.

1224. Holthausen's emendation for MS. *to beholde*.
1228. MS. *schelde brode*.

Who hade done þat dede.   1240
Þay luked vndir þair hande,[24]
Sawe a mekill horse stande,
A blody knyghte liggande
    By a rede stede.
Then said þe lady so brighte,   1245
"ȝondir ligges a knyghte
Þat hase bene in þe fighte,
    If i kane righte rede;
Owthir es ȝone man slane,
Or he slepis hym allane,   1250
Or he in batelle es tane,
    For blody are his wede."

Scho says, "Blody are his wede,
And so es his riche stede;
Siche a knyght in this thede   1255
    Saw i neuer nane.
What-so he es, and he maye ryse,
He es large there he lyse,
And wele made in alle wyse,
    Ther als man sall be tane."[25]   1260
Scho calde appon hir chaymbirlayne,
Was called hende Hatlayne—
The curtasye of Wawayne
    He weldis in wane;[26]—
Scho badd hym, "Wende and see   1265
ȝif ȝon man on lyfe be.
Bid hym com and speke with me,
    And pray hym als þou kane."

Now to pray hym als he kane,
Vndir þe wallis he wane;   1270
Warly[27] wakend he þat mane:
    Þe horse stode still.

---

[24] i.e., just below.   [25] in which a man is judged.   [26] manners.   [27] cautiously.

1262. *Hatlayne* possibly from *chatelain*, the governor or chief-of-staff in a castle.—Holthausen.

Als it was tolde vnto me,
He knelid down on his kne;
Hendely hailsed[28] he þat fre,   1275
    And sone said hym till,
"My lady, lele[29] Lufamour,
Habyddis the in hir chambour,
Prayes the, for thyn honour,
    To come, ʒif ʒe will."   1280
So kyndly takes he þat kyth[30]
Þat vp he rose and went hym wyth,
The man þat was of myche pyth,[31]
    Hir prayer to fulfill.

Now hir prayer to fulfill,   1285
He folowed þe gentilmans will,
And so he went hir vntill,
    Forthe to that lady.
Full blythe was þat birde[32] brighte
When scho sawe hym with syghte,   1290
For scho trowed þat he was wighte,
    And askede[33] hym in hy:
At þat fre gan scho frayne,
Þoghe he were lefe for to layne,[34]
If he wiste who had þam slayne—   1295
    Þase folkes of envy.
He sayd, "I soghte none of tho;
I come the sowdane to slo,
And þay ne wolde noghte late me go;
    Þaire lyfes there refte i."   1300

He sayd, "Belyfe þay solde aby."
And Lufamour, þat lele lady,
Wist ful wele therby
    The childe was full wighte.
The birde was blythe of þat bade[35]   1305
    Þat scho siche an helpe hade:

---

[28] greeted.   [29] worthy.   [30] announcement.   [31] force.   [32] lady.   [33] questioned.
[34] desirous of dissembling.   [35] tidings.

Agayne þe sowdane was fade[36]
  With alle for to fighte.
Faste þe lady hym byhelde:
Scho thoght hym worthi to welde,[37]   1310
And he myghte wyn hir in felde,
  With maystry and myghte.
His stede þay in stabill set
And hymselfe to haulle was fet,
And than, withowtten any let,   1315
  To dyne gun thay dighte.

The childe was sett on þe dese,
And serued with reches[38]
(I tell ȝow withowtten lese)
  Þat gaynely was get[39]—   1320
In a chayere of golde
Bifore þe fayrest, to byholde
The myldeste mayden one molde,[40]
  At mete als scho satt.
Scho made hym semblande so gude,[41]   1325
Als þay felle to þaire fude—
The mayden mengede[42] his mode
  With myrthes at þe mete,—
Þat for hir sake righte tha
Sone he gane vndirta   1330
The sory sowdane to sla,
  Withowtten any lett.

He sayd, withowtten any lett,
"When þe sowdane and i bene mett,
A sadde[43] stroke i sall one hym sett,   1335
  His pride for to spyll."
Then said þe lady so free,
"Who þat may his bon[44] be
Sall hafe þis kyngdome and me,
  To welde at his will."   1340

---

[36] determined. [37] govern. [38] dainties. [39] were properly served. [40] earth. [41] looked on him so pleasantly. [42] mingled; i.e., entertained. [43] severe, hard. [44] bane, death.

He ne hade dyned bot smalle[45]
When worde come into þe haulle
Þat many men with alle
　　Were hernyste[46] one the hill;
For tene[47] þaire felawes were slayne,　　　　1345
　　The cité hafe þay nere tane;
The men þat were within þe wane[48]
　　The comon-belle gun knylle.[49]

Now knyllyn þay þe comon-belle.
Worde come to Perceuell,　　　　1350
And he wold there no lengere duelle,
　　Bot lepe fro the dese—
Siche wilde gerys hade he mo;[50]—
Sayd, "Kynsmen, now i go.
For alle ʒone sall i slo　　　　1355
　　Longe are i sese!"
Scho kiste hym withowtten lett;
The helme on his hede scho sett;
To þe stabill full sone he gett,
　　There his stede was.　　　　1360
There were none with hym to fare;
For no man þen wolde he spare![1]—
Rydis furthe, withowtten mare,
　　Till he come to þe prese.

When he come to þe prese,　　　　1365
He rydes in one a rese;[2]
The folkes, þat byfore hym was,
　　Thaire strenght[3] hade þay tone;
To kepe hym þan were þay ware;
Þaire dynttis deris hym no mare　　　　1370
Þen whoso hade strekyn sare
　　One a harde stone.
Were þay wighte, were þay woke,[4]
　　Alle þat he till stroke,

---

[45] eaten but a little.　[46] armed.　[47] anger that.　[48] stronghold.　[49] did toll the alarm-bell.　[50] i.e., of such impulsive ways had he very many.　[1] forbear, stop.　[2] rush.　[3] full force.　[4] weak.

He made þaire bodies to roke:[5]   1375
Was þer no better wone.[6]
I wote, he sped hym so sone
þat day, by heghe none
With all þat folke hade he done:
One life lefte noghte one.   1380

When he had slayne all tho,
He loked forthir hym fro,
If he myghte fynde any mo
With hym for to fyghte;
And als þat hardy bihelde,   1385
He sese, ferre in the felde,
Fowre knyghtis vndir schelde
Come rydand full righte.
One was Kyng Arthour,
Anothir Ewayne, the floure,   1390
The thirde Wawayne with honoure,
And Kay, þe kene knyghte.
Perceuell saide, withowtten mare,
"To ȝondir foure will i fare;
And if the sowdane be thare,   1395
I sall holde þat i highte."

Now to holde þat he hase highte,
Agaynes thaym he rydis righte,
And ay lay the lady brighte
One þe walle, and byhelde   1400
How many men þat he had slane,
And sythen gane his stede mayne[7]
Foure kempys[8] agayne,
Forthir in the felde.

---

[5] fall back.   [6] manner; i.e., fate.   [7] ride.   [8] warriors.

1380. MS. *lefe*.
1387. I.e., in armor. A knight frequently removed his armor when
riding on a peaceful mission.
1390. For *Ewayne fitz-Asoure*, as in 261? The sequence of rhymes is
much the same.

Then was the lady full wo   1405
When scho sawe hym go
Agaynes foure knyghtys tho,
    With schafte and with schelde.
They were so mekyl and vnryde[9]
Þat wele wende scho þat tyde   1410
With bale þay solde gare hym byde
    Þat was hir beste belde.[10]

Þofe he were beste of hir belde,
As þat lady byhelde,
He rydes forthe in þe felde,   1415
    Euen[11] þam agayne.
Then sayd Arthoure þe Kyng,
"I se a bolde knyghte owt spryng;
For to seke feghtyng,
    Forthe will he frayne.   1420
If he fare forthe to fighte
And we foure kempys agayne one knyght,
Littill menske[12] wold to vs lighte
    If he were sone slayne."
They fore forthward right faste,   1425
And sone keuells[13] did þay caste,
And euyr fell it to frayste[14]
    Vntill Sir Wawayne.

When it felle to Sir Wawayne
To ryde Perceuell agayne,   1430
Of þat fare was he fayne,
    And fro þam he rade.
Euer þe nerre hym he drewe,
Wele þe better he hym knewe,
Horse and hernays of hewe,   1435
    Þat þe childe hade.
"A, dere God!" said Wawayne þe fre,
"How-gates[15] may this be?
If i sle hym, or he me,

---

[9] huge.   [10] reliance.   [11] straight.   [12] honor.   [13] lots.   [14] try.   [15] by what chance.

Þat neuer ȝit was fade,   1440
And we are sister sones two,
And aythir of vs othir slo,
He þat lifes will be full wo
    Þat euer was he made."

Now no maistrys[16] he made,   1445
Sir Wawayne, there als he rade,
Bot houyde[17] styll and habade,
    His concell to ta.
"Ane vnwyse man," he sayd, "am i,
Þat puttis myselfe to siche a foly;   1450
Es þere no man so hardy
    Þat ne anothir es alswa.[18]
Þogfe Perceuell hase slayne þe Rede Knyght,
Ȝitt may anoþer be als wyghte,
And in þat gere be dyghte,   1455
    And taken alle hym fra.
If i suffire[19] my sister sone,
And anothir in his gere be done,[20]
And gete þe maystry me appon,
    Þat wolde do me wa;   1460

It wolde wirke me full wa!
So mote i one erthe ga,
It ne sall noghte betyde me swa,
    If i may righte rede!
A schafte sall i one hym sett,   1465
And i sall fonde firste to hitt;
Þen sall i ken be my witt
    Who weldys þat wede."
No more carpys he þat tyde,
Bot son togedyr gon þay ryde—   1470
Men þat bolde were to byde,[21]

---

[16] warlike manœuvers. [17] remained. [18] i.e., that another may not be his match. [19] i.e., deal gently with. [20] arrayed. [21] were courageous in waiting (for an enemy).

1440. In all four instances in the poem, *fade* seems to mean "eager for trouble."

And styff appon stede;
þaire horse were stallworthe and strange,[22]
þair scheldis were vnfailande;
þaire speris brake to þaire hande,[23]   1475
Als þam byhoued nede.[24]

Now es broken þat are were hale,[25]
And þan bygane Perceuale
For to tell one a tale
 þat one his tonge laye.   1480
He sayde, "Wyde-whare[26] hafe i gane;
Siche anothir sowdane
In faythe sawe i neuer nane,
 By nyghte ne by daye.
I hafe slayne, and i þe ken,   1485
Twenty score of thi men;
And of alle þat i slewe then,
 Me thoghte it bot a playe
Agayne[27] þat dynt þat i hafe tane;
For siche one aughte i neuer nane   1490
Bot i qwyte two for ane,
 Forsothe, and i maye."

Then spake Sir Wawayne—
Certanely, is noghte to layne,
Of þat fare was he fayne,   1495
 In felde there thay fighte:
By the wordis so wylde
At the fole one the felde,
He wiste wele it was þe childe,
 Perceuell þe wighte—   1500
He sayse, "I ame no sowdane,
Bot i am þat ilke man
þat thi body bygan

---

[22] strong. [23] along their whole length. [24] they needs must. [25] whole. [26] far and wide. [27] in comparison with.

1476. If both knights sat firm, and their shields held, the spears must be the parts to break.

In armours to dighte.
I giffe the prise to thi pyth;[28]   1505
Vnkyndely[29] talked thou me with:
My name es Wawayne in kythe,[30]
    Whoso redys righte."

He sayes, "Who þat will rede the aryghte,
My name es Wawayne þe knyghte."   1510
And þan þay sessen of þaire fighte,
    Als gude frendes scholde.
He sayse, "Thynkes þou noghte[31] when
Þat þou woldes þe knyghte brene,
For þou ne couthe noghte ken   1515
    To spoyle[32] hym alle colde?"
Bot þen was Perceuell þe free
Als blythe als he myghte be,
For þen wiste he wele þat it was he,
    By takens[33] þat he tolde.   1520
He dide þen als he gane hym lere:
Putt vp hys vmbrere;[34]
And kyste togedir with gud chere
    Þose beryns[35] so bolde.

Now kissede the beryns so bolde—   1525
Sythen, talkede what þay wolde.
Be then come Arthour þe bolde,
    Þat there was knyghte and kyng—
Als his cosyns hadd done,
Thankede God also sone.   1530
Off mekill myrthis þay mone[36]
    At þaire metyng.
Sythen, withowtten any bade,
To þe castelle þay rade
With þe childe þat thay hade,   1535
    Perceuell þe ȝynge.
The portere was redy þare,

---

[28] acknowledge your spirit. [29] rudely. [30] among my people. [31] do you not recall. [32] plunder. [33] tokens. [34] visor. [35] warriors. [36] recall.

Lete þe knyghtis in fare;
A blythere lady þan . . .

. . . .   1540

"Mi grete socour at[37] þou here sende,
Off my castell me to diffende,
Agayne þe sowdane to wende,
    Þat es my moste foo."
Theire stedis þay sett in þe stalle;   1545
Þe Kyng wendis to haulle;
His knyghtis ȝode hym with alle,
    Als kynde was to go.[38]
Þaire metis was redy,
And þerto went þay in hy,   1550
The Kyng and þe lady,
    And knyghtis also.

Wele welcomed scho þe geste
With riche metis of þe beste,
Drynkes of þe derreste,   1555
    Dightede bydene.
Þay ete and dranke what þay wolde,
Sythen talked and tolde
Off othir estres[39] full olde,
    Þe Kyng and þe Qwene.   1560
At þe firste bygynnyng,
Scho frayned Arthour þe Kyng
Of childe Perceuell þe ȝyng,
    What life he had in bene.
Grete wondir had Lufamour   1565
He was so styffe in stour
And couthe so littill of nurtour
    Als scho had there sene.

Scho had sene with þe childe

---

[37] that.   [38] as was their habit.   [39] stories.

1539. The missing words are torn out of the MS. The scribe omitted
a few lines telling of the lady's welcome to Arthur.

No thyng bot werkes wylde;[40]   1570
Thoghte grete ferly on filde
    Of þat foly fare.[41]
Þen said Arthour þe Kyng
Of bold Perceuell techyng,[42]
Fro þe firste bygynnyng   1575
    [Ti]ll þat he come thar:
[How] his ffadir was slayne,
[And his modi]r to þe wode gane
[For to be t]here hir allane
    [In þe holtis har]e,   1580
Fully feftene 3ere
To play hym with þe wilde dere:
Littill wonder it were
    Wilde if he ware!

When he had tolde this tale   1585
To þat semely in sale,[43]
He hade wordis at wale[44]
    To þam ilkane.
The[n] said Perceuell þe wighte,
"3if i be noghte 3itt knyghte,   1590
Þou sall halde þat þou highte,
    For to make me ane."
Than saide þe Kyng full sone,
"Ther sall oþer dedis be done,
And þou sall wynn thi schone[45]   1595
    Appon þe sowdane."
Þen said Perceuell þe fre,
"Als sone als i þe sowdane see,
Righte so sall it sone be,
    Als i hafe vndirtane."   1600

    He says, "Als i hafe vndirtane

---

[40] acts of violence.   [41] unusual conduct.   [42] training.   [43] hall.   [44] choice.   [45] i.e.,
spurred knight's-shoes.

1576 ff. The words in brackets were supplied by Halliwell and Holthausen; the corner of the leaf is missing.

For to sla þe sowdane,
So sall i wirke als i kanne,
  þat dede to bygynn."
þat day was þer no more dede   1605
With those worthily in wede,
Bot buskede þam and to bedde ȝede,
  The more and the mynn;[46]
Till one þe morne erely
Comes þe sowdane with a cry,[47]   1610
Fonde all his folkes hym by
  Putt vnto pyn.[48]
Sone asked he wha
þat so durste his men sla
And wete hym one lyfe gaa,   1615
  The maystry to wynn.

Now to wynn þe maystry,
To þe castell gan he cry,
If any were so hardy,
  The maistry to wynn,   1620
A man for ane;[49]
þoghe he hadd all his folke slane,
"Here sall he fynde Golrotherame
  To mete hym full ryghte,
Appon siche a couenande   1625
þat ȝe hefe[50] vp ȝour hande:
Who þat may þe better stande
  And more es of myghte
To bryng þat oþer to þe dede,
Browke wele þe londe on brede,[1]   1630
And hir þat is so faire and rede—
  Lufamour þe brighte."

---

[46] less. [47] noise. [48] pain; i.e., dead. [49] man for man. [50] raise. [1] throughout.

1606. *Worthily* is an adjective.
1615. I.e., knew the sultan to be alive, and hence sure to resent it. Saracens are always boastful in the romances.
1620. Probably the right reading is: *With hym for to fyghte.*

Then þe Kyng Arthour
And þe Lady Lufamour
And all þat were in þe towre   1635
    Graunted þerwith.
Thay called Perceuell þe wight;
Þe Kyng doubbed hym to knyghte.
Þofe he couthe littill insighte,[2]
    The childe was of pith.[3]   1640
He bad he solde be to prayse,[4]
Þerto hende and curtayse;
Sir Perceuell the Galayse
    Þay called hym in kythe.
Kyng Arthour in Maydenlande   1645
Dubbid hym knyghte with his hande,
Bad hym, þer he his fo fande,
    To gyff hym no grythe.

Grith takes he nane:
He rydes agayne þe sowdane   1650
Þat highte Gollerotherame,
    Þat felle was in fighte.
In þe felde so brade,
No more carpynge þay made,
Bot sone togedir þay rade,   1655
    Theire schaftes to righte.[5]
Gollerotheram, þofe he wolde wede,[6]
Perceuell bere hym fro his stede
Two londis one brede,
    With maystry and myghte.   1660
At þe erthe þe sowdane lay;
His stede gun rynn away;

---

[2] formal learning.   [3] spirited.   [4] i.e., act worthily.   [5] well aimed.   [6] rage.

1659. The distance traversed by the unfortunate Sultan is uncertain. A land was the part of a field between dead furrows, and was apparently a stable unit of measure. Heroes in romance often cause the weapons of opponents and even the opponents themselves to fly long distances. Cf. "Bevis" A. 1906, where a shield flies three acres. More conservative poets are content with a spear's length.

þan said Perceuell one play,
　"Þou haste þat i the highte."

He sayd, "I highte the a dynt,　　　　　　1665
And now, me thynke, þou hase it hynt.
And i may, als i hafe mynt,
　Þou schalt it neuer mende."
Appon þe sowdan he duelled[7]
To þe grownde þer he was felled,　　　　1670
And to þe erthe he hym helde
　With his speres ende.
Fayne wolde he hafe hym slayne,
This vncely[8] sowdane,
Bot gate couthe he get nane,　　　　　　1675
　So ill was he kende.
Þan thynkes þe childe
Of olde werkes full wylde:
"Hade i a fire now in this filde,
　Righte here he solde be brende."　　　　1680

He said, "Righte here i solde þe brene,
And þou ne solde neuer more then
Fighte for no wymman,
　So i solde the fere!"[9]
Þen said Wawayne þe knyghte,　　　　　1685
"Þou myghte, and þou knewe righte,
And þou woldes of þi stede lighte,
　Wynn hym one were."
The childe was of gamen gnede;[10]
Now he thynkes one thede,[11]　　　　　1690
"Lorde! whethir this be a stede
　I wende had bene a mere?"
In stede righte there he in stode,
He ne wiste noþer of euyll ne gude,[12]
Bot then chaunged his mode　　　　　　1695
　And slaked[13] his spere.

---

[7] blocked, pressed.　[8] luckless.　[9] terrify.　[10] chary of banter.　[11] land; i.e., there.
[12] sc. "manners."　[13] released.

When his spere was vp tane,
The[n] gan this Gollerothiram,
This ilke vncely sowdane,
    One his fete to gete.   1700
Than his swerde drawes he,
Strykes at Perceuell the fre;
The childe hadd no powsté[14]
    His laykes[15] to lett.
The stede was his awnn will:[16]   1705
Saw þe swerde come hym[17] till,
Leppe vp ouer an hill,
    Fyve stryde mett.[18]
Als he sprent forby,[19]
The sowdan keste vp a cry;   1710
The childe wann owt of study[20]
    Þat he was inn sett.

Now ther he was in sett,
Owt of study he gett,
And lightis downn, withowtten lett,   1715
    Agaynes hym to goo.
He says, "Now hase þou taughte me
How þat i sall wirke with the."
Than his swerde drawes he
    And strake to hym thro.[21]   1720
He hitt hym euen one þe nekk-bane,
Thurgh ventale and pesane;[22]
The hede of the sowdane
    He strykes the body fra.
Þen full wightly he ȝode   1725
To his stede, þere he stode;
The milde mayden in mode,
    Mirthe may scho ma!

Many mirthes then he made;
In to þe castell he rade,   1730

---

[14] ability. [15] sword play. [16] i.e., own master. [17] Perceval. [18] and measured five strides. [19] raced past. [20] preoccupation. [21] fiercely. [22] visor and neck armor.

And boldly he there habade
　With þat mayden brighte.
Fayne were þay ilkane
Þat he had slane þe sowdane
And wele wonn þat wymman,　　　　　　　1735
　With maystry and myghte.
Þay said Perceuell þe ȝyng
Was beste worthy to be kyng,
For wele withowtten lesyng
　He helde þat he highte.　　　　　　　　1740
Ther was no more for to say,
Bot sythen, appon þat oþer day,
He weddys Lufamour þe may,
　This Perceuell þe wighte.

Now hase Perceuell þe wight　　　　　　1745
Wedded Lufamour þe bright,
And is a kyng full righte
　Of alle þat lande brade.
Than Kyng Arthour in hy
Wolde no lengare ther ly:　　　　　　　1750
Toke lefe at the lady:
　Fro þam þan he rade:
Left Perceuell the ȝyng
Off all þat lande to be kyng,
For he had [wedded] with a ryng　　　　1755
　Þe mayden þat it hade.
Sythen, appon þe toþer day,
The Kyng went on his way,
The certane sothe, als i say,
　Withowtten any bade.　　　　　　　　1760

Now þan ȝong Perceuell habade
In those borowes so brade
For hir sake, þat he hade
　Wedd with a ryng.
Wele weldede he þat lande,　　　　　　1765
Alle bowes to his honde;

Þe folke, þat he byfore fonde,[23]
   Knewe hym for kyng.
Thus he wonnes in þat wone[24]
Till that the twelmonthe was gone,   1770
With Lufamour his lemman:
   He thoghte on no thyng,
Nor on his moder þat was,
How scho leuyde with þe gres,[25]
With more drynke and lesse,   1775
   In welles, þere þay spryng;

Drynkes of welles, þer þay spryng,
And gresse etys, withowt lesyng!
Scho liffede with none othir thyng
   In þe holtes hare;   1780
Till it byfelle appon a day,
Als he in his bedd lay,
Till hymselfe gun he say,
   Syghande full sare,
"The laste ȝole-day þat was,   1785
Wilde wayes i chese:
My modir all manles[26]
   Leued i thare."
Þan righte sone saide he,
"Blythe sall i neuer be   1790
Or i may my modir see,
   And wete how scho fare."

Now to wete how scho fare,
The knyght busked hym ȝare;
He wolde no lengare duelle thare   1795
   For noghte þat myghte bee.
Vp he rose in þat haulle,

---

[23] came. [24] place. [25] grass. [26] i.e., unprotected.

1770. A year is a conventional period for a mortal to remain in fairyland without recalling his old life. On the subject, see Hartland's "Science of Fairy Tales," Ch. 7.
1775. MS. *with moste.*—Holthausen.

Tuke his lefe at þam alle,
Bot[h] at grete and at smalle;
 Fro thaym wendis he.   1800
Faire scho prayed hym euen than,
Lufamour, his lemman,
Till þe heghe dayes of ȝole were gane,
 With hir for to bee;
Bot it serued hir of no thyng:[27]   1805
A preste he made forthe bryng,
Hym a messe for to syng,
 And aftir rode he.

Now fro þam gun he ryde;
Þer wiste no man þat tyde   1810
Whedirwarde he wolde ryde,
 His sorowes to amende.
Forthe he rydes allone;
Fro þam he wolde euerichone:
Mighte no man with hym gone,   1815
 Ne whedir he wolde lende.[28]
Bot forthe thus rydes he ay,
Þe certen sothe als i ȝow say,
Till he come at a way
 By a wode-ende.   1820
Then herde he faste hym by
Als it were a woman cry:
Scho prayed to mylde Mary
 Som socoure hir to sende.

Scho sende hir socour full gude,.   1825
Mary, þat es mylde of mode:
As he come thurgh the wode,
 A ferly he fande.
A birde,[29] brighteste of ble,
Stode faste bonden till a tre   1830

---

[27] i.e., did her no good. [28] arrive. [29] lady.

1812, 1816. Holthausen transposed these lines; but they may be left as
in the MS. if the second is an ellipsis for "nor (know) whither," etc.

(I say it ȝow certanly),
  Bothe fote and hande.
Sone askede he who,
When he sawe hir tho,
Þat had serued hir so,   1835
  Þat lady in lande.
Scho said, "Sir, þe Blake Knyghte
Solde be my lorde with righte;
He hase me thusgates[30] dighte
  Here for to stande."   1840

Scho says, "Here mon i stande
For a faute[31] þat he fande,
Þat sall i warande,
  Is my moste mone.
Now to the i sall say: 1845
Appon my bedd i lay
Appon þe laste ȝole-day—
  Twelue monethes es gone.
Were he knyghte, were he kyng,
He come one his play[y]nge: 1850
With me he chaungede[32] a ryng,
  The richeste of one.[33]
The body myght i noghte see
Þat made þat chaungyng with me,
Bot what þat euer he be,   1855
  The better hase he tone!"

Scho says, "Þe better hase he tane;
Siche a vertue es in þe stane,
In alle this werlde wote i nane
  Siche stone in a rynge;   1860
A man þat had it in were[34]
One his body for to bere,
There scholde no dyntys hym dere,

[30] in this wise. [31] fault. [32] exchanged. [33] i.e., finest of all. [34] war.

1863. On protective stones, cf. Dickman 181; Joan Evans, "Magical Jewels of the Middle Ages," 111 ff.

Ne to þe dethe brynge."
And then wiste Sir Perceuale   1865
Full wele by the ladys tale
Þat he had broghte hir in bale
Thurgh his chaungyng.
Than also sone sayd he
To that lady so fre,   1870
"I sall the louse[35] fro þe tre,
Als i am trewe kyng."

He was bothe kyng and knyght:
Wele he helde þat he highte;
He loused the lady so brighte,   1875
    Stod bown to the tre.
Down satt the lady,
And ȝong Perceuall hir by;
Forwaked[36] was he wery:
    Rist hym wolde he.   1880
He wende wele for to ryst,
Bot it wolde nothyng laste:
Als he lay althir best,[37]
    His hede one hir kne,
Scho putt on Perceuell wighte,   1885
Bad hym fle with all his myghte,
"For ȝonder comes þe Blake Knyghte;
    Dede mon ȝe be!"

Scho sayd, "Dede mon ȝe be,
I say ȝow, sir, certanly: 1890
Ȝonder out comes he
    Þat will vs bothe sle!"
The knyghte gan hir answere,
"Tolde ȝe me noghte lang ere

---

[35] let loose.   [36] exhausted from being awake.   [37] i.e., most comfortably.

1864. MS. *ne the to.*
1873. This is a preliminary to the enchanter's entrance. Cf. Wimberly
348.
1885. Possibly the right reading is *pult on,* pushed away.

Ther solde no dynttis me dere,   1895
  Ne wirke me no woo?"
The helme on his hede he sett;
Bot or he myght to his stede get,
The Blak Knyght with hym mett,
  His maistrys to mo.   1900
He sayd, "How! hase þou here
Fonden now thi play-fere?[38]
Ʒe schall haby it full dere
  Er þat i hethen go!"

He said, "Or i hethyn go,   1905
I sall sle Ʒow, bothe two,
And all siche othir mo,
  Þaire waryson[39] to Ʒelde."
Than sayd Perceuell þe fre,
"Now sone þan sall we see   1910
Who þat es worthy to bee
  Slayne in the felde."
No more speke þay þat tyde,
Bot sone togedir gan þay ryde,
Als men þat wolde were habyde,[40]   1915
  With schafte and with schelde.
Than Sir Perceuell þe wight
Bare down þe Blake Knyght;
Þan was þe lady so bright
  His best socour in telde:[41]   1920

Scho was þe beste of his belde:[42]
Bot scho had there bene his schelde,
He had bene slayne in þe felde,
  Right certeyne in hy.
Euer als[43] Perceuell the kene   1925

---

[38] paramour.   [39] reward.   [40] i.e., readily engage in war.   [41] tent.   [42] reliance.
[43] just as.

1900. *Mo* is a copyist's substitution; he probably confused the *ma* (make) of the original with *ma* (more), and put in the midland form.
1920. Probably the line should end *in belde*, in relief, defense. The expression in the text is a tag of little meaning.

Sold þe knyghtis bane hafe bene,
Ay went þe lady bytwene
　　And cryed, "Mercy!"
Than þe lady he forbere,[44]
And made þe Blak Knyghte to swere　　　　1930
Of alle euylls þat þere were,
　　Forgiffe the lady;
And Perceuell made þe same othe
Þat he come neuer vndir clothe
To do þat lady no lothe[45]　　　　1935
　　Þat pendid[46] to velany.

"I did hir neuer no velany;
Bot slepande i saw hir ly:
Þan kist i þat lady—
　　I will it neuer layne;—　　　　1940
I tok a ryng þat i fande;
I left hir, i vndirstande[47]
(Þat sall i wele warande),
　　Anothir ther-agayne."[48]
Þofe it were for none oþer thyng,　　　　1945
He swere by Ihesu, Heuen-kyng,
To wete withowtten lesyng,
　　And here to be slayne;
"And all redy is the ryng;
And þou will myn agayne bryng,　　　　1950
Here will i make þe chaungyng,
　　And of myn awnn be fayne."

He saise, "Of myn i will be fayne."
Þe Blak Knyghte ansuers agayne:
Sayd, "For sothe, it is noghte to layne,　　　　1955
　　Thou come ouer-late.
Als sone als i þe ryng fande,
I toke it sone off hir hande;

---

[44] spared.　　[45] injury.　　[46] pertained.　　[47] believe.　　[48] i.e., as a substitute.

1948. I.e., called on heaven to slay him if he spoke falsely. On swearing by one's life, see "Havelok" 186.

To the lorde of this lande
    I bare it one a gate.[49]   1960
Þat gate with grefe hafe i gone:
I bare it to a gude mone,[50]
The stalwortheste geant of one[1]
    Þat any man wate.
Es it nowþer knyghte ne kyng   1965
Þat dorste aske hym þat ryng,
Þat he ne wolde hym down dyng[2]
    With harmes full hate."[3]

Be þay hate, be þay colde,
Than said Perceuell þe bolde—   1970
For þe tale þat he tolde
    He wex all tene—
He said, "Heghe on galous mote he hyng
Þat to þe here giffes any ryng,
Bot þou myn agayne brynge,   1975
    Thou haste awaye geuen!
And ȝif it may no noþer be,
Righte sone þan tell þou me
The sothe: whilke þat es he
    Thou knawes, þat es so kene?   1980
Ther es no more for to say,
Bot late me wynn it ȝif i may,
For þou hase giffen thi part of bothe away,
    Þof thay had better bene."[4]

He says, "Þofe þyn had better bene."   1985
The knyghte ansuerde in tene,
"Þou sall wele wete, withowtten wene,[5]
    Wiche[6] þat es he!
If þou dare do als þou says,
Sir Perceuell de Galays,   1990
    In ȝone heghe palays,

---

[49] i.e., straight. [50] man. [1] all. [2] strike. [3] i.e., fearful injuries. [4] had been even more valuable. [5] doubt. [6] which.

1976. *Geuen* is for the northern form *gein, gen.*

Therin solde he be—
The riche ryng with þat grym![7]
The stane es bright and nothyng dym;
For sothe, þer sall þou fynd hym: 1995
   I toke it fro me;[8]
Owthir within or withowt,
Or one his play þer abowte,
Of the he giffes littill dowte,[9]
   And that sall thou see."   2000

He says, "That sall þou see,
I say the full sekirly."
And than forthe rydis he
   Wondirly swythe.
The geant stode in his holde,[10]   2005
That had those londis in wolde:[11]
Saw Perceuell, þat was bolde,
   One his lande dryfe;
He calde one his portere:
"How-gate[12] may this fare?   2010
I se a bolde man ȝare
   On my lande ryfe.[13]
Go reche me my playlome,[14]
And i sall go to hym sone;
Hym were better hafe bene at Rome,   2015
   So euer mote i thryfe!"

Whethir he thryfe or he the,
Ane iryn clobe takes he;
Agayne Perceuell the fre
   He went than full right.   2020
The clobe wheyhed[15] reghte wele
Þat a freke[16] myght it fele:
The hede was of harde stele,

---

[7] fearful (creature). [8] gave it away. [9] has little fear. [10] castle. [11] power.
[12] by what means. [13] arrive, come. [14] fighting-implement, weapon. [15] weighed.
[16] man, knight.

2018. Cf. "Degaré" 385.

Twelue stone weghte.
þer was iryn in the wande,[17]   2025
Ten stone of the lande,[18]
And one was byhynde his hande,[19]
    For holdyng was dight.
þer was thre and twenty in hale;[20]
Full euyll myght any men smale,   2030
þat men telles nowe in tale,
    With siche a lome[21] fighte.

Now are þay bothe bown,
Mett one a more[22] brown,
A mile withowt any town,   2035
    Boldly with schelde.
þan saide þe geant so wight,
Als sone als he sawe þe knyght,
"Mahown, loued be thi myght!"
    And Perceuell byhelde.   2040
"Art thou hym, that," saide he than,
"That slew Gollerothirame?
I had no brothir bot hym ane,
    When he was of elde."[23]
Than said Perceuell the fre,   2045
"Thurgh grace of God so sall i the,
And siche geanteȝ as ȝe—
    Sle thaym in the felde!"

Siche metyng was seldom sene;
The dales dynned thaym bytwene[24]   2050
For dynttis þat þay gaffe bydene

---

[17] shaft.   [18] i.e., by English standards.   [19] i.e., the handle is bound in iron
weighing one stone.   [20] all.   [21] implement.   [22] moor.   [23] full-grown (a tag).   [24] the
walls of the valleys reëchoed.

2024. A stone was about 14 lb., but varied because of lack of standards.
2031. Writers often represented the men of former times as of unusual stature and strength. Even this poet admits that his own heroes
belong to a past age. Ossian, returning from the otherworld, finds the
men of the day small and puny, and remarks that they are no such
fellows as composed the Fenian band.
2042. On the name, cf. *MPhil.*, 18.220.

When þay so mett.
The gyant with his clobe-lome[25]
Wolde hafe strekyn[26] Perceuell sone,
Bot he þervnder wightely[27] come,   2055
   A stroke hym to sett.
The geant missede of his dynt;
The clobe was harde as þe flynt:
Or he myght his staffe stynt[28]
   Or his strengh lett,   2060
The clobe in þe erthe stode:[29]
To þe midschafte it wode.[30]
The[n] Perceuell the gode,
   Hys swerde owt he get.

By then hys swerde owt he get,   2065
Strykes þe geant withowtten lett,
Merkes euen[31] to his nekk,
   Reght euen þer he stode;
His honde he strykes hym fro,
His lefte fote also;   2070
With siche dyntis as tho
   Nerre[32] hym he ȝode.
Þen sayd Perceuell, "I vndirstande[33]
Þou myghte with a lesse wande[34]
Hafe weledid better thi hande   2075
   And hafe done the some gode;
Now bese it neuer for ane[35]
The clobe of þe erthe tane;
I tell þi gatis alle gane,[36]
   Bi the gude rode!"   2080

He says, "By þe gud rode,
   As euyll als þou euer ȝode,[37]

---

[25] lit., club-weapon. [26] struck. [27] actively. [28] withhold. [29] pierced and remained fixed. [30] i.e., went half its length. [31] thrusts straight. [32] nearer. [33] believe, ween. [34] smaller shaft. [35] will never by one (man). [36] count your roads all traveled; i.e., your career ended. [37] However awkwardly you walk hereafter; i.e., since you are badly crippled.

2064. MS. *He swerde.*

Of þi fote þou getis no gode;
  Bot lepe[38] if þou may !"
The geant gan þe clobe lefe, 2085
And to Perceuell a dynt he ȝefe
In þe nekk with his nefe:[39]
  Sone neghede[40] þay.
At þat dynt was he tene:
He strikes off þe hande als clene 2090
Als þer hadde neuer none bene:
  Þat oþer was awaye.
Sythen his hede gan he off hafe;[41]
He was ane vnhende[42] knaue
A geantberde so to schafe, 2095
  For sothe, als i say !

Now for sothe, als i say,
He lete hym ly there he lay,
And rydis forthe one his way
  To þe heghe holde.[43] 2100
The portare saw his lorde slayne;
Þe kayes[44] durste he noght layne:
He come Perceuell agayne;
  Þe ȝatis he hym ȝolde.
At þe firste bygynnyng, 2105
He askede þe portere of the ryng—
If he wiste of it any thyng;
  And he hym than tolde:
He taughte[45] hym sone to þe kiste[46]
Þer he alle þe golde wiste,[47] 2110
Bade hym take what hym liste
  Of that he hafe wolde.

Perceuell sayde, hafe it he wolde,
And schott owtt all þe golde

---

[38] hop. [39] fist. [40] closed. [41] take. [42] rude. [43] high castle (cf. 1991). [44] keys.
[45] showed. [46] chest. [47] knew (to be).

2092. MS. *alwaye.*—Campion.
2095. Cf. the alliterative "Morte Arthure" 2095; "Ywain" 2400.

Righte there appon þe faire molde;[48]   2115
The ryng owte glade.[49]
The portare stode besyde,
Sawe þe ryng owt glyde,
Sayde ofte, "Wo worthe þe tyde
    þat euer was it made!"   2120
Perceuell answerde in hy,
And asked wherefore and why
He banned it so brothely,[50]
    Bot-if he cause hade.
Then alsone said he,   2125
And sware by his lewté:[1]
"The cause sall i tell the,
    Withowten any bade."

He says, withowtten any bade,
"The knyghte þat it here hade,   2130
Þeroff a presande he made,
    And hedir he it broghte.
Mi mayster tuke it in his hande,
Ressayued faire þat presande:
He was chefe lorde of þis lande,   2135
    Als man þat mekill moghte.[2]
Þat tyme was here fast by
Wonna[n]de a lady,
And hir wele and lely[3]
    He luffede, als me thoghte.   2140
So it byfelle appon a day,
Now þe sothe als i sall say,
Mi lorde went hym to play,
    And the lady bysoghte.[4]

Now þe lady byseches he   2145
Þat scho wolde his leman be;
Fast he frayned þat free,

---

[48] ground, turf. [49] flew. [50] cursed it so violently. [1] fealty. [2] had great power.
[3] truly. [4] importuned.

2138. Campion's emendation.

For any kyns aughte.[5]
At þe firste bygynnyng,
He wolde hafe gyffen hir þe ryng;   2150
And when scho sawe þe tokynyng,
Then was scho vn-saughte.[6]
Scho gret and cried in hir mone;
Sayd, 'Thefe, hase þou my sone slone
And the ryng fro hym tone,   2155
   þat i hym bitaughte?'
Hir clothes ther scho rafe[7] hir fro,
And to þe wodd gan scho go;
Thus es þe lady so wo,
   And this is the draghte.[8]   2160

For siche draghtis als this,
Now es þe lady wode, iwys,
And wilde in þe wodde scho es,
   Ay sythen þat ilke tyde.
Fayne wolde i take þat free,   2165
Bot alsone als scho sees me,
Faste awaye dose scho flee:
   Will scho noghte abyde."
Then sayde Sir Perceuell,
"I will assaye full snelle   2170
To make þat lady to duelle;
   Bot i will noghte ryde:
One my fete will i ga,
þat faire lady to ta.
Me aughte to bryng hir of wa: 2175
   I laye in hir syde."[9]

He sayse, "I laye in hir syde;
I sall neuer one horse ryde
Till i hafe sene hir in tyde,[10]

---

[5] i.e., wealth being no object; on any terms. [6] distressed. [7] tore. [8] course
(of fate), bad luck. [9] i.e., she was my mother. [10] time; at once.

2162. On the mother's madness, see Loomis, Ch. 27.
2175. On the impersonal construction, cf. Int. VII.A.1.

Spede if i may;   2180
Ne none armoure þat may be
Sall come appone me
Till i my modir may see,
　　Be nyghte or by day.
Bot reghte in þe same wode   2185
Þat i firste fro hir ȝode,
That sall be in my mode
　　Aftir myn oþer play;[11]
Ne i ne sall neuer mare
Come owt of ȝone holtis hare   2190
Till i wete how scho fare,
　　For sothe, als i saye."

Now for sothe, als i say,
With þat he helde one his way,
And one þe morne, when it was day,   2195
　　Forthe gonn he fare.
His armour he leued þerin,
Toke one hym a gayt-skynne,
And to þe wodde gan he wyn,
　　Among þe holtis hare.   2200
A seuenyght long hase he soghte;
His modir ne fyndis he noghte;
Of mete ne drynke he ne roghte,
　　So full he was of care.
Till þe nynte day, byfell[12]   2205
Þat he come to a welle
Þer he was wonte for to duelle
　　And drynk take hym thare.

When he had dronken þat tyde,
Forthirmare[13] gan he glyde;   2210
Than was he warre, hym besyde,
　　Of þe lady so fre;
Bot when scho sawe hym thare,
Scho bygan for to dare,[14]

---

[11] deeds; i.e., despite anything.　[12] it chanced.　[13] farther.　[14] hide.

And sone gaffe hym answare,   2215
   Þat brighte was of ble.
Scho bigan to call and cry:
Sayd, "Siche a sone hade i !"
His hert lightened in hy,
   Blythe for to bee.   2220
Be þat he come hir nere
Þat scho myght hym here,
He said, "My modir full dere,
   Wele byde ȝe me !"

Be that, so nere getis he   2225
Þat scho myghte nangatis[15] fle;
I say ȝow full certeynly,
   Hir byhoued þer to byde.
Scho stertis appon hym in tene;
Wete ȝe wele, withowtten wene,   2230
Had hir myghte so mekill bene,[16]
   Scho had hym slayne þat tyde !
Bot his myghte was þe mare,
And vp he toke his modir thare;
One his bake he hir bare: 2235
   Pure[17] was his pryde.
To þe castell, withowtten mare,
Þe righte way gon he fare;
The portare was redy ȝare,
   And lete hym in glyde.   2240

In with his modir he glade,
Als he sayse þat it made;
With siche clothes als þay hade,
   Þay happed[18] hir forthy.
Þe geant had a drynk wroghte;   2245
Þe portere sone it forthe broghte—
For no man was his thoghte
   Bot for that lady.

---

[15] in no wise.   [16] strength been great enough.   [17] poor, little.   [18] clad.

2242. ' As he says who composed the tale."

Þay wolde not lett long thon,
Bot lauede[19] in hir with a spone; 2250
Þen scho one slepe fell also sone,
  Reght certeyne in hy.
Thus the lady there lyes
Thre nyghttis and thre dayes,
And þe portere alwayes 2255
  Lay wakande hir by.

Thus þe portare woke [hir by]—
Ther whills[20] hir luffed se[kerly],—
Till at þe laste the lady
  Wakede, als i wene. 2260
Þen scho was in hir awenn [state][21]
And als wele in hir gate[22]
Als scho hadde nowthir arely ne late
  Neuer þerowte bene.
Thay sett þam down one þaire kne, 2265
Thanked Godde, alle three,
That he wolde so appon þam see[23]
  As it was there sene.
Sythen aftir gan þay ta[24]
A riche bathe for to ma, 2270
And made þe lady in to ga,
  In graye and in grene.

Than Sir Perceuell in hy
Toke his modir hym by,
I say ʒow than certenly, 2275
  And home went hee.

---

[19] poured, dosed. [20] all the while (he). [21] right mind. [22] way; i.e., sane. [23] look graciously. [24] set about.

2257. A corner of the page is missing. Halliwell's conjectures.
2261. Campion's conjecture.
2270. On medieval notions of the properties of colors, cf. W. G. Black, "Folk Medicine," Ch. 7. Cf. also "Eger and Grime." Green was especially effective in soothing and restoring. Grey is the traditional color of wild vegetation; cf. *holtes hore.*
2275. MS. *centenly.*

Grete lordes and the Qwene
Welcomed hym al bydene;
When þay hym one lyfe sene,
   Þan blythe myghte þay bee.   2280
Sythen he went into þe Holy Londe,
Wanne many cités full stronge,
And there was he slayne, i vndirstonde;
   Thusgatis endis hee.
Now Ihesu Criste, heuens Kyng,   2285
Als he es lorde of all thyng,
Grante vs all His blyssyng!
   Amen, for charyté!

QUOD ROBERT THORNTON. EXPLICIT SIR PERCEUELL DE
GALES. HERE ENDYS þE ROMANCE OF SIR PERCEVELL OF
GALES, COSYN TO KYNG ARTHOURE.

2279. *Sene* is preterite plural, *saw.*

THE AVOWING OF ARTHUR

THE AVOWING OF KING ARTHUR, SIR GAWAIN, SIR KAY, AND BALDWIN OF BRITAIN

This romance is in the dialect of the northwest midlands of before 1400. The manuscript is in the possession of Colonel R. Ireland Blackburne; through his kindness and that of the late H. B. Melville, it has been possible to prepare the text from photographs. Robson's edition for the Camden Society, however, is very exact; for convenience, his numbering of the stanzas has been retained. Final -*ll* is expanded to -*lle* only when the cross-stroke is very plain. Final -*h* is crossed except in lines 51 and 474, but since the stroke evidently has little significance (in lines 237, 510, 1036, and others, it is followed by an -*e*), it has usually been ignored. Flourishes after -*n* and other letters have been disregarded.

The story is a skillful compilation: it introduces popular heroes, and blends several familiar anecdotes and traditional practical jokes in a narrative that is by turns swaggering, heroic, comic, and extremely cynical. In all these particulars, it is like the Latin prose tale "Arthur and Gorlagon" (*Harv. St. N.* viii), and may very well have been adapted from a Welsh original. The sources and discussions of the different incidents are indicated in the notes to the text.

On the verse, see *Rom. Rev.* 7.243.

The poem shows several dialectal peculiarities: the omission of relatives, the assimilation of -*n* by pronouns (*thi none*, thine own), plurals in -*us*, preterites in -*ut*, an extra -*u* after -*w* (*dowun; Rowun Tabull*), singular forms where plurals seem called for, and the spelling *qu-* for *wh-* or *w-*. For a careful discussion of the dialect, see *Review of English Studies* 3.54, 186, and especially 328.

I

He þat made vs on þe mulde[1]
And fare fourmet þe folde[2]
Atte his will as he wold,
The see and the sande,

---

[1] earth. [2] formed the dry land.

Giffe hom ioy þat wille here　　　　5
Of duȝti men and of dere,
Of haldurs[3] þat before vs were,
　þat lifd in this londe!
One was Arther the Kinge,
Withowtun any letting;　　　　10
With him was mony lordinge
　Hardi of honde;
Wice and war ofte þay were,
Bold vndur banere,
And wiȝte weppuns wold were,[4]　　15
　And stifly wold stond.

II

Þis is no fantum ne no fabulle:
Ȝe wote wele of þe Rowun Tabull,
Of prest men and priueabulle,[5]
　Was holdun in prise:　　　　20
Cheuetan[6] of chiualry,
Kyndenesse of curtesy,[7]
Hunting full warly,[8]
　As wayt[9] men and wise.
To þe forest þa[y] fare　　　　25
To hunte atte buk and atte bare,[10]
To þe herte[11] and to þe hare,
　Þat bredus in þe rise.[12]
Þe King atte Carlele he lay;
Þe hunter cummys on a day:　　　　30
Sayd, "Sir, þer walkes in my way
　A well grim gryse.[13]

III

He is a balefulle bare;
Seche on segh i neuyr are;

---

[3] elders.　[4] bear.　[5] meritorious.　[6] chief lord.　[7] i.e., (chief of) courteous kindness.　[8] alertly.　[9] brave.　[10] boar.　[11] hart.　[12] thickets.　[13] horror.

29. In northern poems, Carlisle was confused with Caerleon, and became one of Arthur's principal seats.

30. Attached to each court was a professional huntsman, who attended to the mechanical details of the chase.

He hase wroȝte me myculle care,   35
　And hurte of my howundes:
Slayn hom downe slely[14]
　With feȝting full furcely;
Wasse þer none so hardi
　Durste bide in his bandus.[15]   40
On him spild i my spere
　And mycull of my nothir gere;
þer mone no dintus him dere,
　Ne wurche him no wowundes.
He is masly[16] made,   45
　All of fellus[17] þat he bade;
þer is no bulle so brade
　That in frith[18] foundes.

IV

He is heȝer þenne a horse,
　That vncumly corse;[19]   50
In fayth him faylis no force
　Quen þat he shalle feȝte!
And þerto blake as a bere,
　Feye folk will he fere:[20]
þer may no dyntus him dere,   55
　Ne him to dethe diȝte.
Quen he quettus[21] his tusshes,
　Thenne he betus on þe busshes:
All[22] he rinnes and he russhes,
　þat þe rote is vnryȝte.[23]   60
He hase a laythelych luffe:[24]
　Quen he castus vppe his stuffe,[25]

---

[14] craftily.　[15] stay in his neighborhood.　[16] massively.　[17] hide.　[18] field.
[19] bulk.　[20] cowardly folk will he frighten.　[21] whets.　[22] so.　[23] torn up.　[24] i.e.,
a violent rage.　[25] dust cloud.

46. *Bade* for *hade?* But then the tense is wrong.
55. Destructive boars are found in many Celtic pieces, but were not
peculiar to them (cf. "Auberi"). Cf. "Kilhwch and Olwen," "Gawain and
the Green Knight" 1440, "Guy of Warwick" 6417, and "Sir Eglamoure."
Wordsworth is said to have written Cunningham a letter including a
rhyme that "Arthur's boar" was loose and was ravaging the land. (*Rom.
Rev.* 3.192.)

Quo durst abide him a buffe,[26]
Iwisse he were wiʒte."

V

He sais, "In Ingulwode is hee."   65
Þe toþer[27] biddus, "Lette him bee;
We schall þat satnace[28] see,
   Giffe þat he be þare."
Þe King callut on knyʒtis thre:
Himseluun wold þe fuyrthe be;   70
He sayd, "Þere schalle no mo mené
   Wynde to þe bore."
Bothe Kay and Sir Gauan
And Bowdewynne of Bretan,
Þe hunter and þe howundus-squayn[29]   75
   Hase ʒarket[30] hom ʒare.
Þe Kinge hase armut him in hie,
And þo thre buirnes[31] hym bie;
Now ar þay fawre alle redie,
   And furthe conne þay fare.   80

VI

Vnto þe forest þay weynde
Þat[32] was hardy and heynde;
Þe huntur atte þe northe ende
   His bugulle con he blaw,
Vncoupult kenettis[33] as he couthe;   85
Witturly þay soʒte þe southe—
Raches[34] with opon mouthe,
   Rennyng on a raw,[35]
Funde fute[36] of þe bore,
Faste folutte to him thore.   90

---

[26] blow.   [27] i.e., the king.   [28] fiend.   [29] master of hounds.   [30] made ready.
[31] men.   [32] those men who.   [33] loosed the small dogs.   [34] dogs.   [35] row; i.e.,
pack.   [36] scent.

65. Inglewood is a forest in Cumberland, south of Carlisle.

74. Baldwin appears as a knight in Malory, the Morte Arthur poems, and here. As a bishop, he appears in several Gawain poems and the Mabinogion. He seems to have been a Celtic hero. Cf. Loomis 172.

83. I.e., as they entered the forest; they were going south.

Quen þat he herd, he hade care;
  To þe denne conne he draw:
He sloȝe hom downe slely
With feȝting full fuyrsly;
But witte ȝe sirs, witturly,   95
  He stode butte litull awe.[37]

VII

Þay held him fast in his hold;[38]
He brittunt bercelettus[39] bold,
Bothe þe ȝunge and þe old,
  And rafte hom þe rest.[40]   100
Þe raches comun rennyng him by,
And bayes[41] him full boldely,
Butte þer was non so hardy
  Durste on þe fynde fast.[42]
Þenne þe huntur sayd, "Lo, him þare!   105
ȝaw þar such[43] him no mare;
Now may ȝe sone to him fare;
  Lette see quo dose beste!
ȝaw þar such him neuyr more:
I sette my hed opon a store[44]   110
Butte-giffe he slaey ȝo alle fawre,
  Þat griselich geste!"[45]

VIII

Þenne þe hunter turnes home agayn;
Þe King callut on Sir Gauan,
On Bawdewin of Bretan,   115
  And on kene Kay.
He sayd, "Sirs, in ȝour cumpany,
Myne avow make i,
Were he neuyr so hardy,
  ȝone satenas to say;[46]   120

---

[37] had little fear. [38] den. [39] cut hounds to pieces. [40] took away their comfort.
[41] bring him to bay. [42] seize the fiend. [43] need seek. [44] as I value my head.
[45] fearful stranger. [46] attempt, attack.

100. MS. *raste*.
110. MS. *Butte sette*, anticipating the next line.
111. "Slay" has been altered to "flay" in the MS.

To brittun[47] him and downe bringe
Withoute any helpinge,
And i may haue my leuynge[48]
  Hentill to morne atte day!
And now, sir, i cummaunde ȝo   125
To do as i haue done nowe:
Ichone make ȝour avowe."
  Gladdely grawuntutte þay.

IX

Þen vnsquarut Gauan
And sayd godely agayn,   130
"I avowe to[49] Tarne Wathelan
  To wake hit[50] all nyȝte."
"And i avow," sayd Kaye,
"To ride[1] þis forest or daye,
Quo so wernes[2] me þe waye,   135
  Hym to dethe diȝte."
Quod Baudewyn, "To stynte[3] owre strife,
I avow bi my life
Neuyr to be ielus of my wife,
  Ne of no birde[4] bryȝte;   140
Nere werne[5] no mon my mete
Quen i gode may gete;
Ne drede my dethe for no threte,
  Nauthir of king ner knyȝte."

X

Butte now þay haue þayre vowes made,   145
Þay buskute hom and furth rade

---

[47] cut to pieces. [48] if I live. [49] at. [50] keep watch. [1] i.e., patrol. [2] contests.
[3] make an end of. [4] woman. [5] refuse.

127. On the practice of vowing, cf. Koschwitz's later editions of "Karls
des Grossen Reise nach Jerusalem," Introduction; STS 17, xxxv; and 21,
Preface; cf. "Bricriu's Feast," and "The Tournament of Tottenham."
It was usually a sort of literary exercise; but here the vows are actually
carried out. Cf. ESt. 36.337; also MPhil. 25.349.

131. The Tarn Wadling was a small lake about ten miles southeast of
Carlisle. Arthur's knights often found adventures on its shores. It was
drained long ago.

To hold þat þay heȝte hade,
  Ichone sere[6] way.
The King turnus to þe bare;
Gauan, with[oute] any more,   150
To þe tarne[7] con he fore,
  To wake hit to day.
Þenne Kay, as i conne roune,[8]
He rode þe forest vppe and downe.
Boudewynne turnes to toune   155
  Quer þat his gate lay,
And sethun to bed bownus he;
Butte carpe we now of þer[9] othir thre,
How þay preuyd hor wedde-fee,[10]
  Þe sothe for to say.   160

XI

Furst, to carpe of oure Kinge,
Hit is a kyndelich thinge—
  Atte his begynnyng,
    Howe he dedde his dede.
Till his houndus con he hold;[11]   165
The bore, with his brode schilde,[12]
Folut hom fast in þe filde
    And spillutte on hom gode spede.[13]
Þen þe Kinge con crye,
And carputte of venerie;[14]   170
To make his howundus hardi,
    Houut[15] on a stede.
Als sone as he come þare,
Aȝaynus him rebowndet[16] þe bare:
He se neuyr no syȝte are   175
    So sore gerutte him to drede.

---

[6] separate. [7] lake. [8] tell (a tag). [9] these. [10] justified their wager. [11] look at.
[12] hide at the shoulder. [13] worked havoc rapidly. [14] cried out hunting terms.
[15] rode up. [16] rebounded, dashed.

156. MS. *Sum þat.*
160. MS. *þo sothe.*
165. The rhyme-word should probably be *hilde.* Cf. 330.
171. Some of the right words to use to dogs are given in Lord Berners'
"Boke of St. Albans," under the hunting of the hare; all are French.

XII

He hade drede and doute
Of him þat was sturun[17] and stowte;
He began to romy and rowte,[18]
   And gapes and gones.[19]   180
Men myȝte noȝte his cowch kenne
For howundes and for slayn men
þat he hade draun to his denne
   And brittunt all to bonus.[20]
þenne his tusshes con he quette,[21]   185
Opon þe Kinge for to sette;
He liftis vppe, withoutun lette,
   Stokkes[22] and stonis.
With wrathe he begynnus to wrote:[23]
He ruskes[24] vppe mony a rote   190
With tusshes of iii fote,
   So grisly he gronus.[25]

XIII

þenne þe Kinge spanus[26] his spere,
Opon þat bore for to bere;
þer may no dyntus him dere,   195
   So seker was his schilde.[27]
þe grete schafte þat was longe,
All to spildurs[28] hit spronge;
þe gode stede þat was stronge
   Was fallun in þe filde.   200
As þe bore had mente,
He gaue þe King such a dinte,
Or he myȝte his bridull hente,
   þat he myȝte euyr hit fele.
His stede was stonet[29] starke ded: 205
He sturd neuyr owte of þat sted.

---

[17] fierce, stern.   [18] roar and rumble.   [19] yawns; i.e., comes on with open mouth.
[20] stripped to the bones.   [21] whet.   [22] tree trunks.   [23] root (with his tusks).
[24] tears.   [25] rages.   [26] seizes.   [27] tough his hide.   [28] splinters.   [29] struck, stunned.

181. I.e., his lair was concealed by the bones, etc.
193. MS. *span os*.
204. To restore rhyme, read, *That euyr he hit felde.*

To Ihesu a bone he bede,
Fro wothes hym weylde.[30]

XIV

Þenne þe King in his sadul sete
And wiȝtely wan on his fete;   210
He prays to Sayn Margarete
Fro wathes him ware:[31]
Did as a duȝty knyȝte:
Brayd oute a brand bryȝte
And heue[32] his schild opon hiȝte,   215
For spild was his spere.
Sethun he buskette him ȝare,
Squithe, withoutun any mare,
Aȝaynus þe fynde for to fare
That hedoes was of hiere.[33]   220
So þay cowunturt[34] in þe fild,
For all þe weppuns þat he myȝte weld,
Þe bore brittunt his schild
On brest he conne bere.

XV

Þere downe knelus he   225
And prayus till Him þat was so fre,
"Send me þe victoré!
Þis satanas[35] me sekes."
All wroth wex þat sqwyne,
Blu and brayd vppe his bryne;[36]   230
As kylne[37] oþer kechine,
Þus rudely he rekes.[38]
Þe Kynge myȝte him noȝte see,
Butte lenyt[39] him doune bi a tree,

---

[30] perils him to protect. [31] guard. [32] raised. [33] whose hair was hideous. [34] encountered. [35] devil. [36] snorted and raised his brows (rolled his eyes). [37] maltfurnace. [38] vilely he smells. [39] bent.

209. I.e., recovered his balance.
211. St. Margaret is probably the Scotch saint of that name (d. 1093).
224. The relative which should introduce this line is omitted; the construction is common in northern poems.
232. In "The Master of Game" (W. A. and F. Baillie-Grohman), the strong odor of the boar is especially mentioned.

So nyȝe discumford[40] was hee   235
For smelle oþer smekis.[41]
And as he neghet bi a noke,[42]
Þe King sturenly him stroke,
That both his brees con blake;[43]
His maistry he mekes.[44]   240

XVI

Thus his maistry mekes he
With dyntus þat werun duȝté;
Were he neuyr so hardé,
Þus bidus þat brothe.[45]
Þe Kinge, with a nobull brande,   245
He mette þe bore comande:
On his squrd till his hande
He rennes full rathe.
He bare him inne atte þe throte;
He hade no myrth of þat mote:[46]   250
He began to dotur and dote[47]
Os he hade keghet scathe.[48]
With sit siles[49] he adowne.
To brittun him þe King was bowne,
And sundurt in þat sesun   255
His brode schildus bothe.

XVII

Þe King couthe of venery,[50]
Colurt[1] him full kyndely:
Þe hed of þat hardy
He sette on a stake.   260
Sethun brittuns he þe best
As venesun in forest;

---

[40] discomfited.   [41] odors.   [42] drew near an oak.   [43] brows grew pale; i.e., he was stunned.   [44] gets the upper hand.   [45] pauses that fierce (creature).   [46] joy of that encounter.   [47] stagger and reel.   [48] received injury.   [49] pain sinks.   [50] hunting.   [1] cut out the neck.

256. The "schilds" were the shoulder quarters. The boar was to be cut up into thirty-two pieces ("Book of St. Albans"): *The fyrst of theym is the hede, whatteuer befall; An oþer is the coler, and so ye schall hitt call; The sheldys on the sholderis, thereof shall ii be.*

Bothe þe 3onge and lees[2]
He hongus on a noke.[3]
Þere downe knelys hee   265
Þat loues Hur þat is free:
Says, "Þis socur þou hase send me
For þi Sune sake !"
If[4] he were in a dale depe,
He hade no kny3te him to kepe: 270
For-werré[5] slidus he on slepe:
No lengur my3te he wake.

XVIII

The King hase fillut his avowe;[6]
Of Kay carpe we nowe;
How þat he come for his prowe[7]   275
3e schall here more.
Als he rode in þe ny3te,
In þe forest he mette a kny3te,
Ledand a brede[8] bry3te;
Ho[9] wepputte wundur sore.   280
Ho sayd, "Sayn Maré my3te me spede
And saue me my madunhede,[10]
And giffe þe kny3te for his dede
Bothe soro and care !"

XIX

Þus ho talkes him tille,   285
Quille[11] ho hade sayd alle hur wille;
And Kay held him full stille,
And in þe holte houes.[12]
He prekut oute prestely[13]
And aure-hiet[14] him radly,   290

---

[2] strips and slices.   [3] oak.   [4] though.   [5] overweary.   [6] made good his boast.
[7] came to seek his advantage.   [8] maiden.   [9] she.   [10] maidenhood.   [11] until.   [12] remains.   [13] dashed out speedily.   [14] overtook.

263. 3onge for þonge, strip; cf. Layamon 14227.
274. This episode is familiar. See "Ywain and Gawain" for bibliography.
275. MS. *fro his.*
280. MS. *he.*

And on þe knyȝte conne cry,
    And pertely him repreues,
And sayd, "Recraiand[15] knyȝte,
Here i profur þe to fiȝte
Be chesun[16] of þat biurde briȝte!   295
    I bede þe my glouus."
Þe toþer vnsquarut him with skille
And sayd, "I am redy atte þi wille
Þat forward to fulfille
    In alle þat me behouus."   300

XX

"Now quethun art þou?" quod Kay,
"Or quethur[17] is þou on way?
Þi riȝte name þou me say!
    Quere wan þou þat wiȝte?"
Þe toþur vnsquarut him agayn,   305
"Mi riȝte name is noȝte to layn:
Sir Menealfe of þe Mountayn
    My gode fadur hiȝte;
And this lady sum[18] i þe telle:
I fochet[19] hur atte Ledelle,   310
Þer hur frindus con he felle
    As foes in a fiȝte.
So i talket hom tille
Þat muche blode conne i spille,
And all aȝaynus þayre awne wille   315
    Þere wan i this wiȝte."

XXI

Quod Kay, "Þe batell i take
Be chesun[20] of þe birdus sake,

---

[15] treacherous. [16] cause. [17] whither. [18] something. [19] got. [20] cause.

296. On the glove as a challenge, see Hall's note to "King Horn" 793.
300. MS. þe me.
307. If this is the same character as the Meleagant of Chrétien's "Charette," his father's name was Baudemagus. The poet seems confused. See Loomis 211 ff.
311. He may possibly refer to the father; but more probably this is a relapse into indirect discourse. MS. hur selle is expuncted, and he felle written over the line.

And i schalle wurch þe wrake,"[21]
  And sqwithely con squere.[22]   320
Þenne þay rode togedur ryȝte
As frekes[23] redy to fiȝte
Be chesun of þat birde bryȝte,
  Gay in hor gere.
Menealfe was þe more myȝty: 325
He stroke Kay stifly,
Witte ȝe sirs, witturly,
  With a scharpe spere;
All to-schildurt[24] his schilde,
And aure his sadull gerut him to held,[25]   330
And felle him flatte in þe filde,
  And toke him vppeon werre.[26]

XXII

Þus hase he wonnen Kay on werre,
And all to-spild[27] is his spere;
And mekill of [his] othir gere   335
  Is holden to þe pees.[28]
Þenne vnsquarut Kay aȝayn
And sayd, "Sir, atte Tarne Wathelan
Bidus me Sir Gauan,
  Is derwurthe[29] on dese;   340
Wold ȝe thethur be bowne[30]
Or ȝe turnut to þe towne,
He wold pay my rawunsone
  Withowtyn delees."
He sayd, "Sir Kay, þi lyfe i þe heȝte   345
For a cowrce[31] of þat knyȝte !"
Ȝette Menealfe, or þe mydnyȝte,
  Him ruet all his rees.[32]

---

[21] mischief. [22] swore it. [23] men. [24] shattered. [25] sink. [26] i.e., won him as a
captive. [27] broken. [28] forfeited when he desired a truce. [29] prized; i.e., an in-
timate of nobles. [30] betake yourself. [31] encounter. [32] regretted his haste.

344. The form *delees*, delays, is not found in the N.E.D., but the
rhymes with *pees* (>*pais*) and *dese* (>*dais*) indicate that this is the sense
(>*delai*).

XXIII

Þus þay turnut to þe torne[33]
With þe thriuand thorne;[34]   350
Kay callut on Gauan ȝorne:
  Asshes[35] quo is there.
He sayd, "I, Kay, þat þou knawes,
Þat owte of tyme bostus and blawus;[36]
Butte þou me lese with þi lawes,   355
  I lif neuyr more;
For as i rode in þe nyȝte,
In þe forest i mette a knyȝte
Ledand a birde bryȝte;
  Ho wepput wundur sore.   360
Þere togedur faȝte we
Be chesun[37] of þat lady free;
On werre þus hase he wonun me,
  Gif þat me lothe ware.

XXIV

Þis knyȝte þat is of renowun   365
Hase takyn me to presowun,[38]
And þou mun pay my rawunsun,
  Gawan, with þi leue."
Þen vnsquarutte Gauan
And sayd godely agayn,   370
"I wille, wundur fayne:
  Quatt schall i geue?"
"Quen þou art armut in þi gere,
Take þi schild and þi spere
And ride to him a course on werre;[39]   375
  Hit schall þe noȝte greue."
Gauan asshes, "Is hit soe?"
To toþer knyȝt grauntus, "ȝoe;"
He sayd, "Þen togedur schull we goe
  Howsumeuyr hit cheuis!"[40]   380

---

[33] lake. [34] thriving thorn-tree. [35] (Gawain) asks. [36] brag and boast unseasonably. [37] cause. [38] as prisoner. [39] tilting-bout. [40] befalls.

350. Not previously mentioned; but apparently a trysting place.
354. Usually the idiom is "blows boasts."
355. The phrase seems to mean, "unless you release me by acting as surety."

XXV

And these knyȝtus kithun hor crafte,
And aythir gripus a schafte
Was als rude as a rafte;[41]
    So runnun þay togedur.
So somun[42] conne þa[y] hie   385
Þat nauthir scaput forbye;[43]
Gif Menealfe was þe more myȝtie,
    ȝette dyntus gerut him to dedur:[44]
He stroke him sadde[45] and sore.
Squithe squonut he thore;   390
Þe blonke[46] him aboute bore,
    Wiste he neuyr quedur.[47]
Quod Kay, "Þou hase þat þou hase soȝte!
Mi raunnsum is all redy boȝte;
Gif þou were ded, i ne roȝte;   395
    Forþi come i hedur."

XXVI

Þus Kay scornus þe knyȝte,
And Gauan rydus to him ryȝte;
In his sadul sette him on hiȝte,
    Speke[48] gif he may.   400
Of his helme con he draw,
Lete þe wynde on him blaw;
He speke with a vois law,
    "Delyueryt hase þou Kay:
With þi laa hase made him leyce;[49]   405
Butte him is lothe to be in pece,
And þou was aye curtase
    And prins of ich play.[50]
Wold þou here a stowunde bide,
A noþer course wold i ride;   410

---

[41] rough as a beam (hewn by hand).   [42] close.   [43] i.e., slipped past.   [44] tremble.
[45] severely.   [46] horse.   [47] whither.   [48] let him speak.   [49] by accepting the contest, you have freed him.   [50] contest.

381. MS. *kithiun.*

Þis þat houes[1] by my side,
    In wedde[2] i wold hur lay."

XXVII

Thenne vnsquarut Gauan,
Sayd godely agayn,
"I am wundur fayn   415
    For hur for to fiȝte."
These knyȝtus kithun þay[re] gere
And aythir gripus a spere;
Runnun togedure on werre
    Os[3] hardy and wiȝte.   420
So somen þer þay ȝode
Þat Gauan bare him from his stede,
Þat both his brees[4] con blede
    On growunde qwen he liȝte.
Thenne Kay con on him calle   425
And sayd, "Sir, þou hade a falle
And þi wench lost withalle,
    Mi trauthe i þe pliȝte !"

XXVIII

Quod Kay, "Þi leue hase þou loste
For all þi brag or þi boste;   430
If þou haue oȝte on hur coste,[5]
    I telle hit for tente."[6]
Thenne speke Gauan to Kay,
"A mons happe is notte ay;[7]
Is none so sekur of asay[8]   435
    Butte he may harmes hente."
Gauan rydus to him ryȝte
And toke vppe þe toþer knyȝte
Þat was dilfully dyȝte[9]
    And stonet in þat stynte;[10]   440
Kay wurdus tenut[11] him mare
Þenne all þe hapnes[12] þat he hente þare;

---

[1] this (maiden) who rides.   [2] as a prize.   [3] like.   [4] brows.   [5] spent.   [6] I count
it lost.   [7] (good) fortune does not last.   [8] surely proved (by test).   [9] in evil
plight.   [10] check; i.e., collision, onset.   [11] Kay's words angered.   [12] misfortune.

421. MS. *somen þat.*

He sayd, "And we allone ware,
Þis stryf schuld i stynte."[13]

XXIX

"Ȝe, hardely,"[14] quod Kay,   445
"Butte þou hast lost þi fayre may
And þi liffe, i dare lay."[15]
Þus talkes he him tille.
And Gauan sayd, "God forbede,
For he is duȝti in dede;"   450
Prayes þe knyȝte gud spede[16]
To take hit to none ille
If Kay speke wurdes kene.
"Take þou þis damesell schene;
Lede hur to Gaynour þe Quene,   455
Þis forward to fulfille;
And say þat Gawan, hur knyȝte,
Sende hur þis byurde briȝte;
And rawunsun þe[17] anon riȝte
Atte hur awne wille."   460

XXX

Þerto grawuntus þe knyȝte
And truly his trauthe pliȝte,
Inne saue-ward[18] þat byurde bryȝte
To Carlele to bringe.
And as þay houet[19] and abode,   465
He squere on þe squrd brode.
Be he his othe hade made,
Þenne waknut þe King.
Þenne þe day beganne to daw;[20]
Þe Kinge his bugull con blaw;   470

---

[13] put a stop to this abuse. [14] surely. [15] wager. [16] i.e., earnestly. [17] i.e., obtain your own ransom. [18] safe keeping. [19] waited. [20] dawn.

455. Gawain was the queen's special attendant. In another poem in this manuscript, "The Awntyrs of Arthur," he is her escort when she is admonished by the spirit of her mother.

466. The sword was sworn upon because it was iron, which was a magic substance; because it might be the abode of a spirit; or because of its slight resemblance to a cross. See Wimberly 92.

His kny3tus couth hitte welle knaw
His was a sekur thinge.[21]
Sethun þay busket hom 3are,
Sqwith withowtun any mare,
To wete þe Kingus wele-fare,   475
    Withowtun letting.   PRIMUS PASSUS.

XXXI

To þe forest þay take þe way;
Bothe Gawan and Kay,
Menealfe, and þe fare may
    Comun to þe Kinge.   480
Þe bore brittunt[22] þay fande,
Was colurt[23] of the Kingus hande;
If he wore lord of þat londe,[24]
    He hade no horsing.
Downe þay take þat birde bry3te,   485
Sette hur one behinde þe kny3te;
Hur horse for þe King was dy3te,
    Withoutun letting;
Gaue Kay þe venesun to lede,
And hiet hamward gode spede;   490
Bothe þe birde and þe brede[25]
    To Carlele þay bringe.

XXXII

Now as þay rode atte þe way,
Þe Kynge himseluun con say
Bothe to Gauan and to Kay,   495
    "Quere wan 3e þis wi3te?"
Þenne Kay to þe King spake;
He sayd, "Sir, in þe forest as i con wake[26]
Atte þe anturus hoke,[27]
    Þer mette me this kny3te;   500

---

[21] i.e., he had accomplished his aim.   [22] butchered.   [23] cut in sections.   [24] i.e.,
but king though he was, etc.   [25] cuts of meat.   [26] watch.   [27] adventurous oak.

481-2. In the MS., -a and -u are much alike. Though here the reading
is clearly *funde . . . hunde*, the rhyme shows that the vowels have been
confused, possibly in copying from a similar MS.

Þer togedur faȝte we
Be chesun of this lady fre;
On werre hase he þus wonnen me,
    With mayn and wyth myȝte;
And Gawan hase my rawunsun made   505
For a course þat he rode
And felle him in þe fild brode;
    He wanne þis buirde bryȝte.

XXXIII

He toke him þere to presunnere;"
Þen loghe þat damesell dere   510
And louet[28] with a mylde chere
    God and Sir Gawan.
Þenne sayd þe King, opon hiȝte,
All sqwithe to þe knyȝte,
"Quat is þi rawunsun, opon ryȝte?[29]   515
    Þe soth þou me sayn."
Þe tothir vnsquarut him with skille,
"I conne notte say þe þertille:
Hit is atte þe Quene wille;
    Qwi schuld i layne?   520
Bothe my dethe and my lyfe
Is inne þe wille of þi wife,
Quethur ho wulle stynte me of my strife[30]
    Or putte me to payne."

XXXIV

"Grete God," quod þe King,   525
"Gif Gawan gode endinge,
For he is sekur[31] in alle kynne thinge
    To cowuntur with a knyȝte!
Of all playus he beris þe prise,[32]
Loos of þer ladise;[33]   530

---

[28] praised.   [29] truly.   [30] relieve me of my trouble (release me).   [31] to be de-pended upon.   [32] contests he carries off the honors.   [33] praise of ladies.

530. In constructions felt to be genitive or dative, the poet often uses þer for the more usual þe (cf. Norse þeirra).

Menealfe, and þou be wise,
　　Hold þat þou beheȝte,
And i schall helpe þat i maye,"
The King himseluun con saye.
To Carlele þay take þe waye, 535
　　And inne þe courte is liȝte.[34]
He toke þis damesell gente;
Before þe Quene is he wente,
And sayd, "Medame, i am hedur sente
　　Fro Gawan, ȝour knyȝte." 540

XXXV

He sayd, "Medame, Gawan, ȝour knyȝte,
On werre hase wonun me to-nyȝte,
Be chesun of this birde briȝte;
　　Mi pride conne he spille,
And gerut me squere squyftely 545
To bringe the this lady
And my nowne body,
　　To do hit in þi wille.
And i haue done as he me bade."
Now quod þe Quene, "And i am glad; 550
Sethun þou art in my wille stade,[35]
　　To spare or to spille,
I giffe þe to my lord þe Kinge,—
For he hase mestur[36] of such a thinge:
Of knyȝtus in a cowunturinge[37]— 555
　　þis forward to fullfille."

XXXVI

Now þe Quene sayd, "God almyȝte
Saue me Gawan, my knyȝte,
That þus for wemen con fiȝte;
　　Fro wothus him were!"[38] 560
Gawan sayd, "Medame, as God me spede,
He is duȝti of dede,

---

[34] have alighted.　[35] put.　[36] need.　[37] battle.　[38] perils him shield.

A blithe burne[38a] on a stede,
And grayth[39] in his gere."
Þenne þay fochet[40] furth a boke,   565
All þayre laes[41] for to loke;
Þe Kinge sone his[42] othe toke
And squithely gerut him squere;
And sekirly, withouten fabull,
Þus dwellus he atte þe Rowun Tabull,   570
As prest knyȝte and priueabull,[43]
With schild and with spere.

XXXVII

Nowe gode frindus are þay;
Þen carpus Sir Kay:
To þe King con he say: 575
"Sire, a mervaell[44] thinke me
Of Bowdewyns avouyng,
Ȝustur-euyn in þe eunyng,
Withowtun any lettyng,
Wele more thenne we thre."   580
Quod þe King, "Sothe to sayn,
I kepe no lengur for to layn:
I wold wete wundur fayn
How best myȝte be."
Quod Kay, "And ȝe wold gif me leue,   585
And sithun take hit o no greue,[45]
Now schuld i propurly preue,
As euyr myȝte i thee !"

XXXVIII

"Ȝisse," quod þe King, "on þat comande,[46]
Þat o payn on life and on londe   590

[38a] man.   [39] ready, fitly arrayed.   [40] brought.   [41] laws.   [42] Menealfe's.   [43] deserving.   [44] marvel.   [45] as no injury.   [46] these terms.

567. MS. þo kinge.
590. More usual is "on pain of life and of land," i.e., on pain of losing them.

Þat ȝe do him no wrunge,
  Butte saue wele my knyȝte.
As men monly[47] him mete,
And sithun forsette him þe strete:[48]
ȝe fynde him noȝte on his fete![49]   595
  Bewarre, for he is wyȝte.
For he is horsutte full wele
And clene clad in stele;
Is none of ȝo but þat he mun fele[50]
  Þat he may on lyȝte.   600
ȝe wynnun him noȝte owte of his way,"
Þe King himseluun con say;
"Him is lefe, i dar lay,
  To hald þat he heȝte."

XXXIX

Þenne sex ar atte on assente,[1]   605
Hase armut hom and furthe wente,
Brayd owte aure a bente,[2]
  Bawdewyn to mete,
With scharpe weppun and schene,
Gay gowuns of grene   610
To hold þayre armur clene,
  And were hitte[3] fro þe wete.
Thre was sette on ich side
To werne[4] him þe wayus wide:
Quere þe knyȝte schuld furth ride,   615
  For-sette[5] hym þe strete.
Wyth copus[6] couert þay hom thenne,
Ryȝte as þay hade bene vncowthe men,
For þat þay wold noȝte be kennet
  Euyn downe to þayre fete.   620

---

[47] manfully. [48] refuse him the road. [49] i.e., he will be mounted and ready to fight. [50] feel; i.e., be injured. [1] agreed. [2] over a field. [3] protect it. [4] contest. [5] blocked. [6] capes.

591. To restore the rhyme, read *schonde.*
612. Chaucer's Knight also wore a cloth over his armor to preserve its luster (Pro. 75).

XL

Now as þay houut and þay hyild,[7]
þay se a schene vndur schild
Come prekand fast aure þe filde
   On a fayre stede;
Wele armut, and dyȝte   625
As freke[8] redy to fyȝte,
Toward Carlele ryȝte
   He hies gode spede.
He see þer sixe in his way;
þenne to þaymseluun con þay say,   630
"Now he is ferd, i dar lay[9]
   And of his lyfe dredus."
þen Kay crius opon heȝte,
All squyth to þe knyȝte,
"Othir flee or fiȝte: 635
   þe tone behouus þe nede !"[10]

XLI

þenne þay kest þayre copus hom fro;
Sir Bawdewyn se þat hit wasse so,
And sayd, "And ȝe were als mony mo,
   ȝe gerutte me notte to flee.   640
I haue my ways for to weynde
For to speke with a frynde;
As ȝe ar herdmen hinde,[11]
   ȝe marre[12] notte me !"
þenne þe sex sembult[13] hom in fere   645
And squere by Him þat boȝte vs dere,
"þou passus neuyr away here
   Butte gif þou dede be !"
"ȝisse, hardely,"[14] quod Kay,
"He may take anothir way—   650

---

[7] waited and went about. [8] man. [9] afraid, I dare wager. [10] the one (or the other) is incumbent on you. [11] gentle retainers. [12] hinder (subjunctive). [13] gathered. [14] surely.

622. MS. *þay so.* The form here given is the usual spelling in the poem.
632. Probably for *adrede.*
650. The point of view is hastily shifted; Kay addresses first the company, then Baldwin.

And þer schall no mon do nere say[15]
Þat schall greue þe !''

XLII

'Gode þe forȝilde,''[16] quod þe knyȝte,
"For i am in my wais riȝte;
ȝistur euyn i þe King hiȝte   655
To cumme to my mete.
I warne ȝo, frekes, be ȝe bold,[17]
My ryȝte ways wille i holde !''
A spere in fewtre he foldes,[18]
    A gode and a grete.   660
Kay stode nexte him in his way:
He iopput[19] him aure on his play;
Þat heuy horse on him lay;
    He squonet in þat strete.
He rode to þere othir fyue: 665
Þayre schene schildus con he riue,[20]
And faure felle[21] he belyue,
    In hie in þat hete.[22]

XLIII

Hardely, withouten delay,
Þe sex[23] to hom hase takyn vppe Kay;   670
And thenne Sir Baw[d]ewin con say,
    "Will ȝe any more?''
Þe toþer vnsquarutte him þertille,
Sayd, "Þou may weynd quere þou wille,
For þou hase done vs noȝte butte skille,[24]   675
    Gif we be wowundut sore.''

---

[15] do or say (anything).   [16] reward; an exclamation of impatience.   [17] you may be confident (that).   [18] places in rest.   [19] dashed down, pushed over.   [20] split.   [21] four did he fell.   [22] rage.   [23] sixth.   [24] right.

664. MS. *þat squete*. The initial combinations look much alike in the MS. But *squate* (cf. "Ipomadon" 4352) means "heavy tumble."
665. At several points in the manuscript, words have been scrawled on the margin. On fol. 48, at the bottom, are two lines: *Per me Rychardum Lathum; Thomas Yrlond.* After each, in another hand, has been added: *scripsit hoc.*

He brayd aure to þe Kinge,
Withowtun any letting;
He asshed if he hade herd any tithing
    In þayre holtus hore.   680
Þe knyȝte stedit²⁵ and stode;
Sayd, "Sir, as i come thro ȝondur wode,
I herd ne se²⁶ butte gode
    Quere i schuld furthe fare."

XLIV

Thanne was þe Kinge ameruaylet þare   685
That he wold telle him no more.
Als squithur²⁷ þay ar ȝare,
    To masse ar thay wente.
By þe masse wasse done,
Kay come home sone,   690
Told þe King before none,
    "We ar all schente
Of Sir Baudewyn, ȝour knyȝte:
He is nobull in þe fiȝte,
Bold, hardy, and wiȝte   695
    To bide on a bente.²⁸
Fle wille he neuyr more:
Him is much leuyr dee þore.
I may banne²⁹ hur þat him bore,
    Suche harmes haue i hente!"   700

XLV

Noue þe King sayd, "Fle he ne can,
Ne werne his mete to no man;
Gife any buirne³⁰ schuld him ban,
    A meruail hit ware."
Þenne þe King cald his mynstrelle   705
And told him holly³¹ his wille:
Bede him layne atte hit were³² stille:
    Þat he schuld furth fare

---

²⁵ pondered. ²⁶ neither heard nor saw. ²⁷ soon as. ²⁸ field. ²⁹ curse. ³⁰ man.
³¹ entirely. ³² so that it should be.

To Baudewins of Bretan:
"I cummawunde þe, or þou cum agayne,   710
Faurty days, o payne,[33]
  Loke þat þou duelle þere,
And wete me preuely to say
If any mon go meteles[34] away;
For þi wareson for ay,   715
  Do þou me neuyrmore."[35]

XLVI

Þen þe mynstrell weyndus on his way
Als fast as he may;
Be none of þe thryd day,
  He funde þaym atte þe mete,   720
Þe lady and hur mené
And gestus grete plenté;
Butte porter none funde he
  To werne[36] him þe ȝate,
Butte rayket[37] in to þe halle   725
Emunge þe grete and þe smalle,
And loket aboute him aure-alle:
  He herd of no threte,[38]
Butte riall[39] seruys and fyne:
In bollus birlutte[40] þay þe wyne,   730
And cocus[41] in þe kechine
  Squytheli con squete.[42]

XLVII

Þen þe ladi conne he loute,[43]
And þe buirdes all aboute;
Both withinne and withoute,   735
  No faute he þer fonde.
Knyȝte, squyer, ȝoman, ne knaue,
Hom lacket noȝte þat þay schuld haue;
Þay nedut notte aftur hit to craue:
  Hit come to hor honde.   740

---

[33] on penalty.   [34] unfed.   [35] on your eternal welfare, do no more (than this).
[36] deny.   [37] made his way.   [38] threat, constraint.   [39] splendid.   [40] passed.
[41] cooks.   [42] sweat, toil.   [43] bow.

Þenne he wente to þe dece,
Before þe pruddust[44] in prece;
Þat lady was curtase,
And bede him stille stonde.
He sayd he was knoun and couthe,   745
And was comun fro bi southe,[45]
And ho had myrth of his mouthe
To here his tithand.

XLVIII

A senny3te[46] duellut he þare;
Þer was no spense for to spare:[47]   750
Burdes[48] þay were neuyr bare,
Butte euyr couurt clene;
Bothe kny3te and squiere,
Mynstrelle and messyngere,
Pilgreme and palmere   755
Was welcum, i wene.
Þer was plenty of fode:
Pore men hade þayre gode,[49]
Mete and drinke or þay 3ode,
To wete wythoutyn wene.   760
Þe lord lenge[50] wold no3te,
Butte come home qwen him gode tho3te,
And both he hase with him bro3te
The Kinge and þe Quene.   A FITTE.

XLIX

Now þer come fro þe kechine   765
Riall seruice and fine;
Ther was no wonting[1] of wine
To lasse ne to mare.
Þay hade atte þayre sopere
Riche metes and dere;   770
Þe King, with a blythe chere,
Bade hom sle care.[2]

---

[44] proudest.   [45] the south.   [46] week.   [47] spending spared.   [48] tables.   [49] i.e., their needs were filled.   [50] Baldwin tarry (in Arthur's court).   [1] lack.   [2] kill care, be merry.

Þan sayd þe Kinge opon hiȝte,
All sqwithe to þe knyȝte,
"Such a seruice on a nyȝte   775
    Se i neuyr are."
Þenne Bawdewyn smylit and on him logh;
Sayd, "Sir, God hase a gud pluȝe;
He may send vs all enughe:
    Qwy schuld we spare?"   780

L

"Now i cummawunde þe," quod þe King,
"To-morne in þe mornyng
Þat þou weynde on huntyng,
    To wynne vs þe dere.
Fare furthe to þe fenne;[3]   785
Take with þe howundus and men,
For þou conne hom best kenne:
    Þou knoes best here.
For all day to-morne will i bide,
And no forthir will i ride,   790
Butte with þe lades of pride
    To make me gud chere."
To bed bownut[4] þay þat nyȝte,
And atte þe morun, atte days liȝte,
Þay blew hornys opon hiȝte   795
    And ferd furthe in fere.

LI

Þenne þe Kynge cald his huntere,
And sayd, "Felaw, come here !"
Þe toþer, with a blithe chere,
    Knelet on his kne: 800
Dowun to þe Kinge con he lowte.[5]
    "I commawunde þe to be all nyȝte oute;

---

[3] swamp.   [4] went.   [5] bow.

778. "God has a good plough," i.e., he has the means of sending us
enough food.

Bawdewyn, þat is sturun and stowte,
   With þe schall he be.
Erly in þe dawyng[6]   805
Loke þat ȝe come fro huntyng;
If ȝe no venesun bring,
   Full litille reche me."
Þe toþer vnsquarut him þertille,
Sayd, "Sir, þat[7] is atte ȝour aune wille,   810
Þat hald i resun and skille,
   As euyr myȝte i the."

LII

And atte euyn þe King con him dyȝte,
And callut to him a knyȝte,
And to þe chambur full riȝte   815
   He hiees gode waye,[8]
Qwere þe lady of þe howse
And maydyns ful beuteowse,
Were curtase and curiowse,[9]
   Forsothe in bed lay.   820
The Kyng bede, "Vndo;"
Þe lady asshes, "Querto?"[10]
He sayd, "I am comun here, loe,[11]
   In derne[12] for to play."
Ho sayd, "Haue ȝe notte ȝour aune quene here,   825
And i my lord to my fere?
To-nyȝte more neȝe ȝe me nere,[13]
   In fayth, gif i may!"[14]

LIII

"Vndo þe dore," quod þe Kinge,
"For bi Him þat made all thinge,   830

---

[6] dawning.   [7] whatever.   [8] directly.   [9] attentive.   [10] why.   [11] lo!   [12] secret.
[13] nearer shall you not be to me.   [14] i.e., if I have my way.

813. On this incident, see *PMLA* 21.575, where its relationship to
"The Earl of Toulouse" is discussed.
821. MS. *Vnto.*
825. As in other passages, *Ho sayd* is hypermetrical.

þou schall haue no harmynge
Butte in þi none[15] wille."
Vppe rose a damesell squete,
In þe Kinge þat[16] ho lete;
He sette him downe on hur beddus fete,   835
And talkes so hur tille:
Sayd, "Medame, my kny3te
Mun lye with þe all ny3te
Til to-morne atte days li3te;
Take hit on non ille;[17]   840
For als euyr my3te i the,
þou schall harmeles[18] be:
We do hit for a wedde-fee,[19]
The stryue for to stylle."[20]

LIV

Thenne þe Kyng sayd to his kny3te,   845
"Sone þat þou were vndy3te,[21]
And in 3ondur bedde ry3te!
Hie þe gud spede."
þe kny3te did as he him bade,
And qwenne ho se him vnclad,   850
þen þe lady wex drede,
Worlyke in wede.[22]
He sayd, "Lye downe preuely hur by,
Butte neghe no3te þou þat lady;
For and þou do, þou schall dey   855
For þi derfe[23] dede;
Ne no3te so hardy þou stur,[24]
Ne onus turne þe to hur."
þe toþer sayd, "Nay, sur."
For him hade he drede.   860

LV

Thenne þe Kyng asshet a chekkere,[25]
And cald a damesel dere;

---

[15] thine own.   [16] that she should.   [17] i.e., do not be vexed.   [18] unharmed.
[19] wager.   [20] to settle a dispute.   [21] undressed.   [22] prudent one.   [23] presumptuous.   [24] be not so bold as to move.   [25] asked for chess board.

851. Read *adrade*, fearful.

Downe þay sette hom in fere
Opon þe bed-syde.
Torches was þer mony liȝte,   865
And laumpus brennyng full bryȝte;
Butte notte so hardy was þat knyȝte
His hede onus to hide.
Butte fro þay began to play
Quyle[26] on þe morun þat hit was day,   870
Euyr he lokette as he lay,
    Baudewynne to byde.
And erly in þe dawyng
Come þay home from huntyng,
And hertis[27] conne þay home bring,   875
And x buckes of pride.

LVI

Þay toke þis venesun fyne
And hade hit to kechine;
Þe Kinge sende aftur Bawdewine,
    And bede him cum see.   880
To þe chaumbur he takes þe way;
He fyndus þe King atte his play;
A knyȝte in his bedde lay
    With his lady.
Þenne sayd þe King opon hiȝte,   885
"To-nyȝte myssutte[28] i my knyȝte,
And hithir folut i him ryȝte;
    Here funden is hee;
And here i held hom bothe stille
For to do hom in þi wille;[29]   890
And gif þou take hit now till ille,
    No selcouthe thinge[30] me !"

LVII

Þen þe King asshed, "Art þou wroth?"
"Nay, sir," he sayd, "withouten othe,

---

[26] till.   [27] harts.   [28] missed.   [29] put at your disposal.   [30] no marvel seems it to me.

876. The x is a doubtful reading.
879. MS. *sonde.* O- and e- are much alike in the MS.

Ne wille þe lady no lothe;[31]   895
  I telle ʒo as quy:
For hitte was atte hur awen wille;
Els thur[s]t[32] no mon comun hur tille;
And gif i take hitte þenne to ille,
  Muche maugreue[33] haue y.   900
For mony wyntur togedur we haue bene,
And ʒette ho dyd me neuyr no tene,
And ich syn schall be sene
  And sette full sorely."[34]
Þe King sayd, "And i hade þoʒte[35]   905
Quy þat þou wrathis þe noʒte
And fyndus him in bed broʒte
  By þi laydy?"

LVIII

Quod Bawdewyn, "And ʒe will sitte,
I schall do ʒo wele to witte."   910
"ʒisse!" quod þe King, "I þe hete,
  And þou will noʒte layne."
"Hit befelle in ʒour fadur tyme,
Þat was þe Kyng of Costantyne,
Puruayed a grete oste[36] and a fyne   915
  And wente into Spayne.
We werrut on a sawdan
And all his londus we wan,
And himseluun, or we blan;
  Þen were we full fayn.   920
I wos so lufd with þe King,
He gafe me to my leding[37]

---

[31] wish her harm. [32] durst. [33] trouble. [34] if each sin is to be given attention and sternly judged(?). [35] i.e., I marvelled. [36] gathered a large host. [37] under my leadership.

914. In the prose "Merlin," Constant is Uther's father. In Layamon's "Brut," a Constantine, son of Cador, is Arthur's successor. The reference here may be due to a confusion with one of these. Two of Arthur's predecessors were said by Geoffrey of Monmouth to have become emperors of Rome.

Lordus atte my bidding,
Was buxum and bayne.[38]

LIX

He gafe me a castell to gete,[39]   925
With all þe lordschippus[40] grete;
I hade men atte my mete,
Fyue hundryth and mo,
And no wemen butte thre,
Þat owre seruandis schild be.   930
One was bryȝtur of ble
Þen þer othir toe.
Toe were atte one assente:[41]
Þe thrid felow haue þay hente;
Vnto a well ar þay wente,   935
And says hur allso:
"Sithin all þe loce in þe lise,[42]
Þou schall tyne þine aprise;"[43]
And wurchun as þe vnwise,
And tite conne hur sloe.   940

LX

And for þo werkes were we wo,
Gart threte þo othir for to slo.[44]
Þenne says þe tone of þo,
"Lette vs haue oure life,
And we schall atte ȝour bidding be   945
As mycull as we all thre;
Is none of ȝaw in preueté
Schall haue wontyng of wyfe."

---

[38] obedient and ready.   [39] guard.   [40] i.e., supervision of the vassals.   [41] agreed.
[42] praise resides in thee.   [43] fail in thy undertaking.   [44] caused the others to be
threatened with death.

929. This strange story has two analogues: see A. de Montaiglon and
G. Reynaud, "Recueil Général . . . des Fabliaux" I. xxvi; and Johannes
de Garlandia, "Poetria" (a Latin tragedy). Cf. *MLN.* 8.251. For similar
cynicism about women, cf. "Salomon and Marcolf," and "Kittredge Anni-
versary Volume" 209.

þay held vs wele þat þay heȝte,
And diȝte⁴⁵ vs on þe day-liȝte, 950
And þayre body vche nyȝte,
    Withoutun any stryue.
þe tone was more louely,
þat þe toþer hade enuy;
Hur throte in sundur preuely, 955
    Ho cutte hitte with a knyfe.

LXI

Muche besenes⁴⁶ hade we
How þat best myȝte be;⁴⁷
þay asshed cowuncell atte me
    To do hur to dede. 960
And i vnsquarut and sayd, "Nay!
Loke furst qwatt hur seluun will say,
Queþer ho may serue vs all to pay;
    þat is a bettur rede."
þer ho hette vs in þat halle 965
To do all þat a woman schild falle,⁴⁸
Wele for to serue vs alle
    þat stode in þat stede.
Ho held vs wele þat ho heȝte,
And diȝte vs on þe day-liȝte, 970
And hur body iche nyȝte
    Intill oure bed beed.⁴⁹

LXII

And bi this tale i vndurstode,
Wemen þat is of mylde mode
And syne giffes hom⁵⁰ to gode, 975
    Mecull may ho mende;¹
And þo þat giffus hom to þe ille,
And sithin þayre folis² will fullfill,

---

⁴⁵ waited on us. ⁴⁶ perplexity. ⁴⁷ what was best to do. ⁴⁸ work befitting
a woman. ⁴⁹ offered. ⁵⁰ devote themselves. ¹ greatly improve (herself).
² foolish.

965. MS. þer.
974. For evyll mode? As in other passages the numbers are confused.

I telle ʒo wele, be propur skille,[3]
No luffe will inne hom lenge.[4]   980
With gode wille grathely hom gete,
Meke and mylde atte hor mete;
[And] thryuandly, withoutun threte,
Ioy atte iche ende.
Forthi ieluis[5] schall i neuer be   985
For no siʒte þat i see,
Ne no buirdes briʒte of ble;
Ich ertheli thinke[6] hase ende."

LXIII

Þe King sayd, "Þou says wele.
Sir," he sayd, "as haue i sele,[7]   990
I will þou wote hit iche dele;
Þerfore come y.
Þi lady gret me to squere squyftelé,
Or i myʒte gete entré,
Þat ho schuld harmeles[8] be,   995
And all hire cumpany.
Þen gerut i my knyʒte
To go in bed with þe buirde bryʒte,
On þe far[9] syde of þe liʒte,
And lay hur dowun by.   1000
I sette me doune hom besyde,
Here þe for to abide;
He neʒhit neuyr no naked syde
Of þi lady.

LXIV

Forthi, of ielusnes, be þou bold,[10]   1005
Thine avow may þou hold;

---

[3] true reasoning.   [4] dwell.   [5] jealous.   [6] thing.   [7] happiness.   [8] unharmed.
[9] right.   [10] concerning jealousy you may be assured.

981 ff. I.e., select those of good disposition, who are good natured at
the table; and spiritedly, without threatening, be happy at whatever befalls.
984. MS. *And ioy.*
999. Probably a lamp or candle was set in a stick attached to the bed;
but the meaning is not clear.

Butte of þo othir thingus þat þou me told
I wold wete more:
Quy þou dredus notte þi dede[11]
No non þat bitus on þi brede?   1010
As [eu]yr brok i my hede,
   þi ȝatis are euyr ȝare !"[12]
Quod Bawdewyn, "I schall ȝo telle:
Atte þe same castell
Quere þis antur befelle,   1015
   Besegitte we ware.
On a day we vsshet[13] oute
And toke presonerus stoute;
Þe tone of owre feloys[14] hade doute,
   And durst notte furthe fare.   1020

LXV

Þe caytef crope into a tunne[15]
Þat was sette þerowte[16] in þe sunne;
And þere come fliand a gunne,[17]
   And lemet as þe leuyn;[18]
Lyȝte opon hitte,[19] atte þe last,   1025
Þat was fastnut so fast;
All in sundur hit brast,
   In six or in seuyn.
And there hit sluȝe him als
(And his hert was so fals !);   1030
Sone þe hed fro þe hals,[20]
   Hit lyputt full euyn.[21]
And we come fro þe feȝting
Sowunde,[22] withoutun hurting,
And þen we louyd[23] þe King   1035
   Þat heghhest was in heuyn.

LXVI

Þen owre feloys con say,
"Schall no mon dee or his day,

---

[11] death.   [12] i.e., open.   [13] issued.   [14] fellows.   [15] barrel.   [16] outside.   [17] projectile.
[18] gleamed like the lightning.   [19] alighted on the cask.   [20] neck.   [21] i.e., was entirely severed.   [22] sound.   [23] praised.

1019. MS. *foloys.*

Butte he cast himselfe away
Throȝhe wontyng of witte."   1040
And þere myne avow made i—
So dyd all þat cumpany—
For dede neuyr to be drery;²⁴
Welcum is hit:
Hit is a kyndely thing."   1045
"Þou says soth," quod þe King,
"Butte of þi thryd avowyng
Telle me quych is hit:
Quy þi mete þou will notte warne²⁵
To no leuand barne?"   1050
"Ther is no man þat may hit tharne;²⁶
Lord, ȝe schall wele wete.

LXVII

For þe sege aboute vs lay stille;
We hade notte all atte oure wille
Mete and drinke vs to fille: 1055
Vs wontutte þe fode.
So come in a messyngere,
Bade, "Ȝild vppe all þat is here!"—
And speke with a sturun schere²⁷
I nyll, by þe rode!—   1060
I gerutte him bide to none,
Callud þe stuard sone,
Told him all as he schuld done,
As counsell is gud;²⁸
Gerutte trumpe²⁹ on the wall,   1065
And couerd burdes³⁰ in þe hall;
And i myself emunge hom all
As a king stode.

---

²⁴ unhappy. ²⁵ refuse. ²⁶ lack. ²⁷ =*chere;* i.e., I will never speak harshly. ²⁸ as
is a good plan. ²⁹ blow trumpets. ³⁰ set tables.

1053. For parallels, etc., to this story, see *Revue Hispanique* 12.281,
especially 296 ff.; and I. P. McKeehan's "St. Edmund of East Anglia"
(*Colorado Studies* 15.55 ff.).

LXVIII

I gerut hom wasshe, to mete wente;
Aftur þe stuard þen i sente; 1070
I bede þat he schuld take entente[31]
    That all schuld well fare:
Bede bringe bred plenté,
And wine in bollus of tre,[32]
Þat no wontyng schuld be 1075
    To lasse ne to mare.
We hade no mete butte for on day;
Hit come in a nobull aray.
Þe messungere lokit ay
    And se hom sle care.[33] 1080
He toke his leue atte me;
We gerutte him drinke atte þe ȝate,
And gafe him giftus grete,
    And furthe con he fare.

LXIX

But quen þe messyngere was gone, 1085
Þese officers ichone
To me made þay grete mone,
    And drerely con say;
Sayd, "In this howse is no bred,
No quyte wine nere[34] red; 1090
Ȝo behoues ȝild vppe þis stid
    And for oure lyuys pray."
Ȝette God helpus ay his man!
Þe messyngere come agayn þan
Withoute to þe cheuytan,[35] 1095
    And sone conne he say:
"Þoȝhe ȝe sege þis seuyn ȝere,
Castelle gete ȝe none here,
For þay make als mury chere
    Als hit were ȝole-day!" 1100

---

[31] attend to it.   [32] wooden bowls.   [33] saw them make merry.   [34] nor.   [35] chief.

1081. To restore the rhyme, read *me atte.*

1082. The stirrup-cup and the reward were attentions that only people well supplied with food and money could afford.

1090. MS. *nyf red.*

LXX

þen þe messyngere con say,
"I rede ʒo, hie ʒo heþinn away,
For in ʒour oste is no play,
   Butte hongur and thurst."
þenne þe King con his knyʒtis calle;   1105
Sethinn to cowunsell wente þay alle;
"Sythinn no bettur may befalle,
   This hald i þe best."
Euyn atte þe mydnyʒte,
Hor lordis sembelet to a syʒte,[36]   1110
þat were hardy and wiʒte:
   þay remuyt of hor rest.[37]
Mete laynes mony lakke,
And þere mete hor sege brake,
And gerut hom to giffe vs þe bake:[38]   1115
   To preke þay were full preste.

LXXI

And þen we lokit were þay lay
And see oure enmeys away;
And þen oure felawis con say,
   þe lasse and þe mare,   1120
"He þat gode may gete,
And wernys men of his mete,
Gud Gode þat is grete
   Gif him sory care!
For the mete of þe messyngere,   1125
Hit mendutte[39] alle oure chere."
þen sayd þe King, þat þay myʒte here,
   And sqwythely con squere,
"In the conne we fynde no fabull;[40]
þine avowes arne profetabull;"   1130
And þus recordus[41] þe Rownde Tabulle,
   þe lasse and þe more.

---

[36] in plain view (a tag).   [37] left their sleep.   [38] turn their backs on us.
[39] mended.   [40] weakness.   [41] publicly agree.

LXXII

Thenne þe Kinge and his knyʒtis alle,
Þay madun myrthe in þat halle,
And þen þe lady conne þay calle, 1135
  The fayrist to fold;[42]
Sayd Bawdewyn, "And þou be wise,
Take þou þis lady of price,
For muche loue in hur lyce;[43]
  To þine hert hold. 1140
Ho is a buirde full bryʒte,
And þerto semely to þy siʒte,
And þou hase holdinn all þat þou hiʒte,
  As a kniʒte schulde !"
Now Ihesu Lord, Heuyn-kynge, 1145
He graunt vs all his blessynge,
And gife vs alle gode endinge,
  That made vs on þe mulde.[44]   AMEN.

---

[42] to embrace. [43] lies. [44] earth.

1137. *Bawdewyn* is a dative.
1140. The *-d* of *hold* is expuncted.
1148. Ending a poem with the same line with which it begins is a
Celtic device (*Rom. Rev.* 7.243).

COMPOSITES

IPOMADON

This piece is probably more like the erroneous conception of romance generally current than any other in Middle English. The youthful knight falls in love with a princess of a neighboring kingdom without having seen her; spends years in her service without revealing his high rank; wins a tournament of which she is the prize, though he remains in disguise by changing his armor each day; proves himself in many adventures in far lands; and at last appears, still disguised, to champion the lady against an undesired suitor. The complications are numerous; the situations, even those without magic, are wildly improbable; and the pace of the story is deliberate, in spite of the great plenty of incidents.

The English poem is a translation, slightly altered, of the French of Hue de Rotelande, an Englishman (fl. 1190). He made free with the best effects in other romances, but combined them with great literary skill. References to the French are to the edition of Koelbing and Koschwitz.

The dialect is north midland, of the middle of the fourteenth century. The word *fere*, which occurs frequently, is a translation of the French, meaning "proud one" (cf. mod. Fr. *fière*). The scribe often wrote *-ey* where the midland spelling was *-e* (*deyre*, harm). A plural subject sometimes has a singular verb (cf. 390). Final *-ll*, which has a cross-stroke except in a few lines (353, 389, 430, 1137, 1189, 3043, 3138, and 3179), is printed as *-ll*. Final crossed *-h*, which rarely has the stroke, is printed *-he*. The flourish after final *-f* has been printed as *-fe*. Other flourishes (after final *-d*, *-m*, *-n*, and *-g*) have been disregarded.

Through the kindness of the Rev. C. T. E. Phillips and the other authorities of Chetham's Library, it has been possible to prepare the text from rotographs. The numbering is as in Koelbing's edition, which also contains many emendations adopted here; only the less obvious ones are credited to him. Those marked H. are Holthausen's; those marked Z., Zupitza's.

Ipomadon at the Court

After a long journey, the youth and his tutor, Tholomew, arrive at
the lady's court. She has been holding a parliament, to reconcile two
knights who have quarreled.

That day the fere hade made hem frende,
And broughte that grette debate[1] to ende:
   So ys she ware and wyce!
Ladyes, witte that she wille not
Abowtte hur suffyr no debatte,   350
   So grette goodenes in her lyethe.
Her meyny lovyd her euerilke one.
Into the hall comys Ipomadon,
   Amonge thes lordys of price;
An ewen[2] pase forthe he paste,   355
Nother to softe[3] ne to ffaste,
   But at his owne devyce.[4]

Lordys, laydys in the hall
Lokis on hym, men and all,
   And grette mervaylle they þought: 360
He was large of lyme and lythe,[5]
And made so wonder [fayre] therwythe;
   Of ffetter faylyd hym not.[6]
A llyttell wax he rede, for shame;
Full welle that coloure hym became;   365
   Before that high he sowghtte.[7]
His dobelett was of red welvet,
Off bryght golde botuns ibete,[8]
   That worthely was wrovghte.

---

[1] war, contention. [2] even, easy. [3] slow. [4] inclination. [5] limb and joint (a tag).
[6] he lacked nothing in his features; i.e., had good features. [7] went before that
high (princess). [8] covered over with bright gold buttons.

349. Koelbing proposed, *Ladyes wote that she wille nat Abowtte*, etc.
Koeppel suggested, *That she wille not (ladyes wate!)*, etc. MS. *Ladyes
wille that she not wote*. The poem has several admonitions to proud ladies.
351. To help the meter, read *soche* for *so grette*.
362. MS. *then wythe*.

His mantell was of skarlett[9] fyne,   370
Furryd with good armyne:
  Ther myght no better been:
The bordoure all of red sendell;[10]
That araye became hym wele,
  To wete withouten wene.[11]   375
A noble countenavnce he hade:
A blyther and a better made,
  Before they had not sayne,
Also bryght his coloure shone.
All hym lovyd that lokyd hym one,   380
  Bothe lord and lady shene.

And longe he beheldis the fere,
But nothynge chaunges her chere
  For carpynge[12] of the crowde:
[Her] hertte is sett so mekyll of wyte,   385
With love it is not sammyd yte,[13]
  Thow3e she be shene in scherovde;[14]
But aftur sore it bande the fre[15]—
And so i wold that all ye shuld be,
  That is of love so prowde!—   390
The chyld before her knelys than,
And to the lady he began
  To tell his tale on lowde.

He sayd, "Dereworthy[16] damysell,
Grette God kepe the in hele,[17]   395
  And all thy ffayre menye:
Vnder heyvyn is holdyn none
So worthy a lady as thow arte on,
  Ne of so grette beweté.
Ofte sythes this haue i harde saye: 400
A noble[r] courte then thyne allwaye
  There may non holdyn bee.

---

[9] scarlet cloth.   [10] silk.   [11] doubt.   [12] i.e., praise.   [13] her heart is so devoted to
reasoning that it has not yet joined with love.   [14] clothing (a tag).   [15] fettered
that noble (one).   [16] precious; i.e., splendid.   [17] health.

376. MS. *countenavaunce.*
398. For the construction, see Int. VII. 5.

The to serve haue i thowghte;
Thereffore haue i hedyr sought,
   Oute of ffarre contraye.   405

What-as[18] thou wilte put me tow
That longis a gentyll man to doo,
   Gladlye do wille i;
Thereffore i praye the me tell
Whedur thow [wilte] i with the dwell,   410
   Or wynde thedyr i come ffroo;
On asay[19] now shall i see
Yff it be as men say of the
   In countreys many and fell."
The lady satt and hym behylde,   415
And lykyd full wele the tale he tolde,
   When she hym hard[20] say soo,

That he wold hur servand be.
She behylde his grette bewté,
   And in her hertt she thought   420
That he myghte with grette honoure
Haue seruyd kynge or emperoure,
   He was so worthy wroughte.
A thynge in her hert gan ryse,
That she shuld lyke wele hes seruyce: 425
   Forgoo hym wold she note.
She answeryd hym full curtesly,
"Thou arte welcome, Belamye;[21]
   I thanke hym that the browghte.

Syn thou to seruys will be sett,   430
What ys thy name, þou stravnge valete?[22]

---

[18] whatever.   [19] by proof.   [20] heard.   [21] good friend.   [22] attendant.

408, 410. Koelbing's emendations. MS. *do i wille.* Koelbing emended
414 to *and mo* for the rhyme. Since the poet does not elsewhere use
alternate rhyme in the short lines, and since other rhymes are considerably
altered by the scribe, an emendation is necessary.
   419. MS. *behyldys.*
   430 ff. Willert suggested omitting 432, and deleting *name* in 433.
   431. The Oxford Dictionary has no example of "valet" in this sense

Anon that thou tell mee."
"I was callyd at home by the same name,
And borne i was in ferre contré;
   Forther watte ye not for me,   435
Wheddyr ye blysse²³ or blame!"
The lady att his wordys lough:
She sayd sone, "This holde i good inowe:
   It is a noble name!
And thou artte welcome, securly."   440
His mayster sayd, that stode hym by,
   "Gravnte mercy,²⁴ madame."

The lady callyd hur botelere:
"This cupe of gold þou shalte take here,
   And gyffe hit to younde man;   445
To buttrey dore lede hym with the,
Therwith of wyne to serue me:
   We shall se yf he can."
The butteler hym the cuppe betoke,
And he was fayne, and not foresoke;²⁵   450
   To the chylde sayd he thanne,
"It ys my ladyes byddynge
That off wyne thou shall here bring."
   In covrte thus he began.

Rightte in his mantell, as he stode,   455
With the botteler forthe he youde;
   The cupe on hande he bare.
All that lovyd þat chyld beforne
For that dede lovghe hym to skorne,
   Bothe the lesse and the more: 460

---

²³ approve. ²⁴ thanks. ²⁵ did not refuse.

for the Middle English period. In the French, the hero describes himself
to the lady: *Dame, un estrange valet sui* (463).
   433. I.e., at home his name was Belamye. Cf. "Perceval," "Libeaus
Desconus."
   438. As often in this MS., *She sayd* is inserted, to the detriment of
the meter.
   453. MS. *That thou off wyne shall serue here.*

Yffe that he shuld serue one,
It were semande,[26] they sayd ylkone,
 Away his mantell were;
But littill knewe þey his entente:
To the buttery-dore he went,   465
 And offe he caste hit yare.

To the boteler than went hee:
"Syr, this mantell gyffe i the,
 As i haue happe or sele;[27]
And thow wilte take þis sympull gyfte, 470
It shall be mendyd, be my thryfte,
 With efte so good a wille."[28]
The butteler thankyd hym curtesly,
And sayd, "Gentyll syr, gramercy
 Off this ffrenshipe ifelle.[29] 475
In awght þat i can do or saye,
Be grette God, that oweth this day,
 It shall be quytte full wele.

For this vii yere, be my thryfte,
Was not gevyne me suche a gyfte!" 480
 The mantyll he toke hym tille.
All they that thowght skorne before
Thought themselfe folys therefore:
 They satt and held them stille,
And sayden it was a gentill dede; 485
There may no man, so God vs spede,
 Otherwyse say be skylle![30]
All they spake in prevyté,
"A hundyrd men a man may se,
 Yet wott not one his wille." 490

---

[26] fitting. [27] fortune. [28] it shall be pieced out (as I hope for good fortune!) with just as much good will. [29] act of friendship performed. [30] intelligently.

463. When serving, the squire wore his tunic, but no mantle. Cf. the cuts in Wright. Only the marshal wore a mantle.
476. MS. *An in.*—H.
482. MS. *all them.*
489. MS. *men may a man se.*—H.

Ipomadon's Soliloquy

The hero's accomplishments make him a favorite; but his preference
of hunting to more manly sports excites surprise. The princess finally
reproves him, saying that no knight is worthy of a lady's love until he
has proved his valor. Not knowing that she returns his love, he goes
home in despair. The following soliloquy is typical of the method of
the piece. Much of it is a debate between the knight's reason and his
heart.

When the chyld his leve had tane,
To his in[ne] he is ganne   1050
   With sorowys and sykynge sare.
He saw right nought þat was hym leffe:
All thynge he þought dyd hym greffe
   In ye,[31] bothe lesse and more.
His maystur Thelamewe he prayed   1055
That his bedde were redy arayde:
   "Therein i wold i were!"
Off all the nyght he slepyd noþinge,
But lay with many a sore sykynge,
   And mornyethe aye more and more.   1060

"Alas, foule, what alysse[32] the
Soo farre oute of thy owne contré
   Heddur for to come?
Thou dyd as many haue done ayre:[33]
Come to seke sorye care—   1065
   And therof hathe þou sum!
Thou myghttis no man but þiselffe blame:
Thyne owne wille made þe come fro hame;
   Thereffore no man wille the moone.
As euer haue i happe or selle,   1070
That ma[r]kis[34] þat lady, eueri deyle;
   Yet love makis me so dome![35]

---

[31] eye.   [32] ails.   [33] before.   [34] notices.   [35] dumb.

1069. Read *none* for *no man.*—H.; so also in 1067.
1070 ff. MS. *or skylle; þan lady; so deme.* *Selle* is Kaluza's proposal;
dome is Koelbing's.

Be God of heyvyn, now i wott well
That she percevys hit, euery dealee,
   How i with love was tane.   1075
And thoo she gaffe me þat vpbrayde,[36]
Hit was for gode þat she me sayde,
   Thowȝe i toke hit with none.[37]
Therefore spake she all þat þing,
To make me leve my long lokynge,   1080
   That i caste hur vppon!

Thereatt i wotte welle she gave tene
Yet be hur owne cosyn, as i wene;
   She blamyd me forthye!
And sayd it was a skorne, perdé,   1085
That anny suche brothels[38] as we
   Anny ladyes love shuld trye,
That nought þinkyth for to thryve,
Nor neuer gyffys[39] in oure lyve
   To no chevalrye;   1090
But ther was anoþur þinge:
On me she cast an longe lokynge:
   I toke good hede therebye.

A, dere God! what myghte þat meane?
I shall tell the all bedene: 1095
   Younde lady is so whyce,[40]
In fayth, she holdythe me but a foole,
That shuld me melle of lovys scole[41]
   That neuer wanne losse[42] ne price;

---

[36] rebuke.   [37] i.e., badly.   [38] knaves.   [39] devote ourselves.   [40] wise.   [41] busy me in the school of love.   [42] praise.

1076. MS. *gyffe me with vpbrayde.*

1080. Ipomadon had looked very intently at the lady, who perceived the state of his heart. She thereupon rebuked his friend Jason for an imaginary offense of the sort; but all knew that it was intended for Ipomadon.

1083. The meter may be improved by deleting *yet* or *owne.*

1087. Read *A ladyes?*—H. MS. *shuld they.* The French (1150) supports the emendation in the text.

1095. MS. *the tell.*—H.

Now sertys, þat trowe i well, forthy: 1100
She lokyd and spake so angurlye,
And callyd vs euer full nyce.[43]
Of helle yt is the hottis[t] payne
To love and be not lovyd agayne!
Thereon no wysdome lyethe. 1105

Now, hertte, i praye the, lett hur be!
Nay, þat maye i not, pardé,
Yf thow wylte i were[44] slayne!
Yes! Nay, in faythe, i;
For thou, hertte, artte sett[45] so sodenly 1110
Thou wilte not turne agayne.
Why? I watte neuer whereffore;
But dede i had leuer i wore
Than longe to dryȝe[46] this payne!
Dyd neuer love man so deyre; 1115
Had she perte, yet rovghte i neyre;[47]
In faythe then were i ffayne.

We, leef,[48] what dyd thou in this londe?—
I came to seke, and i hur favnde
That aye wille do me deyre.— 1120
He fallythe that puttis hymselfe so farre,
That all his lyffe lon[g]ythe to warre.
Thus darre i savely[49] swere.
Yet is ther non that wotte that,
Ne whens he come, ne what he hatte, 1125
So prevely i am here. . . .
Shalte thou tell them? Sertis, naye!
And gette the schyld and spere,

---

[43] foolish. [44] even though you would have me. [45] fixed. [46] suffer. [47] if she shared it, I should never regret it. [48] alas, my good friend! [49] safely.

1110. Omit *hertte?*—H.
1114. MS. *dryve.*—Z.
1121. The couplet is not in the French, but seems to mean, "He falls who is so distant from other resources that his life (and reputation) depend entirely on ability in war."
1127. The sense of the missing line is, "I shall disclose who I am and whence I come!" (Cf. French 1184.) He at once gives up this course of action, and resolves on proving himself.

And wen the price; and þen may þou
Acordynge be to her avowe,   1130
  For thou have gotten losse![50]
Yet in her cowrte there ys none
That so mekyll of bowrdyng[1] can,
  Ne of all gamus that goothe,
Bothe[2] with schyld and schafte to ryde;   1135
But so that love[3] ys all thy pryde,
  Thereffore all men be thy foos.
In erthe ys none so worthy a knyght
But yf his dede be shewyde in syght,
  Men will no good sopose.   1140

And vnder pryde so arte thow hyde[4]
That for a cowarde art thou kyde
  Bothe with lesse and more;
And yf thou now thyselfe shuld rose,[5]
Men wold say, "All this he dos   1145
  His spendyng[6] for to spare;
Of suche dedis have we not sene
As awauntis hym of bedene;
  Hym semes of bownté[7] bare!"
Therefore thy way i rede the gange;   1150
In faythe, and thou dwell here lange,
  It moo the sorow full sore.

Foole, wille thou lyghttly goo
Fro thy love and lovys the soo?[8]—
  Be God, i may not byde!—   1155

---

[50] honor. [1] entertaining. [2] as well as. [3] i.e., being distinguished in love.
[4] hidden. [5] vaunt. [6] i.e., to avoid the actual practice. [7] i.e., he gives no evidence of wealth of deeds. [8] i.e., and are so in love.

1130. She had vowed that she would have only the best knight in the world.

1131. MS. *gotton*.

1139. From the French, it is clear that the passage means, ". . . that if he brags about his deeds, men will think ill of him." The French further says that prowess must be established in other ways than by talk.

1147. MS. *not sere*.

May thou goo?—Sertis naye.—
Yes, in faythe, i hoope i maye,
  Suche harmys in hertte i take!
To-morowe thou goos, yf þou haue quarte;[9]
Yea, and thou hauc anny hertte,   1160
  Thou turnys[10] not that tyde;
Here has thou take thy leve for aye
That nedys behovys the love allway,
  Where thou shalte goo or ryede.

And here shall thou wynne noþinge   1165
But many a skorne of old and younge.—
  Lo, here[11] this foole forthi![12]
Whoso maye be nere hys love,
Sumtyme love it comys above,[13]
  Be they neuer so slye;   1170
And fere therefro yf he be browghte,
Then shall no man witte his thought
  But his hertte and hee.
On thynge ys, yf he take kepe:[14]
Sore is he bett that darre not wepe,   1175
  Be God and be my lewté.[15]

He hathe no myghte þat mornynge gos,
Ne no ese that sorowe hathe,
  This darre i trewly telle."
Thus lythe he wrynggyng[16] tow and fro   1180
With many a sory syghyng so,
  And mewsus ay in mell;[17]
A while to go he ys in wille,
Anoþur stovnde to hold hym stille
  With þat gay damysell.   1185

---

[9] health; i.e., if you can.   [10] turn back.   [11] listen to.   [12] i.e., on the subject.
[13] wins.   [14] one thing is true, if one notices it.   [15] faith.   [16] writhing.   [17] in the midst (of the sighs) he muses.

1167. MS. *for the.*

1174. The French says, "There is another point;" the next line states it: *mal est batu qe plurer n'ose*—sore is his punishment who dare not weep, i.e., cannot relieve his sorrow by weeping. The hero must keep up appearances if he stays in Calabria; in distant countries he may appear melancholy without exciting attention.

To hymselfe he told þis tale:
"Might i byde, i were all hale—
Be God, i may nought dwell!

For love my herte hathe bovnde so faste
That euermore love will with me last,   1190
To tyme that i shall dye.
It ys full swete to enter in sele,[18]
But ay more and more it bryngys above[19]
To sorowe, and that i se.
Whoso euer ys takyne þerwith   1195
Or wytheinne hem he lyghte,
Full sore schall bovnden be.
Wyth a sorovfull hertte i mon wende,
And sche in quarte[20] mon leve behynde,
And haue no maynde[21] on me!"   1200

The Tournament

To the lady's dismay, Ipomadon leaves her court and returns to his father. He is knighted, and soon acquires a great reputation for valor. Meanwhile the lady's vassals insist that she marry some warrior who will defend her kingdom and keep the lords from quarreling. She is reluctant because of her love for Ipomadon; but after much debate, agrees to make herself the prize of a three-day tournament. The hero appears incognito in the retinue of the Queen of Sicily, whose special attendant he has become; and again he feigns indifference to deeds of arms and the impending contest.

Leve we now this folke there,
And offe the knyght speke we more
That dwellys with the Quene.
To serue hur welle he dyd his tente;[22]
No semblaunte made he to turnament;   2995
Thereat was ladyes tene.

---

[18] happiness.   [19] leads on.   [20] untouched,   heart-whole.   [21] interest.   [22] gave
his attention.

1196. *Lyghte* for *lyethe.*
2993. The queen is the Queen of Sicily.
2996. MS. *there as.*

The maydans hym to skorne louȝghe:
Thereoffe had þey ioye inowghe,
   For he the sothe had sene.
The Quene to hur mete he fett,   3000
And seruyd hyr when she was sett
   Right worthely, i wene.

And sythen vp agayne her ledde,
And kyssyd that lady before her bedde;
   To speke he gan hym spede: 3005
"Madame, lett them turnay to-morn:
I will hunte with hounde and horne,
   And bryng vs home a brayd.[24]
I hold it bettur amonge þe akys[25]
Then in turnament to take strokys;   3010
   I kepe[26] no blod to blede!"
The maydons hym to skorne loughe,
And seyd, "Loo, madam, your drew[27]
   Spekys offe doughtty dedis!"

The Quene cursyd his desteny,[28]   3015
Withoute prowes þat he shuld be,
   That was so fayre offe face;
But sothe ys sayd in olde sawe:
Whedur þat euer love will drawe,
   Lake no lettyng mase.[29]   3020
She louyd hym well for his service,
But oþur damysels of pryse
   Grette skorne at hym have.

---

[24] roast. [25] oaks. [26] intend. [27] lover. [28] evil lot. [29] whoever is in the toils of love, faults are no drawback (to him).

2999. The French (3495) has: *li vilains dist veir* (speak the truth). The English translator seems to have perceived this, and then to have confused *veir* with *veoir* (see). The line is therefore unintelligible.

3003. MS. *agayne vp.*—H.

3004. In accepting the post of special attendant to the Queen, he had stipulated that he be allowed to kiss her each night, and that he be known as the "dru la reine" (queen's lover). These conditions were deliberately strange because he wishes a reputation for eccentricity.

3006. MS. *thy turnay.*

3020. MS. *Lake ne.*

To there skorne toke he no hede,
But toke his leve and forth he yede; 3025
 To the porter he goose.

He gafe the porter a grette gold rynge,
And he sayd, "Sir, i love huntyng
 At rayne-dere and at roos.[30]
And as well wott thow as i, 3030
He that ys not there erlye,
 His best tyde mvst he lose.
Therefore of o thyng i þe praye:
Lett me forthe before the daye."
 "In faythe, sir, i sopposse 3035
Whyles this offyce shall be myn,
Entré and issue shall be thyne,
 For ffrenshipe or for foos!"

Ipomadon to bede goos,
And in the mornyng erly he roosse, 3040
 Or day began to sprynge.
He gerte aray his whyȝte stede,
And all his armore that hym nede,
 Belyve he lett vp brynge.
Soune was covpled all his houndis; 3045
With lowde blowyng forthe he wendis,
 That wakyd ladys yonge.
They sayd, "Lo, madame, your drewe
With horne and hounde se ye may now:
 He hyes to turnayeng!" 3050

The Quene þerto wold take no kepe,[31]
But laye in bedde purposyd to slepe,
 And sore forthought[32] þat tyde

---

[30] roes. [31] pay no attention. [32] regretted.

3042. MS. _gette._
3046. To restore the rhyme, K. suggested _foundis,_ goes.

That he ne was man of prowes;
Whedur[33] she loved hym neuerthelesse: 3055
 In hertt she it hyde.
In the thykest place of all þat woode,
A ermytage he wyst þer stode,
 And thedur gan he ryde.
There he gret araye hym tyte,   3060
His stede and hym all in white:
 He wold no lengur byde.

"Mayster," quod Ipomadon,
"To-day on huntynge mvste ye goone:
 For Goddis love, i you praye,   3065
Yffe God will send you any dere,
Agayne the nyght abyde me here:
 I shall come while i maye."
Fro then vnto the iustyng plase
A full depe dale [betwene] ther was,   3070
 In a deerne[34] waye.
Couyrd-heddyd[35] myght men ryde:
No man myght se hym on no syde
 Yf it were lyghte of day.

His mayster dyd his comaundement;   3075
Ipomadon his waye is went
 Thorow the thike woode.
No man take with hym he lyst
But a chyld þat he on tryste,[36]
 Whiche was bothe fayre and goode: 3080
Of his lond a barons sone,
That wele hym serue con,
 And ofte in stedde hym stoode.[37]

---

[33] yet therefore. [34] hidden. [35] i.e., concealed. [36] trusted. [37] aided him.

3063. The master is the faithful Tholomew. During the day he kills three harts, and thus Ipomadon is able to keep up the fiction of having spent the time in the forest.
3070. *Betwene.*—H. MS. *dede dale.* In the French, it is a *fosse.*

The semely chylde Egyon
Was cosyn[38] to Ipomadon,   3085
　　Right nere sib of his blode.

In the mornynge erly,
He passyd thorow the derne sty
　　Be þat the day gan dawe.[39]
He hovis[40] before that fayre castell;   3090
The wynd wavyd his whyght pensell,[41]
　　And waytis[42] began to blowe;
And ouer the walle þey behylde,
And sawe hym hove in the feld,
　　As whyȝte as any snowe.   3095
He[43] cryed, "Wake, lady bryghte!
For sothe younder hovis a knyghte,
　　The feyrest that euer i sawe.

His stede and he is all in whyȝte;
That syght to se is grette delyȝte,   3100
　　Fro bale as i be broughte!"
The lady weyndis to a wyndowe,
And saw hym hove, as white as snowe;
　　In grette care is she broughte.
Sone she wyst at that day   3105
On whome she shuld her love laye,
　　For in hur h[e]rtte she thought
She wold not the valet chaunge
For emperoure nor for kyng stronge,
　　Gette hym and she movghte.   3110

She beholdys the knyght in whyte,
But what he was, she wot but lite:
　　The more care had the maye.

---

[38] relative.　[39] dawn.　[40] rides.　[41] pennon.　[42] sentinel-minstrels.　[43] i.e., a sentinel.

3098. MS. *i the*.

3109. Koeppel proposed *valet straunge*, and *kyng chaunge*, to make a good rhyme. The former is a common epithet for Ipomadon.

The sonne was vpon lofte be thanne;
All the feld was full of men,   3115
    There armys to assaye.[43]
The Kynge of Spayne, Sir Ottynore,
Sawe the white knyght hove thore
    In armys good and gaye;
To all his folke he sayde syne,[44]   3120
"The fyrste iuste to-day is myne,
    And i hold comnaunte aye!"[45]

With hym was Sir Amfyon;
The Kyng comaundyd hys men ilkone
    Stille they shuld abyde.   3125
He sayd, "Younder is for the fers love
A kyng in white, wele dothe hove;[46]
    And to hym will i ryde!"
A grette spere in honde he nome;
Ipomadon was ware he come   3130
    And blemesshyd on anoþur syde.[47]
Ayther on other brake þer speris:
Ipomadon behynde hym beyris[48]
    Twenty foote þat tyde!

The Kyng laye waltrand[49] in his wede;   3135
Egyon of his hors toke hede,
    And lyghttly lepte þerone.
For all the strengh þat he weldyþe,
The riche Kyng of Spayne hym eldyþe[50]
    To Ipomadon.   3140
Ioyfull was þat lady clere:
How she ordayned[1] now shall ye here:
    Hyr owne cosyne Iosane,

---

[43] try. [44] straightway. [45] keep my agreement. [46] who rides well. [47] crossed the field. [48] strikes him over the back of his steed. [49] writhing. [50] yields. [1] commanded.

3122. In the French (3623): *Kar jo lai assez cuveitee* (craved).
3127. For *kyng* read *knyght*.—K.

That he shuld serue² þerfore [of] speyres,
To what man that best hym beyres   3145
 To the iii dayes were goone.

And þerfore trewly she hym highte
The thryd day he shuld be knyghte,
 His good dedys to alowee.³
A spere to Ipomadon he bare;   3150
As he hadde neuer sene hym ayre,
 He sayd, "Sir, what artt thou?"
"I am the laydis cosyn, sir,
That thus is ordayned here be hur,
 Trewly for to trowe,   3155
That i shall serue here of speris
Two⁴ what man that hym best beris;
 And sertis, that i hold you.

For the man that was of grettis[t] boste
And hym that my lady hatyd moste   3160
 In ffeld here haue ye felde;"
For wele he wyst it was reson.⁵
But he knewe not Ipomadon,
 Togeddur that they had dwellyd;
Togedyr, but it was long beffore.   3165
Ipomadon likyd the more
 The tale that he hym tolde,
And he sayd, "Sir, so God me spede,
My presonere to thy lady lede;
 I wold þat she hym hylde.⁶   3170

Thou shalt haue to þi lady gent
His hors, and saye þat i hit sent—
 The Kyng to hur presone."

---

² furnish. ³ reward. ⁴ to. ⁵ the truth. ⁶ held.

3145. MS. *And what.* ˙The French has *celui ke.*
3152. MS. *And sayd.* Koelbing emends.
3156. The *of* is a result of a literal translation of the French *de lances
servir* (3691).
3158. MS. *sertus.*

Syr Attynore than sorow hade,
But vp he wanne, as he hym bade,   3175
  And rydythe forthe with Iasone.
Whan he came to þat lady bryȝte,
"Madame," he sayd, "younde white knyȝte
  That berythe all oþer downe,
The Kyng offe Spayne takyn hath he,   3180
And he send hym for to bee
  Att your byddyng bowne."

Whereffore was þat lady fayne;
But eft she sayd to Imayne,
  "For ought þat i can see,   3185
Alas! this is a grett myscheffe!
For welle i wott þat my leeffe
  Ys not in this contré.
Certenly he had byn here,
Iosane hym knewe, þat was his fere;   3190
  Now wotte i well, perdé,
That othere [failis] hym manhode
Or he is dede, so God me spede;
  Thereffore full woo is me.

Younde knyght to myne avowe will corde;   3195
And yffe i take hym to my lorde,
  I losse my love, alas!". . .

Ipomadon continues successful, changing the color of his arms each
day, and thus avoiding recognition. Though judged the victor, he does
not reveal himself, and seeks many more adventures before claiming his
reward.

3176. To improve the meter, omit *forthe.*—H.
3184. Imayne is the proud lady's confidante.
3185. MS. *gan see.*
3192. Koelbing's emendation; the rhyme-word is *manhede.*
3195. To avoid hasty marriage proposed by her barons, she had told
her lords that she had vowed to marry only the best knight in the world.
The White Knight fulfills the condition.

EGER AND GRIME

EGER AND GRIME

This poem appears in two versions, one in The Percy Folio Manuscript, c. 1650, and the other in a chapbook printed in Aberdeen in 1711.[1] Of these, the latter is longer by about 1,400 lines, but seems to be a corrupt and expanded version of the source of the former.[2] The present text is from the Percy Folio Manuscript. Through the kindness of the authorities of the British Museum it has been possible to print this text from rotographs of the original.

The earliest mention of the poem is in 1497, when two fiddlers sang it to James IV of Scotland. Its original dialect was northern of the middle or early fifteenth century, but the forms have been greatly altered. It was probably written in and about Linlithgowshire on the Firth of Forth.

The story is of mixed Celtic and Teutonic origins, the latter element being slight and apparently ancient. In Teutonic legend, Grime seems to have been a giant-god who threw up immense dykes; as many as fifteen are ascribed to him in Great Britain. He may possibly be the same person as the Grim in "Havelok," who, according to Skeat's introduction, is said to have thrown down churches. Possibly Eger is the Ægir of Teutonic mythology, god of angry seas, with whose name the fishermen of England were familiar even in Carlyle's time.[3] A Grime's Dyke—an old Roman wall—stretches across the northern part of Linlithgow; the adjacent Firth knew Ægir's wrath sufficiently well. The Teutonic part of the story is thus possibly related to an ancient nature-myth.

With this Teutonic plot has been combined a Celtic account of the Otherworld, similar in many details to the story of Ywain. Gray-steel's country has the usual perilous entrance—a ford defended against invasion—, is located on an island, and is inhabited entirely by women. Gray-steel is the defender of a "perilous princess," and Grime is led to his land by a guide, here rationalized into a squire.

For much useful material on this romance, see the manuscript

---

[1] Edited by Laing, who also had an earlier version printed in 1687 and lacking the name of the printer or place. [2] For the opposite opinion see *ESt.* 19.4ff. [3] See "Heroes and Hero Worship," *Hero as Divinity.*

thesis of Elizabeth Willson (1914) in the University of Chicago Library, Hibbard, and Loomis, many of whose remarks on the Ywain story apply to this. Uncredited emendations are mostly those of Furnivall and Hales.

Off frequently appears for *of;* here it is printed *of.*

It ffell sometimes in the land of Beame
There dwelled a lord within that realme;
The greatest he was of renowne
Eccept the King that ware the crowne.
Thé⁴ called him to name Erle Bragas;   5
He marryed a ladye was fayre of face.
They had noe child but a daughter younge;
In the world was none soe fayre thing.
They called that ladye Winglayne.
Husband wold she neuer haue none,   10
Neither for gold nor yett for good
Nor for noe highnese of his blood,
Without he would with swords dent
Win euery battell where he went.
Soe there were many in that realme rich,   15
But they cold find but few such;
For the Erle rydeth with such a route
Of lords and knights hardye and stout.
There was in that same time
A curteous knight called Sir Grime,   20
And of Garwicke lord was hee;
He was a wise man and a wittye.
Soe there was in that same place
A young knight men called Egace,

---

⁴ *the* for *they; they* for *the,* frequent in the P. F. MS.

1. The land of Beame is a conventional land of romance, now unidentifiable. It has been supposed to be Bohemia. Malory says (XX 18) that Benwyck is Bourges in France; and that *somme men calle it Bayen and somme men calle it Beaume, where the wine of Beaume is.*

9. MS. *winglanye.*

15–6. Laing: *Als there was men in that kinrick Many one, but very few sik* [as she demanded].

21. Garwicke is said by Sir Walter Scott to be Carrick.

24. This form, evidently French, appears only here.

But his name was Sir Eger; 25
For he was but a poore bachlour;[5]
For his elder brother was liuande
And gouerned all his fathers land.
Egar was large of blood and bone,
But broad lands had hee none; 30
But euermore he wan the honour
Through worshipp of his bright armour;
And for loue that he was soe well taught,
Euer he iusted and hee fought.
And because he was soe well proued, 35
The Erles daughter shee him loued.
They ladye granted her good will;
Her father sented[6] there soone till.
He was glad that shee wold,
That shee wold in hart fold[7] 40
For to take vntill her fere
A barun or else a bacheleere.
These knights, Sir Egar and Sir Grime.
They were fellowes good and fine.
They were nothing sib of blood, 45
But they were sworne bretheren good.
They keeped a chamber together att home;
Better loue loued there never none.
Vpon a time Egar he wold forth fare
To win him worshippe as he did ere, 50
Wherby that he might praysed bee
Aboue all knights of high degree.
Soe hee came home vpon a night,
Sore wounded, and ill was he dight:
His kniffe was forth; his sheath was gone; 55

---

[5] young knight, candidate for knighthood. [6] assented. [7] determine.

26. Laing: *And he.* The Percy scribe has probably copied the *for* of l. 27.

39-40. Corrupt. MS. illegible. Laing: *Her friends were fain that she would Once in her heart it for to hold, That she would have to her a pier.*

42. MS. *baru.*

55-6. Laing: *His knife was tint, his sheath was tane, His scabert by his thigh was gane.*

His scaberd by his thigh was done;
A truncheon[8] of a speare hee bore,
And other weapons he bare noe more.
On his bedside he sett him downe;
He siked sore, and fell in swoone.   60
Sir Grime of Garwicke shortlye rose
And ran to Sir Egar and said, "Alas,
For thee, Egar, my hart is woe
That euer I were soe farr thee froe!
For when wee parted att yonder yate,   65
Thou was a mightye man and milde of state;
And well thou seemed, soe God me speede,
To proue thy manhood on a steede.
And now thou art both pale and greene,[9]
And in strong battell thou hast beene.   70
Thou hast beene in strong battell;
It was neuer litle that made thee fayle."
"Now as it hath behappned mee,
God let it neuer behappen thee
Nor noe other curteous knight   75
That euer goeth to the feild to fight
For to win worshipp as I haue done!
I haue bought it deare and lost it soone!
For other lords haue biddn att home
And saued their bodyes forth of shame   80
And kepeed their manhood faire and cleane
Will brook my loue before mine eyen.
And I am hurt and wounded sore,
And manhood is lost for euermore."
Then said Grime to Sir Egar,   85
"Ye greeue you more then meete were;
For that man was neuer soe well cladd,
Nor yett soe doughtye in armes dread,
But in battell place he may be distayned.[10]

---

[8] shaft of a spear.   [9] sickly.   [10] dishonored.

79. Read: "other lords who. . . ." The relative is often omitted.
82. MS. *well broked;* Laing, *will brook.*

Why shold his manhood be reproued,   90
Or his ladye or his loue repine?"
Then said Egar, "Lett be, Sir Grime!
For fairer armour then I had
Was neuer Cristian knight in cladd.
I had a body that seemed well to doe   95
And weapons that well longed therto;
Well I trusted my noble steed,
Soe that I did my good rich weed;
And well I trusted my noble brand.
The best of all I trusted my hart and my hand.   100
I heard tell of a venterous knight
That kept a fforbidden countrye bath day and night
And a fresh iland by the sea,
Where castles were with towers hye.
Ouer the riuer were ryding frythes 2,[11]   105
And soone I chose to the one of tho.
In short while had I rydden
In that land that was fforbidden,
But I heard mouing in the greete[12]
As itt had beene of a steeds feete.   110
My horsse gladedd with that cheere,
Cast vp his head, and was a-steere.
He crope[13] together as he wold haue runen;
I hearkned when more din had comen.
I looked on the way nye before   115
And see a knight come on a sowre.[14]
Red was his sheild, red was his speare,
And all of fresh gold shone his geere;

---

[11] fords to be crossed on horseback. [12] gravel. [13] crept, gathered himself. [14] sorrel.

100. Lines 100 and 102 are hypermetrical. In 100 the first three syllables are probably light, and in 102 the first four. Such lines are common in the P. F. MS.
103. *Iland* illegible in MS. Percy reads *strand*.
113. MS. *groped*.

And by the death that I must thole,[15]
My steed seemed to his but a fole.[16]   120
His speare that was both great and long,
Faire on his brest he cold itt honge;
And I mine in my rest[17] can folde;
I gaue my horsse what head he wold.
Our steeds brought vs together soone.   125
Alas! that meeting I may mone!
For through coate-armour and acton,[18]
Through brest-plate and habergion,[19]
Through all my armour lesse and more,
Cleane through the body he me bore;   130
And I still in my sadle sate;
My good spere on his brest I brake.
The 2[d] time he came againe,
He fayled of me, and my steede he has slaine.
Then I gott vpp deliuerlye,[20]   135
Not halfe soe soone as need had I;
I thought to haue wrocken my steeds bane,
But that great outrage myself hath tane.
I drew a sword of mettle bright,
And egerlye I sought vnto that knight.   140
I stroke at him with all my maine;
I failed of him, and his steed has slaine.
When hee see that itt was soe,
To counter on ffoote he was full throe.[21]

---

[15] suffer. [16] foal. [17] = arest, socket for a spear. [18] stuffed jacket under the coat of mail. [19] coat of mail. [20] quickly. [21] bold.

119. Cf. "Ywain and Gawain," 425–6: *And, bi the ded that i sal thole, Mi stede by his was but a fole.* Laing lacks these lines. A supernaturally large horse belongs to the fairy huntsman in "Geraint, Son of Erbin" in the "Mabinogion"; also in the "Voyage of Mael Duin," *Rev. Celt.* 9.467, and Tale 155 of the "Gesta Romanorum."

122–3. Eger has to rest the butt of his spear in the leather socket at his side. His opponent can stand the encounter with his spear braced against his breast.—Rickert.

127. MS. *ffro.*

137–8. Laing: *For to revenge my steeds bane, The great defoul myself hath tane.*

142. *Has,* northern form of the first person singular.

Hee drew a sword, a worthy weapon; 145
The first dint that on me did happen,
'Throug[h] all my armour, lesse and more,
7 inches into the sholder he me shore.[22]
And I hitt him with whole pith[23]
Aboue the girdle, that he groned with, 150
And with that stroke I cold him lett
Whiles another shortlye on him I sett;
And well I wott I had him gotten,[24]
But with that stroke my sword was broken.
Then I drew a kniffe—I had noe other,— 155
The wh[ich] I had of my owne borne brother,
And he another out of sheath hath tane;
And neerehand together are we gone.
First he wounded me in the face;
My eyen were safe; that was my grace. 160
Then I hitt him vpon the head,
That in his helme my blade I leade.[25]
God lett neuer knight soe woe begon[26]
As I was when all my false weapons were gone!
Yett with the haft that was left in my hand, 165
Fast vpon his face I dange,[27]
That the blood sprang out from vnder the steele.
He lost some teeth; that wott I weele.
My habergion that was of Millaine fine
First my fathers and then was mine, 170
And itt had beene in many a thrust,
And neuer a maile[28] of itt wold burst.
My acton was of Paris worke
Saued me noe more than did my sarke,[29]
For his sword was of noble steele; 175
He strake hard—and it lasted[30] weele—
Through all my armour more and lesse,
And neuer ceaced but in the fleshe.

---

[22] cut.   [23] strength.   [24] killed, conquered.   [25] left.   [26] be so downcast.   [27] struck.
[28] ring.   [29] shirt.   [30] penetrated.

162. Original rhymes were probably *heued—leued.*
163. Cf. *sore bygone,* "Perceval" 349.
169. The famous Milanese steel was a precious possession and heirloom.

Then, fore-foughten,[31] I waxed wearye,
For blood as drye as any tree.   180
I fought soe long, I ffell in swoone,
Till betweene his hands I fell downe.
When I came to myself, my steed was away;
I looked on the land where he lay.
My steed lay slaine a litle me froe,   185
And his backe striken in tow.
Then I was ware of a runing strand,[32]
And thither I crope on foot and hand,
And from my eyen I washt the blood.
All was away shold have done me good.   190
Then I looked on my right hand;
My litle fingar was lackand.
Then I went further on the greene,
Where more strong battells hadden beene.
A slaine knight and spoyled[33] lay;   195
His litle fingar was away,
And by that knight I might well see
That one man had delt both with him and me.
Then of a sadled horsse I gatt a sight,
And by him lay a slaine knight;   200
His steede was both good and fine,
But not halfe soe good as mine.
All that day did I ryde
Till itt was in the euen-tide.
The moone shone fayre; the starres cast light;   205
Then of a castle I gott a sight,
Of a castle and of a towne,
And by an arbour side I light downe;
And there I saw fast me by
The fairest bower that euer saw I.   210
A litle while I tarryed there,

---

[31] tired with fighting.   [32] stream.   [33] plundered.

179. MS. *sore foughten.*

196. The cutting off of a finger may have been done to ensure recognition. The victor wants to be able to recognize the vanquished. Cf. Campbell, "Popular Tales," 1.31, 2.451; "Book of Taliesin" ("Mabinogion"); McInnes and Nutt, "Folk and Hero Tales," 303.

And a lady came forth of a fresh arbor.
Shee came forth of that garden greene,
And in that bower faine wold haue beene.
Shee was cladd in scarlett redd,   215
And all of fresh gold shone her heade;
Her rud was red as rose in raine;
A fairer creature was neuer seene.
Methought her coming did me good,
And straight vpon my feete I stoode.   220
"Good Sir," quoth shee, "what causes you here to lenge?
For ye had me[s]tter of great easmend,[34]
And heere beside is a castle wight,
And there be leeches of great sleight,[35]
Cuning men with for to deale,   225
And wonderous good happ haue for to heale;
And there is the gentlest lady att will
That euer man came in misery till.
Therfore I councell you thither to wend,
For yee had neede of great easmend."   230
"Lady," said Egar, "as itt behappened mee,[36]
I irke to come in any companye.
I beseeche you, lady faire and sweete,
Helpe that I were sounded[37] with one sleepe
And some easment for me and my hackney."   235
"Sir," sayd shee, "I will doe the best I may.
Sir, sith I am first that with you mett,
I wold your neede were the better bett."[38]
Then a faire maid, shee tooke my steede,

---

[34] you have need of relief.   [35] skill.   [36] because of what happened.   [37] made sound.   [38] remedied.

222. MS. meetter.
224. But no physician later appears, and it was usual in the romances for wounded knights to be treated by ladies.
227. This is the lady Loosepaine. The account is confused, so that it is not clear when Eger leaves his guide, one of Loosepaine's attendants, and meets the lady herself.
231. Logically the line should read, *said I.* The meter shows the expression has been added, as it frequently is in this version.

And into a stable shee did him leade; 240
And into a chamber both faire and light,
I was led betweene 2 ladyes bright.
All my bloodye armour of me was done;
The lady searched my wounds full soone.
Shee gaue me drinke for to restore, 245
For neerehand was I bled before;
There was neuer alle nor wine
Came to mee in soe good a time.
A siluer bason she cammanded soone,
And warme water therin to be done. 250
The ladye louesome vnde[r] line,[39]
With her white hands shee did wash mine;
And when shee saw my right hand bare,
Alas! my shame is much the more.
The gloue was whole, the hand was nomen; 255
Therby shee might well see I was ouercomen.
And shee perceiued that I thought shame;
Therfore shee would not aske me my name,
Nor att that word[40] shee sayd noe more,
But all good easments I had there. 260
Then till a bed I was brought;
I sleeped neuer halfe soe soft.
The ladye fayre of hew and hyde,
Shee sate downe by the bedside;
Shee laid a souter[41] vpon her knee; 265
Theron shee plaid full louesomlye.
And yett for all her sweet playinge,
Oftimes shee had full still mourninge;
And her 2 maydens sweetlye sange,
And oft thé weeped, and their hands wrange. 270
But I heard neuer soe sweet playinge,
And euer amongst, soe sore siking.

---

[39] linen.   [40] on that subject.   [41] psaltery.

240. It was courtesy for a lady to disarm a tired knight and attend his wounds, but unusual for her to stable his horse. An instance does occur in the "Mabinogion" in a tale of Ywaine, "The Lady of the Fountain."
255. Laing: *My gloue was hail, my finger was tint.*

In the night shee came to me oft,
And asked me whether I wold ought,
But alwayes I said her nay   275
Till it drew neerr to the breake of day.
Then all my bloodye tents[42] out shee drew;
Againe shee tented my wounds anew.
Wott yee well itt was noe threede,[43]
The tents that into my wounds yeede.   280
They were neither of lake nor line,[44]
But they were silke both good and fine.
Twise the tenting of my wounds
Cost that ladye 20 pounds,
Without spices and salues that did me ease   285
And drinkes that did my body well please.
And then shee gaue me drinke in a horne;
Neuer since the time that I was borne
Such a draught I neuer gatt;
With her hand shee held me after thatt.   290
The drinke shee gaue mee was grasse greene;
Soone in my wounds itt was seene;
The blood was away, the drinke was there,
And all was soft[45] that erst was sore.
And methought I was able to run and stand,   295
And to haue taken a new battell in hand.
The birds sange in the greene arbor;
I gate on foote and was on steere.[46]
The layde came to me where I lay;
These were the words shee to me did say: 300
"I rede you tarry a day or towe

---

[42] dressings of the wounds. [43] thread, cheap cloth. [44] both words mean linen;
lake was the finer. [45] soothed. [46] astir.

286–92. According to a common medieval belief, only if the medicine
appears in the wounds will the patient live. Green was the favorite color
for potions and salves. One of the best known of the latter was composed
chiefly of verdigris. *Take pimpernole also called self-heal and stampe hit
and temper hit with water and gif hym to drinke, and ȝif hit go out at ye
wonde, he schal live.* Cf. "Sir Ferumbras" 510; "Merveilles de Rigomer"
16,954, for similar use of ointment.

Till you be in better plight to goe."
But I longed soe sore to be at home
That I wold needlye[47] take leaue to gone.
Shee gaue me 2 shirts of Raines[48] in fere,   305
Put them next my body; I haue them here.
And my owne shee did abone,[49]
And my bloudye armour on me hath done
Saue my heauy habergion; shee was afrayd
Lest they wold haue mad my wounds to bleede.   310
That ladye with her milke-white hand
To the arson[50] of my saddell shee it bound
With 2 bottels of rich wine,
And therof haue I liued euer sinne.
I sayd, "A! deare, good madam, how may this be?   315
The coningest leeche in this land be yee;
For all my wounds lesse or more,
Of them I feele noe kind of sore,
As I had neuer beene wounded with sword nor speare,
Nor neuer weapon had done mee deere."   320
"Wold God," said shee, "that itt were soe!
But I know well for a day or 2
Froe that loue make you once agast,[1]
Your oyntments may noe longer last.
Sith you will not abyde with mee,   325
Lett your ladye in your countrye
Doe to your wounds as I wold haue done;
Then they will soft and heale full soone."
One thing did my hart great greeffe;
I had nothing that ladye to giue,   330
But my golden beades[2] forth I drew
That were of fine gold fresh and new.
Shee wold not receiue them at my hand,
But on her bedside I lett them liggand.
I tooke leaue of that ladye bright,   335

---

[47] earnestly. [48] of Rennes, Brittany. [49] put above. [50] saddle-bow. [1] when
your love stirs you again. [2] rosary, prayer-beads.

305. Cf. "Squire" 842.
312. MS. *rason*.

And homewards rid both day and night.
I fared full well all that while
Till I came home within 2 mile;
Then all my wounds wrought[3] att once
As kniues had been beaten thorrow my bones.   340
Out of my sadle I fell that fraye;[4]
When I came to myselfe, my steed was away.
Thus haue I beene in this ffarr countrye;
Such a venterous knight mett with mee.
Men called him Sir Gray-steele;   345
I assayd[5] him, and he ffended weele."

2D PARTE

Then spake Grime to Sir Egar
With soft words and faire,
"That man was neuer soe wise nor worthye,
Nor yet soe cuning proued in clergye,[6]   350
Nor soe doughtye of hart nor hand,
Nor yett so bigg in stowre to stand,
But in such companye he may put in[7]
But he is as like to loose as win.
And euer I bade you to keepe you weele   355
Out of the companye of Sir Gray-steele,
For he is called by command[8]
The best knight in any land.
Sith the matter is chanced soe,
Wee will take the choice of wayes 2.   360
From your loue and laydye lained this shal bee;
Shee shall know nothing of our priuitye."
But litle wist Egar nor Sir Grime
Where the lady was that same time;
For the lady that Egars loue was,   365

---

[3] worked, acted . . . as if.   [4] at that seizure.   [5] tested.   [6] learning.   [7] enter.
[8] covenant, general agreement.

354. The scribe may have copied the *but* from line 353.   Perhaps read:
that he. . . .
357. Laing: *For he is called uncannand.*   Cf. *N.E.D.*, *covenant*.
360. MS. *wayes of choice 2.*

Her chamber was within a litle space;
Of Sir Egar shee soe sore thought
That shee lay wakened, and sleeped nought.
A scarlett mantle hath shee tane;
To Grimes chamber is shee gone.   370
Shee heard them att a priuie dain;[9]
Shee stayd without and came not in.
When shee heard that Egars bodye was in distresse,
She loued his body mickle the worse.
Words this lady wold not say,   375
But turned her backe and went awaye;
Yett soe priuilye shee is not gone,
But Grime perceived that there was one.
An vnfolded[10] window opend hee
And saw the way-gate[11] of that ladye.   380
"What is that," said Egar, "maketh that dain?"
Grime sayd, "My spanyell hound wold come in."
To his fellow Sir Egar he said noe more,
But he repented that she came there.
Gryme hath gotten that same night   385
Leeches that beene of great sleight,[12]
Coning men with for to deale
That had good happ wounds to heale;
Yett long ere day word is gone
That Egar the knight is comen home,   390
And hath moe wounds with sword and kniffe
Then had euer man that bare liffe.
17 wounds hee hath tane;
7 beene thorrow his body ran.
The leeches cold doe him noe remede,   395
But all said Egar wold be dead.
In the morning the Erle and the Countesse,
To Grymes chamber can thé passe.

---

[9] din, dispute; cf. 381.   [10] unfastened.   [11] departure.   [12] skill.

371. Laing: *She heard him with a privy din.* MS. one stroke of *u* in *priuie* is lacking.
379. Windows generally opened with a lateral swing and were held in place by a pin.

The Erle said, "How doth Sir Egar the knight?"
Then answered Grime both wise and wight,   400
"He doth, my lord, as you may see."
"Alas!" said the Erle, "how may this bee?"
Grime answered him hastilye,
"My lord, I shall tell you gentleye:
An vncoth land he happened in,   405
Where townes were both few and thinn.
Giffe he rode neuer soe fast,
7 dayes the wildernesse did last.
He heard tell of a venterous knight
That kept a forbbidden countrye day and night,   410
And a mile by the salt sea,
Castles fayre, and towers hye;
On the other side a fayre strand,
A faire fforrest on the other hand.
On the one side run a fresh riuere;   415
There might noe man nighe him nere.[13]
For he that ouer that riuer shold ryde
Strange aventures shold abyde;
Hee shold either fight or flee,
Or a weed[14] in that land leaue shold hee.   420
The wedd[15] that he shold leaue in this land
Shold be the litle ffingar of his right hand;
And or he knew himselfe to slowe,[16]
His litle fingar he wold not forgoe.
Boldlye Egar gaue him battell tho;   425
His helme and his hawberckes he tooke him fro.
Soe did he his sword and his spere
And much more of his golden gayre;
And homewards as he rode apace

---

[13] approach closely. [14] forfeit. [15] forfeit. [16] about to be slain.

405. MS., &, for an, as commonly.
406. MS. where both few.
410. Gray-steel's land is separated from Earl Bragas's by a river over which are two fords. Before crossing the ford, one can see the ocean shore, fair castles, high towers, seven towns, and an island. Cf. 102–5, 933 ff., Laing 122–8 and 1447.
423. He refers to Eger; above (417–22) it is general.

Thorrow the wylde forrest and the wyldenesse,   430
He thought to haue scaped withouten lett.
Then 15 theeues with Egar mett;
They thought Egar for to haue him sloe,
His gold and his good to haue tooke him froe.
Thrise through them with a spere he ran;   435
7 he slew, and the master man.[17]
Yett had hee scaped[18] for all that dread,
They shott att him, and slew his steed.
Hee found a steed when they were gone,
Wheron Sir Egar is come home;   440
For if Sir Egar dye this day,
Farwell flower of knighthoode for euer and aye."
Then the Erle proferred 40[li][19] in land
For a leeche that wold take Egar in hand.
9 dayes were comen and gone   445
Or any leeche wold Egar vndertane.
It was 9 dayes and some deale more
Or his ladye wold come there;
And att the coming of that fayre ladye,
Her words they were both strange and drye.[20]   450
Shee saies, "How doth that wounded knight?"
Then answered Gryme both wise and wight,
"He doth, madam, as yee may see."
"In faith," said the lady, "that's litle pittye.
He might full well haue bidden att home;   455
Worshipp in that land gatt he none.
He gaue a ffingar to lett him gange;
The next time he will offer vp the whole hand."
Gryme was euer wont to gange
In councell with the ladye to stand,   460
And euer told Egar a fayre tale
Till the knight Sir Egar was whole;
For and her want[21] and will had beene to him lenging,[22]
It wold have letted him of his mending.
Soe long the leeches delt with Sir Egar   465

---

[17] chief robber.   [18] would have escaped . . . (but) they shot . . .   [19] pounds.
[20] caustic, unsympathetic.   [21] for if her desire.   [22] delayed, denied.

Till he might stoutlye goe and stirr;
Till itt once beffell vppon a day
Gryme thought the ladye to assaye
Whether shee loued Sir Egar his brother
As well as euer shee did before. 470
Grime said, "Madame, by Godds might,
Egar will take a new battell with yonder knight.
He is to sore wounded yett for to gone;
Itt were worshipp to cause him to abyde at home,
For he will doe more for you then mee." 475
Then answered that fayre lady,
"All that while that Egar was the knight
That wan the degree in euery fight,
For his sake verelye
Manye a better I haue put by; 480
Therfor I will not bidd him ryde,
[Nor att] home I will not bid him abyde,
Nor of his marriage I haue nothing adoe;[23]
I wott not, Gryme, what thou saist therto."
Gryme turned his backe of the ladye faire, 485
And went againe to his brother Sir Egar,
Sett him downe on his bed side,
And talked these words in that tyde:
"Egar," he said, "thou and I are brethren sworne;
I loued neuer better brother borne. 490
Betwixt vs tow let vs make some cast,[24]
And find to make our foemen fast;
For of our enemies wee stand in dread,
And wee lye sleeping in our bedd."
Egar said, "What mistrust haue yee with mee?[25] 495
For this 7 months if I here bee,
Shall neuer man take my matter in hand

---

[23] regret, perturbation.   [24] devise some plan.   [25] doubt . . . of me.

478. MS. *while Egar y^t was.*
478. Cf. "Sir Triamore," P. F. MS., II, p. 103, l. 674, and note.
492. MS. *formen.* Perhaps the line should read: *And fand to make our foemen gast.*
497. *M* of *matter* illegible; Laing: *Shall no man take that deed on hand.*

Till I bee able to auenge myselfe in land."
A kinder knight then Gryme was one
Was neuer bredd of blood nor bone.   500
"Methinke you be displeased with mee,
And that is not your part for to bee;
For sith the last time that ye came home,
I haue knowen priuie messengers come and gone
Betwixt your ladye and Erle Olyes,   505
A noble knight that doughtye is,
Of better blood borne then euer were wee,
And halfe more liuings[26] then such other 3."
Then Egar vp his armes sprang,[27]
And ffast together his hands dange   510
With still mourning and siking sore.
Saith, "Alas! my loue and my ladye fayre,
What haue I done to make you rothe[28]
That[28a] was euer leeue, and now soe lothe?"
Gryme had of him great pittye.   515
"Brother," he said, "be councelled by mee.
If you will doe after my counsaile,
Peraduenture it will greatly preuaile.
Another thing; my liffe I dare lay
That yee shall wed that ladye within this monthes day."[29] 520
"How now?" quoth Egar; "how may that bee?"
"Peace!" said Gryme, "and I shall tell thee.
I haue a brother that men call Palyas,
A noble squier and worthye is.
He is wel beloued within this court   525
Of all the lords round about.
Wee will him call to our councell;
Peraduentur he will vs preuayle,[29a]
And I myselfe will make me sicke at home
Till a certen space be comen and gone,   530
And that such a disease hath taken mee
That I may noe man heare nor noe man see.
Palyas my brother shall keepe you att home,

---

[26] landed estates, sources of income. [27] threw up. [28] angry. [28a] you who. [29] a
month from this day. [29a] transitive: be of use to.

And I myselfe will to that battell gone;
And I shall feitch[30] Gray-steeles right hand,   535
Or I shall leaue another fingar in that land."

3D PARTE

They called Pallyas to their councell,
And he assented soone withouten fayle;
For he loued Sir Egar both euen and morne
As well as he did Gryme his brother borne.   540
"And iff you will to this battell goe,
Yee had neede of good councell betwene vs 2.
Gryme, if thou wilt fight with Sir Gray-steele,
Thou had neede of weapons that stand wold weele;
For weapons may be both fresh and new,   545
Fikle, false, and full vntrue.
When a weapon faileth when a man hath need,
All the worse then may hee speede;
And all I say by Sir Egar,
Where was a better knight knowen any where?   550
When his weapon faild him att most need,
All the worse then did he speede."
Palyas said, "There was sometime in this countrye,
Egar, your vnckle, Sir Egramie;
And when that Egramye was liuand,   555
He had the guiding of a noble brand.
The name of itt was called Erkyin;
Well were that man had it in keeping.[31]
First when that sword was rought,
To King Ffundus it was brought   560

---

[30] fetch.   [31] well were it for that man who . . .

553. MS. *somtimes.*

557. Good swords were named and handed down from generation to
generation. It was not unusual to ascribe a sword to foreign or supernatural workmanship; cf. "Beowulf" 1557 ff. Erkyin appears here only;
otherwise called Egeking, king of swords. Not named in Laing.

560. Fundus is not found in Langlois's index, but Forre (the name in
Laing) is the name of several Saracens in the chansons de geste.

Full far beyond the Greekes sea
For a iewell of high degree.
When the King departed this world hence,
He left it with the younge prince;[32]
And some sayd that Egramye   565
Shold loue that ladye in priuitye;
He desired the sword in borrowing.
The King deceased at that time;
And when that Egrame was liuande,
He had the guiding of that noble brand.   570
That man was neuer of a woman borne
Durst abyde the winde his face beforne.[33]
The ladyes dwelling is heere nye;
She saith there is noe man that sword shall see
Till her owne sonne be att age and land,[34]   575
And able to welde his fathers brande."
Grime sayd, "I will goe thither to-morrow at day
To borrow that sword if that I may."
On the morrow when the sun shone bright,
To Egrames ladie went Grime the knight;   580
Kindley he halcht[35] that ladye faire.
She saith, "How doth my cozin, Sir Egar?"
"Hee will forth, maddam, with all his might
To take a new battell on yonder knight.
He prayeth you to lend him his vnckeles brand,   585
And there he hath sent you the deeds of his land,
And all mine I will leaue with you in pawne
That your sword shall safelye come againe."
Soe he desired that sword soe bright
That shee was loth to withsay[36] that knight;   590
Then shee feitched him forth that noble brand,
And receiued the deeds of both their lands.

---

[32] princess.   [33] endure the wind of the sword on his face.   [34] of age and in possession of his land.   [35] greeted.   [36] deny.

564. Prince frequently feminine throughout the Middle English period. Laing: *Then he betauht it to the queen.*

574. Possibly the weapon is left by a fairy for his son; cf. "Degaré." If so, the situation is rationalized.

She said, "There was noe fault with Egeking
But for want of grace and gouerninge;
For want of grace and good gouerninge   595
May loose a kingdome and a king;
For there is neither lim nor lith[37]
That Egeking my sword meeteth with,
But gladlye it will through itt gone,
That biting sword, vnto the bone.   600
But I wold not for both your lands
That Egeking came in a cowards hands."
And yett was faine Sir Gryme the knight;
To Egar he went againe that night.
Pallyas, he said,[38] "I read you be councelled by mee,   605
And take some gifts to that faire ladye,
To that ladye faire and bright
That lodged Sir Egar soe well the first night."
"The best tokens," said Sir Egar,
"Beene her sarkes of Raines;[39] I haue them here."   610
He tooke broches and beads in that stonde
And other iewells worth 40[li]
To reward that fayre ladye
And thanke her of her curtesie.
"Wherby," sayd Gryme, "shall I her know   615
Amongst other ladyes that stands on a row?"
"I shall tell you tokens," sayd Sir Egar,
"Wherby you may know that ladye faire.
Shee hath on her nose, betweene he[r] eyen,
Like to the mountenance[40] of a pin;   620
And that is red, and the other is white.
There is noe other ladye her like;
For shee is the gentlest of hart and will
That euer man came vntill."

---

[37] limb, i.e., arm nor leg.   [38] i.e., Pallyas said.   [39] shirts from Rennes.   [40] amount.

597. MS. *lin nor light.*   Laing: *Whether that were shank or arm.*
613. MS. *and to.*
619–21. Cf. Laing, 947–51: *Betwixt her een and eke her neise There is the greatness of a peise A spot of red, the lave is white.* This is a "love-spot"; cf. Hibbard, 316.

Early on the other day   625
Theese 2 knights did them array;
Into a window Sir Egar yeede
Bookes of romans for to reede
That all the court might him heare.
The knight was armed and on steere;[41]   630
He came downe into the hall
And tooke his leaue both of great and small.
The Erle tooke Egars hand in his fist;
The Countesse comlye[42] cold him kisse.
His oune lady stood there by;   635
Shee wold bere the knight noe companye.
He sayd, "Ffarwell, my lady faire."
Shee sayd, "God keepe you better then he did ere!"
And all that euer stoode her by
Did marueill her answer was soe dry.[43]   640
He went to the chamber, or he wold blin;
Sir Gryme came forth as he went in,
Stepped into the stirropp that stiffe were in warr,
And Palyas his brother wrought[44] him a spere.
Then wold he noe longer abyde,   645
But towards Gray-steele can he ryde;
To the walls went Winglaine, that lady faire,
For to see the waygate of her loue Sir Egar.
And Gryme the spurres spared not; soe weele
To the steeds sides he let them feele,[45]   650
His horsse bouted[46] forth with noble cheere;
He spowted[47] forward as he had beene a deere
Till he was passed out of her sight.
To Grymes chamber went that ladye bright;
Yett long time or shee came there,   655
Palyas had warned Sir Egar,
Drawen double curtaines in that place
That noe man of Sir Egar noe knowledg hath.

---

[41] astir.   [42] courteously.   [43] caustic.   [44] reached.   [45] be felt.   [46] bolted.
[47] bounded.

650. Laing: *But his steeds sides he made them feel.*
657. The canopy and curtains of his bed.

Palyas was full of curtesie,
And sett a chaire for that faire ladye.   660
Shee said, "At the walls, Palyas, I haue beene there
To see the ryding forth of Sir Egar;
He rydeth feircely out of the towne
As he were a wild lyon.
Alas! hee may make great boast and shoure[48]   665
When there is noe man him before,
But when there is man to man and steed to steede,
To proue his manhood then were it neede!"
Oftentimes Egar both cruell and keene
For her in strong battells oft hath beene,   670
And oftentimes had put himselfe in warr;
And lay and heard her lowte[49] him like a knaue.
He wist not how he might him wrecke,
But cast vp his armes, and thought to speake;
And Palyas was perceiued[50] of that,   675
And by the sholders he him gatt.
He held him downe both sad and sore
That he lay still and sturrd noe more.
Palyas was full of curtesie,
And thus answered that faire ladye: 680
He said, "Maddame, by Gods might,
Egar is knowne for the noblest knight
That euer was borne in the land of Beame,
And most worshipp hath woon to that relme.
That was well proued in heathenesse   685
When the King of Beame did thither passe;
Soe did the lords of this countrye
And alsoe your father, that Erle soe free.
There came a sowdan to a hill
That many Christen men had done ill;   690
The name of him was Gornordine,
That many a Christen man had put to pine;
And he becalled[1] any Cristen knight
Or any 5 that with him wold fight.
500 knights were there that day,   695

---

[48] clamor.   [49] abuse.   [50] aware.   [1] challenged.

And all to that battell they saydden nay.
Egar thought on you att home
And stale to that battell all alone;
They fought together, as I heard tell,
On a mountaine top till Gornordine fell.   700
60 hethen were in a busment² neere,
And all brake out vpon Sir Egar;
Or any reskew came to him then,
He had kild Gornordine and other ten.
Then was he rescewed by a noble knight   705
That euer was proued both hardye and wight;
The name of him was Kay of Kaynes;³
A northeren knight I trow he is.
There were but Egar and other ten,
And thé killed 60 or more of the heathen men;   710
Thus they reschewd the noble Egar
And brought him to the host, as you shall hear.
The King of Beame in that stage
Offered Sir Egar his daughter in marryage;
Yet that gentle knight wold not doe soe;   715
He loued you best [that] now be his foe.
You be his foe; he knowes that nowe
When he standeth in dread, I know."
The lady was soe wroth with Palyas
Shee tooke her leaue and forth shee goth.   720
Now lett vs leaue chyding att home
And speake of Sir Gryme that is to the battell gone.

4D PARTE

All the wildernesse that there bee,
Grime rode it in dayes 3.
He mett a squier by the way;   725
With fayre words Grime can to him say:

---

² ambush.   ³ Caen(?).

707. On the attachment of Kay to Caen, see the selections from the
"Brut."

"Sir," he said, "who is lord of this countrye?"
The squier answered him gentlye,
"It is a lord most worthyest in waine;[4]
Erle Gares is his name."   730
Grime sayd, "How highteth that lords heyre?"
He sayd, "He hath none but a daughter fayre."
Gryme saith, "Who hath that ladye wedd?"
The knight sayd, "Shee neuer came in mans bedd;
But Sir Attelston, a hardye knight,   735
Marryed that lady fayre and bright;
For he gaue battell, that wott I weele,
Vpon a day to Sir Gray-steele.
A harder battell then there was done tho
Was neuer betwixt knights 2;   740
But Gray-steele killed Sir Attelstone,
A bolder knight was neuer none.
Erle Gares sonne and his heyre—
In all the world was none more goodlyere—
He was soe sorry Attelstone was dead   745
He thought to quitt Gray-steele his meede.
Boldlye he gaue him battell vpon a day;
Therfor many a man sayd wellaway,
And there thé both ended att this bane[5]
As many another knight hath done;   750
Ffor I haue wist that tyrant with his hands 2
Kill a 100 knights and some deale moe;
Shamfulye hath driuen them to dead
Withouten succour or any remed."
For all the words he spake in that time,   755
Nothing it feared[6] the knight, Sir Grime.
Gryme sayd, "How ffarr haue wee[7] to that citye
Wheras that ladyes dwelling doth bee?"
The knight said, "But miles 2;

---

[4] customs, character.   [5] at (the hands of) this murderer.   [6] frightened.   [7] have
we (to go).

734. Obviously the line should read: *"The squire sayd. . . ."*
758. MS. *deth.*
759. Again *knight* should be *squire.* Cf. Laing 1167–9.

The one of them I will with you goe."   760
They talked together gentlye
Till he had brought Grime to that citye;
Att a burgesse house his ine[8] he hath tane·
To seeke the ladye Sir Grime is gone.
Then he went into a garden greene   765
Where he saw many ladyes sheene;
Amongst them all he knew her there
By the tokens of Sir Eger.
Egar was hurt vnder the eare;
An oyntment Gryme had drawen there.[9]   770
He held the gloue still on his hand
Where Egers fingare was lackand;
And when that knight came her nye,
He kneeled downe vpon his knee
And thanked her with humble cheere—   775
"Sith the last time, madam, that I was heere."
"Sir," said shee, "excused you must hold mee,
Thus avised[10] I did you neuer see."
Then hee gaue her the shirts of Raines in that stond
And other iewells worth 40li,   780
And thus rewarded that fayre ladye
And thanked her of her curtesie.
"Now sir," sayd shee, "soe haue I blisse,
How fareth the knight that sent me this?"
"I doe, madam, as yee see now;   785
Therof I thanke great God and you."
"Why, sir," said shee, "but is it yee
That in such great perill here did bee?
I am glad to see you so sound in sight."
Hastilye shee rose and kist that knight.   790
Gryme looke vpon that ladye faire:
"Soe faire a creature saw I neuer ere."
For shee was cladd in scarlett redd,
And all of fresh gold shone her head;

---

[8] lodging.   [9] applied (under his own ear as a disguise).   [10] in this guise.

772. MS. *fingars.*
791. MS. *ladyes.*

Her rud was red as rose in raine;
A fairer creature was neuer seene.
As many men in a matter full nice[11]—
But all men in louing shall neuer be wise—,
His mind on her was soe sett
That all other matters he forgett;
And as thé stood thus talkeand,
Shee stale the gloue besids his hand.
When shee saw his right hand bare,
Softlye shee said to him there:
"Sir," said shee, "it was noe marueill though you hidd your
    hand,
For such leeches in this land are none!
There is noe leeche in all this land
Can sett a fingar to a hand
To be as well and as faire
As neuer weapon had done it dere;
But game and bourd let goe together;[12]
Scorning I can well conssider.
It was neuer that knights commandement
Noe scorne hither to mee to send;
If thou be comen to scorne mee,
Ffull soone I can scorne thee."
Before, shee was mild of state;
Now is shee high[13] and full of hate;
And of all the iewells that he hath brought,
Shee curset[14] them to the ground, and wold them naught.
Grime was neuer soe sore in all his day;
He wist neuer a word what he shold say,
And as shee was to the chamber passand,
Grime tooke that ladye by the hand.
Saith, "I beseech you, lady free,
A word or 2 to hearken mee,
And, soe helpe me God and Holy Dame,
I shall tell you how all this matter was done:

---

[11] particular.   [12] make an end of sport and jest.   [13] proud. [14] cast(?).

800. An illegible word inserted above line before *forgett*. Furnivall printed *quite*.

The knight that was heere, he was my brother,
And hee thought me more abler then any other   830
For to take that matter in hand.
He loueth a ladye within his land;
If not in euery fight he win the gree,
Of his loue forsaken must he bee."
Shee sayd, "Yee seeme a gentle knight   835
That answereth a ladye with soe much right."
The iewells the mayden hath vpp tane,
And shee and the knight to chamber are gone.
Shee sent vnto that burgesse place
A mayden that was faire of face;   840
What cost soeuer his steed did take,
Twice double shee wold it make.
A rich supper there was dight
And shortlye sett before that knight;
Meate nor drinke none wold hee,   845
He was soe enamored of that fayre ladye.
He longed sore to [bee] a-bedd,
And to a chamber shee him led,
And all his armour of was done,
And in his bed he was layd soone.   850
The ladye louesome of hew and hyde[15]
Sett her downe by his bedside;
Shée layd a sowter vpon her knee,
And theron shee playd full louesomlye;
And her 2 mayds full sweetlye sang,   855
And euer they wept, and range their hands.
Then spake Gryme to that ladye fayre:
"Of one thing, madam, I haue great marueile,
For I heard neuer soe sweet playinge
And ofetimes soe sore weepinge."   860
Shee commanded her sowter to be taken her froe,
And sore shee wrange her hands 2.

---

[15] skin.

841. "The cost of stabling his steed she offered to pay four times over."
MS. *cast.*
848–63. Largely a repetition of 339 ff.

"Sir," shee sayd, "I must neuer be weele
Till I be auenged on Sir Gray-steele;
For he slew my brother, my fathers heyre,   865
And alsoe my owne lord both fresh and fayre;
For Sir Attelstone shold me haue wedd,
But I came neuer in his bedd.
He gaue a battell, that wott I weele,
Vpon a day to Sir Gray-steele;   870
A harder battell then was done thoe
Was neuer betweene knights 2.
Gray-steele killed Attelstone;
Therfor many a knight made great moane.
Then my brother that was my fathers heyre—   875
In all the world was none more goodlyer—
He was soe sorry for my husband indeed
He thought to haue quitt Gray-steele his meede.
Boldlye he gaue him battell vpon a day;
Therfore many a man sayd wellaway,   880
And there they both ended att that bone
As many another knight hath done.
For I haue wist that tyrant with his hands 2
To haue killed a 100 knights and moe,
And shamefully driuen them to dead   885
Withouten succour or any remed;
And if thou be comen to fight with that knight,
Iesu defend thee in thy right!
There is noe woman aliue that knoweth so weele
As I doe of the condic[i]ouns[16] of Sir Gray-steele;   890
For euerye houre from midnight till noone
Eche hower he increaseth the strenght of a man,
And euery houer from noone till midnight

---

[16] characteristics.

881. *Bone* for *bane;* cf. 749.   878–86 are a repetition of 746–54.
884. MS. *haue a killed a.*
886. MS. *remedeye.*
891–4. Sir Gray-steel here represents the Celtic sun-hero, whose strength grew and diminished each day with the sun. Cf. Miss J. L. Weston's "Gawaine."

Euery hower he bateth[17] the strenght of a knight.
Looke thou make thy first counter[18] like a knight,   895
And enter into his armour bright;
Looke boldlye vpon him thou breake thy spere
As a manfull knight in warr;
Then light downe rudlye[19] for thy best boote;
The tyrant is better on horsbacke then on foote.   900
Presse stiflye vpon him in that stoure
As a knight will thinke on his paramoure;
But I will not bid you thinke on me,
But thinke on your ladye whersoeuer shee bee.
And let not that tyrant, if that he wold,   905
Lett you of that couenant that ladye to holde."
Then shee tooke leaue of that gentle knight;
To her chamber shee is gone with her maidens bright.
Sir Gryme longed sore for the day;
The ostler[20] soone can him arraye.   910
He armed the knight and brought him his steede,
And he gaue him red gold for his meede.
A rich breakfast there was dight,
And shortlye sett before that knight;
But meate nor drinke none wold hee   915
But a cuppe of wine and soppes 3.[21]
He tooke leaue of that ladye cleare
And rydeth towards the fresh riuer.

5D PARTE

Early in that May morning
Merrely when the burds can sing,   920
The throstlecocke, the nightingale,
The laueracke,[22] and the wild woodhall,[23]
The rookes risen in euery riuer,
The birds made a blissfull bere.[24]
It was a heauenly melodye   925

---

[17] grows weaker by.   [18] attack.   [19] quickly.   [20] groom of the chamber.   [21] bread
dipped in wine.   [22] lark.   [23] witwall.   [24] noise.

919–30. A conventional medieval May morning.
925. MS. *molodye.*

For a knight that did a louer bee
On the one side to heare the small birds singing,
On the other side the flowers springing.
Then drew forth of the dales the dun deere;
The sun it shone both fresh and cleere;   930
Phebus gott vp with his golden beames,
Ouer all the land soe light it gleames.
Hee looked vpon the other side,
See parkes and palaces of mickle pryde,
With 7 townes by the salt sea   935
With castles fayre and towers hyee.
Ouer the riuer were ryding places 2,
And soone Grime chose to the one of tho;
And then he wold noe longer abyde,
But into Gray-steeles land can he ryde.   940
And yett was feared Sir Gryme the knight
Lest he wold haue tarryed him[25] till night;
But, God wott, he had noe cause to doe soe,
For Gray-steele had euer waches[26] 2.
They went and told their master anon right: 945
"Into your land is comen a knight,
And 3st he hath rydden about the [plaine],
And now is he bowne to turne home againe."
"Nay," sayd Gray-steele, "by St. Iohn!
This one yeere he shall not goe home,   950
But he shall either fight or flee,
Or a wed in this land leaue shall hee."
They brought him red sheeld and red spere,
And all of fresh gold shone his geere;
His brest plate was purpelye pight;[27]   955
His helmett itt shone with gold soe bright,
Was sett with gold and precious stone;

---

[25] waited (reflexive).   [26] watchmen.   [27] decorated with purple.

926. *For* is abbreviated in the MS.
942. If Gray-steel waited until night, Grime would not have the honor
of fighting him at his strongest.
947. Last word illegible.
955. Read: *purpel ypight?*
957-8 are reversed in the MS.

His shankes full seemlye shone;
His armes with plate and splents[28] dight
Were sett with gold and siluer bright,   960
With his sheelde on his brest him beforne.
Theron was a dragon and a vnicorne;
On the other side a beare and a wyld bore,
In the middest a ramping lyon[29] that wold byte sore.
About his necke, withouten fayle,   965
A gorgett[30] rought with rich mayle,[31]
With his helme sett on his head soe hye;
A mase[32] of gold, full royallye
On the top stoode a carbunckle[33] bright;
It shone as moone doth in the night.   970
His sadle with selcamoure[34] was sett,
With barrs of gold richlye frett;[35]
His petrill[36] was of silke of Inde;
His steed was of a furley[37] kinde
With raines of silke raught to his hand,   975
With bells of gold theratt ringand.
He stepped into his stirropp well armed in war;
A knight kneeled and raught him a spere;
And then wold he noe longer abyde,
But straight to Sir Grime cold he ryde.   980
When Grime was ware of Gray-steele,
Through comfort his hart came to him weele.
He sayd, "Thou wounded my brother Sir Egar;
That deed, traytor, thou shalt buy full sore."
Gray-steele answered neuer a word,   985
But came on Sir Grime as he was woode.
They smoten their steeds with spurres bright
And ran together with all their might,
But Gray-steele came on Sir Grime
Like a lyon in his woodest time;   990
Soe did Grime vpon Sir Gray-steele,

---

[28] splints, overlapping plates for a joint in the armor. [29] lion rampant. [30] armor to protect the neck. [31] chain-mail. [32] mace, war-club. [33] ruby, or any red stone. [34] rich silk. [35] decorated. [36] breast plate. [37] wonderful.

969–70. On shining gems, cf. "Havelok" 2145.

And attilde[38] him a dint that bote[39] full weele.
Thorrow all his armour lesse and more,
Cleane thorrow the body he him bore,
That all his girthers[40] burst in sunder;   995
The knight and salle[41] and all came vnder.
Through the strenght of Gryime and his steede,
He smote downe Gray-steele, and ouer him yeede;
And well perceiued Gray-steele then
That he was macht with a noble man.   1000
Then young Grime start out of stray,[42]
And from his stirropps he light that day.
He thought on that ladye yore,
How shee had taught him to doe before;
He shooke out his sword Egeking;   1005
The other mett him manffully without leasing.
Grime sought[43] him on one side
And raught him with a wound full wyde;
A 100ᵈ mailes[44] he shore assunder
And all the stuffe that was therevnder.   1010
Throughout all his armour bright,
5 inch into the sholder, the sword light,[45]
But Gray-steele neuer with noe man mett
That 2 such dints did on him sett.
Then thought Gray-steele, that warryour wight,   1015
To quitt Sir Grime that noble knight;
He hytt him on the helme on hye
That the fire as flynt out can flye.
Or euer he cold handle Egeking againe,
3 doughtye dints he sett on him certaine   1020
That almost Sir Gryme was slaine;
The least of them might haue beene a mans bane.
Thus these noble burnes[46] in battele
Hacked and hewed with swords of mettle;

---

[38] aimed at him. [39] cut. [40] girths. [41] saddle. [42] astray; jumped clear of his stirrups. Cf. *N.E.D.*, *stray*, sb. II. [43] attacked. [44] links of chain-mail. [45] cut, hit (alighted). [46] men.

1003. In the scribe's source, *yore* may have been *þore*. Rhyme frequently indicates this form. Or the *y* may have been carried over from *ladye; ladye ore*, the favors of the lady.

Through rich mail and myny plee,[47]   1025
The red blood blemished both their blee.
Sir Grime was learned in his childhood
Full noblye to handle a sworde;
With an arkward[48] stroke ffull slee
He hitt Sir Gray-steele on the knee;   1030
If he were neuer soe wight of hand,
On the one foote he might but stand.
"Thou wounded my brother, Sir Egar;
That deed thou shalt abuy full sore."
Then answered Gray-steele, that warryour wight: 1035
"Wherfore vpbraydest thou me with that knight?"
"For he neuer went by watter nor lande,
But he was as good as he, both of hart and hand;
And hee had beene weaponed as well as I,
He had beene worth both thee and mee."   1040
He hitt Sir Gryme on the cainell bone;[49]
A quarter of his sheeled away is gone.
The other he claue in tow
That it ffell into the feyld soe far him froe.
His noble sword, Egeking,   1045
Went from him, without leasing,
But Grime was wight vpon the land;
He followed fast after and gatt his brand.
But-on Gray-steele had had his other foote
To haue holpen him in neede and boote,   1050
I cold not thinke how Gryme the knight
Shold haue comen againe to that lady bright.
When he had gotten againe Egeking,
Fell were the dints he sett on him;
With an arkeward stroke full sore,   1055
Through liuer and longs Gray-steele he bore.

---

[47] many folds (of armor).   [48] backward.   [49] neck-bone.

1025. MS. *many and myny plee.*
1033. MS. *brorther.*
1037–8. No one ever went by water or land (i.e., existed), but Eger was as good as he.
1042. MS. *his gone.*

Gray-steele went walling[50] woode
When his sydes fomed of his harts blood;
Then perceiued the knight Sir Grime
That Gray-steele was in poynt of time.[1]   1060
Grime sayd, "Yeeld thee, Sir Gray-steele,
For thou can neuer doe soe weele."
The other said, "Thou mayst lightlye lye;
That man shall I neuer see,
That man was neuer of woman borne   1065
Shall make me yeelde, one man to one."
He was soe angry att Grimes word
That both his hands he sett on his sword;
And with all his strenght that was in him leade,[2]
He sett itt on Sir Grimes heade   1070
That such a stroke he neuer gate
Nor noe knight that was his mate.
He thought his head roue[3] assunder;
His necke cracked that was vnder;
His eares brushed[4] out of blood;   1075
The knight stackered with that stroke, and stoode.
For and he had once fallen to the ground,
The lady had neuer seene him sound.
Thus they fought together fell and sore
The space of a mile and somthing more;   1080
Gray-steele bled withouten fayle;
His visage waxed wan and pale.
Grime att his gorgett he gate a gripe,
And fast he followed in after itt,
And backward to the ground he him bare;   1085
He let him neuer recouer more;
His brest-plate from him he cast,
And thrise to the hart he him thrust.
Thus vngracious deeds without mending
Can neuer scape without an ill endinge.   1090

---

[50] boiling.   [1] at the point of death.   [2] for *leafde;* left.   [3] rived.   [4] burst.

1060. Possibly read: *in poynt to tyne.*
1077. MS. *for and he and had.*
1082. MS. *pan and wale.*

All this I say by Sir Gray-steele,
For fortune had led him long and weele.
I haue wist that knight with his hands tow
Slay a 100 knights and moe,
Shamefullye driuen them to dead   1095
Without succour or any remed;
And he lyeth slaine with[5] a poore knight
That for his sworne brother came to fight.
Then Gryme looked by him soone;
They steeds were fighting, as they had done.   1100
In sonder he parted the steeds 2;
To Gray-steeles sadle can he goe;
He right[6] the girthes and sadled the steed,
And againe to the dead body he yeede
And pulled forth his noble brand   1105
And smote of Sir Gray-steeles hande.
"My brother left a fingar in this land with thee;
Therfore thy whole hand shall he see."
Hee looked vp to the castle of stone
And see ladyes manye a one   1110
Wringing,[7] and wayling, and riuing there heare;
Striking, and crying with voices full cleere:
"Wight men, they wold not blin
Horsse and harnesse for to win."
It was euer Sir Gray-steeles desiring   1115
That for his death shold be made noe chalishing.[8]
Grime leapt on Sir Gray-steeles steed;
His owne by the bridle he cold him leade,
And he rode towards the fresh riuer.
There was noe man durst nye him nere;   1120
Yett it was an howre within the night

---

[5] by. [6] righted. [7] wringing their hands. [8] mourning(?).

1100. For fighting horses, cf. "Chevelere Assigne" 321; also "Fled Bricrend" (Bricriu's Feast) *Irish Texts Society* 2.89.
1113. The women praise Gray-steel's bravery while mourning him: "Brave men never cease fighting."
1114. *For* is abbreviated in the MS.
1116. Only known occurrence of the word; Laing has *challenging*, i.e., attempted revenge.

Before he came againe to that ladye bright.
He rode strayght to the burgesse dore;
The ostler mett him on the flore.
"O master," he sayd, "now is come that knight   1125
That went hence when the day was light;
He hath brought with him Sir Gray-steeles steede
And much more of his golden weede;
He hath brought with him his chaine of gold—
His sadle harnes is fayre to behold—   1130
With other more[9] of his golden geere;
In all this land is none such to were."
Then to the dore fast cold they hye
Bold men and yeamanrye;
The burgesse asked the knight   1135
Whether he wold lodg with him all night.
Grime sayd, "To lye in a strange land,
And here is a strong castle att hand,
Methinke itt were a great follye;
I wott not who is my freind or my enemye."   1140
Hee tooke the hand and the gloue of gold soe gay;
To the ladyes chamber he tooke the way
Att supper where shee was sett,
But neuer a morsell might shee eate.
"A !" shee sayd, "now I thinke on that knight   1145
That went from me when the day was light !
Yesternight to the chamber I him ledd;
This night Gray-steele hath made his bed !
Alas ! he is foule lost on him;
That is much pittye for all his kine !   1150
For he is large of blood and bone,
And goodlye nurture lacketh he none;
Woe is me for his loue in his countrye !
Shee may thinke longe or she him see,
And he is fayre in armes to fold;   1155

---

[9] more things besides.

1123. Cf. 763.
1130. MS. *behorld.*
1153–4. These lines follow 1156 in the MS.
1155. MS. *his fayre;* cf. 1227.

He is worth to her his waight in gold."
With that shee thought on her Lord Attelstone
That they water out of her eyen ran.
With that Grime knocked att the chamber dore,
And a maiden stoode ther on the flore.   1160
"O madam!" shee said, "now is come that knight
That went hence when the day was light."
And hastilye from the bord she rise
And kissed him 20 sithe.
"How haue you farren on your iourney?"   1165
"Full well, my loue," Sir Grime did say;
"For I haue taken such a surtye[10] on yonder knight
That pore men in his country may haue right;
Merchants may both buy and sell
Within the lands where they doe dwell."   1170
He gaue her the hand and the gloue gay
And sayd, "Lay vp this till itt be day."
Shee tooke the gloue att him,
But shee wist not that they hand was in;
And as they stoode still on the ground,   1175
The hand fell out ther in that stond.
And when shee looked on that hand
That had slaine her brother and her husband,
Noe marueill though her hart did grisse;[11]
The red blood in her face did rise.   1180
It was red rowed[12] for to see,
With fingars more then other three;
On euerye fingar a gay gold ring,
A precious stone or a goodly thing;
And yet shee hath it vp tane   1185
And put into the gloue againe,
And vnto a coffer did shee goe
And vnlocked lockes one or 2.
A rich supper there was dight
And sett before that worthye knight,   1190

---

[10] surety, pledge. [11] tremble (with horror). [12] colored.

1179. *Grisse* has been altered to *griffe*.
1182. Cuchulainn's hands had seven fingers.

But meate nor drinke he might none;
He was soe furbrished,[13] body and bone,
He longed sore to be a-bedd;
And to a chamber shee him ledd,
And all his armour of was done, 1195
And the lady searched his wounds soone.
The ladye was neuer soe sounde
When shee saw hee had no death wound,
For euer thought that fayre ladye
His wedded wife that shee shold bee; 1200
And when shee had this done,
To her owne chamber shee went soone.
She tooke out the hand and the gloue of gold;
To her fathers hall shee sayd shee wold
Att supper when he was sett, 1205
And many lords, withouten lett.
And when shee came into the hall,
Finely shee halched[14] on them all:
"I can tell you tydings, father, will like you well;
Slaine is your enemye Sir Gray-steelee." 1210
Then they laughed all ffull hastilye;
Said, "Maddam, it seemeth to be a lye.
That man was neuer borne of a woman
Cold neuer kill Gray-steele, one man to one."
She cast out[15] the hand and the gloue of gold; 1215
All had marueill did it behold,
For it was red rowed for to see
With fingars more then other 3;
And on euerye fingar a fine gold ring,
A precious stone or a goodlye thing. 1220
The Erle sayd, "Daughter, wher dwelleth that knight?"
Then answered that ladye both faire and bright
And sayth, "Father, his name I cannott myn,[16]
But he was borne in the land of Beame.
He is large of blood and bone, 1225

---

[13] severely bruised, broken. [14] greeted. [15] threw in their midst. [16] tell.

1197. MS. *ladyes . . . soe soe sounde.*
1222. MS. omits *and.*

And goodlye nurture lacketh none.
He is faire in armes to fold;
He is worth his waight in gold;
But he rydeth in the morning when it is day."
"That I sett Gods forbott,"[17] the Erle can say;   1230
"For I wold [not] for a 1000[li]
Of florences red and rounde
Vnrewarded of me that he shold goe
That soe manfully hath uenged mee on my foe."
Earlye on the other day   1235
Sir Gryme radylye can him array;
And as hee was his leaue takeand,
The Erle came att his hand.
And when the Erle came him nye,
Sir Gryme sett him on his knee   1240
And thanked him with humble cheerre
For the great refreshing he had there.
The Erle tooke Gryme by the hand
And said, "Gentle knight, doe thou vpp stand;
And as thou art a warriour wight,   1245
Tarry with me this day and this night."
"My lord," hee said, "I am at your will,
All your commandement to fulfill."
Then a squier tooke the steeds tow,
And to a stable then can he goe.   1250
The Erle tooke Gryme by the hand;
To the pallace thé yode leadand.[18]
A rich dinner ther men might see;
Of meate and drinke was great plentye—
The certaine sooth if I shold say   1255
He was meate-fellow[19] for the ladye gay.
And when the dinner was all done,
The Erle tooke Grime into a chamber soone
And spurred[20] him gentlye,
"Sir, beene you marryed in your countrye?"   1260

---

[17] prohibition.   [18] went hand in hand.   [19] dinner companion.   [20] asked.

1255–7. It is not unlikely that a pun is intended on *meat* (dinner companion) and *meet* (proper fellow).   Cf. 1375–6.

Grime answered him hastilye,
"I had neuer wiffe nor yett ladye.
I tell you truly, by Saint Iohn;
I had neuer wiffe nor yett lemman."
The Erle sayd, "I am glad indeed,   1265
For all the better here may you speede;
For I haue a daughter that is my heyre
Of all my lands, that is soe faire;
And if thou wilt wed that ladye free,
With all my hart I will giue her thee."   1270
Great thankes Gryme to him can make;
Saith, "I loue her to well to forsake."
And afore the Erle and bishopps 3,
Gryime handfasted[21] that faire ladye.
The day of marryage itt was sett,   1275
That Gryme shold come againe without let.
The Erle feitched him in that stonde
2 robes was worth 400[li];
They were all beaten gold begon.[22]
He gaue Egar the better when he came home.   1280
He tooke leaue of the Erle and the ladye,
And rydes home into his countrye.

6D PARTE

He came to a forrest a priuye way,
And leaueth his steed and his palfray;
And when he had soe doone,   1285
He went to his chamber right soone,
And priuylye knocked on the dore;
Palyas his brother stood on the flore.
Palyas was neuer more glad and blyth
When he see his brother come home aliue.   1290
"How fareth Sir Egar?" Sir Grime can say.
"The better that you haue sped on your iourney."
"Rise, Sir Egar, and arme thee weele
Both in iron and in steele,

---

[21] betrothed.   [22] adorned, trimmed.

And goe into yonder forreste free,   1295
And Pallyas my brother shall goe with thee;
And there thou shalt find Sir Gray-steeles steed
And much more of his golden weede.
There thou shalt find his chaine of gold,
His sadle harnesse full fayre to behold   1300
With other more of his golden geere;
In all this land is none such to weare.
To-morrow when the sunn shineth bright,
Looke thou gett into thy ladyes sight,
And looke thou as strange to her bee   1305
As shee in times past hath beene to thee;
For and thou doe not as shee hath done before,
Thou shalst loose my loue for euermore."
Then forth went Egar and Pallyas
Where the steeds and steuen²³ was.   1310
A scarlett mantle Grime hath tane;
To the Erles chamber hee is gone
With still mourning and sighing sore,
"Alas! slaine is my brother, Sir Egar!
For 7 dayes are comen and gone   1315
Sith he promised me to bee att home;
He rode forth wounded verry sore;
Alas! my sorrow is much the more.
The great pride of thy daughter free
Made him in this great perill to bee.   1320
Alas that euer shee was borne!
The best knight that euer was in this world is forlorne!"
Gryme vpon his way can goe;
The Erle and the Countesse were full woe.
Then they bowned them both more and lesse   1325
To the parish church to hear a masse.
When the masse was all done,
To the pallace thé went full soone.
One looked betwene him and the sunn;

---

²³ stuff, goods.

1312. MS. *his gone.*
1319. MS. *thy.*

Sais, "Methinkes I see tow armed knights come." 1330
Another sayd, "Nay indeed,
It is an armed knight ryding, and leads a steede."
And when they knight came them neere,
All wist it was Sir Egar;
But Gryme was the first man 1335
That euer welcomed Sir Egar home.
The Erle tooke Egars hand in his;
The Countesse cold him comlye kisse.
His owne lady Winglaine wold haue done soe;
He turned his backe and rode her froe, 1340
And said, "Parting is a priuye payne,
But old freinds cannott be called againe.
For the great kindnesse I haue found att thee,
Fforgotten shalt thou neuer bee."
He turned his steede in that tyde 1345
And said to Garnwicke he wold ryde.
The lady sooned when he did goe;
The Erle and the Countesse were full woe.
The Erle profered Gryme 40^{li} of land
Of florences that were fayre and round 1350
For to gett the good will of Egar his daughter to;
I hope[24] that was ethe to doe.
Grime went forth on his way
And faire words to Egar can he say.
"Brother," he said, "for charitye, 1355
Abyde and speake a word with mee."
Egar sayd, "Here I am att your will;
Whatere you command, Ile fulfill."
A squier tooke his steeds tow,
And to a stable can he goe. 1360
Gryme tooke Egar by the hand;
To their owne chamber they went leadand,
And all his armour off hath done
And laid it downe where he put it on.
Gryme feitched forth tow robes in that stond; 1365

---

[24] expect.

1354. MS. now illegible after *faire*.

The worse was worth 400^{li};
Thé were all of beaten gold begon.
He put the better Egar on;
Then was Egar the seemlyest man
That was in all christendoume.   1370
Gryme tooke him by the hand;
To the palace thé yode leadand.
A rich dinner there men might see;
Meate and drinke there was plentye—
Certaine sooth if I shold say   1375
He was meate fellow with the ladye gay.
And when the dinner was all done,
Grime tooke the Erle to councell soone:
"As my lord Egar is the knight
That winneth the worshipp in euery fight,   1380
And if hee shall haue your daughter free,
Att your owne will I haue gotten him to bee.
I read anon that it were done."
The Erle and the Countesse accorded soone;
The Erle sent forth his messenger   1385
To great lords both far and neere
That they shold come by the 15 day
To the marryage of his daughter gay.
And there Sir Egar, that noble knight,
Married Winglayne, that ladye bright.   1390
The feast it lasted fortye dayes,
With lords and ladyes in royall arrayes;
And att the 40 dayes end
Euery man to his owne home wend,
Eche man home into his countrye.   1395
Soe did Egar, Grime, and Pallyas, all 3;
They neuer stinted²⁵ nor blan
To Earle Gares land till thé came.
The Erle wist [t]hé wold be there;
He mett them with a royal fere,   1400
With a 100 knights in royall array

---

²⁵ stopped.

1372. MS. *yod*, followed by an erasure.

Mett Egar and Grime in the way
With much myrth of minstrelsye,
And welcomed them into that countrye;
And there Sir Gryme, that noble knight, 1405
Marryed Loosepine, that ladye bright.
Why was shee called Loospaine?
A better leeche was none certaine.
A royall wedding was made there,
As good as was the other before; 1410
And when 5 dayes done did bee,
Egar desired all the Erles meanye
To ryde with him into Gray-steeles land
To resigne all into his brothers hand.
They chose Pallyas to be their captain wight; 1415
The Erle dubd him and made a knight,
And by councell of lords with him did bee,
Hee gaue him a 100^li of fee.
Then wold they noe longer abyde,
But into Gray-steeles land can they ryde; 1420
They brake his parkes and killed his deere,
Rasen[26] his hauens and shipps soe cleere;
They tooken townes and castles of stone.
Gray-steele had neuer a child but one
That was a daughter fayre and free; 1425
Vntill that castle shee did flee.
Egar tooke that lady, as I vnderstand,
And brought her into Earle Gares land.
When that ladye the Earle did see,
Shee kneeled downe vpon her knee 1430
And said, "If my father were a tyrant and your enemye,
Neuer take my land froe me."
The Erle sayd, "For thy curtesye,
All the better the matter may bee.
For to weld thy land and thee, 1435

---

[26] razed.

1411. MS. *did hee.*

1435. According to feudal law, an overlord might compel the heiress of his vassal's land to marry whom he pleased as a protection to his interests.

Choose thee any knight that thou here see."
Amongst all that there was
Shee chose vnto Pallyas.
Glad and blythe was baron and knight;
Soe were Egar and Gryme that were soe wight;   1440
And there Sir Pallyas, that noble knight,
Marryed Emyas that was soe bright.
A royall wedding was made thore,
As good as was the other before.
I neuer wist man that proued[27] soe weele   1445
As did Sir Grine vpon Sir Gray-steele;
For he gate to his brother Sir Egar
An erles land and a ladye faire;
He gate himselfe and erles lande,
The fairest lady that was liuande;   1450
He gate his brother Pallyas
A barrons daughter and a barronage.
Winglaine bare to Sir Egar
15 children that were fayre;
10 of them were sonnes wight   1455
And 5 daughters fayre in sight.
And Loosepine bare to Sir Grime
10 children in short time;
7 of them sonnes was,
And 3 were daughters faire of face.   1460
Emyeas bare to Sir Pallyas
3 children in short spacee;
2 of them sonnes were;
The 3 was a daughter faire and cleere.
After, shee was marryed to a knight   1465
That proued both hardye and wight.
There was noe man in noe countrye
That durst displease those brethren 3;
For 2 of them were erles free;
The 3d was a barron in his countrye.   1470

---

[27] came out well with.

1436. MS. *hee see.*
1465. "Afterwards she, the daughter, was married. . . ."

And thus they liued and made endinge:
To the blisse of heauen their soules bringe!
I pray Iesus that wee soe may;
Bring vs the blisse that lasteth aye.

FFINS.

1471. MS. *an end.*

THE SQUIRE OF LOW DEGREE

THE SQUIRE OF LOW DEGREE

"The Squire of Low Degree" exists complete only in Copland's print of the middle of the sixteenth century. Several leaves of Wynkyn de Worde's edition also exist, and a corrupt version called "The Squier" in the Percy Folio Manuscript. Dialect and date of composition are doubtful, but are probably midland of the late fifteenth century. Through the kindness of the authorities of the British Museum, it has been possible to prepare this text from rotographs of the original.

The poem was carefully edited by W. E. Mead (Ginn and Company, 1904); and the publishers have kindly allowed the use of several of his notes. Emendations not otherwise credited are his.

No source of the story is known. It is probable that the poet assembled such well-known medieval motives and devices as pleased him. Notable among them are the love of persons of unequal rank, the probation of seven years, the wickedness of the steward, and the long descriptive lists. A more unusual motive, the preservation of the body, has a parallel in Keats's "Isabella," derived from Boccaccio's "Decameron" iv. 5.

The, which is sometimes abbreviated in Copland, is always spelled out in this text.

It was a squyer of lowe degre
That loued the Kings doughter of Hungré.
The squir was curteous and hend,
Ech man him loued and was his frend;
He serued the Kyng, her father dere,   5
Fully the tyme of seuen yere;
For he was marshall of his hall,
And set the lords both great and smal.
An hardy man he was, and wight,
Both in batayle and in fyght;   10
But euer he was styll[1] mornyng,

---

[1] secretly.

7–8. The marshal, master of ceremonies, must arrange the king's guests in order of their rank. Cf. "Babees' Book."

And no man wyste for what thyng;
And all was for that lady,
The Kynges doughter of Hungry.
There wyste no wyghte in Christenté   15
Howe well he loued that lady fre;
He loued her more then seuen yere,
Yet was he of her loue neuer the nere.
He was not ryche of golde and fe;
A gentyll man forsoth was he.   20
To no man durst he make his mone,
But syghed sore hymselfe alone.
   And euermore, whan he was wo,
Into his chambre would he goo;
And through the chambre he toke the waye,   25
Into the gardyn, that was full gaye;
And in the garden, as i wene,
Was an arber fayre and grene,
And in the arber was a tre,
A fayrer in the world might none be;   30
The tre it was of cypresse,
The fyrst tre that Iesu chose;
The sother-wood[2] and sykamoure,
The reed rose and the lyly-floure,
The boxe, the beche, and the larel-tre,   35
The date, also the damyse,[3]
The fylbyrdes hangyng to the ground,
The fygge-tre, and the maple round,
And other trees there was mané one,
The pyany, the popler, and the plane,   40
With brode braunches all aboute,
Within the arbar and eke withoute;
On euery braunche sate byrdes thre,

---

[2] wormwood.   [3] damson-plum.

15. C. *chrinstente.*
32. Possibly Christ was supposed to have selected the cypress first before cedar and pine as the materials for the cross. Cf. Mead's long note, pp. 50–7.
33. C. *lykamoure.*

Syngynge with great melody,
The lauorocke[4] and the nightyngale,   45
The ruddocke,[5] the woodwale,[6]
The pee[7] and the popiniaye,
The thrustele saynge both nyght and daye,
The marlyn,[8] and the wrenne also,
The swalowe whippynge to and fro,   50
The iaye iangled[9] them amonge,
The larke began that mery songe,
The sparowe spredde her on her spraye,
The mauys[10] songe with notes full gaye,
The nuthake[11] with her notes newe,   55
The sterlynge set her notes full trewe,
The goldefynche made full mery chere,
Whan she was bente vpon a brere,
And many other foules mo,
The osyll,[12] and the thrusshe also;   60
And they sange wyth notes clere,
In confortynge that squyere.

    And euermore, whan he was wo,
Into that arber wolde he go,
And vnder a bente[13] he layde hym lowe,   65
Ryght euen vnder her chambre wyndowe;
And lened hys backe to a thorne,
And sayd, "Alas, that i was borne!
That i were ryche of golde and fe,
That i myght wedde that lady fre!   70
Of golde good, or some treasure,
That i myght wedde that lady floure!
Or elles come of so gentyll kynne,
The ladyes loue that i myght wynne.
Wolde God that i were a kynges sonne,   75
That ladyes loue that i myght wonne![14]
Or els so bolde in eche fyght,

---

[4] lark. [5] robin. [6] woodpecker. [7] magpie. [8] merlin-hawk. [9] chattered. [10] mavis, song-thrush. [11] nuthatch. [12] blackbird. [13] grassy slope. [14] win.

69. C. *goldy*.

As was Syr Lybius that gentell knyght,
Or els so bolde in chyualry
As Syr Gawayne, or Syr Guy;   80
Or els so doughty of my hande
As was the gyaunte Syr Colbrande.
And [it] were put in ieope[r]de[14]
What man shoulde wynne that lady fre,
Than should no man haue her but i,   85
The Kinges doughter of Hungry."
But euer he sayde, "Wayle a waye!
For pouerte passeth[15] all my paye!"
And as he made thys rufull chere,
He sowned downe in that arbere.   90

    That lady herde his mournyng all,
Ryght vnder the chambre wall;
In her oryall[16] there she was
Closed well with royall glas;
Fulfylled[17] it was with ymagery   95
Euery wyndowe by and by;
On eche syde had there a gynne,[18]
Sperde[19] with many a dyuers pynne.
Anone that lady, fayre and fre,
Undyd a pynne of yueré,   100
And wyd the windowes she open set.
The sunne shone in at her closet;[20]
In that arber fayre and gaye
She sawe where that squyre lay.
The lady sayd to hym anone,   105
"Syr, why makest thou that mone?
And whi thou mournest night and day?

---

[14] jeopardy, to trial. [15] disappears my joy. [16] oriel window opening from a recess in the chamber. [17] covered. [18] device (for keeping the windows closed). [19] fastened. [20] chamber.

78. Lybeaus Desconus, Gawain's son, is the hero of a popular romance mentioned in Chaucer's "Sir Thopas."

82. Colbrand is a giant and Guy the hero in the romance "Guy of Warwick."

83. Ritson supplies *it*.

86. C. *goughter*.

Now tell me, squyre, i thee pray;
And as i am a true lady,
Thy counsayl shall i neuer dyscry;   110
And yf it be no represe to thee,
Thy bote of bale yet shall i be."
And often was he in wele and wo,
But neuer so well as he was tho.

    The squyer set hym on hys kne   115
And sayde, "Lady, it is for thee:
I haue thee loued this seuen yere,
And bought thy loue, lady, full dere.
Ye are so ryche in youre aray
That one word to you i dare not say,   120
And come ye be of so hye kynne,
No worde of loue durst i begynne.
My wyll to you yf i had sayde,
And ye therwith not well apayde,[21]
Ye might haue bewraied me to the Kinge,   125
And brought me sone to my endynge.
Therfore, my lady fayre and fre,
I durst not shewe my harte to thee;
But i am here at your wyll,
Whether ye wyll me saue or spyll;   130
For all the care i haue in be,
A worde of you might comfort me;
And yf ye wyll not do so,
Out of this land i must nedes go;
I wyll forsake both lande and lede,   135
And become an hermyte in vncouth stede;
In many a lande to begge my bread,

---

[21] pleased.

124. C. *þan ye.*

137 ff. The squire threatens to become a pilgrim, not a hermit. Pilgrims went to all spots where the Lord or His mother were thought to have revealed themselves (138). The staff (139) was obligatory if he went on foot; he went barefoot (144) to obtain more merit in heaven; he was sustained (137) by various charitable organizations, and had no business or trade to maintain him. He wore a distinctive habit of rough grey wool (140). Cf. Mead's note.

To seke where Christ was quicke and dead;
A staffe i wyll make me of my spere,
Lynen cloth i shall none were;   140
Euer in trauayle i shall wende,
Tyll i come to the worldes ende;
And, lady, but thou be my bote,
There shall no sho come on my fote;
Therfore, lady, i the praye,   145
For Hym that dyed on Good Frydaye,
Let me not in daunger[22] dwell,
For His loue that harowed hell."
   Than sayd that lady milde of mode,
Ryght in her closet there she stode,   150
"By Hym that dyed on a tre,
Thou shalt neuer be deceyued for me;
Though i for thee should be slayne,
Squyer, i shall the loue agayne.
Go forth, and serue my father the Kynge,   155
And let be all thy styll mournynge;
Let no man wete that ye were here,
Thus all alone in my arbere;
If euer ye wyll come to your wyll,[23]
Here and se, and holde you styll.   160
Beware of the stewarde, i you praye:
He wyll deceyue you and he maye;
For if he wote of your woyng,
He wyl bewraye you vnto the Kynge;
Anone for me ye shall be take   165
And put in pryson for my sake;
Than must ye nedes abyde the lawe,
Perauenture both hanged and drawe.
That syght on you i would not se
For all the golde in Christenté.   170
For and ye my loue should wynne,

---

[22] uncertainty. [23] wish to achieve your desire.

140. I. e., such fine cloth as linen.
150. C. *closed*.
158. C. *arbery*.

With chyualry ye must begynne,
And other dedes of armes to done,
Through whiche ye may wynne your shone;[24]
And ryde through many a peryllous place   175
As a venterous man, to seke your grace,
Ouer hylles and dales and hye mountaines,
In wethers wete, both hayle and raynes,
And yf ye may no harbroughe[25] se,
Than must ye lodge vnder a tre,   180
Among the beastes wyld and tame,
And euer you wyll gette your name;
And in your armure must ye lye,
Eeuery nyght than by and by,[26]
And your meny euerychone,   185
Till seuen yere be comen and gone;
And passe by many a peryllous see,
Squyer, for the loue of me,
Where any war begynneth to wake,
And many a batayll vndertake,   190
Throughout the land of Lumbardy,
In euery cytie by and by.
And be auised,[27] when thou shalt fight,
Loke that ye stand aye in the right;
And yf ye wyll, take good hede,   195
Yet all the better shall ye spede;
And whan the warre is brought to ende,
To the Rodes then must ye wende;
And, syr, i holde you not to prayes
But ye there fyght thre Good Frydayes;   200

---

[21] shoes, i.e., win your spurs.   [25] shelter.   [26] one after the other.   [27] cautious.

183. It was usual not to disarm when in hostile territory.

198. Rhodes was the stronghold of the Hospitallers, one of whose duties it was to shelter a pilgrim on his way to Palestine.

200. According to the "Truce of God" (partially adopted in Europe in the eleventh century; confirmed by the Lateran Council in the twelfth), it was an offence against Holy Church to fight on Friday, Saturday, and Sunday of each week, and during Lent, Advent, and certain other major festivals. But it might be considered commendable to fight heathen on Good Friday as symbolical revenge for Christ's death.

And if ye passe the batayles thre,
Than are ye worthy a knyght to be,
And to bere armes than are ye able,
Of gold and goules[28] sete with sable;[29]
Then shall ye were a shelde of blewe,   205
In token ye shall be trewe,
With vines of golde set all aboute,
Within your shelde and eke without,
Fulfylled with ymagery,
And poudred with true loues by and by.   210
In the myddes of your sheld ther shal be set
A ladyes head, with many a frete;[30]
Aboue the head wrytten shall be
A reason[31] for the loue of me:
Both O and R shall be therin: 215
With A and M it shall begynne.
The baudryke[32] that shall hange therby
Shall be of white, sykerly;
A crosse of reed therin shall be,
In token of the Trynyté.   220
Your basenette[33] shall be burnysshed bryght,
Your ventall[34] shal be well dyght;
With starres of golde it shall be set
And couered with good veluet.
A coronall[35] clene coruen[36] newe,   225
And oy[s]tryche fethers of dyuers hewe.
Your plates[37] vnto you[r] body shal be enbraste,[38]
Sall syt full semely in your waste.
Your cote-armoure[39] of golde full fyne,
And poudred well with good armyne.   230
Thus in your warres shall you ryde,
With syxe good yemen by your syde,

---

[28] gules, heraldic term for red.   [29] heraldic term for black.   [30] ornament.
[31] motto.   [32] belt.   [33] light steel headpiece.   [34] visor.   [35] circlet on helmet.
[36] carved.   [37] back and front of armor.   [38] fastened securely.   [39] tabard, coat worn
over armor.

207. C. *yet*.   Mead alters.
210. "Covered with true-love knots, one after the other." Cf. "Emaré."

And whan your warres are brought to ende,
More ferther behoueth to you to wende,
And ouer many perellous streme,   235
Or ye come to Ierusalem,
Through feytes[40] and feldes and forestes thicke,
To seke where Christe were dead and quycke.
There must you drawe your swerde of were;[41]
To the sepulchre ye must it bere,   240
And laye it on the stone,
Amonge the lordes euerychone;
And offre there florences fyue,
Whyles that ye are man on lyue;
And offre there florences thre,   245
In tokenyng of the Trynyté;
And whan that ye, syr, thus haue done,
Than are ye worthy to were your shone;
Than may ye say, syr, by good ryght,
That you ar proued a venturous knyght.   250
I shall you geue to your rydinge
A thousande pounde to your spendinge;
I shall you geue hors and armure,
A thousande pounde of my treasure,
Where-through that ye may honoure wynn   255
And be the greatest of your kynne.
I pray to God and Our Lady,
Sende you the whele of vyctory,
That my father so fayne may be,
That he wyll wede me vnto thee,   260
And make the king of this countré,
To haue and holde in honesté,
Wyth welth and wynne to were the crowne,
And to be lorde of toure and towne,

---

[40] fights (for *frithes*, fields?).   [41] war.

235. Thus his pilgrimage is from Hungary, through Lombardy (northern Italy) and Rhodes, to the Holy Land.
245. On this practice, cf. "Havelok" 1386.
258. A confusion of the usual medieval metaphor, "the Wheel of Fortune," i.e., unstable luck. Cf. Mead's note.

That we might our dayes endure 265
In parfyte loue that is so pure.
And if we may not so come to,[42]
Other wyse then must we do;
And therfore, squyer, wende thy way,
And hye the fast on thy iournay, 270
And take thy leue of Kinge and Quene,
And so to all the courte bydene.
Ye shall not want at your goyng
Golde nor syluer nor other thyng.
This seuen yere i shall you abyde, 275
Betyde of you what so betyde;
Tyll seuen yere be comen and gone
I shall be mayde all alone."
The squyer kneled on his kne,
And thanked that lady fayre and fre; 280
And thryes he kyssed that lady tho,
And toke his leue, and forth he gan go.
   The Kinges steward stode full nye
In a chambre fast them bye,
And hearde theyr wordes wonder wele, 285
And all the woyng euery dele.
He made a vowe to Heauen-kynge
For to bewraye that swete thynge,
And that squyer taken shoulde be
And hanged hye on a tre; 290
And that false stewarde full of yre,
Them to betraye was his desyre.
He bethought hym nedely,[43]
Euery daye by and by,
How he myght venged be 295
On that lady fayre and fre,
For he her loued pryuely,
And therfore dyd her great enuye.

---

[42] achieve our purpose.   [43] zealously.

271. C. *quenen.*
283. The steward in romances was usually a villain.

Alas! it tourned to wrother heyle[44]
That euer he wyste of theyr counsayle.   300
  But leue we of the stewarde here,
And speke we more of that squyer,
Howe he to his chambre went
Whan he past from that lady gente.
There he araied him in scarlet reed   305
And set his chaplet vpon his head,
A belte about his sydes two,
With brode barres to and fro;
A horne about his necke he caste,
And forth he went at the last   310
To do hys office in the hall
Among the lordes both great and small.
He toke a white yeard[45] in his hande;
Before the Kynge than gane he stande,
And sone he sat hym on his knee   315
And serued the Kynge ryght royally
With deynty meates that were dere,
With partryche, pecoke, and plouere,
With byrdes in bread ybake,
The tele, the ducke, and the drake,   320
The cocke, the curlewe, and the crane,
With fesauntes fayre—theyr were no wane,[46]—
Both storkes and snytes[47] ther were also,
And venyson freshe of bucke and do,
And other deyntes many one,   325
For to set afore the Kynge anone.
And when the squyer had done so,
He serued the hall to and fro.
Eche man hym loued in honesté,

---

[44] misfortune. [45] staff of office (as marshal). [46] lack. [47] snipes.

299. C. *wroth her heyle.* Mead's emendation.

316. C. *kyuge.*

318. The Middle Ages inherited from Rome the practice of cooking in their feathers the swan and the peacock, not very palatable birds, as a display of wealth. Cf. Wright on feasts, especially on cooking birds in their plumage, Ch. XVI.

328. C. *they.*

Hye and lowe in theyr degre; 330
So dyd the Kyng full sodenly,
And he wyst not wherfore nor why.
The Kynge behelde the squyer wele
And all his rayment euery dele;
He thought he was the semylyest man 335
That euer in the worlde he sawe or than.
Thus sate the Kyng and eate ryght nought,
But on his squyer was all his thought.
　　Anone the stewarde toke good hede,
And to the Kyng full soone he yede, 340
And soone he tolde vnto the Kynge
All theyr wordes and theyr woynge;
And how she hyght hym lande and fe,
Golde and syluer great plentye,
And how he should his leue take 345
And become a knight for her sake:
"And thus they talked bothe in fere,
And i drewe me nere and nere.
Had i not come in, verayly,
The squyer had layne her by; 350
But whan he was ware of me,
Full fast away can he fle.
That is sothe: here my hand
To fight with him while i may stand."
　　The Kyng sayd to the steward tho, 355
"I may not beleue it should be so;
Hath he be so bonayre[48] and benyngne,
And serued me syth he was younge,
And redy with me in euery nede,
Bothe true of word and eke of dede, 360
I may not beleue, be nyght nor daye,
My doughter dere he wyll betraye,
Nor to come her chambre nye,

---

[48] courteous, debonair.

353. C., *here my;* W., *here is.*
358. C., *I was.*

That fode[49] to longe[50] with no foly;
Though she would to hym consente,   365
That louely lady fayre and gente,
I truste hym so well, withouten drede,
That he would neuer do that dede
But yf he myght that lady wynne
In wedlocke to welde, withouten synne;   370
And yf she assent him tyll,
The squyer is worthy to haue none yll;
For i haue sene that many a page
Haue become men by mariage;
Than it is semely that squyer   375
To haue my doughter by this manere,
And eche man in his degre
Become a lorde of ryaltye,
By fortune and by other grace,
By herytage and by purchace:[13]   380
Therfore, stewarde, beware hereby;
Defame hym not for no enuy:[14]
It were great reuth he should be spylte,
Or put to death withouten gylte
(And more ruthe of[15] my doughter dere,   385
For[16] chaungyng of that ladyes chere.
I woulde not for my crowne so newe
That lady chaunge hyde or hewe);
Or for to put thyselfe in drede,
But thou myght take hym with the dede.   390
For yf it may be founde in thee
That thou them fame[17] for enmyté,
Thou shalt be taken as a felon
And put full depe in my pryson,

---

[49] child. [50] desire. [13] the acquiring of property in any way other than by inheritance. [14] malice (as usual in Middle English). [15] in the case of. [16] on account of. [17] defame.

364. Perhaps *longe* should be read *fonge*, seize.
375. C. *that the;* Mead emends.
389. *Or for to put* is in parallel structure with ll. 383–4. "It would be a pity to put yourself in jeopardy."
392. C. *enuyte.* Mead emends.

And fetered fast vnto a stone 395
Tyl xii yere were come and gone,
And drawen wyth hors throughe the cyté,
And soone hanged vpon a tre.
And thou may not thyselfe excuse:
This dede thou shalt no wise refuse;[18] 400
And therfore, steward, take good hed
How thou wilt answere to this ded."
The stewarde answered with great enuy,
"That i haue sayd, that i wyll stand therby;
To suffre death and endlesse wo, 405
Syr Kynge, i wyl neuer go therfro;
For yf that ye wyll graunt me here
Strength of men and great power,
I shall hym take this same nyght
In the chambre with your doughter bright; 410
For i shall neuer be gladde of chere
Tyll i be venged of that squyer."
      Than sayd the Kynge full curteysly
Unto the stewarde, that stode hym by,
"Thou shalte haue strength ynough with the, 415
Men of armes xxx and thre,
To watche that lady muche of pryce,
And her to kepe fro her enemyes.
For there is no knyght in Chrystenté
That wolde betray that lady fre, 420
But he should dye vnder his shelde,
And i myght se hym in the feldde;
And therfore, stewarde, i the pray,
Take hede what i shall to the say;
And if the squiere come to-night 425
For to speke with that lady bryght,
Let hym say whatsoeuer he wyll,
And here and se and holde you styll;
And herken well what he wyll say

_____

[18] escape responsibility for this deed.

398. C. *vopn*.
425. C. *come not;* Mead emends.

Or thou with him make any fray;   430
So he come not her chambre win,[19]
No bate[20] on hym loke thou begyn;
Though that he kysse that lady fre
And take his leaue ryght curteysly,
Let hym go, both hole and sounde,   435
Without wemme[21] or any wounde;
But-yf he wyl her chamber breke,
No worde to hym that thou do speke.
But yf he come with company
For to betraye that fayre lady,   440
Loke he be taken soone anone,
And all his meyné euerychone,
And brought with strength to my pr̃yson
As traytour, thefe, and false felon;
And yf he make any defence,   445
Loke that he neuer go thence,
But loke thou hew hym also small
As flesshe whan it to the potte shall.
And yf he yelde hym to thee,
Brynge him bothe saufe and sounde to me: 450
I shall borowe,[22] for seuen yere
He shall not wedde my doughter dere.
And therfore, stewarde, i thee praye
Thou watche that lady nyght and daye."
The stewarde sayde the Kyng vntyll,   455
"All your byddyng i shall fulfyll."
    The stewarde toke his leaue to go.
The squyer came fro chambre tho:
Downe he went into the hall.
The officers sone can he call,   460
Both vssher,[23] panter,[24] and butler,
And other that in office were;

---

[19] within (a contraction).   [20] strife.   [21] injury.   [22] guarantee.   [23] keeper of the door.   [24] keeper of the pantry.

430. C. *made.*
431. For *bin?*   There is a dot over the *w* of *win* in C.
452. C. *uot.*
456. C. *bydgdyng.*

There he them warned sone anone
To take vp the bordes euerychone.
Than they dyd his commaundement,　　　　465
And sythe vnto the Kyng he went;
Full lowe he set hym on his kne,
And voyded his borde[25] full gentely;
And whan the squyre had done so,
Anone he sayde the Kynge vnto,　　　　470
"As ye are lorde of chyualry,
Geue me leue to passe the sea,
To proue my strenthe with my ryght hande
On Godes enemyes in vncouth land,
And to be knowe in chyualry,　　　　475
In Gascoyne, Spayne, and Lumbardy,
In eche batayle for to fyght,
To be proued a venterous knyght."
The Kyng sayd to the squyer tho,
"Thou shalt haue good leue to go;　　　　480
I shall the gyue both golde and fe
And strength of men to wende with thee;
If thou be true in worde and dede,
I shall thee helpe in all thy nede."
The squyer thanked the Kyng anone　　　　485
And toke his leue and forth can gone,
With ioye and blysse and muche pryde,
Wyth all his meyny by his syde.
He had not ryden but a whyle,
Not the mountenaunce[26] of a myle,　　　　490
Or he was ware of a vyllage.
Anone he sayde vnto a page,
"Our souper soone loke it be dyght:
Here wyll we lodge all to-nyght."

---

[25] removed the king's table.　　[26] amount.

464. Cf. Int. III. B.
480. The vassal was looked upon with suspicion if he left the domain of his lord for long; the supposition was that he would attach himself to someone else. Hence the requirement that he be granted formal leave of absence; otherwise he might be treated as an enemy. Cf. Fundenburg 96.

They toke theyr ynnes in good intente,[27]   495
And to theyr supper soone they wente.
Whan he was set and serued at meate,
Than he sayd he had forgete
To take leue of that lady fre,
The Kynges doughter of Hungré.   500
    Anone the squyer made him yare,
And by hymselfe forth can he fare;
Without strength of his meyné,
Vnto the castell than went he.
Whan he came to the posterne[28] gate,   505
Anone he entred in thereat,
And his drawen swerd in his hande.
There was no more with him wolde stande:
But it stode with hym full harde,
As ye shall here nowe of the stewarde.   510
He wende in the worlde none had bene
That had knowen of his pryuité;
Alas! it was not as he wende,
For all his counsayle the stewarde [kende].
He had bewrayed him to the Kyng   515
Of all his loue and his woyng;
And yet he laye her chambre by,
Armed with a great company,
And beset it one eche syde,
For treason walketh wonder wyde.   520
The squyer thought on no mystruste;[29]
He wende no man in the worlde had wyste;
But yf he had knowen, ne by Saynt Iohn,
He had not come theder by his owne![30]
Or yf that lady had knowen his wyll,   525
That he should haue come her chamber tyll,
She would haue taken hym golde and fe,
Strength of men and royalté.

---

[27] took shelter with good will. [28] rear. [29] suspicion. [30] alone.

501. C. *ayre.*
511. M. emended to *be.*
514. Ritson supplies *kende.*

But there ne wyst no man nor grome
Where that squyer was become, 530
But[31] forth he went hymselfe alone,
Amonge his seruauntes euerychone.
Whan that he came her chambre to,
Anone he sayde, "Your dore vndo!
Undo," he sayde, "nowe, fayre lady! 535
I am beset with many a spy.
Lady as whyte as whales bone,
There are thyrty agaynst me one.
Undo thy dore, my worthy wyfe!
I am besette with many a knyfe. 540
Undo your dore, my lady swete!
I am beset with enemyes great;
And, lady, but ye wyll aryse,
I shall be dead with myne enemyes.
Vndo thy dore, my frely[32] floure! 545
For ye are myne, and i am your."
  That lady with those wordes awoke;
A mantell of golde to her she toke;
She sayde, "Go away, thou wicked wyght:
Thou shalt not come here this nyght, 550
For i wyll not my dore vndo
For no man that cometh therto.
There is but one in Christenté
That euer made that forwarde with me;
There is but one that euer bare lyfe, 555
That euer i hight to be his wyfe;
He shall me wedde, by Mary bryght,
Whan he is proued a venterous knyght,
For we haue loued this seuen yere:
There was neuer loue to me so dere. 560
There lyeth on[33] me both kyng and knyght,
Duke, erles, of muche might.
Wende forth, squyer, on your waye,
For here ye gette none other praye;[34]
For i ne wote what ye should be, 565

---

[31] except that. [32] lovely. [33] importune, woo. [34] prey, booty.

That thus besecheth loue of me."
"I am your owne squyr," he sayde,
"For me, lady, be not dysmayde.
Come i am full pryuely
To take my leaue of you, lady."   570
"Welcome," she sayd, "my loue so dere,
Myne owne dere heart and my squyer;
I shall you geue kysses thre,
A thousand pounde vnto your fe,
And kepe i shall my maydenhede ryght   575
Tyll ye be proued a venturous[35] knyght.
For yf ye should me wede anone,
My father wolde make slee you soone.
I am the Kynges doughter of Hungré,
And ye alone that haue loued me,   580
And though you loue me neuer so sore,
For me ye shall neuer be lore.
Go forth, and aske me at my kynne,
And loke what graunt[36] you may wynne;
Yf that ye gette graunt in faye,   585
Myselfe therto shall not say nay;
And yf ye may not do so,
Otherwyse ye shall come to.[37]
Ye are bothe hardy, stronge, and wight;
Go forth and be a venterous knight.   590
I pray to God and our Lady
To send you the whele of victory,
That my father so leue ye be,
That [he] wyll profer me to thee.
I wote well it is lyghtly sayd,   595
'Go forth, and be nothyng afrayde.'
A man of worshyp may not do so:

---

[35] bold, tried. [36] concession, favor. [37] gain your will.

571–636. Kittredge regards these lines as an interpolation because there "is no proper place for love talk or any kind of conversation after l. 570. The Lady at that point learns that it is *her* Squire and that he is in horrible danger." Cf. Mead lxxxiii.

593. C. *he be.*

He must haue what neds him vnto;
He must haue gold, he must haue fe,
Strength of men and royalté.   600
Golde and syluer spare ye nought
Tyll to manhode ye be brought;
To what batayll soeuer ye go,
Ye shall haue an hundreth pounde or two;
And yet to me, syr, ye may saye   605
That i woulde fayne haue you awaye,
That profered you golde and fe
Out of myne eye syght for to be.
Neuerthelesse it is not so:
It is for the worshyp of vs two.   610
Though you be come of symple[38] kynne,
Thus my loue, syr, may ye wynne:
Yf ye haue grace of victory,
As euer had Syr Lybyus or Syr Guy,
Whan the dwarfe and mayde Ely   615
Came to Arthoure, kyng so fre.
As a kyng of great renowne
That wan the lady of Synadowne,
Lybius was graunted the batayle tho;
Therfore the dwarfe was full wo,   620
And sayd, 'Arthur, thou arte to blame.
To bydde this chylde go sucke his dame
Better hym semeth, so mote i thryue,
Than for to do these batayles fyue
At the chapell of Salebraunce!'   625
These wordes began great distaunce;[39]

---

[38] humble. [39] dissensions.

614–32. The references are to the romance "Libeaus Desconus." Libeaus, always victorious (614), is selected by Arthur to accompany a maid Elene and a dwarf to free the lady of Sinadoune; they mock him (620); but when after five preliminary encounters (624), he overcomes the knight of Salebraunce (625), they confess their error (628). *Syr Guy* is Guy of Warwick.

617. Mead suggests that *kyng* should be *knyght*. Very possibly ll. 617–8. should follow l. 614.

The[y] sawe they had the victory;
They kneled downe and cryed mercy;
And afterward, syr, verament,
They called hym knyght absolent:[40]   630
Emperours, dukes, knyghtes, and quene,
At his commaundement for to bene.
Suche fortune with grace now to you fall,
To wynne the worthyest within the wall,
And thynke on your loue alone,   635
And for to loue that ye chaunge none."
    Ryght as they talked thus in fere,
Theyr enemyes approched nere and nere,
Foure and thyrty armed bryght
The steward had arayed hym to fyght.   640
The steward was ordeyned to spy
And for to take them vtterly.
He wende to death he should haue gone;
He felled seuen men agaynst hym one;
Whan he had them to grounde brought,   645
The stewarde at hym full sadly[41] fought.
So harde they smote together tho,
The stewardes throte he cut in two,
And sone he fell downe to the grounde
As a traitour vntrewe, with many a wound.   650
The squyer sone in armes they hente,
And of they dyd his good garmente,
And on the stewarde they it dyd,
And sone his body therin th[e]y hydde,
And with their swordes his face they share,[42]   655
That she should not knowe what he ware;
They cast hym at her chambre dore,
The stewarde that was styffe[43] and store.[44]
Whan they had made that great affraye,
Full pryuely they stale awaye;   660
In arme the[y] take that squyer tho

---

[40] finished, perfect (only occurrence; cf. *N.E.D.*).   [41] determinedly.   [42] cut.
[43] strong.   [44] sturdy.

627. C. *wictory.*

And to the Kynges chambre can they go,
Without wemme[45] or any wounde,
Before the Kynge bothe hole and sounde.
As soone as the Kynge him spyed with eye,   665
He sayd, "Welcome, sonne, sykerly!
Thou hast cast[46] thee my sonne to be;
This seuen yere i shall let thee."

  Leue we here of this squyer wight,
And speake we of that lady bryght,   670
How she rose, that lady dere,
To take her leue of that squyer.
Also naked as she was borne,
She stod her chambre dore beforne.
"Alas," she sayd, "and weale away!   675
For all to long nowe haue i lay;"
She sayd, "Alas, and all for wo!
Withouten men why came ye so?
Yf that ye wolde haue come to me,
Other werninges there might haue be.   680
Now all to dere my loue is bought,
But it shall neuer be lost for nought;"
And in her armes she toke hym there,
Into the chamber she dyd hym bere;
His bowels soone she dyd out drawe,   685
And buryed them in Goddes lawe.[47]
She sered[48] that body with specery,
Wyth wyrgin[49] waxe and commendry;[50]
And closed hym in a maser[1] tre,
And set on hym lockes thre.   690
She put him in a marble stone
With quaynt gynnes many one,
And set hym at hir beddes head;
And euery day she kyst that dead.
Soone at morne, whan she vprose,   695
Unto that dead body she gose;

---

[45] bruise. [46] decided, planned. [47] according to religious practice. [48] covered.
[49] pure. [50] dry cummin (?), an aromatic plant; cf. Mead. [1] maple.

690. C. *lackes*.

Therfore[2] wold she knele downe on her kne
And make her prayer to the Trynité,
And kysse that body twyse or thryse,
And fall in a swowne or she myght ryse.   700
Whan she had so done,
To chyrche than wolde she gone;
Than would she here masses fyue,
And offre to them whyle she myght lyue:
"There shall none knowe but Heuen-kynge   705
For whome that i make myne offrynge."
    The Kyng her father anone he sayde:
"My doughter, wy are you dysmayde,
So feare[3] a lady as ye are one,
And so semely of fleshe and bone?   710
Ye were whyte as whales bone;
Nowe are ye pale as any stone.
Your ruddy[4] read as any chery,
With browes bent[5] and eyes full mery;
Ye were wont to harpe and syng,   715
And be the meriest in chambre comyng;
Ye ware both golde and good veluet,
Clothe of damaske with saphyres set;
Ye ware the pery[6] on your head,
With stones full oryent,[7] whyte and read;   720
Ye ware coronalles of golde,
With diamoundes set many a foulde;[8]
And nowe ye were clothes of blacke;
Tell me, doughter, for whose sake?
If he be so poore of fame   725
That ye may not be wedded for shame,
Brynge him to me anone ryght:
I shall hym make squyer and knight;
And yf he be so great a lorde
That your loue may not accorde,   730
Let me, doughter, that lordynge se;
He shall have golde ynoughe with thee."
    "Gramercy, father, so mote i thryue,

---

[2] on account of it. [3] fair. [4] complexion. [5] arched. [6] jewels. [7] shining. [8] row.

For i mourne for no man alyue.
Ther is no man, by Heuen-kyng,   735
That shal knowe more of my mournynge."
  Her father knewe it euery deale,
But he kept it in counsele:
"To-morowe ye shall on hunting fare,
And ryde, my doughter, in a chare;⁹   740
It shal be couered with veluet reede,
And clothes of fyne golde al about your hed,
With dam[a]ske white and asure-blewe,
Wel dyapred¹⁰ with lyllyes newe;
Your pomelles¹¹ shal be ended with gold,   745
Your chaynes enameled many a folde;
Your mantel of ryche degre,
Purpyl palle¹² and armyne fre;
Jennettes¹³ of Spayne, that ben so wyght,
Trapped¹⁴ to the ground with veluet bright;   750
Ye shall haue harpe, sautry, and songe,
And other myrthes you amonge;
Ye shall haue rumney and malmesyne,
Both ypocrasse and vernage wyne,
Mountrose and wyne of Greke,   755
Both algrade and respice eke,
Antioche and bastarde,
Pyment also and garnarde;
Wyne of Greke and muscadell,
Both claré, pyment, and rochell.   760
The reed your stomake to defye,¹⁵

---

⁹ litter. ¹⁰ embroidered with a pattern, especially a diamond-shaped one.
¹¹ ornamental knobs on the litter. ¹² fine cloth. ¹³ small horses (considered suitable for a lady). ¹⁴ caparisoned. ¹⁵ make active in digestion.

753–62. All the names of kinds of wine. Rumney was a white Spanish wine; Malmsey, a sweet wine; ypocrasse (Hippocrates), a spiced cordial; vernage, an Italian white wine; mountrose appears only here; algrade, a Cretan wine; raspis, "deepe redde enclining to black;" bastarde, a sweet Spanish wine; pyment, wine with honey; garnarde, wine of Granada (or possibly, pomegranates); muscadel, a rich sweet wine; claré, wine mixed with honey and spices; rochelle, wine from La Rochelle; osey, Alsatian wine.

754. C. *ypocraffe*.

And pottes of osey set you by.
You shall haue venison ybake,
The best wylde foule that may be take.
A lese[16] of grehound with you to streke[17]   765
And hert and hynde and other lyke.
Ye shal be set at such a tryst[18]
That herte and hynde shall come to your fyst,
Your dysease[19] to dryue you fro,
To here the bugles there yblow   770
With theyr bugles in that place,
And seuenscore raches[21] at his rechase;[22]
Homward thus shall ye ryde,
On haukyng by the ryuers syde,
With goshauke and with gentyll fawcon,   775
With egle-horne and merlyon.[23]
Whan you come home, your men amonge,
Ye shall haue reuell, daunces, and songe;
Lytle chyldren, great and smale,
Shall syng as doth the nyghtyngale.   780
Than shall ye go to your euensong,
With tenours and trebles among;
Threscore of copes,[24] of damaske bryght,
Full of perles th[e]y shal be pyght;[25]
Your aulter clothes[26] of taffata,   785
And your sicles[27] all of taffetra.
Your sensours[28] shal be of golde,
Endent[29] with asure many a folde.
Your quere nor organ songe shall wante
With countre-note[30] and dyscant,[31]   790
The other halfe on orgayns playeng,

---

[16] a leash. [17] move quickly. [18] a station past which game was driven. [19] discomfort; i.e., unhappiness. [21] dogs hunting by scent. [22] recall. [23] kinds of hawks. [24] vestments (of her choir and priests). [25] decorated. [26] altar-cloths. [27] women's tunics. [28] censers. [29] ornamented. [30] counterpoint. [31] descant.

765. C. *hrehound.*
768. Possibly read *lyst*, pleasure.
771. In 770 *bugles* means "horns;" here, "beagles."
786. Evidently a scribe's mistaken recopying of the preceding line; *taffetra* unknown; possibly read *camaca* as in 835.

With yonge chyldren full fayre syngyng.
Than shall ye go to your suppere,
And sytte in tentes in grene arbere,
With clothes of Aras[32] pyght to the grounde,   795
With saphyres set and dyamonde.
A cloth of golde abought your heade,
With popiniayes pyght, with pery read,
And offycers all at your wyll:
All maner delightes to bryng you tyll.   800
The nightingale sitting on a thorne
Shall synge you notes both euen and morne.
An hundreth knightes truly tolde
Shall play with bowles in alayes colde,
Your disease to driue awaie: 805
To se the fisshes in poles[33] plaie;
And then walke in arbere vp and downe,
To se the floures of great renowne:
To a draw-brydge than shall ye,
The one halfe of stone, the other of tre;   810
A barge shall mete you full ryght
With xxiiii ores full bryght,
With trompettes and with claryowne,
The fresshe water to rowe vp and downe.
Than shall ye go to the salte fome,   815
Your maner[34] to se, or ye come home,
With lxxx shyppes of large towre,
With dromedaryes[35] of great honour,
And carackes[36] with sayles two,
The sweftest that on water may goo,   820
With galyes good vpon the hauen,
With lxxx ores at the fore stauen.[37]
Your maryners shall synge arowe[38]
'Hey, how, and rumbylawe.'[39]

---

[32] Arras, i.e., tapestry. [33] pools. [34] manor. [35] large ships. [36] galleons. [37] stem.
[38] in a row. [39] "a very favorite burden to an ancient sea-song."—M.

804. "Bowling in alleys cooled." They were covered grass alleys.
817. Small castellated towers were sometimes built on battleships; cf. Mead's note.

Than shall ye, doughter, aske the wyne,   825
With spices that be good and fyne,
Gentyll pottes with genger grene,
With dates and deynties you betwene,
Forty torches, brenynge bryght,
At your brydges to brynge you lyght.   830
Into your chambre they shall you brynge,
With muche myrthe and more lykyng.
Your costerdes[40] couered with whyte and blewe,
And dyapred[41] with lyles newe.
Your curtaines of camaca[42] all in folde,   835
Your felyoles[43] all of golde.
Your tester-pery[44] at your heed,
Curtaines with popiniayes white and reed.
Your hyllynges[45] with furres of armyne,
Powdred with golde of hew full fyne.   840
Your blankettes shall be of fustyane,[46]
Your shetes shall be of clothe of Rayne.[47]
Your head-shete[48] shall be of pery pyght
With dyamondes set and rubyes bryght.
Whan you are layde in bedde so softe,   845
A cage of golde shall hange alofte,
With longe peper[49] fayre burnning,
And cloues that be swete smellyng,
Frankensence and olibanum,[50]
That whan ye slepe the taste may come.   850
And yf ye no rest may take,
All night minstrelles for you shall wake."
"Gramercy, father, so mote i the,
For all these thinges lyketh not me."
Vnto her chambre she is gone,   855
And fell in sownyng sone anone
With much sorow and sighing sore;

---

[40] hangings for a bed. [41] adorned. [42] a rich silk cloth. [43] posts of bed. [44] jeweled canopy over bed. [45] coverings. [46] cloth of linen and cotton. [47] Rennes. [48] sheet covering the pillow. [49] pepper used as incense. [50] aromatic gum for incense.

835. C. *curtianes.*
837. C. *fester;* Mead emends.

Yet seuen yeare she kept hym thore.
　But leue we of that lady here,
And speake we more of that squyer,　　　　　860
That in pryson so was take
For the Kinges doughters sake.
The Kyng hymselfe, vpon a daye,
Full pryuely he toke the waye;
Vnto the pryson sone he came;　　　　　865
The squyer sone out he name,
And anone he made hym swere
His counsayl he should neuer discure.[1]
The squyer there helde vp his hande
His byddyng neuer he should withstande:　　　870
The Kyng him graunted ther to go
Upon his iorney to and fro,
And brefely to passe the sea,
That no man weste but he and he;
And whan he had his iurnay done,　　　　875
That he wolde come full soone;
"And in my chambre for to be,
The whyles[2] that i do ordayne for thee;
Than shalt thou wedde my doughter dere
And haue my landes, both farre and nere."　　880
　The squyer was full mery tho,
And thanked the Kynge, and forth gan go.
The Kyng hym gaue both lande and fe.
Anone the squyer passed the se.
In Tuskayne and in Lumbardy,　　　　　885
There he dyd great chyualry.
In Portyngale nor yet in Spayne
There myght no man stan[d] hym agayne;
And where that euer that knyght gan fare,
The worshyp with hym away he bare.　　　890
And thus he trauayled seuen yere
In many a land, both farre and nere;

---

[1] disclose.　[2] times.

869. I. e., "swore that he should never . . ."

Tyll on a day he thought hym tho
Unto the Sepulture for to go;
And there he made his offerynge soone,   895
Right as the Kinges doughter bad him don.
Than he thought hym on a day
That the Kynge to hym dyd saye.
He toke his leue in Lumbardy,
And home he came to Hungry.   900
Unto the Kynge soone he rade,
As he before his couenaunce³ made,
And to the Kyng he tolde full soone
Of batayles bolde that he had done,
And so he did the chyualry   905
That he had sene in Lumbardy.
To the Kynge it was good tydande;
Anone he toke him by the hande,
And he made him full royall chere,
And sayd, "Welcome, my sonne so dere!   910
Let none wete of my meyné
That out of prison thou shuldest be,
But in my chamber holde the styll,
And i shall wete my doughters wyll."

    The Kynge wente forth hymselfe alone   915
For to here his doughters mone,
Right vnder the chambre window,
There he might her counseyle knowe.
Had she wyst, that lady fre,
That her father there had be,   920
He shulde not, withouten fayle,
Haue knowen so muche of her counsayle;
Nor nothing she knew that he was there.
    Whan she began to carke and care,⁴
Unto that body she sayd tho,   925
"Alas that we should parte in two!"
Twyse or thryse she kyssed that body,

---

³ covenant.   ⁴ worry and lament.

894. Christ's tomb at Jerusalem.
923. For *nor* read *but?*

And fell in sownynge by and by.
"Alas!" than sayd that lady dere,
"I haue the kept this seuen yere;   930
And now ye be in powder small,
I may no lenger holde you with all.
My loue, to the earth i shall the brynge,
And preestes for you to reade and synge.
Yf any man aske me what i haue here,   935
I wyll say it is my treasure.
Yf any man aske why i do so,
'For no theues shall come therto':
And, squyer, for the loue of the,
Fy on this worldes vanyté!   940
Farewell golde, pure and fyne;
Farewell veluet and satyne;
Farewell castelles and maners also;
Farewell huntynge and hawkynge to;
Farewell reuell, myrthe, and play;   945
Farewell pleasure and garmentes gay;
Farewell perle and precyous stone;
Farewell my iuielles euerychone;
Farewell mantell and scarlet reed;
Farewell crowne vnto my heed;   950
Farewell hawkes and farewell hounde;
Farewell markes and many a pounde;
Farewell huntynge at the hare;
Farewell harte and hynde for euermare.
Nowe wyll i take the mantell and the rynge   955
And become an ancresse[5] in my lyuynge:
And yet i am a mayden for thee,
And for all the men in Chrystenté.
To Chryst i shall my prayers make,
Squyer, onely for thy sake;   960
And i shall neuer no masse heare
But ye shall haue parte in feare:[6]

---

[5] anchoress, nun.   [6] together; i.e., you shall share the mass.

955. When a nun finished her probation, she was formally married to
the church with bridal costume and ring.

And euery daye whyles i lyue,
Ye shall haue your masses fyue,
And i shall offre pence thre,   965
In tokenynge of the Trynyté."
And whan this lady had this sayde,
In sownyng she fel at a brayde.[7]
 The whyle she made this great mornynge,
Vnder the wall stode har[8] father the Kynge.   970
"Doughter," he sayde, "you must not do so,
For all those vowes thou must forgo."
"Alas, father, and wele awaye!
Nowe haue ye harde what i dyde saye."
"Doughter, let be all thy mournynge: 975
Thou shalt be wedede to a kynge."
"Iwys, father, that shall not be
For all the golde in Christenté;
Nor all the golde that euer God made
May not my harte glade."   980
"My doughter," he sayde, "dere derlynge,
I knowe the cause of your mourny[n]g:
Ye wene this body your loue should be.
It is not so, so mote i the!
It was my stewarde, Syr Maradose,   985
That ye so longe haue kept in close."[9]
"Alas! father, why dyd ye so?"
"For he wrought you all thys wo.
He made reuelation vnto me
That he knewe all your pryuyté,   990
And howe the squyer, on a day,
Unto your chambre toke the way,
And ther he should haue lyen you bi,
Had he not come with company;
And howe ye hyght hym golde and fe,   995
Strengthe of men and royalté;
And than he watched your chambre bryght,

---

[7] suddenly.   [8] her.   [9] confinement.

982. C. *mournyg.*
992. C. *her chambre;* Mead emends.

With men of armes hardy and wyght,
For to take that squyer,
That ye haue loued this seuen yere;   1000
But as the stewarde strong and stout
Beseged your chambre rounde about,
To you your loue came full ryght,[10]
All alone about mydnight.
And whan he came your dore vnto,   1005
Anone 'Lady,' he sayde, 'vndo,'
And soone ye bade hym wende awaye,
For there he gate none other praye:
And as ye talked thus in fere,
Your enemyes drewe them nere and nere;   1010
They smote to him full soone anone.
There were thyrty agaynst hym one:
But with a bastarde large and longe
The squyer presed into the thronge;
And so he bare hym in that stounde,   1015
His enemyes gaue hym many a wounde.
With egre mode and herte full throwe,[11]
The stewardes throte he cut in two;
And than his meyné all in that place
With their swordes they hurte his face,   1020
And than they toke him euerichone
And layd him on a marble stone
Before your dore, that ye myght se,
Ryght as your loue that he had be.
And sone the squier there they hent,   1025
And they dyd of his good garment,
And did it on the stewarde there,
That ye wist not what he were.

---

[10] directly.   [11] bold.

1006. C. *and lady;* cf. 534.
1008. Cf. 564.
1009. C. *he talked thys.* Mead emends.
1013. M. suggests *baslarde,* dagger, since *bastard* usually means a cannon and appears with sword only as a modifying adjective, "large."
1015. C. *bate.*

Thus ye haue kept your enemy here
Pallyng[12] more than seuen yere;   1030
And as[13] the squyer there was take
And done in pryson for your sake.
And therfore let be your mourning;
Ye shal be wedded to a kyng,
Or els vnto an emperoure,   1035
With golde and syluer and great treasure."
"Do awaye,[14] father, that may not be,
For all the golde in Chrystenté.
Alas! father," anone she sayde,
"Why hath this traytour me betraid?   1040
Alas!" she sayd, "i haue great wrong
That i haue kept him here so long.
Alas! father, why dyd ye so?
Ye might haue warned me of my fo;
And ye had tolde me who it had be,   1045
My loue had neuer be dead for me."
Anone she tourned her fro the Kyng,
And downe she fell in dead sownyng.
      The Kyng anone gan go,
And hente her in his armes two.   1050
"Lady," he sayd, "be of good chere:
Your loue lyueth and is here;
And he hath bene in Lombardy,
And done he hath great chyualry,
And come agayne he is to me;   1055
In lyfe and health ye shall him se.
He shall you wede, my doughter bryght:
I haue hym made squier and knyght;
He shal be a lorde of great renowne,
And after me to were the crowne."   1060
"Father," she sayd, "if it so be,
Let me soone that squyer se."

---

[12] fading, decaying.   [13] so.   [14] cease.

1057. On the succession of a foreigner to the throne by marrying the
princess, cf. Frazer ii.280.
  1061. C. *it be so;* Mead alters.

The squyer forth than dyd he brynge,
Full fayre on lyue an[d] in lykynge.
As sone as she saw him with her eye,   1065
She fell in sownyng by and by.
The squyer her hente in armes two,
And kyssed her an hundreth tymes and mo.
There was myrth and melody
With harpe, getron,[15] and sautry,   1070
With rote,[16] ribible,[17] and clokarde,[18]
With pypes, organs, and bumbarde,[19]
Wyth other mynstrelles them amonge,
With sytolphe and with sautry songe,[20]
With fydle, recorde, and dowcemere,[21]   1075
With trompette and with claryon clere,
With dulcet pipes of many cordes;[22]
In chambre reuelyng all the lordes
Unto morne, that it was daye.
    The Kyng to his doughter began to saye,   1080
"Haue here thy loue and thy lyking,
To lyue and ende in Gods blessinge;
And he that wyll departe[23] you two,
God geue him sorow and wo!
A trewe[r] louer than ye are one   1085
Was neuer [yet of] fleshe ne bone;
And but he be as true to thee,
God let him neuer thryue ne thee."
The Kyng in herte he was full blithe;
He kissed his doughter many a sithe,   1090
With melody and muche chere;
Anone he called his messengere,
And commaunded him soone to go
Through his cities to and fro
For to warne his cheualry   1095
That they should come to Hungry,
That worthy wedding for to se,

---

[15] gittern, sort of guitar. [16] zither, played guitar-fashion. [17] lute with two strings. [18] bells. [19] bassoon. [20] song accompanied by citoles and psalteries. [21] flageolet and dulcimer. [22] harmonies. [23] separate.

1085. C. *that ye.*
1086. Additions by Kittredge.

And come vnto that mangeré.[24]
That messenger full sone he wente
And did the Kinges commaundemente.   1100
Anone he commaunded bothe olde and yonge
For to be at that weddyng,
Both dukes and erles of muche myght,
And ladyes that were fayre and bryght.
As soone as euer they herde the crye,[25]   1105
The lordes were full soone redy;
With myrth and game and muche playe
They wedded them on a solempne daye.
A royall feest there was holde,
With dukes and erles and barons bolde,   1110
And knyghtes and squyers of that countré,
And sith with all the comunalté.[26]
And certaynly, as the story sayes,
The reuell lasted forty dayes;
Tyll on a day the Kyng himselfe   1115
To hym he toke his lordes twelfe,
And so he dyd the squyer
That wedded his doughter dere;
And euen in the myddes of the hall,
He made him kyng among them al;   1120
And all the lordes euerychone,
They made him homage sone anon;
And sithen they reuelled all that day
And toke theyr leue and went theyr way,
Eche lorde vnto his owne countré,   1125
Where that hym [semed] best to be.
That yong man and the Quene his wyfe,
With ioy and blysse they led theyr lyfe;
For also farre as i haue gone,
Suche two louers sawe i none:
Therfore blessed may theyr soules be,   1130
Amen, Amen, for charyté!

FINIS.   THUS ENDETH UNDO YOUR DOORE, OTHERWISE
CALLED THE SQUYER OF LOWE DEGRE.

IMPRENTED AT LONDON, BY ME WYLLYAM COPLAND.

---

[24] feast.   [25] announcement.   [26] common folk.

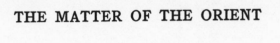
THE MATTER OF THE ORIENT

THE SEVEN SAGES OF ROME

The "Seven Sages of Rome" is the chief Middle English representative among romances of the "framework" story adopted by medieval Europe from the Orient. In such stories—the "Thousand and One Nights," the "Decameron," the "Canterbury Tales," the "Confessio Amantis"—many unrelated tales are linked together through being told by one or more characters of a tenuous main plot. For a full discussion of the legend of the Seven Sages, cf. Campbell's edition, Wells, and Hibbard.

The selections include part of the prologue; two tales of the Sages—the second, "Canis," and the twelfth, "Vidua," with its prologue—and part of the epilogue. For a discussion and bibliography of "Canis," see G. L. Kittredge, *HarvStN.* 8.222, and Campbell lxxviii; of "Vidua," Campbell ci. Ginn and Company have kindly permitted the use of some of Campbell's notes.

After each tale is a "process" carrying on the main plot, then a prologue to the next tale.

The selections in this book are from MS. Cotton Galba E IX (early fifteenth century), edited from rotographs by the kind permission of the authorities of the Department of Manuscripts of the British Museum. Final *-ll* is always crossed.

The story deals with a familiar theme in Oriental literature—the unscrupulousness of women.. The Emperor Diocletian, before he marries a second time, places his only son under the tuition of seven philosophers, who instruct him strenuously for seven years. The selections begin with the end of the sixth year.

> Þe sext ȝere, his maisters thoght   215
> For to asay him, yf þai moght;
> Þai puruaid[1] þam leues sextene,
> Þat war of iubarb[2] gude and grene.
> Þe child lay in a bed o-loft,
> Made ful esely and soft;   220
> Vnder ilka corner of þe bed,

---

[1] procured.   [2] house-leek.

Foure leues þe maysters spred,
Ilkane on oþer, als þam thoght;
Bot þe maisters werk ne wist he noght.
Þe childe went to his bed þat night,   225
And sone him thoght it raised on hight.
Þarfore þat night he sleped noght,
Bot euer in his hert he thoght
Þat þe firmament was satteld³ doun
Wele lawer þan it was won,   230
Or els þe erth was raised bidene
Þe thiknes of foure leues grene.
Þus lay he thinkand al þat night,
And sone, when it was dayes light,
He redied him and went to hall.   235
Þarin he fand his maisters all;
He hailsed⁴ þam, and hendly stode
Al bareheuid, withouten hode.⁵
    Þe childe luked obout him fast;
And hastily his maisters ast⁶   240
What thing he persaiued in þat place.
"Parfay," he said, "a ferly case,
For owþer am i mad or drunken,
Or els þe heuen es sumdel sonken,
Or els raised es þis grounde   245
Þe thiknes of foure leues rounde;
Þis night so mekill higher i lay
More þan it was ȝisterday."
Þe maisters þan wele vnderstode
Þe childes wit was wonder gode.   250
Or þe seuin ȝere war gane,
He past his maisters euerilkane.
    Togeder had þai grete solace,
Bot sone þan fel a ferly case.
Of þe riche Emperoure of Rome   255
I sal ȝow tel, if i haue tome;⁷
Þarfore þe childe now lat we be,
And of his fader speke wil we.

---

³ settled.   ⁴ saluted.   ⁵ bareheaded, without hood.   ⁶ asked.   ⁷ leisure.

His knightes com to him on a day,
And þir[8] wordes gan þai say: 260
"Sir, ȝe lif an anly[9] life;
We wald ȝow rede to wed a wife,
To haue solace bitwix ȝow twa,
And fandes[10] to get childer ma,
For ȝe haue werldes welth, gude wane, 265
To mak þam riche men ilkane."
   Hereof þe Emperowre was payd,
And sone asented als þai said.
Þai puruaid him an emperise,
A gentil lady of mekil prise, 270
Ful lufsom and of high lenage.[11]
Þe Emperoure asked þe mariage;
Þe barnage al þarto asent
Þat he sold wed þat ladi gent.
Þan war þai wed by comun dome;[12] 275
Þat was þe custum þan in Rome.
Þai made grete mirth and mangery,[13]
And samin lufed þai ful trewly.
Þare was grete welth at þaire wedyng,
Als semly was to swilk a thing. 280
   Sone efter þat fel ferly case;
I sal ȝow tel how þat it wase;
For nathing mai ay vnkid[14] be
Bot anely Goddes awin preueté.
Opon a day a seriant nyce[15] 285
Tald vnto þe Emperice
Of þe Emperoure son ful euyn,[16]
And how he wond with maisters seuyn,
And how he sal be emperowre
Efter his fader of þat honowre, 290
And how hir barnes sal be bastardes,

---

[8] these. [9] solitary. [10] attempt. [11] lineage. [12] general consent. [13] feasting.
[14] hidden. [15] foolish servant. [16] entirely; i.e., everything.

283. MS. *vnhid;* *vnkid* suggested by W. H. Browne; cf. Campbell 154.
291. "According to the canonists, bigamy consisted in marrying two virgins successively, one after the death of the other; or in once marrying a widow." *Amer. and Eng. Encyc. of Law,* 2.192, note 1.

And how he sal haue al þe wardes,[17]
And how he sal haue in his hand
Al þe lordship of þat land.
    When þe Emperice herd of þis childe,   295
Hir thoght þat sho was euil bigild,
And in hir hert sho thoght ful sone,
With wichecraft sold he be vndone.
Sho puruaid hir a counsailoure,
A wiche[18] þat cowth hir wele socoure.   300
Þai made couenant bitwen þam twa
Þe Emperours son for to sla.
Þai ordand[19] þus bi þaire asent
A maner of experiment:
Þat if þe childe spak les or mare[20]   305
Fra he into court entred ware
To seuyn daies war went fully,
At þe first word sold he dy;
And if he seuyn daies hald him still,
Efter may he speke at will.   310
Þus was þaire purpose and þaire thoght:
Þe childe sone to dede haue broght;
Bot mani wald greue oþer sare[21]
And to þamself turnes al þe care;
On þe same wise fel it here;   315
Herkins now on what manere.
    Þe Emp[er]oure and his faire wife,
Þat he lufed euer als his life,
On a day þai played þam samen;
And als þai war best in þaire gamen,   320
"Sir," sho said, "bi Heuin-king,
I luf ȝow ouer al oþer thing,
And ȝe luf me noght so trewly;
I sal ȝow say encheson[22] why.
Vntil þis court when þat i come,   325
Ȝe made me Emperice of Rome,

---

[17] guardianships. [18] witch. [19] ordained. [20] i.e., at all. [21] many intend to grieve other people sorely. [22] reason.

323. MS. *lul.*

To be with 3ow at bed and borde,
And wit 3owre cownsail ilka worde.
Bot a thing haue 3e hid fra me
þat i haue moste desire to se.   330
   3e haue a son þat es 3ow dere,
With seuyn maisters for to lere;
He es þi son, sir, and þine ayre,
And als i here say, whise[23] and fayre.
I wald se him bifor me stand,   335
þat es so wise and so cunand;[24]
I luf him wele, for he wil thriue;
Al samyn i wald we led oure liue;
For sertes, sir, sen he es þine,
Me think also he sold be myne;   340
For sertes, sir, it mai fal swa
þat neuer gettes þou childer ma.
If þou wil euer haue ioy of me,
þi faire son þou lat me se!"
Son answerd þe Emperoure,   345
And said, "Dame, by Saint[25] Sauiore,
þou sal him se, yf þat i may,
Tomorn by vnderon[26] of þe day."
   Sho answerd þan with semblant blith,
"Gramercy, syr, a hundereth sith;   350
I sal him honore at my myght,
Als i am halden wele by right."[27]
   þe Emperoure cald currurs[28] twa
And bad þam swith þat þai sold ga
His erand to þe Seuyn Sages,   355
And to þam tald he his message[s]:
"3e sal þam prai, on al manere,
Send hame my son, þat es me dere;
For i wil wit tomorn by prime
How þat he has set[29] his tyme;   360
Miself sal bath se and here
What he has lered þis seuyn 3ere."

---

[23] wise.   [24] knowing, learned.   [25] blessed.   [26] 9 A.M.   [27] according to my power as I am rightly bound to do.   [28] couriers.   [29] employed.

Þe messagers er wightly went
To do þaire lordes cumandment.
Vnto þe place smertly þai come   365
Whare þai wond, withouten Rome.
Into þe hal þai went ful euyn,[30]
And þare þai fand þe Maisters Seuyn
Faire desputand in Latyne
With þe ȝung childe, Florentine.   370
Þe messagers on knese þam set,
And þe maysters faire þai gret;
Þe child also þai gret ful faire,
Als prince of Rome and kindest[31] ayre.

Þai said, "Þe Emperoure of Rome   375
Cumand vs heder to come;
He biddes ȝe sal send hame his son,
And hastily þat it be done,
Þat he cum in his awin presens;
And for ȝowre trauail and ȝowre spens[32]   380
He wil ȝow quite on al manere,
And mak aseth[33] for þis seuyn ȝere."
Þe messagers war welkum þare
With þa maisters, les and mare:
Vnto þe sopere war þai sett,   385
And riche fode bifor þam fett;
Ful wele at ese þare war þai made,
With al gamyns þat men might glade.

Þare þai soiornd al þat night;
Þe mone and sternes bath shined bright.   390
Forth þan went þe maisters all,
And þe childe with þam gan þai call
Preuely to a gardine;
And þare þai teched Florentine
How þat he sold do and say,   395
His lord þe Emperowre to pay.

---

[30] straightway.   [31] most natural, probable.   [32] expense.   [33] recompense.

394. MS. *Floreentine.*

And in þat time þai toke entent[34]
And loked vp to þe fyrmament;
þai saw þe constellaciowne;
þareof a wise man was Catoun;   400
He luked þe sternes[35] and þe mone,
And what he saw he said ful sone:
   "Felous, ȝe sal vnderstand
Slike ferlies neuer bifore i fand;
þe Emperoure has til vs sent   405
To bring him hame his son so gent;
And if we bring him to his lord,
I se þare sal be sone discord;
For if he speke with man or wyfe,
At þe first word he loses his life;   410
And if him swilk vnhap[36] bifall,
þe Emperoure wil ger sla vs all.
And þat it sal þusgat be done
May ȝe se in sternes and mone."
þan þai biheld þe sternes ilkane,   415
And al acorded þai vntil ane:[37]
þat al was soth þat Caton talde.
And Florentine þan gan byhalde
Vnto þe sternes and to þe mone,
And what he saw he said ful sone: 420
He said, "Sirs, se ȝe noght þis tide
A litel stern þe mone bisyde?
Can ȝe me tel, þis pray i ȝow,
What ȝone stern bitakins now?"
þan sayd þe maisters, mare and myn,[38]   425
"Tel vs what þou sese þareyn."
   "Sirs," he said, "i sal ȝow tell
What þe mone and þe sternes menes omel.[39]

---

[34] heed.   [35] stars.   [36] misfortune.   [37] unanimously.   [38] less.   [39] together.

398. For a discussion of astrology in the Middle Ages, see *YaleSt.* 60.103.
399. A "constellation" is a particular astrological position or arrangement of the stars.

Þe mone sais i sal dy with wreke[40]
At þe first word þat i speke; 430
Þe litel stern þan tels me till
If i mai seuyn dayes hald me still
And answer vnto þam nathing,
Þan sal i lif in gude liking,
And i sal be of grete renowne, 435
And saue ȝow fra destrucciowne."
Þe maisters vnderstode ful wele
Þat he said soth ilka dele.
    Þan spak Maister Bausillas,
And said, "Þis es a ferly case. 440
I rede we tak oure kounsail sone
On what maner es best to done."
Þe childe [said], "Sirs, saun fayle,
I sal tel ȝow my counsayle.
Seuen daies sal i hald me still 445
And speke na word, gude ne ill;
And sen ȝe er Seuyn Maysters wise,
In al þe werld maste of prise,
By ȝowre wit me think ȝe may
Ilka man saue me a day, 450
And warand[41] me with ȝowre wisdom
Bifor mi fader, Emperoure of Rome;
And seþin i sal speke for vs all,
And ger oure famen al doun fall;
Þan sal we wele venged be 455
Of þam þat ordans[42] þus for me."
    Þan spak Maister Bausillas,
And said, "Son, by Saint Nicholas,
A dai for þe i sal be bowne."
"And i anoþer," said Maister Caton; 460
And al halely to him þai hight
For to saue him at þaire might
Fra alkin shame and velany;
And he said, "Maisters, gramercy;

---

[40] violence. [41] guard. [42] plot.

443. Campbell adds *said*.

.I mun suffer ful grete turmentes   465
Bot-if 3e haue gude argumentes."
After þir wordes rase þai all
And went ogayn into þe hall.
It was wele passed of þe night;[43]
Vnto bed al went þai right.   470
Þe childes thoght was euer in one:[44]
How þat him was best to done,
And how he sold be war and wise,
And answer noght þe Emperice;
For wele he wist and vnderstode   475
Þat scho wald him litel gude.
    When day was cumen and nyght gane,
Þe maisters rase ful sone ilkane;
Þai cled þe childe in riche wede
And horsed him on a gude stede,   480
And forth þai went fra þat gardyne,
Þat was kald Boys[45] Saynt Martine.
Þai broght þe childe furth in his way,
And at þaire parting gan þai pray
Þat he sold speke wordes nane   485
Til seuyn dayes war cummen and gane:
"Þan sal þou pas fro al þi payne."
When þis was said, þai turned ogayn;
Þe messagers and þe childe hende,
Toward þe court gan þai wende.   490
    When þe Emperi3 herd tiþand
Þat þe childe was nere cumand,
A desterer[46] sone gert sho dyght,
And keped him with many a knyght.
He louted[47] hir and þam ilkane,   495
Bot wordes wald he speke right nane.
In court þai come within a while;
Þe Emperice thoght euer on gile;[48]
Sho toke þe child, þat was so hende,
And vnto chamber gan þai wende,   500

---

[43] i.e., the night was far gone.   [44] on one matter.   [45] wood.   [46] war horse.
[47] bowed to.   [48] trickery.

And doun sho set him on hir bed,
And Florentine was ful adred.
Sho said, "Þou ert of mekil prise,
Hende and curtays, war and wise;'
And sen þi fader has wedded me,   505
Gude reson es þat i luf þe;
And so i do, þe soth to say,
And þarfore, par amore[49] i þe pray
Þat þou me kys and luf me;
And, sir, þi soiet[50] sal i be: 510
Vnto þe, sir, so God me rede,
Haue i keped my maydenhed."[1]

    Sho toke þe childe obout þe hals,[2]
Bot al þat fageing[3] was ful fals.
Þe childe made ay ful heuy chere,   515
And wald noght speke on no manere;
He turned oway with al his might;
And als-sone þan þe lady bryght
Saw sho might noght turn his mode,
And for wa sho was nere wode.   520
"Sir," sho said, "what ayles þe?
Whi wiltou noght speke with me?
And al þi wil, syr, wil i do."
He answerd nothing hir vnto.

    Sho saw þir gaudes[4] might noght gain;   525
Þarfore sho toke anoþer trayn:[5]
Sho lete[6] als sho war wode for wrath,
And sone sho rafe[7] euerilka klath,
And als þe forors[8] of ermyne,
And couercheues[9] of silk gude and fyne.   530
Hir smok[10] also sone rafe sho it,
Als sho wer wode out of hir wit.
Hir faire hare sho al to-drogh;[11]
And sari noys sho made inogh.
Sho al to-raced[12] hir vesage,   535

---

[49] in the name of love.   [50] subject.   [1] maidenhood.   [2] neck.   [3] feigning.   [4] tricks.
[5] stratagem.   [6] behaved.   [7] tore each garment.   [8] furs.   [9] kerchiefs.   [10] under-
garment.   [11] disheveled.   [12] scratched severely.

    525. End of line illegible in MS.

And cried "Harrow!"[13] in grete rage.
  Þe Emperoure was in þe hall,
Carpand with his knightes all;
And when þai herd slike nois and cri,
Fast to chamber gan þai hy.   540
Þai fand þe Emperice al to-rent;[14]
Hir hare, hir face was fouly shent.
Þe Emperoure was ful euil payd,
And vnto hir ful sone he said,
"Tel me wha did þis dishonowre,   545
And sertes it sal be boght ful soure!"
"Þis deuil," sho said, "þat here standes
Has me shent þus with his handes;
Had ȝe noght titter[15] cumen me till,
With me he had done al his will!   550
Þus he haues me al to-rent,
Mi body for he wolde haue shent.
He was neuer cumen, sir, of þi blode;
Ger bind him fast, for he es wode!
He es a deuil, withowten drede!   555
Þarfore, to preson gers him lede;
I tine[16] mi wit—þat wele wit ȝe!—
And i lenger opon hym se."
  Þan hastily þe Emperowre
Cald vnto his turmentoure,[17]   560
And bad þe traitur sold als-sone
Be nakend[18] and in preson done,
And beten als with skowrges sare
For his misdedis and his lare;[19]
"And ger him speke if þat þou may;   565
Here says he nowþer 'ȝa' ne 'nay.'
Bot-if he speke, by God in heuyn,
I sal ger sla his Maisters Seuyn!"
  Alsone þan þe turmentoure
Led þe childe fra þe Emperowre   570
Hastily þe preson vntill;
Þat lyked many a man ful ill;

---

[13] help.   [14] torn to pieces.   [15] very quickly.   [16] lose.   [17] torturer, executioner.
[18] stripped naked.   [19] evil thoughts.

þe knyghtes asked whi it was;
þe turmentoure tald þam þe case:
þai bad þe child sold haue na skath,[20]   575
Bot plenté of mete and drink bath.
þe turmentoure said, "Lattes me allane;
Mete ne drink sal him want nane."
þan þe knightes of grete valure
Went tite vnto þe Emperowre;   580
þai blamed him for þat owtrage,
Withowten cownsail of his barnage;
þai praied him to ses[21] of his sorow
And gif þe childe respite til þe morow,
And þan ger sla him, or els bren,   585
By kownsail of his wisest men.
þat dai þe Emperoure spared his son
And bad no harm þai sold him done,
Bot gif him mete and drink at will,
And hald him so in presown still.   590
Ful wrath he was, þe soth to say;
Bot þus his son was saued þat day.

That evening the Empress tells the Emperor that his son will supplant him, and relates a story to prove her assertion. He arises next morning determined to kill his son, but is dissuaded by the first Sage, who tells the following story.

Þe Secund Tale, of Maister Bausillas.

He said, "Sir, in þis same ceté,   775
On a day of þe Trinité,[22]
Was ordand to be a bowrdice[23]
Of nobil knightes of mekil prise:
In a medow þai made þaire play.
And þus bifel on þat same day,   780
þe knight þat i of tel þis stownde
Had at hame a faire grehownde.
Biside þe medow was his manere,
Al vmclosed[24] with a reuere;

---

[20] harm.   [21] cease.   [22] Trinity Sunday, which follows Pentecost.   [23] festival.
[24] surrounded.

Of ald werk was ilka wall,   785
Ful of creuices and holes ouer-all.
Þe knight had wed a faire lady;
A faire childe sho haued him by.
Þare war thre norices[25] it to ȝeme;
An gaf at sowke,[26] als it wald seme;   790
Þe toþer wasshes it and bathes,
Makes þe bed, and dons þe clathes;
Þe thrid wasshes þe shetes oft
And rokkes it on slepe soft.

   Þis grehund þat i are of talde   795
Was wonder wight and þarto balde,
And þarto was he so wele taght,
Þe knight wald gif him for none aght.[27]
Þe knight was armed in nobil wede,
And sone lepe vp on his stede,   800
With sheld on sholder and shaft in hand,
To iust with knightes of þe land.
Sone he come into þe feld:
Þe lady lay euer and byhelde,
Vp in þe kastell on a vice,[28]   805
Whare sho might se þe faire bourdice.
Þe norices said þat þai wald ga
For to se þe gamyn alswa,
And al þai went out of þe hall
And set þe credil[29] vnder a wall;   810
Þe childe þarein slepand it lay.
Al thre þai went to se þe play,
At a preué place bisyde;
And in þat time þus gan bitide:
   A nedder was norist[30] in þe wall,   815
And herd þe noys of riding all;
He loked out to se þat wonder
And saw þe childe stand him vnder.
Vnto þe erth he went onane;
Þe childe he hopid to haue slane.   820

---

[25] nurses.   [26] one suckled (the child).   [27] possession; i.e., would not give him away for anything.   [28] winding stairway.   [29] cradle.   [30] adder was nourished.

809. *iii* is written above *þai* in the MS.

Þe grehund wanders þareobout
And sese how þe nedder crepis out;
And sone þan gan he him asail,
And toke him ful tite bi þe tayl;
And sone þe nedder bate[31] him sare,   825
Þat he durst hald him na mare.
Out of his mowth when he was gane,
Vnto þe credel he crepis onane;
He fanded fast þe childe to styng;
Þe grehund ogayn to him gan flyng;   830
And sone he hentes [him] by þe bak,
And al obout his eres gan shak.
Bitwix þe nedder and þe grehownd,
Þe credil welterd[32] on þe grownd
Vp-so-down,[33] with þaire fyghting,   835
So þat þe childe lay grouelyng.
Þe foure stulpes[34] held vp þe childe,
Þat he was nowþer hurt ne filde.[35]
Þe nedder bate þe grehund sare
Bath bak and side and eueraywhare.   840
Þe grehund bledes, þe nedder alswa;
Grete batail was bitwix þam twa.
At þe last þe grehund þe neder slogh,
And al to peces he hym drogh.

   By þai had done, withouten dout,   845
Al was blody þam obout.
When þe bourdice was broght til ende,
Þe knightes wald no lenger lende,[36]
Bot ilka man his hernayse[37] hent,
And hastily hame er þai went.   850
Þe norices went to hall in hy,
And ful sone þai war sary;
Þe credel with þe childe þai fand:
Turned on þe stulpes þai saw it stand.

---

[31] bit.   [32] overturned.   [33] upside down.   [34] posts (on top the cradle).   [35] dirtied.
[36] remain.   [37] armor.

830. Campbell supplies *him*.
840. MS. *buth* (?).

Þai wend þe childe ware ded for ay;   855
Þarfore þai luked noght how it lay;
Al obout þare saw þai blode;
Þai had slike wa þai wex nere wode;
Grete sorow had þai in þaire hert.
Þe grehund cried, so euyl him smert;   860
Þai wend he had bene wode and wilde,
And in his wodnes slane þe childe.
Þe lady oft in swown gan fall
Euin[38] omang þam in þe hall.
"Allas," sho said, "þat i was born!   865
Es my faire childe no[w] f[ra] me lorn?"
Þe knight hame come in þat tyde,
And his men on ilka side;
He sese þam wepe and sorow make,
Ilkane for þe childes sake;   870
Þe knight þam asked w[hat] þam was;[39]
And son þai tald him al þe cas.
      Þe lady said, "Sir, þi grehunde
Has etin oure childe on þis grownde.
Bot-if þou reue him sone his life,   875
Miself i sal sla with my knyfe."
Þe knight went withowten let;
His fayre grehund sone him met;
He ran obout both here and þare,
And berked fast, so felde[40] he sare.   880
Of rinyng might he haue no rest:
Þe nedder had venum on him kest.
He fawned[41] his lord fast with his tail;
And þe knyght—for he wald noght fayl—
With his swerd on þe rig he hittes,   885
And sone in sonder he him slittes.[42]
      Þe grehund es ded in þat place;
Þe knight vnto þe credil gase;

---

[38] right.   [39] what was the matter with them.   [40] felt, i.e., out of sympathy.
[41] fawned upon.   [42] cuts.

866. Letters in brackets inserted above line.
883. Cf. "Piers Plowman," B.xv.295, *fauhnede wiþ þe tailes.*

Ay lay þe childe fast slepeand,
And þe wemen sare wepeand.   890
Þe knyght findes þe nedder ded,
In peces casten in þat stede;
Þe credil was blody and þe grund,
Of þe nedder and þe grehund.
Þe credel es turned, þe child es quik;   895
Þareof haue þai grete ferlik.
He sese þe hund þe nedder slogh;
Þan þe knight had sorow inogh;
Ful grete greuance to him bigan:
He said, "Sorow cum to þat man,   900
And sertanly right so it sale,
Þat euer trowes any womans tale!
Allas," he said, "for so did i !"
Þarwith he murned and made grete cri;
He kald his menȝe, les and mare,   905
And shewed þam his sorow sare:
How his childe was hale and sownde,
And slane was his gude grehound
For his prowes and his gude dede,
And also for his wiues rede.   910
   "A !" he said, "sen i þe slogh,
I miself sal by þe wogh;[43]
I sal ken oþer knightes, sanȝ fail,
To trow noght in þaire wife counsail."
He set him down þare in þat thraw,[44]   915
And gert a grome[45] his gere of draw;
Al his gay gere he gaf him fra,[46]
And al barfote forth gan he ga,
Withowten leue of wife or childe.
He went into þe woddes wilde,   920
And to þe forest fra al men,
Þat nane sold of his sorow ken:
Þare tholed[47] he mani a sari stownde
For sorow of his gude grehownde.

---

[43] atone for the evil deed.   [44] (space of) time.   [45] groom, servant.   [46] i.e., gave away.   [47] suffered.

And for þe kounsail of his wife 925
In sorow þus he led his life!
So mai þou haue, Sir Emperoure,
Sorow and shame and dishonoure,
To sla þi son ogains þe right,
Als þe grehund was with þe knyght; 930
For he was fel and ouer hastif,
And wroght by kounsayl of his whif."
þe Emperoure: "By Ihesu fre,
So sal noght bifal to me!
And, maister, i hete þe hardily, 935
þis day sal noght my son dy."
"Sir," said Maister Bausillas,
"Trowes my kownsail in þis cas;
For al þis werld wil þe despise,
To trow þi whif and leue þe wise."[48] 940
þe Emperowre said, "þat ware reson;
I sal noght by hir kownsayl done."
þe childe ogayn to preson es sent;
þe court departes, þe maister es went.

But that evening the Empress tells another tale, and the Emperor changes his mind again until he sees one of the Sages in the morning. So it goes for seven days. The following tale is told by one of the Sages on the sixth day.

Here Bigins þe XII Proloug.

Sone at morn, bifor þe sun,
þe Emperoure rase, als he was won.
He come omang his knyghtes all, 2785
And gert his turmentowre furth call.
He bad his son þat he sold bring,
And on þe galows high him hyng.
For mani knightes and burias come
For to here þe childes dome. 2790

---

[48] forsake the wise.

941. MS. *roson.*
2789. *For* a mistake for *and?*

Þe Emperoure wald haue no rede,
Bot said algates[49] he sold be ded;
And right so cumes into þe hall
Þe sest[50] maister omang þam all.
He said, "Sir Emperoure, lord of prise,   2795
In þi werkes þou ert noght wise;
Ilk man has mater[1] þe to blame;
Þarof þe burd think mekil shame.[2]
Sen þat þou wil trow na whise rede,
Bot wrang[3] wil ger þi son be ded,   2800
Þat ilk chance bifal to þe
Als fel a knyght of þis cuntré,
Þat hurt his whife finger with a knif,
And for þat sorow lost hys life."
Þe Emperoure said, "On al manere,   2805
Maister, þat tale most i here."
He said, "Sir, grant þi son respite,
And i sal tel it þe ful tite."
Þe Emperoure said blethly he sale;
And þan þe mayster tald his tale.   2810

Þe XII Tale Sayd Maister Iesse.

Þe maister said, "Bi God of might,
In þis cuntré wond a knight
Þat wedded had a ful faire whif,
And lufed hir more þan his life,
And sho lufed him wele, als him thoght,   2815
For efter his wil ai sho wroght.
So on a day, bifore his whife,
To þe knight was gifen a fetyce[4] knife;
And als þai plaied with þe knif bare,
A litel in hir fynger he share;[5]   2820
And when he saw þe blude rede,
For sorow he said he sold be ded;
And so he was, sone on þe morow.
Þan þe whife made mekyl sorow:
Sho wrang hir hend and made il chere.   2825

---

[49] in any case. [50] sixth. [1] cause. [2] thereof you should be ashamed. [3] wrongfully. [4] well-fashioned. [5] cut.

þe cors was sone broght on a bere,
With torches and series[6] faire brinand,
And prestes and freres fast singand.
For him þai delt seluer and golde,
And sone he was broght vnder molde.[7]   2830
    When þe knight þus grauen[8] was,
þe lady cried and sayd "Allas !"
And hardily sho said na man
Sold mak hir fra þat graue to gane,
Bot on þat graue ai wald sho ly,   2835
And for hir lordes luf wald sho dy.
Al hir frendes gederd þare
For to cumforth hir of care.
"Dame," þai said, "par charité,
Of þiself þou haue peté.   2840
þou ert faire of hide and hew;
þou may haue knightes nobil inowe;
And sen þou ert both ʒong and fayre,
þou mai haue childer to be þine aire.
It es na bote to mak murning;   2845
Al sal we dy, bath ald and ʒing."
þe lady said oft siþes, "Allas !
Out of þis place sal i neuer pas,
Til i be ded with him alswa !"
þan hir frendes was ful wa: 2850
    Na man might, for na preching,
þe lady fra þe graue bring;
And euil þam thoght þare to dwell.
þarfore þai did als i sal tell:
þai made a loge[9] þe graue biside,   2855
Fra rain and hayl hir for to hide.
þai couerd it ouer ilka dele,
And made a fire þarin ful wele;
Mete and drink þai broght plenté,
And bad þe lady blith sold be.   2860
Bot ett ne drink wald sho nothing.

---

[6] candles.   [7] ground.   [8] buried.   [9] lodge.

Euer sho cried, and made murning.
Hir frendes went oway ilkane,
And þus þe lady leued allane.
   Þat ilk day war outlaws thre   2865
Dampned[10] and hanged on galow-tre,
And knightes war þai euerilkane;
Ful many had þai robbed and slane;
Þarfore war þai hastily hent
And hanged so, by right iugement.   2870
Anoþer knyght of þat cuntré
Fel for to kepe þa theues thre
On þe galows al þat nyght,
Als it was resown and right.
For, sirs, ȝe sal wele vnderstand   2875
He gaf na ferm[11] els for his land
Bot for to kepe þe galows a-night,
When þare hang gentel men or knight;
And if ani þan war oway,
His landes sold he lose for ay.   2880
   Þe knight him cled in nobil wede,
And set him on a stalworth stede,
And went to kepe þe knightes thre
Þat hanged on þe galow-tre.
Þe frost fresed fast þarout;   2885
Þe knight rides euer obout
Biside þe galows, vp and down,
So was he dredand of tresown.
So grete cald[12] come him vnto
Þat he ne wist what he might do.   2890
Toward þe toun luked þe knyght;
He saw a fire brin faire and bright
In þe kirk-ȝerd of þe town,
And þeder fast he made hym boun.

---

[10] condemned. [11] rental. [12] cold.

2862. MS. *sho shïed;* Campbell emends.
2867. Knights and barons often turned bandits; cf. Jusserand 150 ff.
2876. This was his feudal duty; cf. Int. III.E.

Vnto þe loge he come onane;   2895
Þe lady þare he fyndes allane.
To cal and speke wald he noght spare.
Þe lady sais sone, "Wha es þare?"
"I am a knyght þat wald me warm
And wend my way withowten harm."   2900
Þe lady said, "By Him me boght,
Herin, sir, ne cumes þou noght!"
"Lat me cum in, dame, i þe pray."
Þe lady said ful sadly,[13] "Nay."
"A, dame," he said, "me es ful kalde;   2905
A litel while wharm me i walde."
"Sir," sho said, "bi Him me boght,
In þis close[14] ne cumes þou noght!"
"A, dame," he said, "par charyté,
Þare sal na man wit bot we."   2910
Þe knyght spak so with þe lady
Þat in he come, and sat hir by,
And warmed him wele at his will.
Þe lady gret and gaf hir ill.[15]

      Þan said þe knight to hir in hy,   2915
"Dame, whi ertou so sary,
And whi ertou þus here allane,
And so with murni[n]g makes þi mane?
Tel me, gude dame, i þe pray,
And i sal help þe if i may."   2920
Sho said, "Sir, i am wil of rede,[16]
For my lord es fra me dede,
And right here es he laid in graue;
Swilk a lord mun i neuer haue.
He lufed me euer ful stedfastly;   2925
Þarfore here wil i lif and dy."

      Þe knyght said, "Dame, þou ert a fole
Þat þou makes so mekyl dole!
What helpes it so to sorow þe
For thing þat may noght mended be?   2930

---

[13] firmly.   [14] enclosure, shelter.   [15] lamented.   [16] at a loss for advice.

2929. MS. *go.*

Þiseluen mai þou so forfare,
And him ogayn gettes þou na mare.
I rede þou morn na mare þarfore;
Þou may haue ane worth twenti score.[17]
Þarfore, dame, do efter me,   2935
And lat now al þi murning be:
I rede þou luf som oþer knyght,
Þat may þe cumforth day and night."
"Nay," sho said, "sir, by Saint Iohn,
Swilk a lord get i neuer none   2940
Þat so mekil wil mensk[18] me
Ne suffer my will als did he;
For to seke fra hethin till Ynde,
Swilk a lord sold i neuer finde."
      When þe knight had warmed him a while,   2945
He dred þat men sold do him gile
To stele som of þe hanged men
And ger him lose his landes þen.
He toke his leue of þe lady
And went to his hors hastily.   2950
Vnto þe galows rides he,
And sone he myssed ane of þe thre.
Þan was þe knyght ful sary man:
He hopid to tyne[19] his landes ilkane;
He thoght wemen kowth gif gud rede   2955
Vnto men þat had grete nede;
He was noght fer fro þe lady:
Ogayn he rides ful hastily.
He cald als he bifore had done,
And in þan was he laten sone.   2960
He said he had more sorow þan sho,
And assed[20] wat was best to do;
Al þe soth he gan hir say,
How his o knight was stollen oway.
      Þan spak þe lady to þe knight: 2965
"Say me þe soth, sir, if þou myght,
If þou has any whif at hame?"

---

[17] i.e., worth twenty score like him.   [18] honor.   [19] lose.   [20] asked.

"Nay," he said, "by swete Saint Iame,
Whif no leman had i neuer."
"Sir," sho said, "so es me leuyr;[2]   2970
Ful wele sal þou helped be
If þat þou wil wed me."
"3is, dame," he said, "by swete Ihesus !"
When þai had made þaire cownand[22] þus,
"Sir, tak we vp þis cors," sho sayd,—   2975
"Þis ilk day here was he layd—
And hang him vp for him þat failes."
Þe knight was paid of þir counsailes:
Out of þe graue þai toke þe cors;
Þe knight him led opon his hors.   2980
Þan said þe knyght to hir in hy,
"Dame, þou most hang him sertanli,
For if þat i hanged a knight,
Mine honore war lorn by þat vnright."[23]

Þe lady said, "So haue i sele,[24]   2985
I sal hang hym wonder wele."
Sho did þe rape obout his hals[25]—
In hir faith sho was ful fals!—
Sho drogh him vp and fest him fast.
"Lo," sho said, "now sal þis last."   2990
"Dame," said þe knight, "habide a stound:
He þat here hanged had a wonde
In þe forheuyd,[26] wele to knaw;[27]
Swilkane on þis byhoues vs shew,
Or els tomorn, in lytel while,   2995
Wil be percayued al oure gile."
"Sir," sho said, "draw owt þi swerde;
To smite him thar þe noght be lered.[28]
Smite my lord wharesom þe list;
Þan sal noght þi man be mist."   3000

---

[21] i.e., I am the better pleased.   [22] covenant, agreement.   [23] misdeed.   [24] happiness.   [25] rope about his neck.   [26] forehead.   [27] i.e., in truth.   [28] you need not be taught how.

2978. *þir*, these; cf. "The Avowing of Arthur" 530.
2983. He is bound by his oath of knighthood not to injure except in fair combat.

"Nay, dame," he said, "for al þis rike,
A ded knyght wald i noght strike."
Sho said, "Tak me þi swerd þe fra,
And i sal merk him or we ga."
He tald hir whare þat sho sold smyte,   3005
And on þe heuyd sho hit him tite.

    Þan þe knyght wele vnderstode
Þat sho was cumen of vnkind blode.
"Dame," he said, "by heuen-rike,
Ʒit es noght þis þat oþer lyke;   3010
His forteth[29] war al smeten out."
"Sir," sho said, "þarof no dowt;
Smites out his teth; biliue lat se !"
"Nay, dame," he said, "so mot i the
I wil do him no velany;   3015
He was a knyght, and so am i."
Þan þe whif sone toke a stane
And smate his fortheth out ilkane
When sho had on þis wise done,
Sho said vnto þe knight ful sone,   3020
"Sir, now sal þou wed me."
"Nay, dame," he sayd, "so mot i the,
Are wald i swere to wed na wife
Or i with þe sold lede my lyfe,
For þou wald hang me with a cord   3025
Right als þou has done þi lord;
Swilk sorow has þou shewed me now
Þat i sal neuer no wemen trow."

    Þan said þe maister to þe Emperowre,
"I pray Ihesu, our Sauiowre,   3030
Þat to þe fal slike velany
Als did þis knyght of his lady,
If þou for kownsail of þi whife
Reues þi faire son his life.
Spare him, sir, vntil tomorow;   3035
Vnto hir sal fal al þe sorow;
For, sertes, sir, þi son sall speke;

---

[29] front teeth.

By righ[t]wis³⁰ dome þan þou him wreke."
Þe Emperoure said, "So mot i gang,
And i mai wit wha haues þe wrang,   3040
And wha þe right, sir, þan sal i
Deme þam bath ful rightwisly."
Þan þe mayster went hys way;
Þus was þe clerk saued þat day.

After the seventh day, the child tells the final tale of a king's son who,
from overhearing the conversation of some ravens, prophesies he will be
served by his father. The king casts him into the sea; but he survives
to fulfill the prophecy.

Þus þis tale was broght til ende,
And Florentine, with wordes hende   4240
And with reuerence and grete honowre,
Sayd to his fader, þe Emperowre,
"Fader, on þis wise wald ȝe
Ogayns þe right haue gert sla me,
And fully haue ȝe bene my fa.   4245
Dere fader, why do ȝe swa?
I trispast³¹ na mare þan did he,
Þe childe þat was kast in þe se;
And if i myght come to honowre
For to be king or emperowre,   4250
Wene ȝe þat i wald greue ȝow?
Nay, sir, þat sal ȝe neuer trow.
Drawen and brend are wald i be
Or i wald greue my fader fre!
And, fader, ȝowre wife, weterly,   4255
Wald haue gert me lig hir by;
Bot i had leuer haue died als-sone
Þan þat dede to ȝow haue done."
When þe Emperoure herd how he sayd,
Of þat poynt he was noght payd,   4260
And sone he sent efter his whife,
Þat him had made so mekil strife.

---

³⁰ righteous.   ³¹ offended.

"Dame," he sayd, "es þis soth thing?"
"ȝa, syr," sho sayd, "by Heuyn-kyng;
He says al soth in þis sesowne,[32]   4265
And i sal say by what resowne,
For he sold do na harm þe till;
And also for þis sertayn skyll:[33]
Þat mi sons sold be na bastardes,
Bot haue þi landes and be grete lardes.   4270
And, sir, i dred me ȝit alswa
Þat he sold haue þe empire þe fra,
Hereefter when þou cums on elde
And may noght wele þiseluen welde;
Þarfore i wald haue had him dede,   4275
Þat my barnes might be in þi stede.
And on þis wise, sir, haue i soght
To ger hym vnto ded be broght."
"A, dame!" said þe Emperowre,
"Þou haues bene a fals gilowre,[34]   4280
And with þi treson done me tene;
Þat sal now on þiself be sene;
For þi gaudes and þi gilry[35]
I gif þis dome: þat þou sal dy.
Sakles[36] þou wald my son haue slayne: 4285
Þiself sal haue þe same payne;
Þi witchecraft and þi sorceri
Sal þou now ful dere aby.
Þou grantes þiself here al þe gilt;
Þarfore es reson þou be spilt.   4290
If þou lifed lenger, it war wath,[37]
For ful sone wald þou shend vs bath;
And sen þou grantes þi werkes wrang,
It nedes no quest on þe to gang.[38]
Þou ert worthy þe ded to take,   4295
By rightwis dome, for my son sake."
Þe Emperoure gert bifor hym call
His knightes and hys menȝe all,

---

[32] at this time.   [33] reason.   [34] deceiver.   [35] tricks and deceptions.   [36] guiltless.
[37] harm.   [38] no jury need examine you.
4294. Cf. "Gamelyn" 840.

And sayd, "Sirs, smertly for my sake,
A grete fire þat ჳe ger make,   4300
Hastily at þe towns end;
For þaryn sal þis whif be brend,
With mekyl dole, þis day or none,[39]
For þe tresown þat sho has done;
And loke ჳe spare hyr neuer a dele,   4305
For sho has serued[40] it ful wele."
Þe barons war al of ane asent
Þat sho sold haue þat same iugement,
And al þe knyghtes fast gan cri,
"Do to ded þat fals lady,   4310
Þat with hir wichecraft and hir rede
Wald haue gert þe childe be ded!"
    Sone þai made, onane right,
A faire fire, brinand ful bright.
Þan þai tok þat faire lady;   4315
Yt helpid hyr noght to ask mercy:
Þai band hir fast, bath fote and hand,
Þat sho myght nowþer rise ne stand.
Hir fete þai fest vnto hir swyre,
And lete hir flye in myddes þe fire.   4320
Þus was þe ladies ending-day,
And þus was sho quit hir iornay.[41]
Þe childe lifed with grete honowre,
And efter his fader was emperoure,
And led his life with werkes wise,   4325
And ended seþn in Goddes seruyse.
Þusgate endes al þis thing;
Ihesu grante vs his blyssyng!
                                    AMEN.

---

[39] before noon.   [40] deserved.   [41] repaid her for pains.

KING ALEXANDER

KING ALEXANDER

In the Middle Ages, the history of Alexander the Great suffered the same fate as the Troy-legend: it was known only through a late Latin romance, considerably expanded by French writers of the twelfth century. (See Wells, and M. Schlauch's "Medieval Narrative" 281; the different rescensions are discussed by G. L. Hamilton in *Speculum* 2.113.) The source of the English poem is Thomas of Kent's "Roman de Toute Chevalerie," which has not yet been printed entire. A few passages, including an index to the divisions, are in Meyer's selections. Those quoted here are from a rotograph of the Durham Cathedral MS. (Library of Congress, Modern Language Association Deposit No. 59).

The text is from Hale MS. 150, and is prepared from a rotograph, made with the kind permission of the Librarian and Library Committee of Lincoln's Inn Library. The right numbering of the lines in the two extracts is 3835–4261 and 5418–5467; but here Weber's numbering has been followed, both as likely to be serviceable and because a forthcoming edition of the poem will follow the same practice.

The dialect is southern, of the early fourteenth century. The language shows two common southern peculiarities: *-e-* is often broken into *-eo-* (*beo, þreo*); and *-u-* often is written where the midland form had *-i-* (*hulle*, hill; *fuf*, five). The sense often suffers from the writer's attempt to compress the French original and preserve its idiom, and hence several passages are obscure. In the manuscript, final *-ll* always has a cross-stroke; final *-g* and *-k* always, and final *-r* sometimes, are followed by a flourish.

There is only a mild undercurrent of history in the story. Alexander invades the east and encounters King Darius on the banks of the Tigris, where a bloody battle takes place. The following incident illustrates the generosity and magnanimity for which Alexander's name was a byword in the Middle Ages.

Darie fauȝte wel douȝtyliche
And dude swiþe muche wo;
To on side he drough him to;
He blew his horn, saun doute;[1]   3860
His folk come swiþe aboute,
And he heom saide wiþ voys clere,
"Y bidde, freondes, ȝe me here!
Alisaundre is ycome in þis lond
Wiþ stronge knyȝtis and myȝty of hond;   3865
Ȝef he passeþ[2] wiþ honour,
Oure is þe deshonour!
Y am of Perce deschargid,[3]
Of Mede and of Assyre aquyted;[4]
Ac ȝef þer is among vs   3870
Ony knyȝt so vertuous[5]
Þat Alisaundre myȝte slen,
We scholde parten ows bytweon
Alle my londis, euen atwo,[6]
And ȝet he schal haue þerto   3875
Cristaline, my douȝter flour,[7]
And þoruȝ and þoruȝ[8] al my tresour.
Now let seo ȝef ony is so hardy
Þat durste hit him afyȝe!"[9]
Þey þouȝten þoruȝ,[10] noþeles,   3880
Ȝef he myȝte come on cas[11]

---

[1] indeed. [2] goes through. [3] deprived of Persia. [4] relieved of Media and Assyria.
[5] valorous. [6] right in two. [7] white. [8] i. e., quite. [9] trust himself at it. [10] unanimously. [11] be in a situation.

3857. In the margin is a gloss: *Quomodo Darius viviter pugnauit cum Alex.* The last word has a flourish. The passage is a translation of sections LXV ff. in the French.

3859. The second *to* for *tho?*

3860. Weber's numbering contains some errors, and this number is assigned by him to the line beginning *And dude.* He corrects the numbering later. Except for minor differences such as this, his numbering is followed.

3866. The French has *ist*, comes away, for *passeth.*

3876. The French has, *ma fille au gent corps.*

Wher he myȝte yseo him abaye,[12]
Oþir bygile oþir bytreye.
Lord Crist, þat þis world eyȝte,[13]
Is lyf[14] to duyk and to knyȝte: 3885
Þer nys non so slow[15] wiþinne,
And he wiste to haue muche wynne,[16]
Þat he no wolde for gret tresour
Don himseolf in antoure![17]
Among þo of Perce was a knyȝt, 3890
Hardy and stalworþe, queynte and lyȝt;[18]
A knyȝt of Grece sone he slowe,
And his armure of he drowe,
And quyk armed him þerynne,
And þouȝte Alisaundre wynne. 3895
Alisaundre of him nouȝt ȝaf,[19]
Ac Perciens tofore him he drof:
Somme he kyt[20] of þe arme
And somme þe hed, and dude heom harm.
He bad his folk fyȝte harde 3900
Wiþ spere, mace, and sweord,
And he wolde, after fyȝt,
Rome londis to heom dyȝt.[21]
Þis forsaide knyȝt rod him by
As he weore his amy;[22] 3905
Whan he Alisaunder besy[23] seoþ,
To him anon he geþ;
He tok a launce, so y fynde,
And rod Alisaundre byhynde;
He smot him harde on þe hawberk.[24] 3910
Hit was mad of strong werk;
Þe Kyng was sumdel agast;
He huld faste: þeo spere tobarst:

---

[12] brought to bay. [13] owns. [14] gracious. [15] sluggish. [16] profit. [17] risk himself. [18] clever and spirited. [19] paid no heed. [20] cut. [21] make over. [22] comrade. [23] busy. [24] coat of mail.

3882. MS. *akaye*. The construction is loose: they preferred seeing him at bay, or beguiled, etc. (to engaging him openly). It is an addition by the English poet.

He sat faste, and lokid aȝeyn,
And saw on armed so hit weore his men.[25] 3915
"Fy!" he saide, "apon þe, lechour!"[26]
Þow schalt dye as a traytour!"
"Certis," quod þe aliene knyȝt,
"Y am no traytour, ac an aliene knyȝt;
Y dude a gyn,[27] þe to slene; 3920
And ded þow hadest for soþe ybeon;
At auenture for þe fyȝt,[28]
Þis victorie is þe ydyȝt.
Of Perce y am, feor by west;[29]
Þis hardinesse y dude for a byheste[30] 3925
Þat Darie byheyȝte, to whom þat myȝte,
Þe to slene in þis fyȝte:
He scholde haue half his kynriche,
And his douȝter, sikirliche.
Þis was, Kyng, al my chesoun;[31] 3930
No myȝt þou fynde here no treson
Ac þat y me putte in dedly cas
For to haue þat faire byheste!"
Þe Kyng by chyn him schoke,
And his seriauns he him toke 3935
And bad him loke[32] in prisoun:
He nolde him sle bote by resoun.[33]
He was don in god warde,[34]
And bounde faste in bondis harde.
Þe Kyng brouȝte forþ Bulsifall,[35] 3940
And metiþ of Perce an admyrall;
He smot him þoruȝ body and scheld,
And cast him ded in to þe felde.

---

[25] one armed as were his men.   [26] wretch.   [27] performed a trick.   [28] by the chances of war.   [29] to the west.   [30] bold act I did because of a promise.   [31] reason.   [32] lock.   [33] according to law.   [34] safe-keeping.   [35] Bucephalus.

3922. MS. *Ac.*
3924. The French says, *Ainz sui nee de Perse, al chef vers orient* (at the end of the orient).
3934. I.e., handled him roughly. The Fr. has only *Alixandre prist le Persanz.*
3943. *þe* not clearly written; may be *þeo.*

Þer myȝte men in heorte reowe[36]
How noble knyȝtis ouerþreowe;[37] 3945
Hors totraden þeo boukes[38]
Of noble barouns and dukis.
Þicke weore þe stretis[39] of knyȝtis yslawe,
And medewe and feld, hyȝ and lowe.
Non no myȝte heom bytweone 3950
Wite who scholde maister beon;
In boþe halue,[40] wiþ sweord and spere
Was ydo gret lore:[41]
Mony faire knyȝt þat day was schent,
Hors totorn, hauberke torent; 3955
Mony fair eyȝe wiþ deþ yblent,[42]
And mony a soule to helle went.
Þeo day failiþ, þeo nyȝt is come;
Wery buþ þe gentil gome.[43]
In boþe halue, mony gent 3960
Wenten hom to heore tent
And tokyn reste til amorwe,
Makyng ful gret sorwe
For heore lordis and for heore kyn
Þat laien yslayn in þe fen.[44] 3965
Alisaundre arisen is,
And sittiþ on his hyȝ deys:
His duykes and his barouns, saun doute,
Stondiþ and sittiþ him aboute.
He hette brynge forþ þat felawe 3970
Þat him wolde haue yslawe;
He is forþ brouȝt, and þe Kyng
Ȝeueþ him acoysyng:[45]
"Þow," he saide, "traytour,
Ȝursturday þow come in aunture, 3975
Yarmed so on of myne;[46]
Me byhynde at my chyne[47]
Smotest me wiþ þy spere;
No hadde myn hawberk beo þe strengore,

---

[36] regret. [37] fell. [38] bodies. [39] roads. [40] sides. [41] caused great loss. [42] blinded.
[43] fine warriors. [44] mud. [45] accusation. [46] armed like one of my men.
[47] back.

Þou hadest me vyly[48] yslawe.   3980
Þou schalt beo honged and todrawe,
And beo tobrent al to nouȝt,
For þou soche traytory wrouȝtest."
"Sire," quoþ þeo Perciens knyȝt,
"Ȝef ȝe doþ me lawe and ryȝt,   3985
No worþ y todrawe no anhonge,
For hit weore[49] al wiþ wronge.
Darie byhette to eche of his
To make pere to him, ywis,
Who þat myȝte þe wynne,   3990
Oþir by gile oþir by gynne.
Darie was my ryȝte lord:
Y fonded to do his word—
His fo to quelle in eche manere;[50]
And of treson me wol y skere;[1]   3995
Ȝef ony wol oþer preoue,
Aȝeyns him, lo, here my gloue!"
Antiochus saide, "Þow no myȝt þe skere!
Þow hast denied[2] þyself here
Þo þow for mede or byhotyng   4000
Stal[3] byhynde on oure Kyng,
Him to slen so þeofliche![3a]
Founde[4] þow schalt beon openliche:
Þow schalt sterue[5] on soche deþ hard!
Þis dom y ȝeue to þe-ward!"[6]   4005
Tholomeus þeo marchal vpstod,
Wyȝt in bataile and in counsail god,
And saide, "Þe Kyng may do his wille,
Saue þat Percien knyȝt or spille;
Ac he no haþ no ryȝt cheson,[7]   4010

---

[48] basely. [49] would be. [50] kill in any wise. [1] clear, acquit. [2] i.e., contradicted (by stealing). [3] stole. [3a] like a thief. [4] confounded. [5] die. [6] upon thee. [7] cause.

3989. MS. *þere*.

3997. On the glove as a challenge, cf. Hall's note on "Horn" 793; "Avowing" 296; "Earl of Toulouse" 1100.

4003. In the French, Antiochus accepts the challenge; this line is his defiance.

For he no dude no treson.
His dede nas bote honest,[8]
For he dude his lordes hest:[9]
Euery man to sle his fo,
Diuers gyn[10] he schal do.   4015
For his lord, nymeþ god cure,[11]
He dude his lif in aunture;
He nas nouȝt sworn to my lord,
Bote wiþ spere and wiþ sweord
Lefliche[12] is euery fo   4020
How he may oþir slo.
Ȝe mowe wel him do brenne and honge,
Ac y sigge hit where wiþ wrong!"
Vp stode Sire Mark of Rome
And entermetyd[13] of þis dome: 4025
"Certes," he saide, "he dude wowȝ
Þat he a knyȝt of Grece slowȝ
And dispoyled him of his armes
By treson, to oure harmes,
And ioyned him vs among   4030
So on of al þis was wrong,[14]
And so stal on oure Kyng,
Him to brynge to eyndyng!
Y iugge he schal anhonged beo!
Barouns of court, what sey ȝe?"   4035
Eueriche saide, "He schal beo slawe,
Forbrent,[15] hongid, and todrawe!"
Non no spak him on word fore[16]
Bote þat he scholde beo lore.
Þo Alisaunder say þis,   4040
Heriþ what he saide, ywis

---

[8] honorable.   [9] command.   [10] sleight.   [11] note carefully.   [12] every fighter may practice any sleight to slay another.   [13] interposed.   [14] so this (act) was wholly wrong.   [15] burned up.   [16] one word in his favor.

4020. *Lefliche* for *lefful?* The French has, *Car de son enemy deust prendre vengeison En tot manere sanz fere traison.*

4031. The French has, *M'est auis de donc en fist tres malement* (I think that in it all he did very evilly).

(Hit is ywrite, euery þyng
Himseolf schewiþ in castyng;[17]
So hit is of lewed[18] and clerk:
Hit schewiþ in his werk): 4045
He saw þat no knyȝt hende
Nul more þat knyȝt schende,
And saide, "Knyȝt, he weore wod
Þat wolde do þe ouȝt bote god;
Treson þou no dudest, no feyntise,[19] 4050
Ac hardy dede, in queyntise.[20]
For þat dede, by myn hod,[21]
Ne schaltow haue bote god!"
Richeliche he deþ him schrede[22]
In spon-neowe[23] knytis wede, 4055
And sette him on an hyȝ corsour,[24]
And ȝaf him muche of his tresour,
And lette him to Darie wende hom;
No ȝaf he him non oþir dom.[25]

Mury[26] hit is in þe dawenyng[27] 4060
Whan þe foules bygynneþ to syng,
And iolyf[28] heorte bygynneþ to spryng;
In muche loue is gret mornyng;
To sone hit þenkiþ þeo slowe gadelyng;[29]
In muche nede is gret þankyng. 4065

. . . .

Erly þe Kyng ariseþ, and makiþ bost,
And hoteþ quyk arme al his host;

---

[17] under trial. [18] ignorant. [19] nor cowardice. [20] ingeniously. [21] order (rank as king). [22] clothe. [23] newly spun. [24] charger. [25] sentence. [26] merry. [27] dawn. [28] joyous. [29] sluggish knave.

4042. MS. *ywrite in.* Most of the passage is not in the French.

4047. *Shend* is a translation of the French *defent,* defend. Although the Oxford Dictionary gives no example of its use in this sense before 1530, this is evidently an early occurrence of it.

4060. The different sections of the poem are not indicated in the MS. by capitals, but each has a little preface constructed like this one: an observation on the season, then some disconnected reflections or proverbs.

4068. Before this line, Weber has two others not in this manuscript. The numbering is made to conform to his, though the lines are omitted. The phrase *makith bost* probably means that he announces his intention of doing something surprising.

Þey beon alle armed quykliche,   4070
And alle him sywiþ,[30] sikirliche,
Ouer a water, into a forest,
And alle doþ heore lordes hest:
Bowes of diuers treoes þey kyttiþ[31]
And to heore hors tayl kneottiþ.[32]   4075
To Darie-ward[33] alle þey fariþ;
Þeo bowes þeo dust areriþ;[34]
Of drawyng of bowes and stikke,
Þeo eyr bycam þo trouble[35] and þikke,
Þat to Daries ost[36] hit ferde   4080
So on heom com þe myddelerd.[37]
Anon þey tolden hit Darie,
And bad him he scholde warye,[38]
"For Alisaundre comeþ wiþ his pray:[39]
His folk srediþ al þe contray."   4085
Darie hy3t al his men
Remuwe his tentis of þe fen[40]
And setten his bysyde Estrage,
A cold water and a sauage;
A castel he hadde in þat ryue:[41]   4090
Nas non strenger in al his lyue.
Anon was alle Daries ost
Ylogged by Estrages acost,[42]
Þere þey wolde fonde aspye
Al Alisaundres folye.   4095
Alisaunder þis tellen herd;
Wiþ his ost he after ferd,
And þere he loggiþ anon
Þer Darie hadde beon erst apon.[43]
Now is ywrye[44] al þe contray   4100
Bytweone heom as feole myle way.[45]
Ofte þer was bytweone heom rydyng,[46]
And mony a wy3t batailyng.

---

[30] follow.   [31] cut.   [32] tie.   [33] toward Darius.   [34] the boughs raise the dust.
[35] murky.   [36] host.   [37] as if the earth were descending on them.   [38] beware.
[39] company.   [40] remove his tents from the flats.   [41] river.   [42] shore.   [43] i.e.,
had camped.   [44] hidden, covered.   [45] for many a mile.   [46] i.e., scouting, etc.

Þeo whiles[47] [of] Alisaunder þe Kyng
Listeniþ now a woundur þyng: 4105
In a more-tyde[48] hit was;
Þeo dropes hongyn on þe gras;
Þeo maydenes lokyn in þe glas,
For to tyffen[49] heore fas.
Kyng Alisaundre is out yride,   4110
And þreo noble kny3tis him myde,
Pryueliche, in a gret myst;
His grete ost hit no wist.
He doþ þeo þreo, wiþoute reuþe,[50]
Ply3te to him heore treowþe,   4115
"Þat 3e ne schal me bywry3en[1]
Of þat y wol to 3ow sayn."
Þey doþ al his wille,
And he heom gan telle
He wolde wende swiþe snel   4120
To Darye þe feolle,
To seo þe contynaunce[2]
Of Daries court, saun demorrance.[3]
No kny3t no rod wiþoute stede,
No wiþouten yren wede;   4125
To þe water þey come ry3t:
Of his stede þe Kyng aly3t,
And of dude al his armure,
And dude on a robe of peolour![4]
Apon a palfray he leope,[5]   4130
And saide, "Kny3tis, nymeþ kepe[6]
To Bulsifall, my destrere,[7]
And abideþ me ry3t here:
Y wol come whan y may."
Quyk he doþ him in his way.   4135
Þeo þreo kny3tis of whom y saide,
Þat on het Amas of Cartage,
Þat oþir hette Philotas,

---

[47] meanwhile. [48] morning. [49] adorn. [50] i.e., severely. [1] betray. [2] appearance.
[3] delay. [4] fur. [5] leapt. [6] take care. [7] charger.

4104. *Of* supplied by Weber from other MSS.

And þe þridde Perditas:
Þer nere better knyʒtis þreo   4140
In al þe Kyngis maigné;
Þis þreo Alisaundre abyde,
Wel yarmed, by þe water syde.
Now sit Darye on an hulle,[8]
Folk of his ost to telle;   4145
Alisaunder to him comeþ and nouʒt stet,[9]
And saide, "Kyng Alisaunder þe Gret,
He is ycome to þe parlement
For to ʒulde þe þy rent.[10]
Tweyes he haþ þe ouercome,   4150
Þy wif and þy children ynome:
Feole þow hast yslawe of his.
He sent þe sigge[11] þus ywis:
'Hit schal beo ful deore abouʒt,
Þeo tole[12] þat was in Grece ysouʒt!   4155
Greyþeþ armes and ʒarkiþ[13] scheldis:
He ʒow abideþ in þe felde!' "
Darie was ful sore anoyed
Of þat Alisaunder haþ to him saide,
And saide, "Of tale beo [þou] smart![14]   4160
Alisaundre þyseolf þow hit art!"
Alisaundre saide, "Hit is nouʒt so:
He is whitter, wiþowte no,[15]
And his lokkes buþ nouʒt so crolle;[16]
Ac he is waxe more to þe fulle.[17]   4165
Ac y am hoten Antygon,
Þat mony a message haue ydon."
Darie saide, "Messanger, alyʒt,
And go we eten anon ryʒt,
And after mete þow schalt beore   4170

---

[8] hill.   [9] did not hasten.   [10] tribute.   [11] he sends to say to thee.   [12] tribute.
[13] make ready.   [14] your speech is impudent.   [15] fairer, unquestionably.   [16] curly.
[17] attained a better growth.

4160. MS. *table*. Possibly for *fable*, lie? The other MSS. read *tale*.
The French has, *Et ly dit, D'un rien* (thing) *me sui aperceuz: Vous estes
Alixandre: as dis la y entenduz* (by your words it is known).

To þy lord aȝeyn onswere."

. . . .

Alisaundre, wiþoute fable,
He set at his owne table.   4175
Þey weore serued wiþ gret plenté:
Wiþ fresch and salt and alle deynté,
And dronke wyn and eke pyment,[18]
Whyt and red, al to talent.[19]
Þere was coppes riche ywrouȝt;   4180
Alisaunder him byþouȝt
How he myȝte do sum þyng
Of to speke wiþoute eyndyng.
Þer of a coppe to him he dronk;
He hit afongiþ wiþ muche þonk.   4185
He dronk of þat wyn rede;
Þe coppe he putte vndur his grede.[20]
Þeo coppe was of red gold;
A botileir hit haþ al byholde,
And tolde Darie al þe soþe,   4190
And he bycom ryȝt wroþe,
And saide, "Haþ he do me þat schond?[21]
Men schal speke of Grece-londe
Of þe vengaunce þat he schal þole,[22]
Haue he my coppe ystole!"   4195
Þeo botiler takiþ vp his grede
And fynt þeo coppe of gold rede.
Darie to Alisaunder gan to sigge,
"Ey, felaw! theof! þow schalt abygge!
Y set þe at table myn   4200
For reuerence of lord þyn:
My coppe þow hast ystole,
And vndur þy barm hole![23]

---

[18] spiced wine.   [19] desire.   [20] bosom; i.e., under his robe.   [21] injury.   [22] suffer.
[23] concealed in thy bosom.

4171. After this line, Weber inserted two more, so that the numbering
is disturbed.

4185. "He accepts it gratefully."   Darius drinks to Alexander from a
cup, then hands it to him to complete the ceremony; Alexander takes it
and drinks to Darius.

Þow art ynome hond-habbyng;[24]
Þow schalt honge wiþ þe wynd!"   4205
Quoþ Alisaundre, þe Kyng so heynde,
"Of þefþe[25] y wol me defende
Aȝeyn knyȝt, swayn, and baroun,
Þat y no am no laroun:[26]
Y come to ȝow on message,   4210
And wende ȝe hadde soche an vsage
So haueþ my lord in court his—
For þy richesse and for þy pris,
Þat þow hast oþer tofore;[27]
Ac þat honour þou hast lore,   4215
For ȝef kyng sente, or kayser,
To my lord a messanger,
And he beo worþy, saun fable,
He schal sitte at his table,
And whan my lord him drynkiþ to,   4220
Þe coppe he schal to wille[28] vp do;
Y wende ȝe hadde also here
Of oure court þe manere!
Y am repentand, seþ ȝe no doþ:[29]
For harme no dude y hit, forsoþ."   4225
Darie, þauȝ he weore agramed,[30]
Of his[31] onswar he was aschamed;
Stille sate ȝonge and olde,
And heo gonne him byholde.
A knyȝt þer was þat hyȝte Pertage: 4230
Alisaundre he kneow in þe vysage:
. . . .
He saw Alisaundre vnder his hod.
Wel Alisaunder hit vndurstod: 4235

---

[24] i.e., red-handed.   [25] theft.   [26] thief.   [27] which you have in excess of other rulers.   [28] at his pleasure.   [29] sorry, since you do not do so.   [30] angered.   [31] Alexander's.

4218. The MS. has, *And ha* (flourish) *worþy*. Weber's emendation.
4230. MS. *Percage?* The French has, *Qui fu tenu per sage* (who was thought a wise man). The English translator takes this as a proper name.
4232. Weber here inserted two lines from the Auchinleck MS.

Hit ran in Alisaundres corage
Þat qued of him reumed[32] Per[t]age,
And þat he of him to Darie spak.
Ouer þeo table he leop arape;[33]
Quyk in his way he him dyȝt,[34]   4240
Darie after wiþ al his myȝt.
A sweord Alisaunder hadde, certes,
Þat was to him faste ygurd;[35]
Out he brayd hit in hond;
Non nolde in his way stonde.   4245
He mette a knyȝt wiþ a spere,
So God wolde, on a iustere;[36]
He smot him swyftly in þe swyre,
Þat he laide his hed to hyre;[37]
He schof him quycly adoun   4250
And leop himseolf in þe arsoun;[38]
He smot þe stede, and he forþ glyt;[39]
Alisaunder quyk away ryt:[40]
Þat day no schole þey him take!
Darie gynneþ after schake:[41]   4255
Prynce and duyk, knyȝt and swayn
Dasscheþ after wiþ gret mayn.
Euerichon þey doþ for nouȝt:
Alisaunder haþ þeo water cauȝt.[42]
Hit was brod, and eke Estrage   4260
Deope stremes and sauage:
He smot þe hors and in he leop.
Hit was swiþe brod and deop:
Hors and Kyng, wiþ alle hater,[43]
Was auntred vndur þe water.   4265
Alisaunder tofore[44] no seoþ:
He was sore adred of deþ.
Noþeles his hors was god,

---

[32] whispered evil of him.   [33] in haste.   [34] i.e., started away.   [35] girded. [36] charger.   [37] left his head as a forfeit.   [38] saddle.   [39] rushed.   [40] = rideth. [41] dash.   [42] attained.   [43] trappings.   [44] ahead.

4260. This seems to mean, "and likewise was Estrage a deep stream," etc. The French has, *Venuz est a l' Estrage, dont le ewe* (water) *fu bruant* (roaring).

And keouerid[45] vp abowe þe flod,
And swam to þat oþir syde, 4270
Þere his kny3tis him dude abyde.
Þay halp him vp, and his stede,
And anon chaungeþ his wede.
3ette he hadde þe coppe in hond
Þat he on Daries table fond; 4275
To his ost he fariþ, god schour,[46]
And tolde heom his auenture.
Þeo 3onge þerof hadden game:
Þeo olde wyse nome hit agrame,[47]
And saiden wel, þat cas 4280
Of gret folye don hit was.

When Alexander passes through her territory, Candace, a queen, falls in love with him, though she has never seen him. She sends him this letter:

"To Alisaundre þe Emperour,
Of alle kayseris pris kyng and flour: 6685
Þe Quene Candace, wiþ alle honour,
Sendiþ þe gretyng par amour.
O, Alisaundre, dure[48] sire,
Ouer alle men y þe desyre!
Tak me tofore alle to þy qwene! 6690
Riche schal þy mede beone:
Y wol charge,[49] saun faile,
Wiþ besauns[50] a þousand camailes;
Y wol 3eue þe 3ymmes and by3es[1]
Ten þousand caries;[2] 6695
Y wol cha[r]gen al þe bestis
Wiþ pellis and siglatouns[3] honeste;
Y wol þe 3eue gentil men—

---

[45] recovered, got.   [46] at a good speed.   [47] were angered.   [48] dear.   [49] load.
[50] gold coins.   [1] gems and rings.   [2] pack-horses.   [3] fur garments and genuine satins.

6684. This episode is adapted from § CCV of the French.
6695. The French has *somer*, pack-horses, for *caries*.

Ten þousand wyȝte Ethiopen,
ȝonge knyȝtis, flumbardynges,[4]   6700
Wyȝte in euery batalynges,
And an C þousand noble knyȝtis
To þy seruyse, gode and wyȝte;
And of gold a coroune bryȝt,
Ful of preciouse stones ypyȝt:[5]   6705
Gold no seoluer, so y sigge,
No myȝte þe stones to worþ bugge.[6]
ȝet þou schalt haue six hundred rinoceros,
And V C olifauns and VII C pardos,[7]
And two hundred vnycornes,   6710
And fuf M boles wiþ on hornes,[8]
And four hundred lyouns whyte,
And a þousand þat wel can byte
Olifans, and in playn,
Stronge houndis of Albayne,   6715
And fyf hundred ceptres[9] of gold,
And my lond to þy wold,[10]
And an C þousand gentil sqwyers
Þat konne þe serue in eche mesters,[11]
And þrytty þousand maidenes bryȝt,   6720
For to serue þyne knyȝtis—
Alle eorlis, duykes, and barouns,
Ful of cortely wones![12]

---

[4] fiery warriors.   [5] adorned.   [6] buy at their true worth.   [7] panthers.   [8] with one horn.   [9] scepters.   [10] power.   [11] art.   [12] ways.

6699. The French has *blauns Ethiopiens.*

6700. The French has, "beardless youths."

6709. The French also has *pardos;* the usual English form is *pardes.*

6711. The French has, *Mil blanc tors que ont les corns lusanz.* The last word may have puzzled the English translator, so that he took it to be some form of the word *sanz,* without.

6713. This line is misplaced by the English translator; it belongs after 6715, as the French shows.

6714. Other MSS. read *and lyouns in playn,* following the French.

6719. Plurals should not be taken too seriously in the work of this scribe.

6723. MS. *cortesy?* This may be an error for the familiar phrase *corteys wones.*

O, Alisaundre, riche Kyng,
Beo my lord and my derlyng!   6725
Y wol þe serue to hond and fot,
By nyȝt and day, ȝef y mot."
Of þis lettres was muche pris[13]
Wiþ Alisaundre and alle his;
Þe messangers aȝeyn heom dyȝtis,   6730
And ȝaf heom riche ȝeftis,
And wiþ wordes bonere[14]
Heom answeriþ swiþe faire.
Þer was ycome wiþ þe messangers
A queynte[15] mon, a metal ȝeoter,[16]   6735
Þat couþe caste in alle þyng.[17]
He avysed[18] þan þe Kyng,
And þo he com hom, sykirliche,
He caste a forme þe Kyng yliche:
In face, in eyȝnen, in nose, in mouþ,   6740
In leynthe,[19] in membres, þat is selcouþ;[20]
Þe Qwene sette him in hire boure,
And kepiþ hit in gret honour.

---

[13] was highly regarded. [14] courteous. [15] skillful. [16] caster. [17] i.e., any sort
of thing. [18] looked closely at. [19] length. [20] marvelous.

THE DESTRUCTION OF TROY

THE DESTRUCTION OF TROY

This piece, the full title of which is "The Gest Historiale of the Destruction of Troy," is in a manuscript in the Hunterian Museum at Glasgow. Mr. W. R. Cunningham, Librarian of Glasgow University, and Keeper of the Hunterian Books and Manuscripts, has very kindly compared the proof of the text with the manuscript.

The Troy-legend was known to the Middle Ages, not through the work of Homer, but through Latin versions of the Christian era. (For a brief account, see C. H. A. Wager's "Seege of Troy," Introduction.) These were distinguished by sympathy for the cause of the Trojans, from whom many western races thought themselves descended; and this preference is apparent in every medieval version. Achilles is reduced from a hero to a cowardly murderer; Helen's conduct is made the occasion for a disapproving sermon; the gods are carefully suppressed; war is conducted in terms of medieval chivalry, with castles, cavalry, captives, cross-bows, mining, etc.

The immediate source, which the Middle English poem follows closely, is the "Historia Destructionis Troiæ" of Guido della Colonne. The dialect is northern of before 1400. Few pieces in Middle English can approach the poem in sustained excellence; there is scarcely a dull passage in its 14,000 lines. The three selections below show the peculiar merits and point of view of the piece.

On the verse, see Introduction VI.B.2.

The vocabulary contains several words common in alliterative poetry and rare elsewhere. The most useful of these are the following: *wegh, shalk, lede, buern, gome*—man; *wees*—men; *bent*—field; *stithe, dern*—fierce; *euyn*—right, quite; *gird*—strike, rush; *braid*—rushed; *hor*—their; and *greme*—rage. The participles often end in *-it*.

Prologue

Maistur in Magesté, Maker of alle,
Endles and on,[1] euer to last!

---

[1] one.

1. The prologue is a paraphrase of Guido's own.

Now, God, of þi grace graunt me þi helpe,
And wysshe me with wyt þis werke for to end
Off aunters ben[2] olde, of aunsetris nobill   5
And slydyn vppon shlepe by slomeryng of age;[3]
Of stithe men in stoure, strongest in armes,
And wisest in wer to wale[4] in hor tyme,
Þat ben drepit[5] with deth and þere day paste,
And most out of mynd for þere mecull age.   10
Sothe stories ben stoken vp and straught[6] out of mynd
And swolowet into swym[7] by swiftenes of yeres
For new, þat ben now, next at our hond,
Breuyt[8] into bokes for boldyng of hertes,—
On lusti to loke, with lightnes of wille,[9]   15
Cheuyt[10] throughe chaunce and chaungyng of[11] peopull;
Sum tru for to traist, triet[12] in þe end,
Sum feynit o fere,[13] and ay false vnder.
Yche wegh as he will warys[14] his tyme
And has lykyng to lerne þat hym list after;   20
But olde stories of stithe þat astate helde[15]
May be solas to sum þat it segh neuer:[16]
Be writyng of wees þat wist it in dede—
With sight for to serche of hom þat suet after[17]—
To ken all the crafte how þe case felle,   25
By lokyng of letturs þat lefte were of olde.
    Now of Troy for to telle is myn entent euyn:[18]
Of the stoure and þe stryff when it distroyet was;
Þof fele yeres bene faren syn þe fight endid
And it meuyt[19] out of mynd, myn[20] hit i thinke   30

---

[2] events that are.   [3] lapsed into sleep in the slumbering (oblivion) of age.
[4] choose, who could be chosen. [5] struck down. [6] locked away and gone out.
[7] swallowed up in confusion. [8] written. [9] i.e., agreeable as light reading.
[10] gained, come by. [11] exchanging among. [12] trust, tried. [13] altogether fictitious. [14] spends. [15] fierce (men) who were prominent. [16] i.e., do not know the
story. [17] followed; i.e., to read the work of their successors. [18] plain. [19] moved,
removed. [20] to recall.

5. Historians thought the English descendants of the Trojans.

13. This prologue is like that of the "Cursor Mundi" in its recognition
of the power and attractiveness of the new fiction and its distrust of the
influence of that fiction.

23. Dares and Dictys professed to have been eye-witnesses of the
struggle.

Alss wise men haue writen the wordes before—
Left it in Latyn for lernyng of vs.
But sum poyetis full prist[21] þat put hom þerto
With fablis and falshed fayned þere speche,
And made more of þat mater þan hom maister[22] were;   35
Sum lokyt ouer-little, and lympit[23] of the sothe.
Amonges þat menye, to myn hym be nome,
Homer was holden haithill[24] of dedis
Qwiles his dayes enduret, derrist of other,[25]
Þat with the Grekys was gret and of Grice comyn.   40
He feynet myche fals was neuer before wroght,
And turnet[26] þe truth, trust ye non other.[27]
Of his trifuls[28] to telle i haue no tome[29] nowe,
Ne of his feynit fare þat he fore with:
How goddes foght in the filde, folke as þai were,   45
And other errours vnable,[30] þat after were knowen,
That poyetis of prise have preuyt vntrew—
Ouyd, and othir þat onest were ay—
Virgill þe virtuus, verrit for nobill—:
Thes dampnet his dedys, and for dull[31] holdyn.   50
But þe truth for to tell, and þe text euyn,
Of þat fight, how it felle in a few yeres,
Þat was clanly compilet with a clerk wise—
On[32] Gydo, a gome þat graidly[33] hade soght
And wist all þe werkes by weghes[34] he hade,   55
That bothe were in batell while the batell last,
And euþer sawte and assembly[35] see with þere een.
Thai wrote all þe werkes wroght at þat tyme,

---

[21] i.e., officious.   [22] i.e., authority.   [23] i.e., were inattentive, and failed.
[24] worthy.   [25] finest of all.   [26] distorted.   [27] i. e., else.   [28] inaccuracies.   [29] leisure.   [30] unfortunate.   [31] condemned his deeds and thought them unfortunate.   [32] one.   [33] thoroughly.   [34] i.e., authorities.   [35] every assault and meeting.

44. "The fictitious material with which he dealt;" medieval poets were willing to concede that the gods of Greece had existed, but thought they were merely men and women elevated by poets and priests to the dignity of gods after their deaths. Cf. article on Euhemerism, *Speculum* II.396.

49. Maybe *verrit* for *verdit*, attested; but the Oxford Dictionary gives no example of the verb so early.

In letturs of þere langage, as þai lerned hade:
Dares and Dytes were duly þere namys.   60
Dites full dere was dew[36] to the Grekys—
A lede of þat lond, and loged[37] hom with;
The tothyr was a tulke[38] out of Troy selfe—
Dares, þat duly the dedys behelde.
Aither breuyt[39] in a boke, on þere best wise,   65
That sithen at a sité somyn were founden—
After at Atthenes, as aunter befell;—
The whiche bokes barely,[40] bothe as þai were,
A Romayn ouerraght,[41] and right[42] hom hymseluyn,
That Cornelius was cald to his kynde name.   70
He translated it into Latyn, for likyng to here;
But he shope it so short þat no shalke might
Haue knowlage by course[43] how þe case felle;
For he brought it so breff, and so bare leuyt,[44]
Þat no lede might have likyng to loke þerappon,   75
Till þis Gydo it gate, as hym grace felle,
And declaret it more clere, and on clene wise.
In this shall faithfully be founden, to the fer ende,
All þe dedes bydene, as þai done were:
How þe groundes[45] first grew and þe grete hate;   80
Bothe of torfer[46] and tene þat hom tide aftur.
And here fynde shall ye faire of þe felle peopull:
What kynges þere come of costes[47] aboute;
Of dukes full doughty and of derffe[47a] erles
That assemblid to þe citie þat sawte to defend;[48]   85
Of þe Grekys þat were gedret, how gret was þe nowmber—
How mony knightes þere come, and kynges enarmed;[49]
And what dukes thedur droghe for dedis of were;
What shippes þere were shene and shalkes within,
Bothe of barges and buernes[50] þat broght were fro Grese;   90

---

[36] belonged. [37] lodged, stayed. [38] warrior. [39] wrote. [40] entirely. [41] recovered.
[42] corrected. [43] duly. [44] left it so bare. [45] causes. [46] injury. [47] regions.
[47a] fierce. [48] repulse. [49] under arms. [50] warriors.

59. The book of Dictys was said to have been written in Phoenician characters; but it survives only in a Latin abridgment of the fourth century A.D. Dares' book is also preserved only in a Latin summary, declared to be by Cornelius Nepos, but actually by a later writer.

And all the batels on bent, þe buernes betwene—
What duke þat was dede throughe dyntes of hond;
Who falin was in ffylde, and how it fore after;
Bothe of truse and of trayne[1] þe truthe shall þou here,   95
And all the ferlies þat fell, vnto the ferre ende.[2]
Fro this prologe i passe, and part me þerwith:
Frayne will i fer, and fraist[3] of þere werkes:
Meue[4] to my mater, and make here an ende.

EXPLICIT PROLOGUS

The Taking of Tenedos

The island of Tenedos was one of the outposts of Troy, and was taken
by the Greeks before they attacked the city.

Þai past fro þat port with pillage þai hade
And turnyt vnto Tenydon, taryt no lengur.   4700
Þere arof[5] all the rowte with þere ranke[6] shippes;
Cast ancres with cables þat kene were of byt;[7]
Lete sailes doune slide; slippit into botis;
Festnet with fuerse[8] ropis the flete in þe hauyn,
And buskit vnto banke, the boldist ay first.   4705
At this Tenydoun truly was a tried[9] castell,
Wele wroght for the werre, with walles full stronge,
Evyn[10] fild full of folke, fuerse men and noble,
And riches full rife; rank[11] men within;
Wele viteld,[12] iwisse, for winturs ynoghe.   4710
Hit was sothely but sex myle fro the cité euyn,
As i told haue tomly[13] in a tale here before.
The folke in þat fuerse hold[14] were ferde of hom selfe;[15]
Arait hom full radly, right to the werre;

---

[1] truce and treachery.   [2] to the very last.   [3] make trial.   [4] proceed.   [5] arrived.
[6] proud.   [7] holding power, grip.   [8] strong.   [9] strong.   [10] quite.   [11] powerful.
[12] provisioned.   [13] at length.   [14] castle.   [15] feared for their lives.

4699. For information about the tactics, cf. Charles Oman, "A History of the Art of War in the Middle Ages," especially VI.vii.3.
4704. The ships were tied together, instead of being separately berthed, for security against storms and attacks.

In defense[16] of hor fos, þat on flete[17] lay,   4715
Wenton out wightly wale[18] men of armys,
And bateld hom on the banke, as hom best thught.
When the Grekes were gethurt and to ground comen,
Mony fightyng folke in a fuerse nowmbur,
The pepull with hor power put[19] hom agayne,   4720
And foght with hom felly, þof þai few were.
Bold was þat biker[20] opon bothe haluys:[21]
Mony deid bydene of the derfe[22] Grekes,
And Troiens with tene tynt[23] of hor pepull,
But not so fele at þe first as of the ferre side.[24]   4725
The Grekes full greatly greuyt þerat,
Oppresset hom with payne and preset þere faster,
Fought full felly, and fele were þere slayne.
Of the Troiens þat tyme tynt were þe mo;
The fresshe[25] was so felle of the furse Grekes,   4730
And the nowmber so noyous[26] þat neghed in hast,
That the Frigies[27] floghen, and the fild leuyt:
Turnyt vnto Troy, and the toune entrid.
And þo at fore[28] not to flight ne of forse[29] were,
The Grekes gird[30] hom to gro[u]nd with hor grym swerdes,   4735
And brittenit[31] on the bent þat abide wold;
Comyn to the castell, vnclosit[32] it aboute,
Foghten with the folke þat defens made;
Shottyn[33] vp sharply at the shene wallis
With glayues and gonnes;[34] girdyn doun toures;   4740
Dryuen vp dartes, gyffen depe woundes.
With alblasters also, amyt[35] full streght,
Whappet in wharels, whellit[36] of the pepull;
With speris full dispitiously spurnit[37] at the yates;
Dongen on dernly,[38] with mony dede-hurttes   4745
In diffens[39] of þe folke þat affroi[40] made.

---

[16] to repel.   [17] afloat.   [18] picked.   [19] with all their might thrust them back.
[20] struggle.   [21] sides.   [22] fierce.   [23] lost.   [24] i.e., their opponents.   [25] ferocity.
[26] grievous.   [27] Phrygians, Trojans.   [28] those who took.   [29] strong.   [30] struck.
[31] butchered.   [32] encircled.   [33] cast.   [34] spears and missiles.   [35] cross-bows
aimed.   [36] shot in bolts, killed.   [37] violently beat.   [38] struck angrily.   [39] attacking.   [40] resistance.

4728. MS. *were þere þai slayne.*
4740. MS. *gomes.*

But the wallis thé were, for all the wo yet,[41]
And fele of hor fos fellyn without.
Þen gone furthe the Grekes, graithet engynes,
Batold[42] hom all abrode vmbe[43] the bare walles,   4750
Layn ladders alenght,[44] and oloft wonnen.
At yche cornell[45] of þe castell was crusshyng of weppon;
Fell was the feght þo fuerse men amonge:
Mony Greke in þere gremþ gird[46] on the hed,
Till þai lept of the ladder, light in the dyke,   4755
The brayne out-brast, and the brethe leuyt;
And mony dongen[47] to dethe with dynttes of hond.
The Troiens full tit were terghit[48] for fight:
Wondit and weré, þat þai were noght;[49]
And the Grekes in so grete nowmber gedrit hom till,   4760
Wonyn on the wallis wightly with ladders,
At wyndous on yche wiss[50] a wondurfull nombur.
The grete toures þai toke, tiruyt[1] the pepull:
Was no lede opon lyfe þat alofte stode.
Thé chefe[2] into chambers and oþer chere[3] hallis,   4765
And yche freke þat þai found, felly þai slogh,
Old men and other, with ournyng[4] to dethe,
Tyll no lede of þat lynage[5] vpon lyfe was.
All the caves[6] in the castell clenly þai sought,
Robbit the riches and the rife goodes,   4770
Prayet and piket þat[7] proffet was in,
And wonnyn[8] it wightly þe wallis withoute,
Till all was bare as a bast, to þe bigge woghes ![9]
Mynours than mightely the moldes[10] did serche;

---

[41] protect, despite all their misfortune.   [42] drew up.   [43] about.   [44] end to end.
[45] battlement.   [46] fury (were) struck.   [47] beaten.   [48] exhausted.   [49] so that they
had no strength.   [50] staircase.   [1] threw over.   [2] make their way.   [3] fine.
[4] running down (like beasts of the chase).   [5] race.   [6] vaults.   [7] plundered and
looted whatever.   [8] took.   [9] wand, to the strong walls.   [10] earthworks.

4755. Castles were usually set on mounds, formed by heaping up earth;
the resulting excavation around the mound was called the ditch, or moat,
and was a part of the defenses.
4766. The Greeks are always represented as butchers by Guido. They
succeed only because of overwhelming numbers (cf. 4758), not superior
valor.

Ouertyrnet the toures and the tor[11] walles; 4775
All dusshet[12] into the diche, doll to beholde;
Betyn doun the buyldynges and brent[13] into erthe
Tyll the place was playne[14] and out of plite broght[15]
And hegh Tenydon with tourys tyrnyt all vnder.
When þai hade wasted the won and wonen the gre, 4780
All the tresour thay toke and turnyt to ship.
This fight is the first, and firre vs behouus.[16]

The Death of Hector

Though his wife has dreamed that he will die and his father has therefore kept him from the battle, Hector cannot restrain himself when one
of his brothers is killed by the Greeks.

Ector, wode of his wit for woo of his brother,
Haspit[17] on his helme and his horse toke,
Went out wightly, vnwetyng[18] his fader.
Two dukes full derne he to dethe broght, 8595
And manly with mayn mellit[19] with other;
Kyld[20] downe knightes, karve hom in sondur.
Mony wondet the weghe and to woo caste,[21]
Britnet hom on bent, and on bake[22] put.
The Grekes for his greffe girdyn[23] hym fro: 8600
Thay knew hym full kyndly be caupe[24] of his sword.
Then the Troiens full tyte to the towne floghen,
Issuet out egurly Ector to helpe,
Gird evyn to the Grekes, and hor ground toke;[25]
Foghten full felly, and hor fos harmyt. 8605
Polidamas the pert[26] was presset so fast
Þat he was wonen in wer, and away led.
Than Ector in yre egerly faght,
And the Grekes in his grem gird[27] he to dethe—

---

[11] strong. [12] dashed. [13] burnt to the ground. [14] levelled. [15] i.e., rendered
harmless. [16] it behooves us to proceed further. [17] fastened. [18] without the
knowledge of. [19] and manfully with might contended. [20] struck. [21] made sorrowful. [22] i.e., overthrew. [23] because of the harm he did, fled. [24] blow.
[25] took up a position. [26] brave. [27] rage struck.

4775. Undermining walls was the easiest way of destroying them. The
miners removed the earth at key-points, and the walls fell of themselves.
8606. Polydamas was the son of the Trojan prince Antenor.

Two hundreth in hast, þat the hend led[28]— 8610
And deliuert the lede with his lyfe hole!
This a grete[29] of the Grekes graidly[30] beheld,
Had meruell full mekyll, macchet hym to Ector:
Liochydes the large, so þe lord hight;
He wend the prinse in the prese haue put out of lyue. 8615
Ector wrathit hym with,[31] and the wegh hit
þat he deghit of the dynt er he doun fell.
Achilles this chaunse choisly[32] beheld,
þat so mony of þaire men were marrid by hym;[33]
He hopit but if happely þat hardy were slayne, 8620
þat neuer Greke shuld haue grace the ground for to wyn,
Ne neuer Troye for to take, terme of hor lyue.[34]
He bethoght hym full thicke,[35] in his thro[36] hert,
And all soteltie soght, serchit his wit
On all wise in this world þat werke for to end, 8625
And the prinse with his power put vnto dethe.
As he stode þus in stid, starit hym vpon,
Policenes—a pert duke þat in prese rode,
þat was chere[37] to Achilles, cherisit with loue,
And thidur soght for his sake his sistur to haue; 8630
A mon he was of More Ynde, mighty of godes,—
þere hit auntrid full euyn þat Ector hym met,
And the lede with a launse out of lyue broght.
Achilles the chaunse cheuit[38] for to se,
Vne[39] wode of his wit, walt[40] into angur: 8635
The dethe of þat duke he dight hym to veng.
To Ector full egurly he etlit[41] anon;
Ector keppit[42] the kyng er he caupe[43] might,

---

[28] who led Polydamas (as captive). [29] great (hero). [30] completely; i.e., saw it all. [31] raged against him. [32] especially. [33] Hector. [34] during their lives. [35] hard. [36] fierce. [37] dear. [38] managed; happened. [39] even, quite. [40] burst. [41] rushed. [42] struck. [43] give a blow.

8610. For such feats in battle see "Havelok" 1919.

8628. The sentence is never completed; the following four lines are in apposition with *hym* (8632).

8631. Greater India was the eastern part, around the Bay of Bengal; Lesser India was along the western coast.

8638-9. Most of the principal warriors are described as kings by Guido, and hence have some right to the title; but the poet also calls them princes, dukes, lords, barons, or men, if these words suit the alliteration.

Drof at hym with a dart, and þe duke hit.
Hit was keruond[44] and kene, and the kyng hurt,   8640
And woundit hym wickedly thurght the waist euyn,
þat he sesit of his sute;[45] soght he no ferre!

The Dethe of Ector, By Achilles Traturly Slayn

Achilles for the chop cherit[46] hym not litle:
Braid out of batell, bound vp his wounde,
Stoppet the stremys stithly[47] agayne,   8645
Lep vp full lyuely, launchit on swithe,
To þat entent truly, as the trety[48] sais,
To deire Ector with dethe or degh þere hymseluyn.
As Ector faght in the fild fell[49] of þe Grekes,
He caupit[50] with a kyng, caght hym anon,   8650
Puld[1] hym as a prisoner of prise for to wyn
With strenght thurgh the stoure, as the story tellus.
His sheld on his shulders shot[2] was behynd
And his brest left bare: so the buerne rode
To weld hym more winly[3] þat worthy to lede.   8655
Achilles grippit a gret speire with a grym wille;
Vnpersayuit of the prince, prikit hym to;
Woundit hym wickedly as he away loked,
Thurgh the body with the bit of the bright end,[4]
That he gird to þe ground and the gost yald.   8660
This Sedymon segh, þat soght out of Troy;
Evyn wode for þat worthy was of lyue done,
He cheuet[5] to Achilles with a chop felle,
þat he braid to þe bent with a brem[6] wound,
And for ded of þat dynt the duke þere hym leuit.   8665

---

[44] penetrating.   [45] ceased in his pursuit.   [46] blow altered his course.   [47] strongly.
[48] book, history.   [49] encountered . . . many.   [50] engaged.   [1] drew, led away.
[2] slung.   [3] manage more readily.   [4] cutting edge of the bright point.   [5] reached.
[6] terrible.

8643. Heading—The text is full of such headings, which also appeared in the Latin MSS. (See George Neilson's "Huchowne of the Awle Riale" 25 and *Speculum* II.114.n.9.)

8651. Prisoners were desired because large ransoms could be exacted for their return.

The Myrmaidons,[7] his men, þaire maistur can take,
Bere hym on his brade sheld to his big tent,
There left hym as lyueles, laid hym besyde;[8]
But yet deghit not the duke, þof hym dere tholet.[9]
Then the Troiens with tene turnyt them backe,   8670
Soghten to þe citie with sorow in hert,
Entrid al samyn, angardly[10] fast,
And the body of the bold prinse broghtyn hom with.

---

[7] Myrmidons.   [8] to one side.   [9] suffered great injury.   [10] very.

8673. The scene in which Priam begs his son's body of Achilles is not in Guido's version.

MISCELLANEOUS

FLORIS AND BLANCHEFLOUR

The romance has the two peculiarities of having been current in English at an early date (c. 1250) and of dealing well with sentiment, a merit not common in early romances. On the history of the legend, see Hibbard 184 ff. For a complete introduction, see A. B. Taylor's edition (Oxford, 1927).

The text given here is that of the Trentham Manuscript (now Egerton 2862), which is reproduced from rotographs taken and used with the kind permission of the officials of the Department of Manuscripts of the British Museum. Though not the earliest or best text, this is nearly complete, and is hence most suitable for literary study.

The dialect is that of the east midlands; but late and northern forms have been freely substituted. The scribe seems not to have been familiar with the use of final -e in the earlier dialects, and ends many words with a flourish that might be expanded into -e; but in transcribing, this has usually been disregarded after final -n or -m, and expanded after -d. In other occurrences, it has been invariably disregarded.

The numbering is as in McKnight's edition for the Early English Text Society, and the work of Hausknecht and Taylor has also been consulted; but only the more ingenious emendations and conjectures have been carefully credited. References to the French are to Du Meril's edition, usually to his first text.

The beginning of the story is lost in all the English manuscripts; from the French, it may be summarized as follows: A Christian woman of high rank, taken by a heathen king during a raid, bears a daughter at the same time that the queen, her mistress, gives birth to a son. In honor of the feast of Pasque-florie (Palm Sunday), they are named Florie and Blanceflor. They are brought up together, the Christian mother being nurse to both.

Heading. The MS. has *Fflorence and Blanchefloure.*

Ne thurst[1] men neuer in londe
After feirer children fonde.
þe Cristen woman fedde hem þoo;
Ful wel she louyd hem boþ twoo.
So longe she fedde hem in feere   5
þat þey were of elde of seuen ȝere.
þe Kyng behelde his sone dere,
And seyde to him on this manere:
þat harme it were muche more
But his son were sette to lore   10
On þe book letters to know,
As men don, both hye and lowe.
"Feire sone," she seide, "þou shalt lerne;
Lo, þat þou do ful ȝerne!"
Florys answerd with wepyng,   15
As he stood byfore þe Kyng;
Al wepyng seide he,
"Ne schal not Blancheflour lerne with me?
Ne can y noȝt to scole goon
Without Blaunchefloure," he seide þan,   20
"Ne can y in no scole syng ne rede
Without Blaunchefloure," he seide.
þe King seide to his soon,
"She shal lerne, for þy loue."
To scole þey were put;   25
Boþ þey were good of wytte.
Wonder it was of hur lore,
And of her loue wel þe more.[2]
þe children louyd togeder soo
þey myȝt neuer parte a twoo.   30
When þey had v ȝere to scoole goon,
So wel þey had lerned þoo,
Inowȝ þey couþ of Latyne,
And wel wryte on parchemyne.[3]
þe Kyng vnderstod þe grete amoure[4]   35
Bytwene his son and Blanchefloure,

---

[1] need.   [2] i.e., the greater wonder.   [3] parchment.   [4] love.

3. In the French, the Christian mother acts as nurse for both children.

And þou3t when þey were of age
þat her loue wolde no3t swage,[5]
Nor he my3t no3t her loue withdrawe
When Florys shuld wyfe[6] after þe lawe.   40
Þe King to þe Queene seide þoo
And tolde hur of his woo—
Of his þou3t and of his care
How it wolde of Floreys fare.
"Dame," he seide, "y tel þe my reed: 45
I wyl þat Blaunchefloure be do to deed.
When þat maide is yslawe
And brou3t of her lyf-dawe,[7]
As sone as Florys may it vnder3ete,[8]
Rathe he wylle hur for3ete.   50
Þan may he wyfe after reed."[9]
Þe Queene answerde þen and seid,
And þou3t with hur reed
Saue þe mayde fro þe deed.
"Sir," she seide, "we au3t to fonde   55
Þat Florens lyf with menske[10] in londe,
And þat he lese not his honour
For þe mayden Blauncheflour.
Who so my3t [reue] þat mayde clene,
Þat she were brou3t to deþ bydene,   60
Hit were muche more honour
Þan slee þat mayde Blancheflour."
Vnneþes þe King g[ra]unt þat it be soo:
"Dame, rede vs what is to doo."
"Sir, we shul oure soon Florys   65
Sende into þe londe of Mountargis;
Blythe wyl my suster be,
Þat is lady of þat contree;
And when she woot for whoom
Þat we have sent him vs froom,   70
She wyl doo al hur my3t,

---

[5] abate.   [6] marry.   [7] days of life, life.   [8] realize.   [9] i.e., advisedly.   [10] honor.

59. Hausknecht's emendation: in l. 289, *reve* is used to translate *tolir*, which also occurs here in the corresponding French passage.

Boþ by day and by ny3t,
To make hur loue so vndoo
As it had neuer ben soo.
And, sir," she seide, "y rede eke 75
Þat þe maydens moder make hur seeke.[11]
Þat may be þat other resoun
For þat ylke encheson,[12]
Þat she may not fro hur moder goo."
Now ben þese children swyþ woo, 80
Now þey may not goo in fere;
Drewryer[13] þinges neuer noon were.
Florys wept byfore þe Kyng
And seide, "Sir, without lesyng,
For my harme out 3e me sende, 85
Now she ne my3t with me wende;
Now we ne mot togeder goo,
Al my wele is turned to woo!"
Þe King seide to his soon aply3t,[14]
"Sone, withynne þis fourteny3t, 90
Be her moder quykke or deede,
Sekerly," he him seide,
"Þat mayde shal com þe too."
"3e, sir," he seid, "y pray 3ow it be soo.
3if þat 3e me hur sende, 95
I rekke neuer wheder y wende."
Þat þe child graunted, þe Kyng was fayn,
And him betau3t his chamburlayn.
With muche honoure þey þeder coom,
As fel to[15] a ryche kynges soon. 100
Wel feire him receyuyd þe Duke Orgas,
Þat king of þat castel was,
And his aunt wiþ muche honour;
But euer he þou3t on Blanchefloure.
Glad and blythe þey ben him withe; 105
But for no ioy þat he seith
Ne my3t him glade game ne gle,
For he my3t not his lyf[16] see.

---

[11] feign sickness. [12] cause. [13] sadder. [14] straightway. [15] befitted. [16] dear one.

His aunt set him to lore
Þere as other children wore,   110
Boþ maydons and grom;
To lerne mony þeder coom.
Inowȝ he sykes, but noȝt he lernes;
For Blauncheflour euer he mornes.
Yf eny man to him speke,   115
Loue is on his hert steke.[17]
Loue is at his hert roote,
Þat no þing is so soote:[18]
Galyngale[19] ne lycorys
Is not so soote as hur loue is,   120
Ne no thing ne non other.[20]
So much he þenkeþ on Blancheflour,
Of oo day him þynkeþ þre,
For he ne may his loue see;
Þus he abydeth with muche woo,   125
Tyl þe fourtenyȝt were goo.
When he saw she was nouȝt ycoome,
So muche sorow he haþ noome
Þat he loueth mete ne drynke,
Ne may noon in his body synke.[21]   130
Þe chamberleyn sent þe King to wete[22]
His sones state, al ywrete.
Þe King ful sone þe waxe to-brake
For to wete what it spake;
He begynneth to chaunge his moode,   135
And wel sone he vnderstode,
And with wreth he cleped þe Queene,
And tolde hur alle his teene,
And with wraþ spake and sayde,
"Let do bryng forþ þat mayde!   140
Fro þe body þe heued shal goo."
Þenne was þe Quene ful woo;
Þan spake þe Quene, þat good lady,

---

[17] fastened. [18] sweet. [19] a spice. [20] no other person. [21] consume. [22] advise of.

111. "Grom" is the masculine equivalent of "maiden"; i.e., an unmarried youth.

"For Goddes love, sir, mercy!
At þe next hauen þat here is,   145
Þer ben chapmen[23] ryche, ywys,
Marchaundes of Babyloyn ful ryche,
Þat wol hur bye blethelyche.
Than may ȝe for þat louely foode[24]
Haue muche catell[25] and goode;   150
And soo she may fro vs be brouȝt
Soo þat we slee hur nouȝt."
Vnneþes[26] þe King graunted þis,
But forsoth, so it is.
Þe King let sende after þe burgeise,   155
Þat was hende and curtayse,
And welle selle and bygge couth,
And moony langages had in his mouth.
Wel sone þat mayde was him betauȝt,
An to þe hauen was she brouȝt;   160
Ther haue þey for þat maide ȝolde[27]
xx mark of reed golde,
And a coupe good and ryche;
In al þe world was non it lyche.
Þer was neuer noon so wel graue;[28]   165
He þat it made was no knave.
Þer was purtrayd on, y weene,
How Paryse ledde awey þe Queene;
And on þe couercle[29] aboue
Purtrayde was þer bother[30] love;   170
And in þe pomel[31] þeron
Stood a charbuncle stoon:
In þe worlde was not so depe soler[32]
Þat it nolde lyȝt þe botelere
To fylle boþ ale and wyne;   175
Of syluer and golde boþ good and fyne.
Enneas þe King, þat nobel man,

---

[23] merchants. [24] maid. [25] chattels. [26] not readily. [27] given. [28] engraved, decorated. [29] lid. [30] of them both. [31] knob on the lid. [32] cellar.

147. Babyloyn is Old Cairo in Egypt.—Taylor.
170. MS. *per both her*.
176. A condensation of several lines of description in the French.

At Troye in batayle he it wan,
And brouȝt it into Lumbardy,
And gaf it his lemman, his amy.   180
Þe coupe was stoole fro King Cesar;
A þeef out of his tresour-hous it bar;
And sethe þat ilke same þeef
For Blaunchefloure he it ȝeef;
For he wyst to wynne suche þree,[33]   185
Myȝt he hur bryng to his contree.
Now þese marchaundes saylen ouer þe see
With þis mayde, to her contree.
So longe þey han vndernome[34]
Þat to Babyloyn þey ben coom.   190
To þe Amyral of Babyloyne
Þey solde þat mayde swythe soone;
Rath and soone þey were at oon:
Þe Amyral hur bouȝt anoon,
And gafe for hur, as she stood vpryȝt,   195
Seuyn sythes of golde her wyȝt,[35]
For he þouȝt without weene
Þat faire mayde haue to Queene;
Among his maydons in his bour
He hur dide, with muche honour.   200
Now þese merchaundes þat may belete,[36]
And ben glad of hur byȝete.[37]
    Now let we of Blancheflour be,
And speke of Florys in his contree.
Now is þe bu[r]gays to þe King coom   205
With þe golde and his garyson,[38]
And haþ take þe King to wolde[38a]
Þe seluer and þe coupe of golde.
They lete make in a chirche
A swithe feire graue wyrche,[39]   210
And lete ley þervppon

---

[33] three as good.   [34] persisted.   [35] weight.   [36] abandoned the maid.   [37] their profit from her.   [38] payment.   [38a] in keeping.   [39] made a fine tomb.

180. *Amy*, beloved. She was Lavinia, daughter of Latinus.—Taylor.
210. MS. *as swithe.*

A new feire peynted ston,
With letters al aboute wryte
With ful muche worshippe.
Whoso couth þe letters rede,   215
Þus þey spoken and þus þey seide:
"Here lyth swete Blaunchefloure,
þat Florys louyd par amoure."
Now Florys haþ vndernome,[40]
And to his ffader he is coome: 220
In his ffader halle he is lyȝt.
His ffader him grette anoon ryȝt,
And his moder, þe Queene also,
But vnneþes myȝt he þat doo[41]
Þat he ne asked where his lemman bee;   225
Nonskyns[42] answere chargeþ[43] hee.
So longe he is forth noome,[44]
In to chamber he is coome.
Þe maydenys moder he asked ryȝt,
"Where is Blaunchefloure, my swete wyȝt?"   230
"Sir," she seide, "forsothe ywys,
I ne woot where she is."
She beþouȝt hur on þat lesyng
Þat was ordeyned byfoore þe King.
"Þou gabbest[45] me," he seyde þoo;   235
"Þy gabbyng doþ me muche woo!
Tel me where my leman be!"
Al wepyng seide þenne shee,
"Sir," shee seide, "deede." "Deed!" seide he.
"Sir," sche seide, "for sothe, ȝee."   240
"Allas, when died þat swete wyȝt?"
"Sir, withynne þis ffourtenyȝt
þe erth was leide hur aboute,

---

[40] journeyed. [41] scarcely might he perform that act without, etc. [42] no sort
of answer. [43] awaits. [44] made his way. [45] mock.

226. *Chargeþ* is a result of confusion for the French: *Il* (his parents)
se tardent de respons rendre. The Cotton MS. has *targeþ*, and the rest of
the context is more like the French. The idiom "charge to answer,"
demand an answer, may have been intended.
243. The rhyme requires *hur above.*

And deed she was for thy loue."
Flores, þat was so feire and gent,   245
Sownyd þere, verament.
Þe Cristen woman began to crye
To Ihesu Crist and Seynt Marye.
Þe King and þe Queene herde þat crye;
Into þe chamber þey ronne on hye,   250
And þe Queene seȝe her byforne[46]
On sowne þe childe þat she had borne.
Þe Kinges hert was al in care,
Þat sawe his son for loue so fare.
When he awooke and speke moȝt,   255
Sore he wept and sore he syȝt,
And seide to his moder ywys,
"Lede me þere þat mayde is."
Þeder þey him brouȝt on hyȝe;
For care and sorow he wolde dyȝe.   260
As sone as he to þe graue com,
Sone þere behelde he þen
And þe letters began to rede,
Þat þus spake and þus seide:
"Here lyth swete Blauncheflour,   265
Þat Florys louyd par amoure."
Þre sithes Florys sownydde nouth,[47]
Ne speke he myȝt not with mouth.
As sone as he awoke and speke myȝt,
Sore he wept and sore he syȝt.   270
"Blauncheflour!" he seide, "Blauncheflour!
So swete a þing was neuer in boure!
Of Blauncheflour is þat y meene,[48]
For she was com of good kyn.
Lytel and muche loueden þe   275
For þy goodnesse and þy beauté.
Ȝif deþ were dalt aryȝt,
We shuld be deed boþ on oo nyȝt.
On oo day born we were;

---

[46] saw that before her her own child was swooning, etc.   [47] now.   [48] bemoan.

251. MS. *Queene herde her. Herde* is carelessly repeated from l. 249.

We shul be ded boþ in feere. 280
Deeþ," he seide, "ful of enuye
And of alle trechorye,
Refte þou hast me my lemman;
For soth," he seide, "þou art to blame.
She wolde haue leuyd, and þou noldest, 285
And fayne wolde y dye, and[49] þou woldest.
After deeþ clepe no more y nylle,
But slee my selfe now y wille."
His knyfe he braide[50] out of his sheth;
Himself he wolde haue doo to deth 290
And to hert he had it smeten,
Ne had his moder it vnderȝeten;
Þen þe Queene fel him vppon,
And þe knyfe fro him noom:
She reft him of his lytel knyf, 295
And sauyd þere þe childes lyf.
Forþ þe Queene ranne, al wepyng,
Tyl she come to þe Kyng.
Þan seide þe good lady,
"For Goddes loue, sir, mercy! 300
Of xii children haue we noon
On lyue now but þis oon;
And better it were she were his make[1]
Þan he were deed for hur sake."
"Dame, þou seist soþ," seide he; 305
"Sen it may noon other be,
Leuer me were she were his wyf
Þan y lost my sonnes lyf."
Of þis word þe Quene was fayne,
And to her soon she ran agayne. 310
"Floryes, soon, glad make the:
Þy lef þou schalt on lyue see.
Florys, son, þrouȝ engynne[2]
Of þy ffaders reed and myne,
Þis graue let we make, 315
Leue sone, for þy sake.

---

[49] if. [50] plucked. [1] mate. [2] device.

ʒif þou þat maide forgete woldest,
After oure reed wyf þou sholdest."
Now euery worde she haþ him tolde
How þat þey þat mayden solde.   320
"Is þis soth, my moder dere?"
"For soth," she seide, "she is not here."
Þe rowʒ³ stoon adoun þey leyde
And sawe þat [þere] was not þe mayde.
"Now, moder, y þink þat y leue may.   325
Ne shal y rest nyʒt ne day—
Nyʒt ne day ne no stounde—
Tyl y haue my lemmon founde.
Hur to seken y woll wende,
Þauʒ it were to þe worldes ende !"   330
To þe King he goþ to take his leue,
And his ffader bade him byleue.⁴
"Sir, y wyl let for no wynne;⁵
Me to bydden it it were grete synne."
Þan seid þe King, "Seth it is soo,   335
Seþ þou wylt noon other doo,
Al þat þe nedeþ we shul þe fynde.
Ihesu þe of care vnbynde !"
"Leue ffader," he seide, "y telle þe
Al þat þou shalt fynde me: 340
Þou mast me fynde, at my deuyse,⁶
Seuen horses al of prys;
And twoo ycharged⁷ vppon þe molde⁸
Boþ with seluer and wyþ golde;
And twoo ycharged with moonay   345
For to spenden by þe way;
And þree with clothes ryche,
Þe best of al þe kyngryche;⁹
Seuen horses and seuyn men,
And þre knaues without hem;¹⁰   350
And þyne owne chamburlayne,
Þat is a wel nobel swayne:¹¹

---

³ rough.   ⁴ remain.   ⁵ pleasure.   ⁶ disposal.   ⁷ loaded.   ⁸ ground (a tag).
⁹ realm.   ¹⁰ in addition.   ¹¹ fellow.

He can vs both wyssh[12] and reede,
As marchaundes we shull vs lede."
His ffader was an hynde king;   355
Þe coupe of golde he dide him bryng,
Þat ilke selfe coupe of golde
Þat was Blauncheflour for ȝolde.[13]
"Haue þis, soon," seide þe King,
"Herewith þou may þat swete þing   360
Wynne, so may betyde[14]—
Blauncheflour with þe white syde,
Blauncheflour, þat faire may."
Þe King let sadel a palfray,
Þe oone half[15] so white so mylke,   365
And þat other reed so sylke.
I ne can telle nouȝt
How rychely þat sadel was wrouȝt.
Þe arson[16] was of golde fyn;
Stones of vertu[17] stode þeryne,   370
Bygon aboute wit orfreys.[18]
Þe Queene was kynde and curtays:
Cast hur toward þe Kyng,
And of hur fynger she brayde a ryng:
"Haue now þis ylke ryng: 375
While is it þyne, douȝt no þyng
Of fire brennyng ne water in þe see;
Ne yren ne steele shal dere thee."
He took his leue for to goo;
Þer was ful muche woo;   380
Þey made him noon other chere
Þan her soon were leide in bere.[19]
Furþ he went with al his mayne;[20]
With him went þe chamberlayne.
So haue þey her hauyn nome   385
Þat þey ben to þe hauyn come
Þere Blaunchefloure was al nyȝt.

---

[12] guide.   [13] given in payment for.   [14] as may befall.   [15] side.   [16] saddle-peak.
[17] worth.   [18] fringed with gold fringe.   [19] bier.   [20] might.

385. Probably *hauyn* is an error for *wey*.

Wel rychely þey ben dyȝt;
Þe lord of þe ynne was welle hende;
Þe childe he sette next þe ende   390
In al þe feirest seete.
Alle þey dronken and al þey ȝete:[21]
Ete ne drynke myȝt he nouȝt;
On Blaunchefloure was al his þouȝt.
Þe lady of þat vnderȝat[22]   395
Þat þe childe mornyng sat,
And seide to her lord with styl dreme,[23]
"Sir, nym now goode ȝeme[24]
How þe childe mournyng syttes:
Mete and drynke he forȝetes;   400
Lytel he eteþ, and lasse he drynkeþ;
He is no marchaund, as me þynkeþ."
To Flores þen seide she,
"Al ful of mournyng y the see.
Þer sate þer þis sender day[25]   405
Blauncheflour, þat swete may.
Heder was þat mayde brouȝt
With marchaundes þat hur had bouȝt;
Heder þey brouȝt þat mayde swete;
Þey wold haue solde hur for byȝete;[26]   410
To Babyloyn þey wylle hur bryng,
Boþ of semblant and of mornyng."
When Florys herd speke of his lemman,
Was he neuer so glad a man,
And in his hert bygan to lyȝt;[27]   415
Þe coupe he let fulle anoon ryȝt:
"Dame," he seide, "þe fessel[28] is þyne,
Boþ þe coupe and þe wyne—
Þe wyne and þe gold eke,

---

[21] ate.   [22] perceived.   [23] quiet voice.   [24] heed.   [25] recently.   [26] profit.   [27] grow lighter.   [28] vessel.

390. This table was not on a dais, but a single long one, the carver sitting at one end, and the seat of honor being at his right.
402. MS. *He is a.* The reading is from the Cambridge MS.
405. For *þis ender*, a recent.
412. For this line the Cambridge MS. has, *þou art hire ilich of alle þinge.*

For þou of my leman speke. 420
On hur y þou3t; for hur y sy3t;
I ne wyst where i hur fynde my3t.
Wynde ne weder shal me assoyne[29]
Þat y ne shal seche hur in Babyloyne."
Now Florys resteþ him al a ny3t. 425
At morn, when it was day ly3t,
He dide him into þe wylde floode.
Wynde and weder with him stoode;
Sone so Florys com to londe,
Þere he þanked Goddes sonde[30] 430
To þe londe þer his lyf ynne is:
Him þou3t he was in paradyse.
Sone to Florys tydyng men tolde
Þat þe Amyral wold ffest holde;
His erls, barons, comyn sholde, 435
And al þat wolde of him lond holde,
For to herkyn his hest,
And for to honoure his ffeest.
Glad was Florys of þat tydyng.
He hoped to com to þat gestnyng,[31] 440
3if he my3t in þat halle
His lemman see among hem alle.
    Now to þat citee Florys is come:
Feire he hath his ynne ynoome
At a palaise; was non it lyche; 445
Þe lord of þat ynne was fulle ryche;
He hadde ben ferre and wyde.
Þe childe he set next his syde
In al þe feirest seete.
Alle þey dronken and ete, 450
Al þat þerynne were:
Al þey made good chere;
Þey ete and dronke echoon with other;
But Florys þou3t al another:
Ete ne drynke he my3t no3t; 455
On Blauncheflour was al his þou3t.

---

[29] provide excuse.   [30] sending (him).   [31] entertainment.

þan spake þe burgays,
þat was hende and curtays:
"Ow,[32] child, me þynkeþ welle
þat muche þou þynkest on my catelle."   460
"Nay, sir, on catel þenke y nouȝt"
(On Blauncheflour was al his þouȝt),
"But y þynke on al wyse
For to fynde my marchaundise;
And ȝit it is þe most woo,   465
When y it fynd, y shal it forgoo."
þan spak þe lord of þat ynne,
"Þis sender day, þer sate hereyn
þat faire maide Blauncheflour,
Boþ in halle and in boure.   470
Euer she made mornyng chere,
And bement[33] Florys, her lyf fere;
Ioye ne blis made she noon,
But for Florys she made her moon."
Florys toke a coupe of syluer clere,   475
A mantyl of scarlet with menyuere:[34]
"Haue þis, sir, to þyn honour:
þou may þonke it Blauncheflour.
He myȝt make myn hert glade
þat couþ me tel wheder she is ladde."   480
"Child, to Babyloyn she is brouȝt;
þe Amyral hur haþ bouȝt:
He gafe for hur, as she stood vpryȝt,
Seuen sithes of gold hur wyȝt;
For he þenkeþ, without weene,   485
þat feire may haue to Queene.
Among his maydons in his toure
He hur dide, with muche honoure."
Now Flores resteþ him þere al nyȝt,
Tyl on þe morow þe day was lyȝt;   490

---

[32] oh. [33] bemoaned. [34] fur.

461. Such riddling replies were common in romances. Cf. "Horn,"
"Havelok," "Beryn."
477. MS. *Houe.*

He roos on þe morownyng.
He gaf his ost an hundryd shelyng,
To his ost and to his ostesse,
And toke his leue, and feire dide kysse;
And ȝerne his ost he besouȝt,   495
Þat he him help, ȝif he myȝt ouȝt[35]—
Ȝif he myȝt, with any gynne,[36]
Þat feire may to him wynne.
"Childe," he seide, "to a brygge[37] þou shalt com;
The senpere fynde at hoom: 500
He woneth at þe brygges ende;
Curtays man he is, and hende;
We arn bretheren, and trouthes plyȝt:
He can þe wyssh[38] and rede aryȝt.
Þou shalt bere him a rynge   505
Fro myself, to tokenynge,
Þat he help þe in boure and halle
As it were my self befalle."
Florys takeþ þe rynge and nemeþ leue,
For longe wolde he nouȝt beleue.[39]   510
By þat it was vndern hyȝe,
Þe brygge com he swyth nye.
Þe senperes name was Darys:
Florys gret him wel feire, ywys,
And he him þe rynge arauȝt,[40]   515
And ful feire it him betauȝt.
Þrowȝ þe token of þat ilk ryng
Florys had ful faire gestnyng[41]
Off ffyssh and flessh and tender breede,
Of wyn, both white and reede: 520
And euer Florys sate ful colde,
And Dares bygan þe childe beholde:
"Leue child, what may þis be,
Þus þouȝtful, as y the see?

[35] could in any way. [36] trick. [37] bridge. [38] direct. [39] tarry. [40] handed over.
[41] entertainment.

500. *Senpere* translates *pontonnier* and *portier* in the French. But other English translations show that their French source had *burgeis;* and this may account for the peculiar *senpere*, man of good rank.

Art þou nouȝt al in feere,[42]   525
Þat þou makist þus sory chere,
Or þou lykkest noȝt þis yn?"
Þan Floreys answerd him:
"ȝis, sir, by Goddes ore,
So good ne had y mony day ȝore;   530
God let me abyde þat daye
Þat y þe quyte wel may!
But y þenke on al wyse
Most vppon my marchaundyse;
And ȝit it is most woo,   535
When y hit ffynde, y shal it forgoo."
"Childe, woldest þou telle me þy gryf,[43]
To hele[44] þe, me were ful lyf."
Euery word he haþ him tolde—
How þe mayde was fro him solde,   540
And how he was of Spayn a kynges son,
For grete loue þeder ycome
To fonde, with quayntyse and with gyn,[45]
Blauncheflour for to wynne.
"Now," seith Dares, "þou art a ffolt"[46]—   545
And ffor a ffoole þe childe he halt—;
"Now y woot how it gooth:
Þou desirest þyn own deeth.
Þe Amyral haþ to his iustinges[47]
Oþer[48] half hundred of ryche kinges;   550
And þe alder-rychest king
Durst not begynne suche a þing.
ȝif Amyral myȝt it vnderstonde,
He shulde be drawe in his owne londe.
About Babyloyn, y wene,   555
Six longe myle and tene;
At euery myle is a walle þerate,

---

[42] well.   [43] grief.   [44] heal.   [45] slyness and trickery.   [46] dunce.   [47] tournaments.
[48] half a hundred other.

543. MS. *quanytyse*.

555. The scribe has condensed without noting that this is a description
of the city: "it is six and ten long miles around the city."

557. The Cambridge MS. has, *Abute þe walle þer buþ ate Seue siþe
tuenti ȝates.* The passage is different in the French.

Seuen sithes twenty ȝate;[49]
And xx toures þer ben ynne,
Þat euery day chepyng[50] is ynne;   560
Euery day and nyȝt þrouȝout þe ȝere
Þe chepyng is ylyche plenere;[1]
And þauȝ al þe men þat ben bore
Had on hur lyf swore
To wynne þat maide feire and free,   565
Al shul þey die, so moot y the.
In þat bour, in mydward ryȝt,
Stondeþ a toure, y the plyȝt:[2]
An hundryd fathum it is hye;
Whosoo beholdeþ hit, fer or nere,   570
An hundred fathum it is yfere;
It is made without pere,[3]
Of lyme and of marbul stone;
In al þis world is suche noone.
Now is þe morter made so wele,   575
Ne may it breke iren ne steele.
Þe pomel[4] þat aboue is leide,
It is made with muche pride,
Þat man ne þar[4a] in þe tour berne
Nouther torche ne lanterne,   580
Suche a pomel was þer bygone:[5]
Hit shyned anyȝt so doþ þe soone.
Now arn in þat ilke toure
Twoo and fourty nobell boure;
Wel were þat ilke man   585
Þat myȝt woon in þat oon!
Ne durst him neuer more, ywys,
Couete after more blysse.
Naw arn þer seriauntes in þat stage[6]
Þat seruen þe maydons of hyȝe parage:[7]   590

---

[49] gates. [50] trading. [1] in full progress. [2] assure. [3] equal. [4] ornamental globe
on top. [4a] need. [5] set. [6] set of apartments. [7] lineage.

561. MS. þrouȝtout.
570. The rhyme requires nye for nere.
580. MS. torthee.

But no serieaunt may serue þerynne
þat bereþ in his breche þat gynne[8]
To serue hem day and nyȝt,
But he be as a capoun[9] dyȝt.
At þe ȝate is a ȝatewarde;   595
He is not a cowarde:
He is wonder proude withalle;
Euery day he goþ in ryche palle.[10]
And þe Amyral haþ a wonder woon,
þat he þat is com of Cristendom,   600
Euery ȝere to haue a new wyf;
þen he louiþ his Queene as his lyf.
Then shul men bryng doun of þe toure
Al þe maidens of grete honoure,
And bryng hem into an orcharde,   605
þe feirest of al mydlerde:[11]
þeryn is mony fowles song;
Men myȝt leue þeryn ful long.
About þe orchard is a walle;
þe fowlest stone is cristall;   610
And a well spryngeþ þerynne
þat is made with muche gynne:
þe wel is of muche prys:
þe stremes com froo Paradyse;
þe grauel of þe ground is precious stoones.   615
And al of vertu[12] for þe noones.
Now is þe well of muche auȝt:[13]
Ȝif a woman com þat is forlauȝt
And she be doo to þe streeme
For to wesshe her honndes clene,   620
þe water wylle ȝelle as it were woode
And bycome red as bloode.
On what maide þe water fareþ soo,

---

[8] i.e., has manhood.   [9] eunuch.   [10] rich cloth.   [11] the earth.   [12] peculiar power.
[13] power.

600. Apparently interpolated without meaning. It is not in the French
or the other MSS.
618. *Forlauȝt* seems to be a bad form, made on the analogy of *auȝt* (in
other MSS. *eye*, fear), from *forleie*, unchaste.

Sone she shal to deþ be doo;
Þoo þat ben maidens clene,   625
Þey may wessh þeryn, y wene;
Þe water woll stonde feire and clere;
To hem makeþ it no daungere.[14]
At þe walles hed stondeþ a tree—
Þe feirest þat on erthe may be;   630
It is cleped þe Tree of Loue;
Floures and blossomes spryngen aboue.
Þen þey þat maydons clene bene,
Þei shul be brouȝt vnder þe trene,
And which so falleþ þe floure[15]   635
Shal be queene with muche honour.
Ȝif any mayden þer is
Þat þe Amyral telleþ of more pris,
Þe flour shal be to her sent
Þrouȝ art of enchauntement.   640
Þe Amyral cheseþ hem by þe flour,
And euer he herkeneþ after Blauncheflour."
Thre sithes Flores sownyd anoon
Riȝt byfore hem euerychoon.
When he awoke and speke myȝt,   645
Sore he wept and sore he syȝt,
And seide, "Dares, y worth now deede,
But þat y hope of þe som reede."
"Leue soon, wyl ȝe see
Þat þy trust is muche on me.   650
Þen is þe best reed þat y can—
Other reed ne can y noon—
Wende to-morn to þe toure
As þou were a good gynoure;[16]
Take on þy honde squyer and scantlon[17]   655
As þou were a freemason.

---

[14] resistance.   [15] the one upon whom, etc.   [16] craftsman.   [17] square and measure (mason's tools).

642. The French says, *Blanceflor dist qu'adont prendra* (1837). The English means, "He listens eagerly for the announcement that it will be Blancheflour."

649. "Dear son, well you see that," etc.; but ȝe should be i.

Behold þe tour vp and doun;
Þe porter is cruel and ffeloun;
Wel sone he wyl com to the
And aske what maner man þou be,   660
And bere[18] on þe ffelonye,
And sey þou art com to be a spye.
And þow shalt answere swetlyche,
And sey to him myldelyche;
Sey þou art a gynoure   665
To beholde þat feire toure,
For to loke and for to fonde
To make suche another in þy londe.
Wel sone he wyl com þe nere
And wyl byd þe pley at þe chekere.[19]   670
When þou art at cheker brouȝt,
Without seluer [be] þou nouȝt;
Þou shalt haue redy with the
xx marke beside þy knee.
Ȝif þou wynne ouȝt of his,   675
Þow tel þerof lytel prys;
And yf he wynne ouȝt of þyn,
Loke þow leue it with hym.
So þou shalt, al with gynne,[20]
Þe porters loue forsoth wynne,   680
Þat he þe help on þis day:
But he þe helpe, no man may.
Wel ȝerne he wyl þe bydde and pray
Com anoþer day to playe;
Þou shalt seye þou wylt soo;   685
Þou shalt take with þe suche twoo.
Þe þrydde day, take an hundred pound
And þy coupe hool and sound;
Ȝeue him markes and poundes of þy male;[21]
Of þy tresoure tel þou no tale.[22]   690
Wel ȝerne he wyl þe bydde and pray
To lay[23] þy coupe, and to play;

---

[18] impute.   [19] chess.   [20] a trick.   [21] wallet.   [22] keep no account.   [23] wager.

686. I.e., "twice as much money."

Þou shalt answere alþerfirst,[24]
Lenger to play þe ne lyst.
Ful muche he wylle for þe coupe bede,   695
Ȝif he myȝt þe better spede;[25]
Þou shalt it blethly ȝeue him,
Ȝif[26] it be of gold fyne;
And he wol ful muche loue þe,
And to þe bowe also, pardé,   700
Þat he wyl falle to þy foote
And becom þyn, ȝif he moote;
And homage þou shalt fonge,
And þe trouþ[27] of his honde."
As he seide, he dide ywys;   705
And as he ordeyned, so it is:
Þe porter ys Florys man bycom
For his gold and his warysone.[28]
Florys seide, "Now art þou my moon,[29]
Al my trust is þe vppon;   710
Now my consel y wyl þe shewe;
Rede me ryȝt, ȝif þou be trew."
Now euery word he haþ him tolde—
How þe mayde was fro him solde,
And how he was of Spayn a kynges soon,   715
For grete loue þeder ycoom
To fonden, with some gynne,
Þat feire mayde for to wynne.
Þe porter þat herde, and sore syȝt,
And seide, "Y am betrayde aryȝt;   720
Þrouȝ þy catel y am dismayde;
Þerfore y am wel euyl apayde.[30]
Now y woot how it gooþ;
For þe shal y suffer deth!
I shal þe faile neuermoo,   725
Þe while y may ryde and goo;

---

[24] at the very first.   [25] i.e., in the hope of succeeding better.   [26] though.
[27] pledge of faith.   [28] reward.   [29] companion, fellow.   [30] little pleased.

711. MS. *new.*
714. MS. *sholde.*

Þy fforwardes shal y holde alle,
Whatsoeuer may befalle.
Wynde now hoom to þyn ynne,
While y beþenke me of sum gynne; 730
Bytwene þis and þe þrydde day,
Fonde³¹ y shal what y do may."
Flores spake and wept among,³²
And þou3t þe terme al to long.
Þe porter þou3t þe best reed, 735
And let geder floures in a meede;
He wist it was þe maydons wylle.
To lepes³³ he lete of floures fylle:
Þat was þe best reed, as him þou3t þoo,
Floures in þat oon lep to doo. 740
Twoo maydens þe lepe bore;
So heuy charged³⁴ neuer þey wore,
And bade God 3eue hem euyl fyne³⁵—
To³⁶ mony floures he dide þerynne!
To Blaunchefloures chamber þey shulde tee;³⁷ 745
Þey 3ede to anoþer, and let þat be;
Þey shuld haue gon to Blaunchefflour,
And 3ede to swete Clarys boure,
And cursed him³⁸ so fele brou3t to honde;
Þey 3ede hoom, and lete hem stonde. 750
Clarys to þe lepe com wolde,
Þe flores to hondel and to beholde;
Florys wende it hadde be his swete wy3t;
Of þe lepe he stert vpry3t,
And þe mayde, al for drede, 755
Bygan to shrelle and to grede.³⁹
When he saw3 it was not shee,
Into þe lepe a3en stert he,
And held him betrayde clene;
Of his lyf tolde⁴⁰ he not a beene. 760
Þer com maydons, and to Clarys lepe
By ten, by twelf, on an heepe,⁴¹

---

³¹ try. ³² as well. ³³ baskets. ³⁴ loaded. ³⁵ an evil end. ³⁶ too. ³⁷ hasten.
³⁸ him who. ³⁹ shriek and cry. ⁴⁰ thought worth. ⁴¹ group, body.

And þey asked what hur were,[42]
And why she made suche a bere.[43]
Clarys byþouȝt hur anoon ryȝt   765
Þat hit was Blauncheflour þe white,
And gaue þe maydons answere anoon,
Þat to her chamber were goon,
Þat to þe lepe com she wolde,
Þe fflowres to hondel and to beholde;   770
"And or y it e[ue]re wyst,
A botterfleye [cam] ageynst my brest!
I was so soore adrad þan
Þat y loude crye can."
Þe maydons þerof hadden glee,   775
And turned hem and lete hur be.
As sone as þe maydons were gone,
To Blauncheflour she ȝede anoon,
And seide boldly to Blauncheflour,
"Felow, come and see a feire fflour!   780
Suche a flour þe shal wel lyke,
Haue þou it sene a lyte."
"Awey, Clarys!" quod Blauncheflour;
"To scorne me, it is none honoure.[44]
I here, Clarys, without gabbe,[45]   785
Þat þe Amyral wyl me to wyf habbe;
But þat day shal neuer be
Þat he shal euer haue me—
Þat y shal be of loue so vntrewe,
Ne chaunge my loue for no newe;   790
For no loue, ne for noon aye,[46]
Forsake Florys in his contraye.
Now[47] y shal swete Florys mysse,

---

[42] what was wrong with her.   [43] outcry.   [44] to mock me is a small distinc-
tion.   [45] mockery.   [46] fear.   [47] i.e., since.

765–6. A careless translation of the French: *Cele se fu rasseuree, Et de
Blanceflor porpensee; Ce fu ses amis, bien le sot. . . . Blauncheflour* is a
genitive; but the reading proposed by Taylor, *Blauncheflour swete wiȝt*,
is better than the text.
772. MS. *An otter fleyȝ.* The reading is conjectured from the other
MSS., which do not rhyme on the same words found here.

Ne shal noon other of me haue blysse."
Clarys stood and beheld þat rewth   795
And þe trewnesse of hur trewth,[48]
And seide, "Lady Blaunchefloure,
Goo we see þat ilke floure."
To þe lepe þey went both;
Ioyful man was Florys þoo,   800
For he had herde al þis.
Of þat lepe he stert ywys;
Wel sone Blauncheflour chaunged hewe;
Ayther of hem other knewe:
Withoute speche togeder þey lepe,   805
And klippt[49] and kyst wonder swete.
Clarys beheld al this,
Her countenaunce and her blysse,
And seide þen to Blaunchefloure,
"Felow, knowist þou auȝt þis flour?   810
She shul konne ful muche of art
Þat þou woldest þerof geue part."[50]
Now Blauncheflour and Florys,
Boþ þese swete þinges ywys,
Cryen her mercy, al wepyng,   815
Þat she ne wrey hem to þe King.
"Ne douȝt no more of me in alle
Þan it were myself byfalle:
Wete ȝe wel weturly,
Heele[51] y wyl ȝoure drury."[21]   820
To a bedde þey ben brouȝt
Þat is of palle and of sylke wrouȝt,
And þere þey sette hem doun
And drowȝ hemself al aroom:[22]
Þer was no man þat myȝt radde[23]   825
Þe ioye þat þey twoo madde.
Florys þen to speke bygan,
And seide, "Lord, þat madest man,

---

[48] trustworthiness of her pledged word.   [49] embraced.   [50] i.e., only a most artful woman could induce you to share him.   [51] conceal.   [21] love.   [22] aside.   [23] express.

799. MS. *lope*. The rhyme-word should be *bo*.

I it þonke Goddes Sone
Þat al my care i haue ouercome;   830
Now my leue i haue yfounde,
Of al my care y am vnbounde."
Clarys hem seruyd al at wylle,
Boþ dernlyche²⁴ and stylle.

Clarys with þe white syde   835
Rose vp on morne tyde,
And cleped after Blaunchefloure
To wende with her in to þe toure.
She²⁵ seide, "Y am commaunde;"²⁶
But her answere was slepaunde.²⁷   840
Þe Amyral had suche a woone
Þat euery day shulde com
Twoo maydons of hur bour
Vp to him in to þe toure
With water and clooth and basyn   845
For to wesshe his hondes ynne:
Þat day þey seruyd him feire;
Anoþer day com another peire;
But most were wonyd²⁸ into þe toure
Clarys and Blauncheflour.   850
Clarys come þenne aloon:
Þe Amyral asked anoon,
"Where is Blauncheflour so free?
Why comeþ she not heder with þe?"
"Sir," she seide anoon ryȝt,   855
"She haþ wakyd²⁹ al þis nyȝt,
And ycryde and yloke³⁰
And yredde on hur booke,
And ybede to God her orysone³¹
Þat He geue þe his benysone,   860
And þat He holde long þy lyf;
And now þe mayde slepeþ swyth;
She slepeþ so fast, þat mayde swete,

²⁴ secretly.   ²⁵ Blancheflour.   ²⁶ coming.   ²⁷ given sleepily.   ²⁸ used (to go).
²⁹ been awake.   ³⁰ gazed (in meditation).   ³¹ offered her prayer.

838. MS. *with him.*

þat she may not com ȝete."
"Certes," seide þe Kyng,   865
"Now is she a swete þing:
Wel auȝt me ȝerne[32] her to wyf
þat so preyeth for my lyf."
Anoþer day Clarys erly aryst,
þat Blauncheflour well wyst,   870
And seide, "Y com anoone,"
When Clarys her clepe bygan,
And fel in a slepe newe;
Sone after it made hem to rewe!
Clarys to þe pyler cam;   875
A basyn of gold in hond she nam,
And cleped after Blaunchefloure
To wende with hur into þe toure.
þe Amyral asked after Blaunchefloure,
"What! is she not com ȝet?   880
Now she me douteþ al t[o lyte."]
Forþ he cleped his chamburlayne
And bade him wende with his mayne
"To wete why she wyl not com
As she was wonyd to doon."   885
þe chamburlayn is forth noom;
In to chamber he is coom,
And stondeþ byfore hur bedde,
And fyndeþ þere, nebbe to nebbe,[33]
Nebbe to nebbe, and mouþ to mouþ.   890
To þe Amyral it was sone couþ;
Vp in to þe toure he steyȝ[34]
And told his lord al þat he seyȝ.
þe Amyral lete him his swerd bryng,
For wete[35] he wolde of þat tydyng.   895
He went to hem þere þey lay:
Ȝit was she aslepe þere ay.[36]

---

[32] desire. [33] face. [34] ascended. [35] learn the truth. [36] ever, still.

875. In a passage preserved in the French and other MSS., it is ex-
plained that the water supply of the castle is circulated through a pipe
of brass, here called a pillar.

The Amyral lete þe clothes doun cast
A lytel bynethe hur brest,
And sone he knew anoon   900
Þat oon was woman, and þat oþer groom.
He quaked for tene þere he stood;
Hem to sloon was in his moode;
Ʒit he þouʒt, or he hem quelde,
What þey were, þey shuld him telle,   905
And seth he wyl with dome hem done.[37]
Þe children wakyd swyth soone,
And saw þe swerde ouer hem drawe;
Þey ben adrad and in awʒe.
Þan seide Florys to Blauncheflour,   910
"Of oure lyf is no socour."
But þey cryde him mercy swyth,
For to length[38] her lyue.
Vp he bade hem sytte booth,
And do on boþ her cloþ;   915
Seþ he dide hem bynde fast
And in prison lete hem be cast.
Now haþ he after his barons sent,
To wreke him after iugement.[39]
Now han þe barons vndernome,[40]   920
And to þe Amyral þey ben coom.
He stood vp among hem al
With semblaunt wroþ withalle,
And seide, "Lordynges with much honour,
Ʒe herde speke of Blauncheflour: 925
Þat y bouʒt hur dere aplyʒt[41]
For seuen sithes of golde hur wyʒt;[42]
For y wende, without wene,
Þat feire mayde to haue had to quene.
Among my maydons in my toure   930
I hur dide, with muche honoure;

---

[37] bring judgment on them.   [38] prolong.   [39] avenge him according to law. [40] set out.   [41] indeed.   [42] weight.

904. The rhyme shows that the right form is the present: *quelle*, kill.
917. On the judicial procedure, cf. notes to the trial in "Havelok."

Byfore her bedde my self y coom;
I fonde þeryn a naked man.
Þan were þey to me so looþ,
I þou3t to haue sleyn hem booþ,   935
I was so wroþ and so woode;
3it y withdrow3 myn hoot bloode[43]
Tyl y haue sende after 3ow, by assent,
To wreke me with iugement.
Now 3it 3e woot how it is goone;   940
Wreke me soon of my foon."
Þan spake a kyng of þat londe,
"We haue herd al þis shame and shonde;[44]
But or we hem to deth deme,
Lat vs hem see, 3if it þe queeme,[45]   945
What þey wolde speke or sygge,[46]
3if þey wyl au3t ageyn vs legge:[47]
Hit were nou3t ry3t iugement
Without answere make acoupement.[48]
Til þis is herde of more and lasse,   950
What myster is to bere wytnesse?"[49]
After þe children haue þey sent—
To brenne hem was his entent—;
Two serieauntes hem gan bryng
Toward hur [deþ] al wepyng.   955
Drery booþ þese children goo;
Ayther bemeneþ[50] oþeris woo.
Þan seide Florys to Blauncheflour,
"Of oure lyf is no socour:
Yf kinde of man it þole my3t,[1]   960
Twyes y shuld dye with ry3t,
Oones for myself, anoþer for the,
For þy deeþ þou hast for me."
Blauncheflour seyde þoo,
"Þe gylt is myn of oure woo."   965

---

[43] withheld my rage.   [44] injury.   [45] please.   [46] say.   [47] set forth against our decree.   [48] accusation.   [49] what is the use of passing judgment?   [50] laments.   [1] if man's nature were such as to endure it.

955. *Deþ* supplied from other MSS.

Florys drouȝ forþ þat ryng
Þat his moder him gaff at her partyng:
"Haue þis ryng, lemman myn;
Þou shalt not dye while it is þyn."
Blaunchefloure seide þoo,   970
"So ne shal it neuer goo[2]
Þat þis ryng shal help me,
And þe deed on þe see."
Florys þat ryng hur rauȝt,
And she it him agayn betauȝt: 975
Nouther ne wyl other deed seene;
Þey let it falle hem bytwene.
A king com after; a ryng he fonde,
And brouȝt it forth in his honde.
Þus þe children wepyng com   980
To þe fire and hur doom;
Byfore þe folk þey were brouȝt.
Drery was her bothes[3] þouȝt;
Þere was noon so stern man
Þat þe children loked oon,   985
Þat þey ne wolde, al wel fawe,[4]
Her iugement haue withdrawe,
And with grete catel hem bygge,
Ȝif þey durst speke or sygge;
For Flores was so feire a ȝonglyng,[5] 990
And Blaunchefloure so swete a þing,
Þer wyst no man whor[6] hem were woo
For no semblaunt þat þey made þoo.
Þe Admyral was so woode,
Ne myȝt he nouȝt kele[7] his hoot bloode. 995
He bade þe children fast be bound
And in to þe fire slong.[8]
Þat ilke king þat þe ryng fonde,

---

[2] be done, come to pass.   [3] of both of them.   [4] gladly.   [5] youth.   [6] whether.
[7] cool. [8] cast.

973. The construction is confused: "The ring shall not help me (if) I am to see you dead."

992. Another MS. says that they in their sorrow seemed more fair than others who were glad.

To Amyral he spake and rounde,[9]
And wolde hem saue to þe lyf,   1000
And told how for þe ryng þey gon stryf.
Þe Amyral lete hem ageyn clepe,[10]
For he wolde here hem speke,
And asked Florys what he heete,
And he tolde him ful skeete:[11]   1005
"Sir," he seide, "yf it were þy wylle,
Þou ne getest not þat maide to spylle;[12]
But, goòd sir, quel[13] þou me,
And late þat maide on lyue be."
Blauncheflour seide byne,[14]   1010
"Þe gylt of oure dedes is myn."
Þe Admyral seide þoo,
"Iwys, ȝe shul dye boo!"[15]
His swerd he breide[16] out of his sheeth,
Þe children to haue don to deeth.   1015
Blaunchefloure put forþ hur swire,[17]
And Florys dide her agayn to tyre,[18]
And seide, "I am man; i shal byfore:
With wrong hast þou þy lyf loore!"
Florys forth his swere putte,   1020
And Blauncheflour agayn him tytte.[19]
Þe king seide, "Drery mot ȝe be,[20]
Þis rouþ by þis children to see!"
Þe king þat þe ryng hadde,
For routh of hem sone he radde,[21]   1025
And at þe Amyral wyl he spede[22]
Þe children fro þe deþ to lede.
"Sir," he seide, "it is lytel prys
Þese children for to slee, ywys;
And it is wel more worship   1030

---

[9] whispered.   [10] be called back.   [11] quickly.   [12] kill.   [13] kill.   [14] within, i.e., interjected.   [15] both.   [16] plucked.   [17] neck.   [18] draw.   [19] drew back.   [20] i.e., bad luck to you.   [21] spoke.   [22] succeeded.

1007. Other MSS. have, *þu nauȝtest,* you should not.
1020. MS. *swerd.*
1022. MS. *dredry.*
1027. *Amyral* is a genitive.

Florys counsel þat ȝe weete:
Who him tauȝt þat ilke gynne,
Þy toure for to com ynne,
And who him brouȝt þare,
And other,[23] þat ȝe may be ware." 1035
Þan seide þe Amyral, "As God me saue,
Florys shal his lyf haue
ȝif he me telle who him tauȝt þerto.". . .
. . . . Of Florys, "þat shal y neuer doo."
Now þey bydden al ywys 1040
Þat þe Admyral graunted þis,
To forȝeue þat trespas
ȝif Florys told how it was.
Now euery word he haþ him tolde:
How þat maide was for him solde, 1045
And how he was of Spayn a kynges sone,
For grete loue þeder ycom
For to fonde, with sum gynne,
Þat feire maide for to wynne,
And how þe porter was his man bycom 1050
For his gold and for his warysoun,[24]
And how he was in þe ff.lorys borne;
Alle þe lordinges lowȝ þerforne.
Now þe Admyral—wol him tyde![25]—
Florys setteþ next his syde, 1055
And efte he made him stonde vpryȝt
And dubbed him þere knyȝt,
And bade he shulde with him be
Þe furthermast[26] of his meyné.
Florys falleþ doun to his feet 1060
And prayeþ geue[27] him his sweet.
Þe Amyral gaf him his lemman:
Al þat þere were þankyd him þanne.
To a chirche he let hem bryng,
And dede let wed hem with a ryng. 1065

---

[23] more things too. [24] reward. [25] good luck to him! [26] foremost. [27] that he give.

1039. This is all that is left of a speech in which Floris refuses to betray his accomplices unless they are pardoned.

Boþ þese twoo swete þinges, ywys,
Fel his feet for to kysse;
And þrouȝ consel of Blauncheflour,
Clarys was fet doun of þe toure,
And Amyral wedded hur to queene.   1070
Þere was fest swythe breeme;[28]
I can not telle al þe sonde,[29]
But rycher fest was neuer in londe.
Was it nouȝt longe after þan
Þat to Florys tydyng cam   1075
Þat þe King his ffader was deed.
Þe baronage gaf him reed
Þat he shuld wende hoom
And fonge his feire kyngdoom.
At þe Amyral þey toke leue,   1080
And he byddeþ þem byleue.[30]
Hom he went with royal array,
And was crownyd within a short day.

---

[28] fine.   [29] dishes, viands.   [30] remain.

1083. The end of the story is not found in the MS.; but in another
version are found the usual benediction of the hearers and the assurance
that the couple lived happily.

CHEVELERE ASSIGNE

CHEVELERE ASSIGNE

The romance is in the east midland dialect (with some northern forms) of the late fourteenth century. With the consent of the Department of Manuscripts of the British Museum, it has been edited from rotographs of the unique manuscript, Cotton Caligula A II.

The story is apparently a condensation of about the first 1100 lines of the French "Chevalier au Cygne," a 6000-line composite of the late twelfth century. A long English prose version was printed by Copland and again by Wynkyn de Worde.

This romance is related to the cycle of Godfrey of Bouillon, famous crusader and one of the Nine Worthies, who was reputed to have descended from a swan—a legend which attached itself to some noble English families also. The changing of a human being into a swan is a well-known theme in folklore; its origin may be traced to totemism (cf. Lang, "Myth, Ritual, and Religion," 1.168; also E. S. Hartland, "The Science of Fairy Tales," last chapters).

The manuscript is peculiar in its interchange of -th and -d (swyde for swythe, 158; bygyleth for bygyled, 78) so that many preterites and past participles resemble the present tense. These forms have been retained. Because of doubt of the scribe's intentions, final -m and -n with a flourish and final crossed -ll and -th have not been doubled or expanded to -lle, etc.

Gibbs's edition (*EETS.*) is referred to in the notes as G.

All-weldynge[1] God   ·   whenne it is His wylle,
Wele He wereth[2] His werke   ·   with His owne honde;
For ofte harmes were hente   ·   þat helpe we ne myȝte,
Nere þe hyȝnes[3] of Hym   ·   þat lengeth in heuene.
For this i saye by a lorde   ·   was lente[4] in an yle   5
That was kalled Lyor—   ·   a londe by hymselfe.
The Kynge hette Oryens   ·   as þe book telleth,

---

[1] omnipotent.   [2] protects.   [3] were it not for the supremacy.   [4] dwelt.

6. A corruption of the Lillefort of the French poem, where it is no island. Possibly the scribe took it to be some form of *l'île forte.* Cf. Krüger, *Arch.* 77.169.

And his Qwene, Bewtrys[5] · þat bryȝt was and shene.
His moder hyȝte Matabryne · þat made moche sorwe,
For she sette her affye[6] · in Sathanas of helle.　　　10
This was chefe of þe kynde · of Cheualere Assygne;[7]
And whenne þey sholde into a place— · it seyth full wele where,—
Sythen aftur his lykynge · dwellede he þere
With his owne Qwene · þat he loue myȝte;
But all in langour he laye · for lofe of here one　　　15
That he hadde no chylde · to cheuenne[8] his londis,
But to be lordeles of his[9] · whenne he þe lyf lafte;
And þat honged in[10] his herte · i heete þe for sothe.
　As þey wente vpon a walle · pleynge hem one,
Bothe þe Kynge and þe Qwene · hemselfen togedere,　　20
The Kynge loked adowne · and byhelde vnder
And seyȝ a pore womman · at þe ȝate sytte
With two chylderen her byfore · were borne at a byrthe;
And he turned hym þenne · and teres lette he falle.
Sythen sykede he on hyȝe · and to þe Qwene sayde,　　25
"Se ȝe þe ȝonder pore womman · how þat she is pyned
With twynlenges[11] two · and þat dare i my hedde wedde."[12]
　The Qwene nykked hym with nay[13] · and seyde, "It is not to leue:
Oon manne for oon chylde · and two wymmen for tweyne,
Or ellis hit were vnsemelye þynge · as me wolde þenke,　30
But eche chylde hadde a fader · how manye so þer were."
　The Kynge rebukede here · for her worþes ryȝte þere,
And whenne it drowȝ towarde þe nyȝte · þey wenten to bedde;
He gette on here þat same nyȝte · resonabullye manye.
The Kynge was witty[14] · whenne he wysste her with chylde,35
And þankede lowely our Lorde · of his loue and his sonde;
But whenne it drowȝe to þe tyme · she shulde be delyuered,

---

[5] Beatrice.　[6] trust.　[7] Knight of the Swan.　[8] possess.　[9] without a lord of his blood.　[10] weighed on.　[11] twins.　[12] wager.　[13] contradicted.　[14] overjoyed.

17. Violation of parallel structure is common in the romances.
28–31. I.e., the same man did not father both children. Twins were considered infallible sign of adultery; cf. Westermarck, "Origin and Development of Moral Ideas," I. 408.

Ther moste no womman come her nere · but she þat was
   cursed,
His moder Matabryne · þat cawsed moche sorowe;
For she thow3te to do[15] þat byrthe · to a fowle ende.   40
   Whenne God wolde þey were borne · þenne brow3te she
   to honde
Sex semelye sonnes · and a dow3ter, þe seueneth,
All safe and all sounde · and a seluer cheyne[16]
Eche on of hem hadde abowte · his swete swyre;
And she lefte[17] hem out · and leyde hem in a cowche.   45
And þenne she[18] sente aftur a man · þat Markus was called
That hadde serued herseluen · skylfully longe;
He was trewe of his feyth · and loth for to tryfull.
She knewe hym for swych · and triste[19] hym þe better,
And seyde, "Þou moste kepe counsell · and helpe what þou
   may.   50
The fyrste grymme watur · þat þou to comeste,
Looke þou caste hem þerin · and lete hem forth slyppe;
Sythen seche to þe courte · as þou now3te hadde sene,
And þou shalt lyke full wele · yf þou may lyfe aftur."
Whenne he herde þat tale · hym rewede þe tyme,   55
But he durste not werne[20] · what þe Qwene wolde.
The Kynge lay in langour · sum gladdenes to here,
But þe fyrste tale þat he herde · were tydynges febull.[21]
   Whenne his moder Matabryne · brow3te hym tydynge,
At a chamber dore · as she forth sow3te,   60
Seuenne whelpes she sawe · sowkynge þe damme;
And she kaw3te out a knyfe · and kylled þe bycche.

---

[15] bring.   [16] silver chain.   [17] lifted.   [18] i.e., Matabryne.   [19] trusted.   [20] refuse.
[21] unpleasant.

40. In the French version, the king ravishes his bride from the other-world, a fact which explains Matabryne's hostility. Cf. "Emaré."

42. A similar story is told about Irmentrude, Countess of Altorfe, ancestress of the Guelphs (whelps), who bore twelve sons at a birth after having accused the mother of triplets of adultery. Cf. Gibbs xi. For a full discussion and parallels of this incident, see M. Schlauch, "Chaucer's Constance and Accused Queens," 21.

52. MS. *hym forth.*

57. In the French story, the children are born during the king's absence.

She caste her þenne in a pytte · and taketh þe welpes
And sythen come byfore þe Kynge · and vpon hyȝe she seyde,
"Sone, paye þe with þy Qwene · and se of her berthe !"[22] 65
Thenne syketh þe Kynge · and gynnyth to morne,
And wente wele it were sothe · all þat she seyde.
Thenne she seyde, "Lette brenne her anone · for þat is the beste."
"Dame, she is my wedded wyfe · full trewe as i wene
As i haue holde her er þis · our Lorde so me helpe !" 70
"A, kowarde of kynde," quod she · "and combred[23] wrecche,
Wolt þou werne wrake[24] · to hem þat hit deserueth?"
"Dame, þanne take here þyselfe · and sette her wher þe lyketh,
So þat i se hit noȝte · what may i seye elles?"
    Thenne she wente her forth · þat God shall confounde, 75
To þat febull,[25] þer she laye · and felly she bygynneth,
And seyde, "Aryse, wrecched Qwene · and reste þe her no lengur;
Thow hast bygyleth[26] my sone · it shall þe werke sorowe.
Bothe howndes and men · haue hadde þe a wylle;[27]
Thow shalt to prisoun fyrste · and be brente aftur." 80
Thenne shrykede þe ȝonge Qwene · and vpon hyȝ cryeth.
"A, lady," she seyde · "where ar my lefe chylderen?"
Whenne she myssede hem þer · grete mone she made.
    By þat come tytlye · tyrauntes[28] tweyne,
And by þe byddynge of Matabryne · anon þey her hente, 85
And in a dymme prysoun · þey slongen here deepe
And leyde a lokke on þe dore · and leuen here þere.
Mete þey caste here adowne · and more God sendeth.
And þus þe lady lyuede þere · elleuen ȝere,
And mony a fayre orysoun · vnto þe Fader made 90

[22] see what she has borne.   [23] troubled.   [24] deny punishment.   [25] wretched woman.   [26] beguiled.   [27] at their pleasure.   [28] evildoers.

65. For information and parallels to the old queen's accusation against the young, cf. M. R. Cox's "Cinderella" 199, 486.
68. "Burning for adultery is common in the romances, but appears to have no basis in medieval custom," Child 2.113. Cf. J. D. Bruce, "Mort Artu," 282; W. Foerster, "Ywain," 3rd. ed., ix; Pio Rajna, "Le Fonti dell' Orlando Furioso," 2nd ed., 154. Cf. also "Layamon" 28,181; "Emaré" 533.

That saued Susanne fro sorowefull domus · [her] to saue als.
Now leue we þis lady in langour and pyne
And turne aȝeyne to our tale · towarde þese chylderen
And to þe man Markus · þat murther hem sholde,
How he wente þorow a foreste · fowre longe myle 95
Thyll he come to a water · þer he hem shulde in drowne,
And þer he keste vp þe cloth · to knowe hem bettur;
And þey ley and lowȝe on hym · louelye all at ones.
"He þat lendeth wit," quod he · "leyne²⁹ me wyth sorowe
If i drowne ȝou to-day · thowgh my deth be nyȝe." 100
Thenne he leyde hem adowne · lappedde in þe mantell,
And lappede hem and hylyde³⁰ hem · and hadde moche rewthe
That swyche a barmeteme³¹ as þat · shulde so betyde.
Thenne he taketh hem to Cryste · and aȝeyne turneth,
But sone þe mantell was vndo · with mengynge³² of her
legges. 105
They cryedde vpon hyȝe · with a dolefull steuenne;
They chyuered³³ for colde · as cheuerynge chyldrenn.
They ȝoskened³⁴ and cryde out · and þat a man herde;
An holy hermyte was by · and towarde hem cometh.
Whenne he come byfore hem · on knees þenne he fell, 110
And cryede ofte vpon Cryste · for somme sokour hym to
sende
If any lyfe were hem lente³⁵ · in þis worlde lengur.
Thenne an hynde kome fro þe woode · rennynge full swyfte
And fell before hem adownne · þey drowȝe to þe pappes.³⁶
The heremyte prowde³⁷ was þerof · and putte hem to
sowke;³⁸ 115
Sethen taketh he hem vp · and þe hynde foloweth,
And she kepte hem þere · whyll our Lorde wolde.
Thus he noryscheth hem vp and Criste hem helpe sendeth.
Of sadde³⁹ leues of þe wode · wrowȝte he hem wedes.
Malkedras þe fostere⁴⁰— · þe fende mote hym haue!— 120

---

²⁹ reward. ³⁰ concealed. ³¹ progeny. ³² entangling. ³³ shivered. ³⁴ sobbed.
³⁵ remained in them. ³⁶ teats. ³⁷ gratified. ³⁸ suck. ³⁹ fallen. ⁴⁰ forester.

91. The apocryphal story of the saving of Susannah from the false
charges of the elders was popular in the Middle Ages. G. supplies *her*.
99. MS. *lendeth wᵗ* the usual contraction for *with*.

That cursedde man for his feyth[41] · he come þer þey weren,
And was ware in his syȝte— · syker[42] of þe chyldren.
He turnede aȝeyn to þe courte · and tolde of þe chaunce,
And menede byfore Matabryne · how many þer were.
"And more merueyle þenne þat · dame, a seluere cheyne 125
Eche on of hem hath · abowte here swyre."
She seyde, "Holde þy wordes in chaste[43] · þat none skape
    ferther;
I wyll soone aske hym · þat hath me betrayed."
    Thenne she sente aftur Markus · þat murther hem sholde,
And askede hym in good feyth[44] · what fell of þe chyldren. 130
Whenne she hym asked hadde · he seyde, "Here þe sothe:[45]
Dame, on a ryueres banke · lapped in my mantell
I lafte hem lyynge there · leue þou for sothe.
I myȝte not drowne hem for dole · do what þe lykes!"
Thenne she made here all preste · and out bothe hys yen.135
Moche mone was therfore · but no man wyte moste.
    "Wende þou aȝeyne, Malkedras · and gete me þe cheynes,
And with þe dynte of þy swerde · do hem to deth;
And i shall do þe swych a turne— · and þou þe tyte hyȝe—
That þe shall lyke ryȝte wele · þe terme[46] of þy lyue." 140
    Thenne þe hatefull thefe · hyed hym full faste;
The cursede man in his feyth · come þer þey were.
By þenne was þe hermyte go into þe wode · and on of þe
    children,
For to seke mete · for þe other sex
Whyles þe cursed man · asseylde þe other.   145
And he out with his swerde · and smote of þe cheynes;
They stoden all stylle · for stere[47] þey ne durste.
And whenne þe cheynes fell hem fro · þey flowenn vp swannes
To þe ryuere bysyde · with a rewfull steuenne;

---

[41] i.e., accursed because of his allegiance (to a wicked woman). [42] sure. [43] box, i.e., be secret. [44] i.e., to tell in good faith. [45] here is the truth; cf. "Alex." 3997. [46] for the length of. [47] stir.

127. Hypermetrical *she seyde*, added by a copyist; fairly common in later romances. Cf. "Eger and Grime."

135. MS. has *putt* in different ink, but much the same hand, and a caret between *and* and *out*. Verbs of motion are frequently omitted. Cf. 146. Cf. also Int. VII.A.3.

And he taketh vp þe cheynes · and to þe cowrte turneth, 150
And come byfore þe Qwene · and here hem bytaketh;
Thenne she toke hem in honde · and heelde ham full stylle.
She sente aftur a goldesmyȝte[48] · to forge here a cowpe,[49]
And whenne þe man was comen · þenne was þe Qwene blythe.
She badde þe wessell were made · vpon all wyse,[50]   155
And delyuered hym his weyȝtes[1] · and he from cowrte wendes.
   The goldesmyȝth gooth and beetheth[2] hym a fyre · and
      breketh a cheyne,
And it wexeth in hys honde · and multyplyeth swyde.
He toke þat oþur fyue · and fro þe fyer hem leyde
And made hollye þe cuppe · of haluendell þe sixte;   160
And whenne it drowȝe to þe nyȝte · he wendeth to bedde,
And thus he seyth to his wyfe · in sawe[3] as i telle:
"The olde Qwene at þe courte · hath me bytaken
Six cheynes in honde · and wolde haue a cowpe,
And i breke me a cheyne · and halfe leyde in þe fyer,   165
And it wexedde in my hande · and wellede[4] so faste
That i toke þe oþur fyve · and fro þe fyer caste,
And haue made hollye þe cuppe · of haluendele þe sixte."
"I rede þe," quod his wyfe · "to holden hem stylle.
Hit is þorowe þe werke of God · or þey be wronge wonnen; 170
For whenne here mesure is made · what may she aske more?"
And he dedde as she badde · and buskede hym at morwe.
He come byfore þe Qwene · and bytaketh here þe cowpe,
And she toke it in honde · and kepte hit full clene.
"Nowe lefte ther ony ouur vnwerketh[5] · by þe better
      trowthe?"[6]   175
And he recheth her forth · haluenndele a cheyne,
And she rawȝte hit hym aȝeyne · and seyde she ne rowȝte,
But delyuered hym his seruyse[7] · and he out of cowrte
      wendes.

---

[48] goldsmith. [49] cup. [50] at all hazards. [1] amount of gold. [2] mended. [3] speech.
[4] boiled up. [5] unused. [6] to the best of your belief. [7] pay.

155 and 156 are reversed in the MS. The first four words in 157 probably should be replaced with *He*. The word "mended," rather than
"kindled," is generally used of fires, since fires were kept banked because
of the difficulty of lighting them.

"The curteynesse of Criste," quod she · "be with þese oþur cheynes.

They be delyuered out of þis worlde · were þe moder eke! 180
Thenne hadde i þis londe · hollye to myne wyll;
Now all wyles[8] shall fayle · but i here deth werke."
  At morn she come byfore þe Kynge · and byganne full keene,
"Moche of þis worlde, sonne, · wondreth on þe allone,
That thy Qwene is vnbrente · so meruelows longe   185
That hath serued[9] þe deth · if þou here dome wyste.[10]
Lette sommene þy folke · vpon eche a syde,
That þey bene at þy syȝte · þe xi day assygned."
And he here graunted þat · with a grymme herte,
And she wendeth here adown · and lette hem anone warne.
                           190

  The nyȝte byfore þe day · þat þe lady shulde brenne,
An angell come to þe hermyte · and askede if he slepte.
The angell seyde, "Criste sendeth þe worde · of þese six chyldren,
And for þe sauynge of hem · þanke[11] þou haste serueth.
They were þe Kynges Oriens · —wytte þou forsothe— 195
By his wyfe Betryce · she bere hem at ones
For a worde on þe wall · þat she wronge seyde,
And ȝonder in þe ryuer · swymmen þey swannes.
Sythen Malkedras þe forsworn þefe · byrafte hem her cheynes,
And Criste hath formeth þis chylde · to fyȝte for his moder."
                           200

"Oo lyuynge God þat dwellest in heuene," · quod þe hermyte þanne,
"How sholde he serue for suche a þynge · þat neuer none syȝe?"
"Go brynge hym to his fader courte · and loke þat he be cristened—
And kalle hym Enyas to name · for awȝte þat may befalle—
Ryȝte by þe mydday · to redresse his moder; 205

---

[8] tricks.   [9] deserved.   [10] i.e., knew what her doom should be.   [11] thanks.

179. The line seems to mean: "Now heaven's blessing go with these other chains"; i.e., "good riddance to."

For Goddes wyll moste be fulfylde · and þou most forth
  wende."
The heremyte wakynge lay · and thow3te on his wordes.
Soone whenne þe day come · to þe chylde he seyde,
"Criste hath formeth þe, sone, · to fy3te for þy moder."
He asskede hymm þanne · what was a moder. 210
"A womman þat bare þe to man · sonne, and of here re-
  redde."[12]
"3e, kanste þou, fader, enforme me · how þat i shall fy3te?"
"Vpon a hors," seyde þe heremyte · "as i haue herde seye."
"What beste is þat," quod þe chylde · "lyonys wylde?
Or elles wode · or watur?"[13] quod þe chylde þanne. 215
"I sey3e neuur none," quod þe hermyte · "but by þe mater[14]
  of bokes.
They seyn he hath a feyre hedde · and fowre lymes hye,
And also he is a frely beeste · forthy he man serueth."
"Go we forth, fader," quod þe childe · "vpon Goddes
  halfe."[15]
Thé grypte eyþur a staffe in here honde · and on here wey
  straw3te.[16] 220
Whenne þe heremyte hym lafte · an angell hym suwethe,[17]
Euur to rede þe chylde · vpon his ry3te sholder.
  Thenne he seeth in a felde · folke gaderynge faste,
And a hy3 fyre was þer bette · þat þe Qwene sholde in brenne,
And noyse was in þe cyté · felly lowde, 225
With trumpes and tabers · whenne þey here vp token,
The olde Qwene at here bakke · betynge full faste.
The Kynge come rydynge afore · a forlonge and more.
The chylde stryketh[18] hym to · and toke hym by þe brydell.
"What man arte þou," quod þe chylde · "and who is þat þe
  sveth?"[19] 230
"I am þe Kynge of þis londe · and Oryens am kalled,
And þe 3ondur is my Qwene— · Betryce she hette—

---

[12] i.e., nourished, fed thee. [13] i.e., wood-beast or water-beast—G. [14] con-
tents. [15] behalf, i.e., in God's name. [16] set forth. [17] follows. [18] ran. [19] follows.

210 ff. Cf. "Perceval."

In þe ȝondere balowe-fyre[20] · is buskedde[21] to brenne.
She was sklawnndered[22] on hyȝe · þat she hadde taken
    howndes,
And ȝyf she hadde so done · here harm were not to charge."[23]
                                       235
"Thenne were þou noȝt ryȝ[t]lye sworne,"[24] quod þe chylde ·
    "vpon ryȝte iuge,
Whenne þou tokest þe þy crowne— · kynge whenne þou
    made were—
To done aftur Matabryne · for þenne þou shalt mysfare;
For she is fowle, fell, and fals · and so she shall be fownden,
And bylefte with þe fend · at here laste ende."   240
That styked styffe in here brestes[25] · þat wolde þe Qwene
    brenne.
"I am but lytull and ȝonge," quod þe chylde · "leeue þou
    forsothe,
Not but[26] twelfe ȝere olde · euenn at þis tyme;
And i woll putte my body · to better and to worse
To fyȝte for þe Qwene · with whome þat wronge seyth."[27] 245
    Thenne graunted þe Kynge · and ioye he bygynneth,
If any helpe were þerinne · þat here clensen myȝte.
By þat come þe olde Qwene · and badde hym com þenne:
"To speke with suche on as he · þou mayste ryȝth loth
    thenke."
"A, dame!" quod þe Kynge · "thowȝte ȝe none synne? 250
Thow haste forsette[28] þe ȝonge Qwene · þou knoweste well
    þe sothe.
This chylde þat i here speke with · seyth þat he woll preue
That þou nother þy sawes · certeyne be neyther."[29]
And þenne she lepte to hym · and kawȝte hym by þe lokke[30]
That þer leued in here honde · heres an hondredde. 255

---

[20] blazing fire. [21] prepared. [22] accused. [23] of no importance. [24] badly advised;
see note. [25] this remark stuck in the breasts of those who. [26] only. [27] against
whoever makes the accusation. [28] opposed. [29] thou nor thy sayings, neither
is trustworthy. [30] hair.

233. The scribe has confused the bale-fire (blazing, outdoor fire) of his
original with the adjective *balwe*, deadly. Cf. 344.

236. The second half is a mistranslation of the French: *Nas pas a
droit iugé comme roy loyaument.*

"A, by lyuynge God," quod þe childe · "þat bydeste in
    heuene!
Thy hedde shall lye on þy lappe · for þy false turnes.[31]
I aske a felawe anone · a fresh knyȝte aftur,[32]
For to fyȝte with me · to dryue owte þe ryȝte."[33]
    "A, boy," quod she, "wylt þou so? · þou shalt sone mys-
    karye;   260
I wyll gete me a man · þat shall þe sone marre."
She turneth her þenne to Malkedras · and byddyth hym
    take armes,
And badde hyme bathe his spere · in þe boyes herte;
And he of suche one · gret skorne he þowȝte.
An holy abbot was þer by · and he hym þeder boweth[34] 265
For to cristen þe chylde · frely and feyre.
The abbot maketh hym a fonte · and was his godfader;
The Erle of Aunnthepas · he was another;
The Countes of Salamere · was his godmoder.
They kallede hym Enyas to name · as þe book telleth.   270
Mony was þe ryche ȝyfte · þat þey ȝafe hym aftur.
Alle þe bellys of þe close[35] · rongen at ones
Withoute ony mannes helpe · whyle þe fyȝte lasted;
Wherefore þe[y] wyste well · þat Criste was plesed with here
    dede.
    Whenne he was cristened · frely and feyre,   275
Aftur þe Kynge dubbede hym knyȝte · as his kynde wolde.[36]
Thenne prestly he prayeth þe Kynge · þat he hym lene wolde
An hors with his harnes · and blethelye he hym graunteth.
Thenne was Feraunce fette forth · þe Kynges price stede,
And out of an hyȝe towre · armour þey halenne,[37]   280
And a whyte shelde with a crosse · vpon þe posse honged,
And hit was wryten þer vpon · þat to Enyas hit sholde;[38]
And whenne he was armed · to all his ryȝtes,
Thenne prayde he þe Kynge · þat he hym lene wolde
Oon of his beste menne · þat he moste truste   285

---

[31] tricks. [32] (I ask) for a strong knight. [33] bring out the truth by fighting.
[34] goes. [35] abbey grounds. [36] i.e., as befitted his condition. [37] bring. [38] i.e.,
should belong.

281. As Gibbs noted, *posse* is probably an error for *poste.*

To speke with hym but · a speche-whyle.[39]
A kny3te kaw3te hym by þe hande · and ladde hym of þe
rowte.
   "What beeste is þis," quod þe childe · "þat i shall on
houe?"[40]
"Hit is called an hors," quod þe kny3te · "a good and an
abull."
"Why eteth he yren;" quod þe chylde · "wyll he ete no3th
elles?   290
And what is þat on his bakke · of byrthe or on bounden?"[41]
"Nay, þat in his mowth · men kallen a brydell,
And that a sadell on his bakke · þat þou shalt in sytte."
"And what heuy kyrtell[42] is þis · with holes so thykke;
And þis holowe on my hede · i may no3t here?"   295
"An helme men kallen þat on · and an hawberke[43] þat other."
"But what broode on[44] is þis on my breste? · Hit bereth
adown my nekke."
"A bry3te shelde and a sheene · to shylde þe fro strokes."
"And what longe on is þis · that i shall vp lyfte?"
"Take þat launce vp in þyn honde · and loke þou hym hytte,
        300
And whenne þat shafte is schyuered · take scharpelye[45]
another."
"3e, what yf grace be · we to grownde wenden?"
"Aryse vp ly3tly on þe fete · and reste þe no lengur,
And þenne plukke out þy swerde · and pele[46] on hym faste,
Allwey eggelynges[47] down · on all þat þou fyndes.   305
His ryche helm nor his swerde · rekke þou of neyþur;
Lete þe sharpe of þy swerde · schreden[48] hym small."
"But woll not he smyte a3eyne · whenne he feleth smerte?"[49]
"3ys—i knowe hym full wele— · both kenely and faste.
Euur folowe[50] þou on þe flesh · tyll þou haste hym falleth, 310
And sythen smyte of his heede · i kan sey þe no furre."

---

[39] time for conversation. [40] remain. [41] i.e., is it natural or bound on. [42] shirt. [43] body-armor. Cf. Int. III.D. [44] i.e., thing. [45] quickly. [46] strike. [47] edgewise. [48] shred. [49] the sting. [50] keep on striking.

295. Originally *holowe on on;* one *on* assimilated by the other.—G.

"Now þou haste tawȝte me," quod þe childe · "God i þe
    beteche;
For now i kan of þe crafte · more þenne i kowthe."
    Thenne þey maden raunges[1] · and ronnen togedere
That þe speres in here hondes · shyuereden to peces,   315
And for rennenge aȝeyn · men rawȝten hem other
Of balowe[2] tymbere and bygge · þat wolde not breste;
And eyther of hem · so smer[t]lye smote other
That all fleye in þe felde · þat on hem was fastened,
And eyther of hem topseyle[3] · tumbledde to þe erthe. 320
Thenne here horses ronnen forth · aftur þe raunges,
Euur Feraunnce byforne · and þat other aftur.
Feraunnce launces[4] vp his fete · and lasscheth out his yen.
The fyrste happe other hele[5] was þat · þat þe chylde hadde
Whenne þat þe blonk[6] þat hym bare · blente[7] hadde his
    fere.   325
    Thenne thei styrte vp on hy · with staloworth shankes,
Pulledde out her swerdes · and smoten togedur.
"Kepe þy swerde fro my croyse" · quod Cheuelyre Assygne.
"I charge[8] not þy croyse," quod Malkedras · "þe valwe of
    a cherye;[9]
For i shall choppe it full small · ere þenne þis werke ende."
                                 330
An edder[10] spronge out of his shelde · and in his body
    spynneth;[11]
A fyre fruscheth[12] out of his croys · and [f]rapte[13] out his yen.
    Thenne he stryketh a stroke— · Cheualere Assygne—
Euenn his sholder in twoo · and down into þe herte,

---

[1] marked off a tilting course. [2] deadly. [3] upside down. [4] kicks. [5] advantage. [6] horse. [7] blinded. [8] value. [9] amount of a cherry. [10] adder. [11] hurls itself. [12] rushes. [13] struck.

316. MS. *rennenne.*
323. For fighting horses, cf. "Eger and Grime" 1100.
325. MS. *þe chylde þat.* Obviously wrong; G. suggests *blonk.*
328. MS. *cheuelrye.*
329. MS. *charde.*
332. Cf. *A fire þan fro þe crosse gane frusche,* "Sege of Melayne" 469. Here the fire burns the eyes of a Saracen who has attempted to destroy the cross.
334. Understand *stryketh* from 333.

And he boweth hym down · and ȝeldeth vp þe lyfe. 335
"I shall þe ȝelde," quód þe chylde · "ryȝte as þe knyȝte me
 tawȝte."
He trusseth his harneys[14] fro þe nekke · and þe hede wynneth;
Sythen he toke hit by the lokkes · and in þe helm leyde.
Thoo thanked he our Lorde lowely · þat lente hym þat grace.
  Thenne sawe þe Qwene Matabryne · her man so mur-
   dered, 340
Turned her brydell · and towarde þe towne rydeth;
The chylde foloweth here aftur · fersly[15] and faste.
Sythen browȝte here aȝeyne · wo for to drye,[16]
And brente here in þe balowe-fyer[17] · all to browne askes.[18]
The ȝonge Qwene at þe fyre · by þat was vnbounnden. 345
The childe kome byfore þe Kynge · and on hyȝe he seyde,
And tolde hym how he was his sone · "and oþur sex childeren
By þe Qwene Betryce · she bare hem at ones
For a worde on þe walle · þat she wronge seyde,
And ȝonder in a ryuere · swymmen þey swannes 350
Sythen þe forsworne thefe Malkadras · byrafte hem her
 cheynes."
"By God," quod þe goldsmythe · "i knowe þat ryȝth wele.
Fyve cheynes i haue · and þey ben fysh-hole."[19]
  Nowe with þe goldsmyȝth · gon all þese knyȝtes;
Toke þey þe cheynes · and to þe watur turnen 355
And shoken vp[20] þe cheynes · þer sterten vp þe swannes;
Eche on chese to his[21] · and turnen to her kynde,
But on was alwaye a swanne · for losse of his cheyne.
Hit was doole for to se · þe sorowe þat he made:
He bote[22] hymself with his byll · þat all his breste bledde, 360
And all his feyre federes · fomede vpon blode
And all formerknes[23] þe watur · þer þe swanne swymmeth.
There was ryche ne pore · þat myȝte for rewthe

---

[14] plucks the armor. [15] fiercely. [16] suffer. [17] blazing fire. [18] ashes. [19] as sound
as a fish. [20] rattled. [21] chose his own. [22] bit. [23] darkens.

358. In the French poem, also, the sixth son remains a swan, who
guides his brother, the Chevelere, on many adventures; but in the English
prose story, Queen Beatrice, following the guidance of a dream, restores
him to his true form by having a mass said over him and over the two
cups which were made from his chain.

Lengere loke on hym ·   but to þe courte wenden.
Thenne þey formed a fonte ·   and cristene þe children,   365
And callen Vryens þat on, ·   and Oryens another,
Assakarye þe thrydde ·   and Gadyfere þe fowrthe;
The fyfte hette Rose ·   for she was a mayden.
The sixte was fulwedde[24] ·   —Cheuelere Assygne—
And þus þe botenynge of God ·   browȝte hem to honde.[25] 370

EXPLICIT.

[24] had been baptized.   [25] the succour of God saved them.

369. *Cheuelere Assygne* must be in apposition with *sixte*, since he was christened Enyas.

SIR CLEGES

SIR CLEGES

"Sir Cleges" is in the north midland dialect of the late fourteenth, or possibly very early fifteenth, century. The poem exists in two manuscripts of the fifteenth century: (1) the Edinburgh manuscript, 19.1.11* in the National Library of Scotland (formerly the Advocates' Library), from rotographs of which this text is printed with the kind permission and assistance of the authorities of the Library; (2) the Oxford manuscript, Ashmole 61. The two versions can be compared in Treichel's edition, *ESt.* 22.345.

Both of the main incidents, the miraculous fruit and the choosing of blows as a reward, were very popular in the Middle Ages (for variants and parallels, cf. G. H. McKnight's edition of the Oxford manuscript in his "Middle English Humorous Tales in Verse," lxi ff.); but the actual source of the romance is unknown. It is both a fabliau—a comic tale—and an exemplum—a moral tale to be used in sermons. In its present form it is clearly also a Christmas tale which minstrels told "to encourage liberality at Yule-tide feasts" (McKnight lxiii).

The following spellings peculiar to this manuscript should be noted: *nere* for *nor*, *ar* for *or*, *will* for *well*, and the intrusion of an inorganic -ʒ (*prowʒd*, proud, 448).

Plurals of nouns are abbreviated in the manuscript in the usual fashion; they have been expanded as *-is*, which seems to be the scribe's favorite form. The scribe is prodigal with *ff-*. At the beginning of lines, this has been printed *F-;* elsewhere, *ff-*. The following final letters are always crossed or flourished in the manuscript, but have not been expanded: *-ll*, *-ch*, *-m*, (except in *hym*, 123), *-n* (except in *in*, where it is never flourished). Final *-ng* and *-t*, which are nearly always crossed or flourished, have not been expanded; nor has *-d*, which is flourished in about half its occurrences. Final flourished *-r* has been expanded to *-re*.

* Formerly Jac.V.6.21; the editors are grateful to Mr. H. W. Meikle of the National Library of Scotland for this correction.

Will ye lystyn, and ye schyll here
Of eldyrs that before vs were,
Bothe hardy and wyʒt,

In the tyme of kynge Vtere,
That was ffadyr of kynge A[r]thyr,   5
    A semely man in siȝt.
He hade a knyȝt, þat hight Sir Cleges;
A dowtyar was non of dedis
    Of the Rovnd Tabull right.
He was a man of hight[1] stature   10
And therto full fayre of ffeture,
    And also of gret myȝt.

A corteysear knyȝt than he was on
In all the lond was there non;
    He was so ientyll and fre.   15
To men þat traveld in londe of ware[2]
And wern fallyn in pouerté bare,
    He yaue both gold and ffee.
The pore pepull he wold releve,
And no man wold he greve;   20
    Meke of maners was hee.
His mete was ffre to euery man
That wold com and vesite hym than;
    He was full of plenté.

The knyȝt hade a ientyll wyffe;   25
There miȝt non better bere life,
    And mery sche was on siȝte.
Dame Clarys hight þat ffayre lady;
Sche was full good, sekyrly,
    And gladsum both day and nyȝte.   30
Almus[3] gret sche wold geve,
The pore pepull to releue;
    Sche cherisschid many a wiȝt.
For them hade no man dere,
Rech ar pore wethyr they were;   35
    They ded euer ryght.

_____

[1] tall.   [2] suffered in a war-swept country.   [3] alms.

21. MS. _manres._

Euery yer Sir Cleges wold
At Cristemas a gret ffest hold
  In worschepe of þat daye,
As ryall in all thynge   40
As he hade ben a kynge,
  Forsoth, as i you saye.
Rech and pore in þe cuntré abouȝt
Schuld be there, wythoutton douȝtt;
  There wold no man say nay.   45
Mynsstrellis wold not be behynde,
For there they myȝt most myrthis fynd;
  There wold they be aye.

Mynsstrellys, whan þe ffest was don,
Wythoutton yeftis schuld not gon,   50
  And þat bothe rech and good:
Hors, robis, and rech ryngis,
Gold, siluer, and othyr thyngis,
  To mend wyth her modde.[4]
Ten yere sech ffest he helde   55
In the worschepe of Mari myld
  And for Hym þat dyed on the rode.
Be that, his good began to slake[5]
For the gret ffestis that he dede make,
  The knyȝt ientyll of blode.   60

To hold the feste he wold not lett;
His maners he ded to wede sett;[6]
  He thowȝt hem out to quyȝtt.
Thus he ffestyd many a yere
Many a knyȝt and squire   65
  In the name of God all-myȝt.
So at the last, the soth to say,
All his good was spent awaye;
  Than hade he but lyȝt.
Thowe his good were ner[h]and leste,   70

---

[4] to cheer their spirits with. [5] decrease. [6] he put up his estates as security.

Yet he thowȝt to make a feste;
In God he hopyd ryght.

This rialté[7] he made than aye,
Tyll his maneris wern all awaye;
   Hym was lefte but on,   75
And þat was of so lytyll a value
That he and his wyffe trewe
   Miȝt not leve thereon.
His men that wern mekyll of pride
Gan slake[8] awaye on euery syde;   80
   With hym there wold dwell non
But he and his childyrn too;
Than was his hart in mech woo,
   And he made mech mone.

And yt befell on Crestemas evyn,   85
The knyȝt bethowȝt hym full evyn;[9]
   He dwellyd be Kardyfe syde.[10]
Whan yt drowe toward the novn,
Sir Cleges fell in svounnyng sone,
   Whan he thowȝt on þat tyde   90
And on his myrthys þat he schuld hold
And howe he hade his maners sold
   And his renttis wyde.[11]
Mech sorowe made he there;
He wrong his handis and wepyd sore,   95
   And ffellyd was his pride.

And as he walkyd vpp and dovn
Sore syȝthyng, he hard a sovne
   Of dyvers mynstrelsé:
Of trompus, pypus, and claraneris,[12]   100

---

[7] magnificence.   [8] disappear.   [9] pondered deeply.   [10] near Cardiff.   [11] large income.   [12] trumpeters.

82. O. *Bot hys wife and.* . . .
86. MS. *kynge.*
99. MS. *mynstrelses;* Treichel emends.
100. Most of these instruments are illustrated in Wright.

Of harpis, luttis, and getarnys,
  A sitole and sawtré,[13]
Many carellys[14] and gret davnsyng;
  On euery syde he harde syngyng,
    In euery place, trewly.   105
He wrong his hondis and wepyd sore;
  Mech mone made he there,
    Syghynge petusly.

"Lord Ihesu," he seyd, "Hevyn-kynge,
  Of nowȝt Thou madyst all thynge;   110
    I thanke The of Thy sond.
The myrth that i was wonte to make!
  At thys tyme for Thy sake,
    I fede both fre and bond.
All that euer cam in Thy name   115
Wantyd neythyr wyld nere tame[15]
    That was in my lond;
Of rech metis and drynkkys good
That myȝt be gott, be the rode,
    For coste i wold not lend."[16]   120

As he stod in mornyng soo,
  His good wyffe cam hym vnto,
    And in hyr armys hym hent.
Sche kyssyd hym wyth glad chere;
  "My lord," sche seyd, "my trewe fere,   125
    I hard what ye ment.
Ye se will, yt helpyth nowȝt
To make sorowe in youre thowȝt;
    Therefore i pray you stynte.[17]
Let youre sorowe awaye gon,   130

---

[13] lutes and gitterns, a citole and psaltery.   [14] carols.   [15] lacked neither game nor domestic animal.   [16] hesitate.   [17] cease.

102. MS. *sotile;* O. *sytall.*
103. Carols were dances accompanied by singing; cf. the famous example in "Handlyng Synne" 8987 ff.
128. MS. *your hart;* O. *thouȝt.*

And thanke God of hys lone[18]
Of all þat He hath sent.

For Crystis sake, i pray you blyne[19]
Of all the sorowe þat ye ben in,
   In onor of thys daye.   135
Nowe euery man schuld be glade;
Therefore i pray you be not sade;
   Thynke what i you saye.
Go we to oure mete swyth
And let vs make vs glade and blyth,   140
   As wele as we may.
I hold yt for the best, trewly;
For youre mete is all redy,
   I hope, to youre paye."

"I asent," seyd he tho,   145
And in with hyr he gan goo,
   And sumwatt[20] mendyd hys chere.
But neuerþeles hys hart was sore,
And sche hym comforttyd more and more,
   Hys sorewe away to stere.[21]   150
So he began to waxe blyth
And whypyd[22] away hys teris swyth,
   That ran dovn be his lyre.
Than they wasschyd and went to mete
Wyth sech vitell[23] as they myȝt gett   155
   And made mery in fere.

Whan they hade ete, the soth to saye,
Wyth myrth they droffe þe day away,
   As will as they myȝt.
Wyth her chyldyrn play they ded   160
And after soper went to bede,
   Whan yt was tyme[24] of nyȝt.
And on the morowe they went to chirch,

---

[18] gift. [19] stop. [20] somewhat. [21] guide. [22] wiped. [23] food. [24] i.e., the proper time.

Godis service for to werch,
    As yt was reson and ryȝt.   165
[Up þei ros and went þeþer,
They and þer chylder togeþer,
    When þei were redy dyȝht.]

Sir Cleges knelyd on his kne;
To Ihesu Crist prayed he   170
    Becavse of his wiffe:
"Gracius Lord," he seyd thoo,
"My wyffe and my chyldyrn too,
    Kepe hem out of stryffe!"
The lady prayed for hym ayen   175
That God schuld kepe hym fro peyne
    In euerlastyng lyf.
Whan service was don, hom they went,
And thanked God with god entent,
    And put away penci[ffe].[25]   180

Whan he to hys place cam,
His care was will abatyd than;
    Thereof he gan stynt.
He made his wife afore hym goo
And his chyldyrn both to;   185
    Hymselfe alone went
Into a gardeyne there besyde,
And knelyd dovn in þat tyde
    And prayed God veramend,
And thanked God wyth all hys hartt   190
Of his dysese and hys povertt,[26]
    That to hym was sent.

As he knelyd on hys knee
Vnderneth a chery-tre,
    Makyng hys preyere,   195
He rawȝt a bowe ouer hys hede

---

[25] pensiveness, melancholy. [26] poverty.

166. The three lines in brackets are supplied from O.

And rosse vpe in that stede;
  No lenger knelyd he there.
Whan þe bowe was in hys hand,
Grene leves thereon he fonde,   200
  And rovnd beryse in fere.
He seyd, "Dere God in Trenyté,
What manere of beryse may þis be,
  That grovyn²⁷ þis tyme of yere?

Abowȝt þis tyme i sey neuer ere,   205
That any tre schuld frewȝt²⁸ bere,
  As for²⁹ as i haue sowȝt."
He thowȝt to taste yf he cowþe;
And on he put in his mowth,
  And spare wold he nat.   210
After a chery þe reles³⁰ was,
The best þat euer he ete in place,
  Syn he was man wrowȝt.
A lytyll bowe he gan of-slyve,³¹
And thowȝt to schewe yt to his wife,   215
  And in he yt browȝt.

"Loo! dame, here ys newelté;³²
In oure gardeyne of a chery-tre
  I fond yt, sekerly.
I am aferd yt ys tokynnyng   220
Of more harme that ys comynge;
  For soth, thus thynkkyth me."
[His wyfe seyd, "It is tokenyng
Off mour godness þat is comyng;
  We schall haue mour plenté.]   225
But wethyr wee haue les or more,
Allwaye thanke we God therefore;
  Yt ys best, trewly."

---

²⁷ grow.   ²⁸ fruit.   ²⁹ far.   ³⁰ taste.   ³¹ cut off.   ³² novelty.

208. MS. *caste;* O. *tayst.*
222. The lines in brackets are supplied from O.
226. MS. *more or les;* Tr. alters.

Than seyd the lady with good chere,
"Latt vs fyll a panyer[33]   230
   Of þis þat God hath sent.
To-morovn, whan þe day doþe spryng,
Ye schill to Cardyffe to þe kynge
   And yeve hym to present;
And sech a yefte ye may haue there   235
That þe better wee may fare all þis yere,
   I tell you, werament."
Sir Cleges gravntyd sone thereto:
"To-morovn to Cardiffe will i goo,
   After youre entent."   240

On the morovn, whan yt was lyȝt,
The lady hade a panere dyght;
   Hyr eldest son callyd sche:
"Take vpp thys panyere goodly
And bere yt forth esyly   245
   Wyth thy fadyr fre !"
Than Sir Cleges a staffe toke;
He hade non hors—so seyth þe boke—
   To ryde on hys iorny,
Neythyr stede nere palfray,   250
But a staffe was hys hakenay,[34]
   As a man in pouerté.

Sir Cleges and his son gent
The right waye to Cardiffe went
   Vppon Cristemas daye.   255
To the castell he cam full right,
As they were to mete dyȝt,
   Anon, the soth to saye.
In Sir Cleges thowȝt to goo,
But in pore clothyng was he tho   260
   And in sympull araye.

---

[33] basket. [34] horse.

248. The source is unknown; for analogues, see McKnight.
258. O. *at none.*

The portere seyd full hastyly,
"Thou chorle, withdrawe þe smertly,
   I rede the, without delaye;

Ellys, be God and Seint Mari,   265
I schall breke thyne hede on high;
   Go stond in beggeris rowȝt.[35]
Yf þou com more inward,
It schall þe rewe afterward,
   So i schall þe clowȝt."[36]   270
"Good sir," seyd Sir Cleges tho,
"I pray you, lat me in goo
   Nowe, without dowȝt.
The kynge i haue a present browȝtt
From Hym þat made all thynge of nowȝt;   275
   Behold all abowȝt !"

The porter to the panere went,
And the led[37] vppe he hentt;
   The cheryse he gan behold.
Will he wyst, for his comyng   280
Wyth þat present to þe kyng,
   Gret yeftis haue he schuld.
"Be Hym," he seyd, "that me bowȝt,
Into thys place comste þou nott,
   As i am man of mold,[38]   285
The thyrde part but þou graunte me
Of þat the kyng will yeve þe,
   Wethyr yt be syluer or gold."

Sir Cleges seyd, "I asent."
He yaue hym leve, and in he went,   290
   Wythout more lettyng.
In he went a gret pace;
   The vsschere at the hall-dore was

---

[35] crowd.   [36] beat.   [37] lid.   [38] earth; i.e., mortal man.

266. MS. higȝt; Tr. emends.
267. Cf. Int. III.A.2 and "Horn" 1080.

Wyth a staffe stondynge,
In poynte[39] Cleges for to smyȝt: 295
"Goo bake, þou chorle," he seyd, "full tyȝt,
   Without teryyng!
I schall þe bette euery leth,[40]
Hede and body, wythout greth,
   Yf þou make more pressynge."[41]   300

"Good sir," seyd Sir Cleges than,
"For Hys loue þat made man,
   Sese[42] youre angrye mode!
I haue herr a present browȝt
From Hym þat made all thynge of nowȝt,   305
   And dyed on the rode.
Thys nyȝt in my gardeyne yt grewe;
Behold wethyr it be false or trewe;
   They be fayre and good."
The vsschere lyfte vp þe lede smartly   310
And sawe the cheryse verily;
   He marveld in his mode.

The vsschere seyd, "Be Mari swet,
Chorle, þou comste not in yett,
   I tell þe sekyrly,   315
But þou me graunte, without lesyng,
The thyrd part of þi wynnyng,
   Wan þou comste ayen to me."
Sir Cleges sey non othyr von;[43]
Thereto he grauntyd sone anon;   320
   It woll non othyr be.
Than Sir Cleges with hevi chere

---

[39] ready. [40] limb. [41] importunity. [42] cease. [43] supposition; i.e., no alternative.

295. Ushers were attendants at the doors who kept the rabble from annoying guests at a feast; cf. Wright, Ch. V.
296. MS. transfers *full tyȝt* to the beginning of l. 297.
306. MS. *on rode tre;* Tr. emends.
315-6. These lines are written as one in the MS.; also 333-4.

Toke hys son and hys panere;
Into the hall went he.

The styward walkyd there withall   325
Amonge the lordis in þe hall,
  That wern rech on wede.
To Sir Cleges he went boldly
And seyd, "Ho made the soo hardi
  To com into thys stede?   330
Chorle," he seyd, "þou art to bold!
Wythdrawe the with thy clothys old
  Smartly, i the rede!"
"I haue," he seyd, "a present browȝt
From oure Lord, that vs dere bowȝt   335
  And on the rode gan blede."

The panyere he toke the styward sone,
And he pullyd out the pyne[44] [anon],
  As smertly as he myȝt.
The styward seyd, "Be Mari dere,   340
Thys sawe i neuer thys tyme of yere,
  Syn i was man wrowȝt.
Thou schalt com no nere the kynge,
But yf thowe graunt me myn askyng,
  Be Hym þat me bowȝt: 345
The thyrd partt of the kyngis yefte,
That will i haue, be my threfte,[45]
  Ar forthere gost þou nott!"

Sir Cleges bethowȝt hym than,
"My part ys lest bethwyxt þes men,   350
  And i schall haue no thynge.
For my labor schall i nott get,
But yt be a melys mete."[46]
  Thus he thouȝt syynge.

-----

[44] pin, fastener.   [45] thrift.   [46] a meal's food.

338. Tr. supplies *anon* from O.

He[47] seyd, "Harlot, hast þou noo tonge?   355
Speke to me and terye nat longe
    And graunte me myn askynge,
Ar wyth a staffe i schall þe wake,
That thy rebys schall all toquake,[48]
    And put þe out hedlynge."[49]   360

Sir Cleges sey non othyr bote,
But his askyng graunte he most,
    And seyd with syynge sore,
"Whatsoeuer the kyng reward,
Ye schyll haue the thyrd part,   365
    Be yt lesse ar more."
[When Sir Cleges had seyd þat word,
The stewerd and he wer acorde
    And seyd to hym no more.]
Vpe to the desse Sir Cleges went   370
Full soborly and with good entent,
    Knelynge the kynge beforn.

Sir Cleges oncowyrd[50] the panyere
And schewed the kynge the cheryse clere,
    On the grovnd knelynge.   375
He seyd, "Ihesu, oure savyore,
Sent the thys frewȝt with honore
    On thys erth growynge."
The kynge sye thes cheryse newe;
He seyd, "I thanke Cryst Ihesu;   380
    Thys ys a fayre neweynge."[1]
He commaunndyd Sir Cleges to mete,
And aftyrward he thowȝt with hym to speke,
    Wythout any faylynge.

The kynge thereof made a present   385
And sent yt to a lady gent
    Was born in Cornewayle.

---

[47] i.e., the steward.   [48] that your ribs shall be shattered.   [49] headlong.   [50] un-
covered.   [1] novelty.

362. *Most* for *mote.*

Sche was a lady bryght and schene
And also ryght will besene,[2]
   Wythout any fayle.   390
The cheryse were servyd thorowe þe hall;
Than seyd þe kynge, þat lord ryall:
   "Be mery, be my cunnsell!
And he þat browȝt me þis present,
Full will i schall hym content;   395
   Yt schall hym will avayle."

Whan all men were mery and glade,
Anon the kynge a squire bade,
   "Brynge nowe me beforn
The pore man þat the cheryse browȝt!"   400
He cam anon and teryde natt,
   Wythout any skorn.
Whan he cam before the kynge,
On knese he fell knelynge,
   The lordis all beforn.   405
To the kyng he spake full styll;
"Lord," he seyd, "watte ys your will?
   I am youre man fre-born."

"I thanke the hartyly," seyd þe kynge,
"Of thy yeft and presentynge,   410
   That þou haste nowe idoo.
Thowe haste onowryd[3] all my fest,
Old and yonge, most and lest,
   And worschepyd me also.
Wattsooeuer þou wolt haue,   415
I will the graunnte, so God me saue,
   That thyne hart standyth to.[4]
[Wheþer it be lond our lede
Or oþer gode, so God me spede,
   How-þat-euer it go."]   420

---

[2] circumspect.   [3] honored.   [4] desires.

388. O. says that afterwards this lady was his queen, a reminiscence of
the story of Uther and Ygerne.

He seyd, "Gramarcy, lech[5] kynge!
Thys ys to me a comfortynge,
    I tell you sekyrly.
For to haue lond or lede
Or othyr reches, so God me spede,   425
    Yt ys to mech for me.
But seth i schall chese myselfe,
I pray you graunt me strokys xii
    To dele were lykyth me;
Wyth my staffe to pay hem all   430
To myn aduerseryse in þe hall,
    For Send[6] Charyté."

Than aunsswerd Hewtar[7] þe kynge,
"I repent my grauntynge
    That i to þe made.   435
God!" he seyd, "so mott i thee,
Thowe haddyst be better[8] haue gold or fee;
    More nede thereto þou hade."
Sir Cleges seyd with awaunt,[9]
"Lord, yt ys youre owyn graunte;   440
    Therefore i am full glade."
The kynge was sory therefore,
But neuer the lesse he grauntyd hym there;
    Therefore he was full sade.

Sir Cleges went into þe hall   445
Amonge þe gret lordis all,
    Without any more.
He sowȝt after the prowȝd styward,
For to yeve hym hys reward,
    Becavse he grevyd hym sore.   450
He yaffe the styward sech a stroke,
That he fell dovn as a bloke[10]
    Before all þat therein were,

_____

[5] liege.   [6] saint.   [7] Uther.   [8] it would be better for you to.   [9] boast; i.e., boldly.
[10] block.

434. MS. _grauntetynge_.
436. MS. _Good_.
437. Written as two lines in the MS.

And after he yafe hym othyr thre;
He seyd, "Sire, for thy corteci,   455
   Smyʒte me no more!"

Out of the hall Sir Cleges went;
Moo to paye was hys entent,
   Wythout any lett.
He went to þe vsschere in a breyde:[11]   460
"Haue here sum strokys!" he seyde,
   Whan he wyth hym mete,
So þat after and many a daye
He wold warn[12] no man þe waye,
   So grymly he hym grett.   465
Sir Cleges seyd, "Be my threft,
Thowe haste the thyrd part of my yefte,
   As i the behight."

Than he went to the portere,
And iiii strokys he yaue hym there;   470
   His part hade he tho,
So þat after and many a daye
He wold warn no man þe waye,
   Neythyr to ryde nere goo.
The fyrste stroke he leyde hym on,   475
He brake in to hys schuldyr bon
   And his on arme thereto.
Sir Cleges seyd, "Be my threfte,
Thowe haste the thyrd parte of my yefte;
   The comnaunnte[13] we made soo."   480

The kynge was sett in hys parlore[14]
Wyth myrth, solas, and onor;
   Sir Cleges thedyr went.
An harpor sange a gest[15] be mowth
Of a knyʒt there be sowth,   485

---

[11] rush.   [12] deny.   [13] agreement.   [14] small, private audience-room.   [15] tale.

455. MS. *sore;* O. *sir.*
471. MS. *there;* O. *tho.*

Hymselffe, werament.
Than seyd the kynge to þe harpor,
"Were ys knyȝt Cleges, tell me here;
   For þou hast wyde iwent.
Tell me trewth, yf þou can: 490
Knowyste þou of þat man?"
   The harpor seyd, "Yee, iwysse:

Sum tyme forsoth i hym knewe;
He was a knyȝt of youris full trewe
   And comly of gesture.   495
We mynstrellys mysse hym sekyrly,
Seth he went out of cunntré;
   He was fayre of stature."
The kynge sayd, "Be myn hede,
I trowe þat Sir Cleges be dede,   500
   That i lovyd paramore.[16]
Wold God he were alyfe;
I hade hym levere than othyr v,
   For he was stronge in stowre."

Sir Cleges knelyd before þe kynge;   505
For he grauntyd hym hys askynge,
   He thanked hym cortesly.
Specyally the kynge hym prayed,
To tell hym whye tho strokis he payed
   To hys men thre.   510
He seyd þat he myȝt nat com inward,
"Tyll euerych i graunttyd þe thyrd⁺partt
   Of þat ye wold yeve me.
With þat i schuld haue nowȝt myselfe;
Werefore i yaue hem strokis xii;   515
   Me thowt yt best, trewly."

The lordes lowe, both old a[nd] yenge,
And all that wern with þe kynge,

---

[16] fervently.

488. MS. *herere.*

They made solas inowe.
The kynge lowe, so he myȝt nott [sitte];   520
He seyd, "Thys ys a noble wyȝt,[17]
   To God i make a wove."[18]
He sent after his styward:
"Hast þou," he seyd, "thy reward?
   Be Cryst, he ys to lowe."[19]   525
The styward seyd with lokes grym,
["I thynke neuer to haue ado[20] with hym;]
   The dewle hym born on a lowe!"[21]

The kynge seyd to hym than,
"What ys thy name? tell me, good man,   530
   Nowe anon rygh[t]!"
"I higȝt Sir Cleges, soo haue i blysse;
My ryght name yt ys iwysse;
   I was ȝoure owyn knyȝt."
"Art thou Sir Cleges, þat servyd me,   535
That was soo ientyll and soo fre
   And so stronge in fyght?"
"Ye, sir lord," he seyd, "so mott i thee;
Tyll God in hevyn hade vesyte[22] me,
   Thus pouerte haue me dyȝt."[23]   540

The kynge yaue hym anon ryȝt
All þat longed to a knyȝt,
   To rech[24] hys body wyth;
The castell of Cardyffe he yaue hym thoo
[With all þe pourtenans[25] þerto,   545
   To hold with pes and grythe.
Than he made hym hys stuerd
Of all hys londys afterwerd,
   Off water, lond, and frythe.[26]

---

[17] wit, jest. [18] vow. [19] be praised. [20] to do. [21] may the devil burn him in a fire. [22] blessed. [23] afflicted. [24] enrich. [25] appurtenances. [26] woods.

520. O. *sytte;* Tr. supplies.

A cowpe[27] of gold he gafe hym blythe,   550
To bere to Dam Clarys, hys wyfe,
    Tokenyng of ioy and myrthe.]

The last page of the Edinburgh manuscript is lacking. The Oxford manuscript has two more stanzas. The king makes Sir Cleges' son a squire. They return to Dame Clarice and live long and happy lives thereafter.

---

[27] cup.

THE TALE OF BERYN

THE TALE OF BERYN

This piece is one of the spurious Canterbury Tales in the Duke of Northumberland's manuscript (after 1400), where it is assigned to the Merchant on the return journey. The text is that of the edition of Furnivall and Stone for the Early English Text Society (*Extra Series* 105), with normalized capitals and punctuation and restoration of many readings of the manuscript. A flourish at the end of a word has been transcribed as *-e*. Most of the purely metrical emendations of previous editors have been removed.

The meter is that of "Gamelyn": a doggerel line tending to seven stresses and an iambic cadence.

The poem is very like a French romance, "L'Histoire du Chevalier Berinus," known in a manuscript of the fifteenth century and in a print of the sixteenth. This, in turn, has several oriental analogues, and, despite the Roman names and setting, the source of the tale is certainly oriental. Discussions of the story are in the edition mentioned above, and in "The Book of Sindibad," E. Comparetti (*Folk Lore Society* 1882), and by W. A. Clouston (privately printed, Glasgow, 1884), who lists eight oriental versions and one Spanish. Like most oriental pieces, this has been unduly neglected.

The scribe's most troublesome mannerism is omission of relatives (2924, etc.).

The extract is the trial scene, the first of its kind in the English romances. Beryn's father, Faunus, turns against him because of his profligacy and the enmity of a stepmother. As a parting gift, Beryn receives five merchant ships and their cargoes. After a storm, the fleet lands at Falsetown, where the inhabitants make a business of swindling strangers. In their courts, no matter how preposterous the testimony, no rebuttal or negative evidence is permitted; and they abet each other in swearing to falsehoods. They find Beryn easy prey: as the loser in a game of chess, he must drink all the salt water in the sea or give up his ships; a merchant, Hanybald, offers to exchange for the cargo five shiploads of such goods as Beryn shall find in his house, but removes all the goods before Beryn can seize them; a blind man accuses him of having stolen his eyes; a woman of the town asks damages because he has deserted her; and another knave, Macaigne, sells Beryn a knife, and then accuses him

899

of having murdered Macaigne's father with it. Beryn is indicted
on each count, and is in sore straits when Geffrey, a Roman exile
a hundred years old, so abused by the Falsetowners that he must
masquerade as a crippled beggar, offers his services. Beryn accepts,
and the accusers, fearful that he will put to sea before the trial,
appear before his ships to summon him.

When Beryn hem aspied: "Now, Geffrey, in thy honde 2910
Stont lyff and goodis; doth with vs what the list;
For all our hope is on the—comfort, help, and trist;[1]
For we must bide aventur such as God woll shape,
For nowe i am in certen we mow no wise scape."[2]
"Have no dout," quod Geffrey, "beth mery; let me aloon: 2915
Getith a peir sisours,[3] sherith my berd anoon;
And aftirward lete top[4] my hede, hastlych and blyve."
Som went to with sesours, som with a knyfe;
So what for sorowe and hast, and for lewd tole,[5]
There was no man alyve bet like to[6] a fole 2920
Then Geffrey was. By þat tyme þey had al ido,
Hanybald clepid out Beryn, to motehall[7] for to go,
And stood oppon the brigg, with an huge route.[8]
Geffrey was the first to Hanybald gan to loute,[9]
And lokid out a-fore-shipp. "God bles ȝew, sir!" quod he. 2925
"Where art þow now, Beryn? com nere! behold and se!
Here is an huge pepill irayd and idight;[10]
All these been my children, þat been in armys bryȝte.
Ȝistirday i gate[11] hem: [is it] nat mervaill
That þey been hidir icom, to be of oure counsaill, 2930
And to stond by vs, and help vs in oure ple.
A, myne owne childryn, blessid mut ye be!"
Quod Geffrey, with an hiȝe voise, and had a nyce[12] visage,
And gan to daunce for ioy, in the fore-stage.[13]
Hanybald lokid on Geffrey as he were amasid,[14] 2935
And beheld his contenaunce, and howe he was irasid;[15]

---

[1] trust. [2] escape. [3] scissors. [4] cut hair off the top. [5] unsuitable instruments.
[6] more like. [7] assembly-hall, court. [8] throng. [9] bow. [10] crowd dressed up and
ready. [11] begot. [12] silly. [13] forecastle. [14] dazed. [15] shaved.

2917. This is done to show that he is a professional jester. Cf. "Robert
of Sicily" 170 ff.
2927. MS. *in dight*.

But evir-more he þou3t þat he was a fole,
Naturell of kynde, and had noon othir tool,[16]
As semed by his wordis and his visage both;
And þou3t it had been foly to wex with hym wroth,   2940
And gan to bord[17] ageyn, and axid hym in game,
"Sith þow art oure ffadir, who is then oure dame?
And howe and in what plase were wee begete?"
"3istirday," quod Geffrey, "pleying in the strete
Att a gentill game þat clepid is the quek:[18]   2945
A longe peny-halter was cast about my nekk,
And iknet[19] fast with a ryding-knot,[20]
And cast ovir a perche and hale[d][21] along my throte."
"Was þat a game," quod Hanybald, "for to hang þyselve?"
"So þey seyd about me, a Ml[22] ech by hymselff."   2950
"How scapiddist þow," quod Hanybald, "þat þow were nat
      dede?"
"Thereto can i answere, without eny rede:
I bare thre dise[23] in myne owne purs—
For i go nevir without, fare i bettir or wors;
I kist[24] hem forth al thre, and too fil amys-ase,[25]   2955
But here now what fill aftir—ri3t a mervelouse case !—
There cam a mows lepe forth, and ete þe þird boon,[26]
That puffid out hire skyn, as grete as she my3t goon;
And in this manere wise, of þe mouse and me
All yee be icom, my children faire and fre.   2960
And 3it, or it be eve, fall wol such a chaunce,
To stond in my power 3ew alle to avaunce;
For and wee plede wele to-day, we shull be riche inow3e."
Hanybald of his wordis hertlich lou3e,

---

[16] silly by nature and without other device (intent). [17] jest. [18] checkers. [19] tied.
[20] slip-knot. [21] projection, and drawn. [22] thousand. [23] dice. [24] cast. [25] double-
aces (the lowest possible throw). [26] bone, die.

2945. Geffrey's answers are deliberately silly; the force of this one is,
"We were playing a harmless game: they were about to hang me." *Quek*
means checkers, and is also used in the morality play "Mankind" (801)
to imitate the sound of a man strangling.
2956. MS. *mervolouse*.
2962. The infinitive stands for a complement of *such*, this fortune:
namely, to advance you, etc.

And so did al þat herd hym, as þey myȝte wele,   2965
And had grete ioy with hym for to telle,
For þey knewe hym noon othir but a fole of kynde;
And al was his discrecioune; and þat previd þe ende.[27]
  Thus whils Geffrey iapid[28], to make hire hertis liȝte,
Beryn and his company were rayid and idiȝte,   2970
And londit hem in botis, ferefull howe to spede;
For all hir þouȝtis in balance stode betwene hope and drede.
But ȝit they did hir peyn[29] to make liȝtsom chere,
As Geffrey hem had enfourmed, of port[30] and al manere
Of hire governaunce,[31] al the longe day,   2975
Tyll hir plee were endit. So went they forth hire wey,
To the court with Hanybald. Then Beryn gan to sey,
"What nedith this, Sir Hanybald, to make such aray,
Sith wee been pese-marchantis, and vse no spoliacioune?"[32]
"For soth, sire," quod Hanybald, "to me was made relacioune
Yee were in poynt to void;[33] and yef ye had do so,   2981
Yee had lost yeur lyvis, without wordis mo."
Beryn held hym still; Geffrey spak anoon;
"No les wed þen lyvis![34] whi so, good Sir Iohne?
That were somwhat to much, as it semeith me!   2985
But ye be ovir-wise þat dwell in this ceté:
For[35] yee have begonne a thing makith ȝewe riȝte bold;
And ȝit, or it be eve, as folis shul ye be hold.
And eke yee devyne;[36] for in shipmannys crafft,
Wotith litill what longith to afore-þe-shipp and bafft;[37] 2990
And namelich[38] in the dawnyng, when shipmen first arise."
"My good ffrend," quod Hanybald, in a scornyng wise,
"Ye must onys enfourme me, þurh yeur discrecioune;
But first ye must answer to a questioune:

---

[27] it was all ingenuity on his part, and the outcome proved it. [28] jested. [29] i.e., did their best. [30] demeanor. [31] conduct. [32] practice no robbery. [33] leave. [34] forfeit not only bail, but life too. [35] that. [36] make guesses. [37] the front and stern of a vessel. [38] especially.

2984. "Sir John" is a jesting name for a priest. It was first a name very commonly assumed by members of the priesthood; then it became a soubriquet for "priest;" and at length it was often used disparagingly. See Skeat's Chaucer, "Pro." 1172.
  2990. MS. *and wotith.*

Why make men cros-saill in myddis of þe mast?" 2995
[Gef.] "For to talowe þe shipp, and fech[e] more last."[39]
[Han.] "Why goon the ȝemen[40] to bote, ankirs to hale?"[41]
[Gef.] "For to make hem redy to walk to þe ale."
[Han.] "Why hale they vp stonys by the crane-lyne?"
[Gef.] "To make the tempest sese, and the sonne shyne." 3000
[Han.] "Why close they the port with the see-bord?"[42]
[Gef.] "For the mastir shuld awake atte first word."[43]
[Han.] "Thow art a redy reve,"[44] quod Hanybald, "in fay."
[Gef.] "Yee sir trewly, for sothe is þat yee sey."
Geffrey evir clappid[45] as doith a watir myll, 3005
And made Hanybald to lauȝe al his hert fell.[46]
"Beryn," quod this Geffrey, "retourn thy men ageyne;
What shull they do with the[m] at court? No men on hem
       pleyne.[47]
Plede thy case thyselve, riȝt as þow hast iwrouȝt;
To bide with the shippis my purpos is and þouȝt." 3010
"Nay, for soth," quod Hanybald, "þow shalt abyde on lond;
Wee have no folis but the," and toke hym by þe hond,
"For thow art wise in lawe to plede al the case."
"That can i bettir," quod Geffrey, "þen eny man in this plase!
What seyst þow therto, Beryn? shall i tell thy tale?" 3015
Hanybald likid his wordis wele, and forward gan hym hale.[48]
Beryn made hym angry,[49] and siȝhid wondir sore,
For Geffrey hym had enfourmyd of euery poynt tofore,
How he hym shuld govern all the longe day.
Geffrey chas[t]id[50] hym ageyne: "Sey me ȝe or nay! 3020
Maystowe nat ihere speke som maner word?"
"Leve thy blab, lewd[1] fole! me likith nat thy bord![2]

---

[39] grease the bottom and give more displacement. [40] sailors. [41] haul up. [42] a
plank to cover the ports. [43] i.e., quickly. [44] overseer. [45] rattled on. [46] heart's
fill. [47] accuse them. [48] draw. [49] feigned grief. [50] rebuked. [1] ignorant, stupid.
[2] humor.

2995 ff. The cross-sail is the square sail used in going rapidly before the
wind. The anchors were dropped at some distance from the ship, often
in shallow water; and hence at least one had to be dislodged and recovered
from a small boat. The stones are being put in for ballast, Beryn's cargo
having been removed by Hanybald's men.
3008. MS. man.

I have anothir þou3t," quod Beryn, "whereof þowe carist lite."[3]
"Clepeist þow me a fole," quod Geffrey; "al þat i may þe wite?[4]
But first, when wee out of Rome saillid both in fere,　　　3025
Tho i was thy felawe and thy partynere;
For tho the marchandise was more þen halff myne;
And sith þat þowe com hidir, þowe takeist al for thyne.
But 3it or it be eve, i woll make oon behest:[5]
But þowe have my help, thy part shal be lest."　　　　3030
"Thyn help!" quod Beryn; "lewde fole, þow art more þen
　　masid!"[6]
Dres the to þe shippis ward,[7] with thy crowne irasid,
For i my3t nevir spare the bet! trus, and be agoo!"[8]
"I wol go with the," quod Geffrey, "where þow wolt or no,
And lern to plede lawe, to wyn both house and londe."　　3035
"So þow shalt," quod Hanybald, and led hym by the honde,
And leyd his hond oppon his nek; but, and he had iknowe
Whom he had led, in sikirnes he had wel levir in snowe
Have walkid xl myle, and rathir then faill more;[9]
For he wisshid that Geffrey had ibe vnbore　　　　3040
Ful offt-tyme in that day, or the ple were do;[10]
And so did al þat wrou3t Beryn shame and woo.
　　Now yee þat list abide and here of sotilté[11]
Mow knowe how þat Beryn sped in his ple,
And in what aray to the court he went;　　　　3045
And howe Hanybald led Geffrey, disware[12] of his entent.
But 3it he axid of Geffrey, "What is þy name, i prey?"
"Gylhochet," quod Geffrey, "men clepid me 3istirday."
"And where weer þow ibore?" "I note, i make avowe,"
Seyd Geffrey to this Hanybald; "i axe þat of 3ewe;　　3050
For i can tell no more, but here i stond nowe."
Hanybald of his wordis hertlich. low3e,
And held hym for a passing[13] fole to serve eny lord.
Thus þey romyd ianglyng[14] into þe court ward;

---

[3] i.e., his impending trial. [4] though I may protect you. [5] vow. [6] befuddled.
[7] hasten to the ship. [8] get out and begone! [9] and (walked) many more (even)
more readily. [10] suit was completed. [11] trickery. [12] unaware. [13] excellent.
[14] bandying words.

But or they com ther, the Steward was iset,   3055
And the grettest of þe towne, a company imet
And gon to stryve fast who shuld have þe good
That com was with Beryn ovir þe salt flood.
Som seyd oon, and som seyde anothire;
Som wold have the shippis, þe parell, and þe rothir;[15]   3060
Som his eyen, som his lyff wold have, and no les;
Or els he shuld for hem fyne,[16] or he did pas.
And in the mene-whils[17] they were in this afray,
Beryn and these Romeyns were com, in good aray
As myȝt be made of woll and of coloure greynyd;[18]   3065
They toke a syde-bench þat for hem was ordeyned.
    When all was husst[19] and still, Beryn rose anoon
And stode in the myddis of þe hal, tofore hem everychone,
And seyd, "Sir Steward, in me shall be no let:
I am icom to answere as my day is set.   3070
Do me ryȝte and reson: i axe ȝewe no more."
"So shall [i]," quod the Steward, "for þerto i am swore."
    "He shall have ryȝt," quod Geffrey, "where þow wolt or no.
For, and þow mys onys thy iugement on do,[20]
I woll to þe Emperour of Rome, my cosyne;   3075
For of o cup he and i ful offt have dronk þe wyne,
And ȝit wee shull hereaftir, as offt as wee mete,
For he is long[21] the gladdere when i send hym to grete."
Thus Geffrey stode oppon a fourme,[22] for he wold be sey
Above all the othir the shuldris and the cry,[23]   3080
And starid al aboute, with his lewd[24] berd,
And was ihold a verry[25] fole of ech man [þat] hym herd.
    The Steward and þe officers and þe burgeyssis alle

---

[15] tackle and rudder.   [16] pay ransom.   [17] while.   [18] wool and fast-dyed colors.
[19] hushed.   [20] impose your judgment wrongly.   [21] by far.   [22] bench.   [23] above
the shoulders and tumult of all the others.   [24] absurd.   [25] true.

3055. Evander the Steward is in league with the accusers, and has
already given decisions against Beryn.
3056. The right reading probably is *town in company imet*. The loose
syntax of the next clause is of no importance.—F.
3083. The various accusations and the solutions are all in the French
original; but the English story is more ingenious in not disposing of each
accusation as it is made, but waiting until the charges are complete.

Lauȝhid at hym hertlich; the crioure gan to calle
The burgeys þat had pleyd with Beryn atte ches; 3085
And he aros quiklich, and gan hym for to dres²⁶
Afore the Steward atte barr, as þe maner is.
He gan to tell his tale with grete redynes;
"Here me, Sir Steward! þis day is me set,
To have ryght and reson—i ax ȝewe no bet,— 3090
Of Beryn, þat here stondith, þat with me ȝistirday
Made a certen covenaunt, and atte ches we did pley:
That whoso were imatid²⁷ of vs both too
Shuld do the todirs byddyng; and yf he wold nat so,
He must drynke al the watir þat salt were in the se; 3095
Thus i to hym surid,²⁸ and he also to me.
To preve my tale trewe, i am nat al aloon."
Vp rose x burgeysis quyklich anoon,
And affermyd evir[y] word of his tale soth;
And made hem al redy for to do²⁹ hire othe. 3100
    Evandir the Steward, "Beryn, now," quod he,
"Thow must answere nede; it wol noon othir be;
Take thy counsell to the: spede on! have i doon."
Beryn held hym still: Geffrey spak anoon:
    "Now be my trowith," quod Geffrey, "i mervell much of
        ȝewe 3105
To bid vs go to counsell, and knowith³⁰ me wise inowȝ,
And evir ful avisid, in twynkelyng of an eye,
To make a short answere, but yf my mowith be dry.
Shuld wee go to counsell for o word or tweyne?
Be my trowtith we nyl! let se mo that pleyne!³¹ 3110
And but he be ianswerd, and þat riȝt anoon,
I ȝeve ȝewe leve to rise and walk out, everychoon,
And aspy redely yf ye fynd me there.
In the meen-whils, i wol abide here.
Nay, i telle trewly, i am wiser þen yee ween; 3115

---

²⁶ go. ²⁷ mated, beaten. ²⁸ assured. ²⁹ take. ³⁰ knowing me to be. ³¹ i.e.,
produce other complainants.

3103. Line 3102 is repeated after this.
3113. I.e., if the plaintiffs are not answered, it will be because Geffrey
is out of the courtroom.

For þere nys noon of ȝewe woot redely what i meen."
Every man gan lawȝe al his hert fill
Of Geffrey and his wordis; but Beryn held hym still,
And was cleen astonyd,—but ȝit, nere-þe-lattir,[32]
He held it nat al foly þat Geffrey did clatir,[33]   3120
But wisely hym governyd, as Geffrey hym tauȝte,
For parcell of his wisdom tofore he had smaught.[34]
"Sire Steward," quod Beryn, "i vndirstond wele
The tale of þis burgeyse; now let anothir tel,
That i may take counsell, and answer al att onys."   3125
"I graunt," quod the Steward, "thyn axing, for þe nonys,
Sith þow wolt be rewlid by þy folis rede;
For he is ryȝte[35] a wise man to help the in thy nede!"
    Vp arose the accusours, queyntlich[36] anoon;
Hanybald was the first of hem evirichone,   3130
And gan to tell his tale with a proud chere:
"ȝistirday, soverens, when i was here,
Beryn and thes burgeyse gon to plede[37] fast
For pleying atte ches; so ferforth,[38] atte last,
Thurh vertu of myne office, þat i had in charge   3135
Beryns fyve shippis, for[39] to go at large,
And to be in answere here þis same day.
So, walkyng to the strond ward, wee bargeynyd by the wey
That i shuld have the marchaundise þat Beryn with hym brouȝte
(Wherof i am sesid,[40] as ful sold and bouȝte),   3140
In covenaunt that i shuld his shippis fill ageyne
Of my marchaundise, such as he tofore had seyne
In myne owne plase, howsis to or thre,
Ful óf marchandise as they myȝt be.
And i am evir redy: when-so-evir he woll,   3145
Let hym go or sende, and charge[41] his shippis full
Of such marchandise as he fyndith there:
For in such wordis wee accordit[42] were."
    Vp rose x burgeysis—not tho þat rose tofore,
But oþir,—and made hem redy to have swore   3150

---

[32] nevertheless. [33] babble. [34] for he had tasted a bit of his wisdom before.
[35] indeed. [36] with alacrity. [37] have a dispute over. [38] to such an extent. [39] i.e.,
so as to permit him. [40] in possession. [41] load. [42] agreed.

That every word of Hanybald, from þe begynnyng to þe ende,
Was soth and eke trewe; and with all hir mende[43]
Ful prest they were to preve; and seyd þey were present
Atte covenaunte makeing, by God omnipotent.
"It shall nede," quod Geffrey, "whils þat i here stonde;   3155
For i woll preve it myself with my riȝt honde.
For i have been in foure batellis heretofore,
And this shall be the ffifft; and therfor i am swore;
Beholdith and seith!" and turnyd hym aboute.
The Steward and þe burgeyse gamyd[44] al aboute;   3160
The Romens held hem still, and lawuȝid but a lite.
   With that cam the blynd man, his tale to endite,[45]
That God hym graunte wynnyng riȝte as he hath aservid.[46]
Beryn and his company stood al astryvid
Betwene hope and drede, riȝte in hiȝe distres;   3165
For of wele or of woo þey had no sikirnes.[47]
"Beryn," quod this blynd, "þouȝe i may nat se,
Stond nere ȝit the barr: my comyng is for the:
That wrongfullich þowe witholdist my both to eyen,[48]
The wich i toke the for a tyme, and quyklich to me hyen,   3170
And take hem me ageyn, as our covenant was.
Beryn, i take no reward[49] of othir mennys case,
But oonlich of myne owne, that stont me most an hond.[50]
Nowe blessid be God in heven, þat brouȝt þe to this lond!
For sith our laste parting, many bittir teris   3175
Have i lete for thy love, þat som tyme partineris[1]
Of wynnyng and of lesing[2] were, ȝeris fele;
And evir i fond the trewe, til at the last þow didist stele
Awey with my too eyen that i toke to the

---

[43] memory.   [44] jested.   [45] say over.   [46] deserved.   [47] certainty.   [48] both my two eyes.   [49] regard.   [50] is especially pressing to me.   [1] partners.   [2] losing.

3158. I.e., he jestingly proposes a trial by combat, and offers himself as experienced in such affairs.

3164. The rhyme-word is probably *asterued*, in bad condition, nearly dead.

3170. The construction is: "Which I gave you (so that you might) come soon to me and give them back, as we agreed."

3176. Though the syntax is involved, the meaning is clear. The antecedent of *þat* is *our*.

To se the tregitour[i]s pley,[3] and hir sotilté,   3180
As ʒistirday here in this same plase
Tofore ʒewe, Sir Steward, rehersid as it was.
Ful trewe is that byword,[4] 'a man to seruesabill
Ledith offt Beyard from his owne stabill.'
Beryn, by the i meen, þouʒe þowe make it straunge;[5]   3185
For þow knowist trewly þat i made no chaunge[6]
Of my good eyen for thyne, þat badder[7] were."
Therewith stood vp burgeys four, witnes to bere.

   Beryn held hym still, and Geffrey spak anoon:
"Nowe of þy lewde[8] compleynt and thy masid moon,[9]   3190
By my trowith," quod Geffrey, "i have grete mervaill.
For þouʒe þow haddist eyen-sight, [y]it shuld it litil availl:
Thow shuldist nevir fare þe bet, but þe wors, in fay;
For al thing may be stil nowe for the[10] in house and way;
And yf thow haddist þyn eyen, þowe woldist no counsell hele.[11]
I knowe wele by thy fisnamy,[12] thy kynd were to stele;   3196
And eke it is thy profite and thyne ese also
To be blynd as þowe art; for nowe, whereso þow go,
Thow hast thy lyvlode,[13] whils þow art alyve;
And yf þowe myʒtist see, þow shuldist nevir thryve."   3200
Al the house þurhout, save Beryn and his feris,
Lawʒid of [14] Geffrey, þat watir on hire leris
Ran downe from hir eyen, for his masid[15] wit.

   With that cam þe vomman—hir tunge was nat sclytt[16]—
With xv burgeysis and vommen also fele[17]   3205
Hir querell[18] for to preve, and Beryn to apele,[19]
With a feire knave-child iloke[20] within hir armys;
And gan to tell hir tale of wrongis and of armys,[21]

---

[3] jugglers' performance. [4] proverb. [5] of you I complain though you feign lack
of acquaintance. [6] exchange. [7] worse. [8] stupid. [9] muddled lament. [10] for all
that you can do. [11] hide; i.e., use discretion. [12] face. [13] sustenance. [14] at.
[15] perverse. [16] slit; i.e., she was not dumb. [17] as many. [18] complaint. [19] accuse. [20] clasped. [21] injuries.

3183. Bayard was a common name for a horse; and since horses were
valuable property, "Bayard" was often used as a symbol of treasure or
wealth. The proverb means that a man too kind to others will assist
them to take his own best treasure.
3200. I.e., he would be hanged for stealing.

And eke of vnkyndnes, vntrowith,[22] and falshede
That Beryn had iwrouȝt to hire, þat queyntlich[23] from hire ȝede
Anoon oppon hire wedding, when he his will had doon,   3211
And brouȝt hir with child, and lete her sit aloon
Without help and comfort from þat day; "and noweȝ
He proferid me nat to kis onys with his mowith,
As ȝistirday, Sir Steward, afore ȝewe eche word   3215
Was rehersid here; my pleynt is of record,
And this day is me set for to have reson:[24]
Let hym make amendis, or els tell encheson[25]
Why hym ouȝt nat fynd[26] me, as man ouȝt his wyffe."
These fifftene burgeysis, quyklich also blyve,   3220
And as fele vymmen as stode by hire there,
Seyd that they were present when they weddit were,
And that every word þat þe vomman seyde
Was trewe, and eke Beryn had hire so betrayd.

    "Benedicite!" quod Geffrey, "Beryn, hast þowe a wyff?   3225
Now have God my trowith, the dayis of my lyff
I shall trust the þe las! Þow toldist me nat tofore
As wele of thy wedding and of thy sone ibore.
Go to, and kis hem both, thy wyff and eke thyn heire!
Be þow nat ashamyd, for þey both be feyr!   3230
This wedding was riȝt pryvy, but i shal make it couthe:
Behold, thy sone, it semeth, crope[27] out of þy mowith,
And eke of thy condicioune both sofft and some.
Now am i glad þyne heir shall with vs to Rome;
And i shall tech hym as i can whils þat he is ȝong,   3235
Every day by the strete to gadir houndis doung,[28]
Tyll it be abill of prentyse to crafft of tan[e]ry,[29]
And aftir i shall teche hym for to cache a fly,
And to mend mytens[30] when they been to-tore,
And aftir to cloute shoon,[31] when he is elder more: 3240

---

[22] untruth. [23] craftily. [24] reckoning. [25] cause. [26] provide for. [27] crept; i.e., the resemblance is strong. [28] dung. [29] till the child is able to be apprenticed to the business of tanning. [30] mittens. [31] patch shoes.

3223. MS. *vommen*.

3233. The more usual spelling is *saught and some* (accordant and fitting).

3237. *Taury*, as printed by Urry, means whitening leather. Either reading makes nonsense.

Ʒit, for his parentyne, to pipe as doith a mowse,
I woll hym tech, and for to pike a snayll out of his house,
And to berk as doith an hound, and sey 'Baw bawe!'
And turne round aboute, as a cat doith with a strawe;
And to blete as doith a shepe, and ney as doith an hors, 3245
And to lowe as doith a cowe; and as myne owne corps[32]
I woll cherissh hym every day, for his modirs sake;"
And gan to stapp[33] nere, the child to have itake,
As semyd by his contenaunce, alþouʒe he þouʒt nat so.

Butte modir was evir ware, and blenchid[34] to and fro, 3250
And leyd hire hond betwene, and lokid somwhat wroth;
And Geffrey in pure wrath beshrewid[35] hem al bothe;
"For by my trowith," quod Geffrey, "wel masid is thy pan![36]
For i woll teche thy sone the craftis þat i can,
That he in tyme to com myʒt wyn his lyvlood. 3255
To wex therfor angry, þow art verry wood!
Of husbond, wyff, and sone, by the Trynyté,
I note wich is the wisest of hem al[le] thre!"
"No, sothly," quod the Steward, "it liith al in þy noll,[37]
Both wit and wisdome, and previth by þy poll."[38] 3260
For al be that Geffrey wordit[39] sotilly,
The Steward and þe burgeysis held it for foly,
Al that evir he seyd, and toke it for good game,
And had ful litill knowlech he was Geffrey þe lame

Beryn and his company stode still as stone, 3265
Betwene hope and drede, disware[40] how it shuld goon;
Saff Beryn trist in party[41] þat Geffrey wold hym help;
But ʒit into þat houre he had no cause to ʒelpe,[42]
Wherfor þey made much sorow, þat dole was, and peté.
Geffrey herd hym siʒe sore; "What devill is[43] ʒewe?" quod he;
"What nede ʒew be sory, whils i stonde here? 3271

---

[32] body. [33] step. [34] twisted. [35] cursed, abused. [36] head. [37] pate. [38] (shaven)
crown. [39] spoke. [40] uncertain. [41] except that Beryn trusted in part. [42] boast.
[43] is (wrong with).

3241. The only examples of *parentyne* in the *Oxford Dictionary* are from
this poem, where it is glossed "parentage." It seems rather to mean
"training."
3249. MS. *nat nat.*
3264. Geffrey was well known to them; they had robbed him of all
'.is money, and he had pretended to be a cripple so as to escape death.

Have i nat enfourmyd ȝewe how and in what manere
That i ȝew wold help, and bryng hem in the snare?
Yf yee coude plede as wele as i, ful litill wold yee care.
Pluke[44] vp thy hert!" quod Geffrey; "Beryn, i speke to the!"
"Leve þy blab leude!"[45] quod Beryn to hym a-ye,   3276
"It doith nothing availl þat[46] sorowe com on thy hede!
It is nat worth a fly, al þat þowe hast seyde!
Have wee nat els nowe for to thynk oppon,
Saff here to iangill?"[47] Machyn rose anoon,   3280
And went to the barr, and gan to tell his tale:
He was as fals as Iudas, þat set Criste at sale.

   "Sir Steward," quod this Machyn, "and þe burgeysis all,
Knowith wele howe Melan, with purpill and with pall,[48]
And othir marchandise, seven ȝere ago   3285
Went toward Rome; and howe þat i also
Have enquerid sith, as reson woll, and kynde,
Syth he was my ffadir, to knowe of his ende.
For ȝit sith his departyng, til it was ȝistirday,
Met i nevir creature þat me coude wissh[49] or say   3290
Reedynes[50] of my ffadir, dede othir alyve.
But blessid be God in heven, in this thevis sclyve,[1]
The knyff i gaff my ffadir was ȝistirday ifound.
Sith i hym apele,[2] let hym be fast ibound.
The knyff i knowe wel inowe; also þe man stont here   3295
And dwellith in this towne, and is a cotelere,[3]
That made þe same knyff with his too hondis,
That wele i woot þere is noon like, to sech al Cristen londis;
For iii preciouse stonys been within the hafft[4]
Perfitlych icouchid, and sotillich by crafft[5]   3300
Endendit[6] in the hafft, and þat riȝt coriously:[7]

---

[44] pluck.   [45] ignorant babble.   [46] i.e., to prevent.   [47] except here to have words.
[48] rich cloth.   [49] inform.   [50] sure knowledge.   [1] sleeve.   [2] accuse.   [3] cutler.
[4] handle.   [5] set and expertly by skill.   [6] fixed.   [7] with careful art.

3283. A close parallel to this incident is in the Irish "Echtra Cormaic i Tir Tairngiri," which otherwise is little like the "Tale of Beryn."
3292. The sleeve was a convenient place for carrying small articles. Cf. the proverb, "The friar preached against stealing when he had a pudding up his sleeve."

A saphir and a salidone and a rich ruby."
The cotelere cam lepeing forth with a bold chere,
And seyd to the Steward, "þat Machyn told now here,
Every word is trew: so beth the stonys sett;   3305
I made þe knyff myselff—who myȝt know it bet?—
And toke the knyff to Machyn, and he me payd wele:
So is this felon gilty; there is no more to tell."
Vp arose burgeysis, by to, by iii, by iiii,
And seyd þey were present, þe same tyme and houre,   3310
When Machone wept sore, and brouȝt his ffadirs gownd, [8]
And gaff hym þe same knyff oppon the see stronde.
"Bethe there eny mo pleyntis of record?"
Quod Geffrey to the Steward. And he ageynward:
"How semeth the, Gylhoget? beth þere nat inowȝe?   3315
Make thyne answere, Beryn, case [9] þat þow mowe;
For oon or othir þow must sey, alþouȝe it nat availl;
And but þowe lese or þowe go, me þinkith grete mervaill."
Beryn goith to counsell, and his company;
And Geffrey bode behynde, to here more, and se,   3320
And to shewe the burgeyse somwhat of his hert,
And seyd, "But i make the pleyntyfs for to smert,
And al þat hem meyntenyth, for auȝt þat is iseyd,
I woll graunte ȝewe to kut þe eris fro my hede.
My mastir is at counsell, but counsell hath he noon;. 3325
For but i hym help, he is cleen vndoon.
But i woll help hym al þat i can, and meynten hym also
By my power and connyng; so i am bound thereto.
For i durst wage batell [10] with ȝewe, þouȝe yee be stronge,
That my mastir is in the trowith, and yee be in the wrong: 3330
For and wee have lawe, [11] i ne hold ȝew but distroyed
Iń yeur owne falshede, so be ye now aspied; [12]
Wherfor, ȝit or eve i shall abate yeur pride,
That som of ȝew shall be riȝt feyne to sclynk [13] awey and hyde."

---

[8] gown.   [9] if.   [10] agree to a judicial duel.   [11] i.e., right judgment.   [12] found out.   [13] slink.

3302. A celidony was red or black, and was thought to come from the stomach of a swallow. Cf. "Anglo-Norman Lapidaries," P. Studer and J. Evans.

The burgeysis gon to lawȝe, and scornyd hym thereto.   3335
"Gylochet," quod Evander, "and þow cowdist so
Bryng it þus about, it were a redy way."[14]
"He is a good fool," quod Hanybald, "in fay,
To put hymselff aloon in strengith, and eke in witt,
Ageyns al the burgeysis þat on þis bench sit."   3340
   "What clatir is this," quod Machyn, "al day with a fole?
Tyme is nowe to worch with som othir tole.
For i am certeyn of hir answere þat they wolle faill;
And lyf for lyf of my ffadir,[15] what may þat availl?
Wherfor beth avisid, for i am in no doute,   3345
The goodis been sufficient to part al aboute;
So may euery party-pleyntyff have his part."
   "That is reson," quod the blynd; "a trew man þow art;
And eke it were vntrowith, and eke grete syn,
But ech of vs þat pleynyth myȝt somwhat wyn."   3350
   Hanybald bote[16] his lyppis, and herd hem both wele:
"Towching the marchandise, o tale i shall ȝew tell,
And eke make avowe, and hold my behest:[17]
That of the marchandise yeur part shall be lest;
For i have made a bargeyn þat may nat be vndo;   3355
I woll hold his covenaunt, and he shall myne also."
   Vp roos quyklich the burgeyse Syrophanes:
"Hanybald," quod he, "the lawe goith by no lanys,[18]
But hold forth the streyt wey, even as doith a lyne;
For ȝistirday when Beryn with me did dyne,   3360
I was the first persone þat put hym in arest;
And for he wold go large, þow haddist in charge and hest[19]
To sese both shipp and goodis, til i were answerid;
Then must i first be servid: þis knowith al men ilerid."
   The vomman stode besidis, and cried wondir fast: 3365
"Ful soth is þat byword,[20] 'to pot who comyth last,
He worst is servid;' and so it farith by me:
Ȝit nethirles, Sir Steward, i trust to yeur leuté,[21]
That knowith best my cause and my trew entent;
I ax ȝewe no more but riȝtfull iugement.   3370

---

[14] easy way (out of trouble).   [15] i.e., if Beryn is killed in reprisal.   [16] bit.
[17] promise.   [18] by-paths.   [19] command.   [20] proverb.   [21] uprightness.

3358. L. 3352 is repeated here in the MS.

Let me have part with othir, sith he my husbond is:
Good sirs, beth avisid: i axe ȝew nat amys."
Thus they gon to stryve, and were of hiȝe[22] mode
For to depart[23] among hem othir mennys good,
Where they tofore had nevir properté,   3375
Ne nevir shuld þereaftir, by doom of equyté,
But they had othir cause þen þey had tho.
Beryn wås at counsell; his hert was ful woo,
And his meyny sory, distrakt, and al amayide;[24]
For tho they levid noon othir but[25] Geffrey had hem trayde: 3380
Because he was so long, they coude no maner rede;
But everich by hymselff wisshid he had be dede:
"O myȝtfull God!" þey seyd, "i trow, tofore this day
Was nevir gretter tresoun, fere, ne affray[26]
Iwrouȝt onto mankynde, þen now is to vs here;   3385
And namelich[27] by this Geffrey, with his sotil chere!
So feithfulle he made it[28] he wold vs help echone;
And nowe we be imyryd,[29] he letith vs sit aloon!"
"Of Geffrey," quod Beryn, "be as it be may:
Wee mut answere nede;[30] ther is noon oþir way;   3390
And therfor let me know yeur wit and yeur counsaille."
They wept and wrong hire hondis, and gan to waille
The tyme þat they were bore; and shortly, of þe lyve
The[y] wisshid þat þey were. With þat cam Geffrey blyve,
Passing hem towardis, and began to smyle.   3395
Beryn axid Geffrey wher he had be al the while;
"Have mercy oppon vs, and help vs as þowe hiȝte!"
"I woll help ȝew riȝt wele, þurh grace of Goddis myȝte;
And i can tell ȝew tyding of hir governaunce:
They stond in altircacioune and stryff in poynt to praunce[31] 3400
To depart[32] yeure goodis, and levith verryly
That it were impossibill ȝewe to remedy.
But hire hiȝe pryde and hir presumpcioune
Shal be, ȝit or eve, hir confusioune,
And to make amendis, ech man for his pleynt.   3405
Let se therfor yeur good avise, howe þey myȝt be ateynt."[33]

---

[22] angry. [23] divide. [24] dismayed. [25] nothing else except that. [26] fear or
fright. [27] especially. [28] professed. [29] stuck in the mire. [30] must needs answer.
[31] on the verge of swaggering away. [32] share. [33] convicted.

The Romeyns stode still, as who had shore hire hed.[34]
"In feith," quod Beryn, "wee con no maner rede;
But in God and ȝewe we submit vs all,
Body, lyffe, and goodis, to stond or to fall;   3410
And nevir for to travers[35] o word þat þow seyst:
Help vs, good Geffrey, as wele as þow maist !"
"Depardeux,"[36] quod Geffrey, "and i wol do me peyn
To help ȝewe, as my connyng wol strech and ateyne."
The Romeyns went to barr, and Geffrey al tofore,   3415
With a nyce contenaunce, barefote, and totore,
Pleyng with a ȝerd[37] he bare in his honde,
And was evir wistlyng[38] att euery pase comyng.
The Steward and the burgeysis had game inowȝe
Of Geffreyis nyce comyng, and hertlich lowȝe,   3420
And eche man seyd, "Gylhochet, com nere:
Thowe art ryȝt welcom, for þowe makist vs chere."
"The same welcom," quod Geffrey, "þat yee wol vs,
Fall oppon yeur hedis, i prey to God, and wers !"
They held hym for a verry fole, but he held hem wel more:[39] 3425
And so he made hem in breff tyme, alþouȝ þey wer nat shore.
"Styntith[40] nowe," quod Geffrey, "and let make pese !
Of myrthis and of iapis[41] tyme is now to cese,
And speke of othir mater þat wee have to doon,
For and wee hewe amys eny maner spone,[42]   3430
We knowe wele in certeyn what pardon wee shull have.
The more is our nede vs to defend and save.
My mastir hath bee at counsell, and ful avisid is
That i shall have the wordis,—speke i wele or mys.[43]
Wherfor, Sir Steward and yee burgeysis all,   3435
Sittith vpryȝt and wriith nat,[44] for auntris þat may fall.
For and yee deme vntrewly or do vs eny wrong,
Wee shull be refourmyd,[45] be ye nevir so strong,

---

[34] cut their heads off. [35] oppose. [36] by heaven. [37] stick. [38] whistling. [39] greater
(fools). [40] stop. [41] jesting. [42] chip; i.e., make any sort of mistake. [43] badly.
[44] conceal nothing. [45] redressed.

3407. See the note to line 3779.
3425. MS. *hym wel.* I.e., he held them greater fools than himself, and
made them appear so, although their heads were not shorn like his own.
3438. MS. *Yee shull.*

Of euery poynt and iniury, and þat in grete hast,
For he is nat vnknowe to vs þat may ȝewe chast.[46]   3440
Hold forthe the riȝt wey, and by no side-lanys!

And ás towching the first pleyntyfe Syrophanes,
That pleyde with my mastir ȝistirday atte ches
And made a certen covenaunte, who þat had þe wers
In the last game (alþouȝe i were nat there)   3445
Shuld do the todirs bidding, whatsoevir it were,
Or drynk al the watir þat salt were in the see;
Thus, i trowe, Sir Steward, ye woll record þe ple:
And yf i have imyssid[47] in lettir or in word
The lawe, wol i be rewlid aftir yeure record;[48]   3450
For we be ful avisid in this wise to answere."

Evander þe Steward and al men þat were there
Had mervill much of Geffrey, þat spak so redely,
Whose wordis ther[to]for semyd al foly,
And were astonyed cleen, and gan for to drede;   3455
And euery man til othir lenyd with his hede,
And seyd, "He reportid the tale riȝt formally;[49]
He was no fool in certen, but wise, ware, and scly:[50]
For he hath but iiapid[1] vs, and scornyd heretofore,
And wee have hold hym a fole; but wee be wel more!"[2]   3460 .
Thus they stodied[3] on Geffrey, and lauȝid þo riȝt nauȝt.

When Geffrey had aspied they were in such þouȝt,
And hir hertis trobelid, pensyff, and anoyed,
Hym list to dryv in bet þe nayll, til they were fully cloyid.[4]
"Soveren sirs," he seyd, "sith þat it so is   3465
That in reportyng of our ple yee fynd nothing amys—
As previth wele yeur scilence,—eke yee withseyith[5] not
O word of our tale, but [fynde it] clene without spot;[6]
Then to our answere i prey ȝewe take hede,
For wee wol sey al the trowith, riȝt as it is indede.   3470
For this is soth and certeyne: it may nat be withseyd:
That Beryn, þat here stondith, was þus ovirpleid[7]

---

[46] chastise.   [47] misstated.   [48] corrected by your remembrance.   [49] in good form.
[50] cunning.   [1] made fun of.   [2] i.e., greater fools.   [3] pondered.   [4] sharply pricked.
[5] deny.   [6] defect.   [7] outdone.

3440. A reference to the wise Isope, the ruler of the country.
3468. Words supplied by Furnivall.

In the last game, when wagir was opon;
But þat was his sufferaunce,[8] as ye shul here anoon.
For in al this ceté ther nys no maner man 3475
Can pley bettir atte ches þen my mastir can;
Ne bet þen i, þouʒe i it sey, can nat half so much.
N[ow]e how he lost it be his will, the cause i wol teehe:
For ye wend, and ween, þat ye had hym engyned;[9]
But yee shul fele in every veyn þat ye be vndirmyned 3480
And ibrouʒt at ground, and eke ovirmusid.[10]

   And aʒenst the first[11] þat Beryn is acusid,
Hereith nowe entyntyflich:[12] when wee were on the see,
Such a tempest on vs fill þat noon myʒt othir se,
Of þundir, wynd, and liʒtenyng, and stormys ther among; 3485
xv dayis duryng[13] the tempest was so strong,
That ech man til othir began hym for to shryve,
And made hire avowis, yf þey myʒte have þe lyve,
Som to sech the Sepulkir, and som to oþir plase,
To sech holy seyntis, for help and for grace; 3490
Som to fast and do penaunce, and som do almys-dede;
Tyl atte last, as God wold, a voise to vs seyde,
In our most turment, and desperate of mynde,
That yf we wold be savid, my mastir must hym bynde
Be feith and eke by vowe, when he cam to londe, 3495
To drynke al the salt watir within the se-stronde,
Without drynkyng any sope[14] of þe fressh watir,
And tauʒt hym al the sotilté: how and in what manere
That he shuld wirch by engyne[15] and by a sotill charme
To drynk al the salt watir, and have hymselff no harme: 3500
But stop the ffressh ryvers by euery cost side,
That they entir nat in the se þurh þe world wyde!

---

[8] condescension.   [9] tricked.   [10] bewildered.   [11] with regard to the first (charge).
[12] attentively.   [13] lasting; i.e., continuously.   [14] bit.   [15] trickery.

3477. [Nor can anyone play] better than I, though I say it, [who] know, etc.

3489. MS. *se the the.* Vipan's emendation. The Holy Sepulcher at Jerusalem was the most famous of medieval shrines, and pilgrimages to it were thought especially meritorious; but many had to be content with visits to the less distant shrines of the saints (3490).

3493. The usual word is *desperaunce,* despair.

The voyse we herd, but nauȝt wee sawe, so were our wittis
    ravid:[16]
For this was [the] end fynally,[17] yf we lust be savid.
Wherfor my mastir Beryn, when he cam to this port,   3505
To his avowe and promys he made his first resort,[18]
Ere that he wold bergeyne[19] any marchandise.
And riȝt so doith these[20] marchandis in the same wise,
That maken hir avowis in saving of hire lyvis:
They completyn hire pilgremagis or þey se hir wyvis.   3510
So mowe ye vndirstond þat my mastir Beryn
Of fre will was imatid, as he þat was a pilgrym,
And myȝt nat perfourme by many-þowsand part[21]
His avowe and his hest, without riȝt sotil art,
Without help and strengith of many mennys myȝte.   3515
Sir Steward and Sir Burgeyse, yf we shul have riȝte,
Sirophanes must do [the] cost and aventur[22]
To stopp al the ffressh ryvers into þe see þat entir.
For Beryn is redy in al thing hym to quyte;
Ho-so be in defaute must pay for the wite.[23]   3520
Sith yee been wise all, what nede is much clatir?[24]
There was no covenaunte hem betwen to drynk fressh water.''

    When Sirophanes had iherd al Geffreyis tale,
He stode al abasshid, with coloure wan and pale,
And lokid oppon the Steward with a rewful chere   3525
And on othir frendshipp and neyȝbours he had there,
And preyd hem of counsell, the answere to reply.
    "These Romeyns," quod the Steward, "been wondir scly,[25]
And eke riȝt ynmagytyff, and of sotill art,
That i am in grete dowte howe yee shull depart   3530
Without harm in oon side.[26] Our lawis, wel þowe wost,
Is to pay damagis and eke also the cost
Of euery party-plentyff þat fallith in his pleynt.

---

[16] taken away. [17] i.e., final terms. [18] i.e., gave his first attention. [19] barter.
[20] i.e., all. [21] by the many-thousandth part. [22] must pay for the expense and
the risk. [23] whosoever is in arrears must pay for his offense. [24] rambling
talk. [25] clever. [26] i.e., in either event.

3520. MS. *So ho.*
3529. *Ynmagytyff* is not in the *Oxford Dictionary*, but is intended for
imaginatif, inventive.

Let hym go quyte, i counsell, yf it may so be queynt."[27]
"I merveill," quod Syrophanes, "of hir sotilté; 3535
But sith þat it so stondith and may noon othir be,
I do woll be[28] counsell;" and grauntid Beryn quyte.
But Geffrey þou3t anothir, and without respite,
"Sirs," he seyd, "wee wetith wele þat yee wol do vs ri3te,
And so ye must nedis, and so yee have vs hi3te; 3540
And therfor, Sir Steward, ye occupy [y]our plase;
And yee knowe wele what law woll in this case.
My mastir is redy to perfourme his avowe."
"Geffrey," quod the Steward, "i can nat wete howe
To stop all the ffressh watir were possibilité." 3545
"3is, in soth," quod Geffrey, "who had of gold plenté
As man coude wissh, and it my3t wel be do.
But þat is nat our defaute he hath no tresour to.[29]
Let hym go to[30] in hast, or fynd vs suerté
To make amendis to Beryne for his iniquité, 3550
Wrong, and harm, and trespas, and vndewe wexacioune,
Loss of sale of marchandise, disese and tribulacioune,
That wee have sustenyd þurh his iniquité.
What vaylith it to tary[31] vs? for þou3 [ye] sotil bee,
Wee shull have reson, where yee woll or no. 3555
So wol wee þat ye knowe what þat wee wol do:
In certen, ful avisid to Isope for to pase,
And declare euery poynt, þe more and eke the lase,
That of yeur opyn errours hath pleyn[32] correccioune;
And ageyns his iugement is noon proteccioune! 3560
He is yeur lord riall, and soveren iugg and lele;[33]
That, and ye wrie in eny poynt,[34] to hym liith oure apele."
So when the Steward had iherd, and þe burgeysis all,
Howe Geffrey had isteryd, þat went so ny3e the gall,[35]

[27] settled. [28] will act according to. [29] for the purpose. [30] set about his task.
[31] hinder. [32] full. [33] judge and worthy. [34] go amiss in any particular.
[35] managed, who came so near to the sore spot.

3547. The syntax is poor, but the sense apparent. Render *who* (3546)
as "[grant that] some one."
3552. MS. *lost.*
3554. MS. *þou3t sotil pry.* The emendation is on analogy with 3592.—
Vipan.
3562. MS. *ye work.* Cf. 3436.

What for shame and drede of more harme and repreff,[36]   3565
They made Syrophanes, weer hym looth or leffe,
To take Beryn gage,[37] and plegg fynd also,
To byde þe ward[38] and iugement of þat he had mysdo.
"Nowe ferthermore," quod Geffrey, "sith þat it so is
That of the first pleyntyff wee have sikirnes,   3570
Nowe to the marchant wee must nedis answere,
That bargayned[39] with Beryn al þat his shippis bere,
In covenaunte þat he shuld his shippis fill ageyne
Of othir marchandise, þat he tofore had seyne
In Hanybaldis plase, howsis too or thre,   3575
Ful of marchandise as they myȝt be.
Let vs pas thidir, yf eny thing be there
At our lust and likeing, as they accordit were."[40]
"I graunt wele," quod Hanybald; "þow axist but riȝte."
Vp arose these burgeysis,—"þowe axist but riȝte:"—   3580
The Steward and his comperis[41] entrid first þe house,
And sawe nothing within, strawe ne leffe ne mowse,
Save tymbir and þe tyle-stonys and þe wallis white.
"I trowe," quod the Steward, "the wynnyng woll be but lite
That Beryn wol nowe gete in Hanybaldis pleynte;   3585
For i can se noon othir but they wol be atteynt."[42]
And clepid hem in echone, and went out hymselve.
As soon as they were entrid, they sawe no maner selve[43]
For soris of hir hert; but as tofore is seyd,
The house was cleen iswept. þen Geffrey feir þey preyde 3590
To help [hem] yf he coude. "Let me aloon!" quod he,
"ȝit shull they have the wors, as sotill as þey bee."
    Evander the Steward in the mene while
Spak to the burgeyse, and began to smyle:
"Thouȝe Syrophanes by ihold these Romeyns for to curs,   3595

---

[36] shame. [37] pledge. [38] award. [39] exchanged. [40] i.e., under the terms of the
agreement. [41] fellows. [42] convicted; i.e., refused a decree. [43] salve.

3567. "To give Beryn a pledge," usually a glove. This served as a
public acknowledgment of the debt.
3580. Recopied from the preceding line.
3595. The reading is bad, the usual expression being *be biholden*, be
constrained.

ʒit i trow þat Hanybald woll put hym to þe wers;
For i am suyr and certeyn, within they shul nat fynde."
"What sey yee be my pleynt, sirs?" quod the blynde,
"For i make avowe i wol nevir cese
Tyl Sirophanes have of Beryn a pleyn[44] relese,   3600
And to make hym quyte of his submyssioune;[45]
Els woll i have no peté of his contricioune,
But folow hym also fersly as i can or may,
Tyl i have his eyen, both to, away."
"Now in feith," quod Machyn, "and i wol have his lyffe!   3605
For þouʒe he scape ʒewe all, with me wol he nat stryffe,
But be riʒt feyn in hert al his good forsake[46]
For to scape with his lyff, and to me it take."
Beryn and his feleshipp were within the house,
And speken of hir answere, and made but litill rouse;   3610
But evir preyd Geffrey to help yf he coude ouʒt.[47]
"I woll nat faill," quod Geffrey, and was tofore beþouʒt[48]
Of too botirfliis, as white as eny snowe:
He lete hem flee within the house, þat aftir on the wowe[49]
They clevid[50] wondir fast, as hire kynde woll,   3615
Aftir they had flowe, to rest anothir quile.
When Geffrey sawe the botirfliis cleving on þe wall,
The Steward and þe burgeys in he gan call:
"Lo, sirs," he seyde, "whosoevir repent,[1]
Wee have chose marchandise most to oure talent,[2]   3620
That wee fynd herein. Behold, Sir Hanyball,
The ʒondir bottirflyis, þat clevith on þe wall:
Of such yee must fille oure shippis al fyve.
Pluk vp thy hert, Beryn, for þow must nedis thryve!
For when wee out of Rome, in marchantfare went,   3625
To purchase buttirflyes was our most entent.[3]
ʒit woll i tell the cause especial and why:

---

[44] complete. [45] i.e., relieved of his obligation. [46] relinquish. [47] i.e., any means.
[48] had before thought (to bring). [49] wall. [50] clung. [1] regret it. [2] liking.
[3] principal purpose.

3597. *Nat find* is used absolutely for "not find anything."
3610. The *Oxford Dictionary* lists *rouse* as an isolated occurrence. The
senses under *roose*, boast, flatter, are satisfactory in this poem.
3616. MS. *anothir pull.*

There is a leche in Room þat hath imade a cry[4]
To make an oyntement to cure al tho been blynde
And all maner infirmytees þat growith in man-kynde.   3630
The day is short, the work is long: Sir Hanyball, ye mut hy!"
  When Hanybald herd this tale, he seyd pryuely
In counsell to the Steward, "In soth i have þe wors:
For i am sikir by þis pleynt þat i shal litil purs."[5]
  "So me semeth," quod the Steward, "for in þe world rounde 3635
So many botirflyis wold nat be founde,
I trowe, o shipp to charge.[6] Wherfor me þinkith best,
Lete hym have his good ageyn, and be in pese and rest.
And 3it is an auntir and[7] þowe scape so,
Thy covenaunt to relese without more ado."   3640
  The burgeysis everichon þat were of þat ceté
Were anoyid sore when they herd of þis plee.
Geffrey with his wisdom held hem hard and streyte,[8]
That they were accombrit[9] in hire owne disceyte.
  When Hanybald with his ffrendis had spoke of þis matere, 3645
They drowe hem toward Beryn, and seid in þis manere:
"Oonly for botirflyes ye com fro yeur contrey;
And wee 3ewe tell in sikirnes, and opon oure fey,
That so many botirflyes wee shul nevir gete:
Wherfor we be avisid othirwise to trete:[10]   3650
That Hanybald shall relese his covenaunt þat is makid,
And delyvir the good ageyn þat from 3ewe was ransakid,[11]
And wexe[12] 3ewe no more, but let 3ew go in pese."
  "Nay, for soth," quod Geffrey, "vs nedith no relese!
Yee shull hold oure covenaunt, and wee shul yeurs also,   3655
For wee shull have reson, where ye wol or no.
Whils Isope is alyve, i am nothing aferd;
For i can wipe al this ple cleen from yeur berd

---

[4] publicly announced his intention.   [5] be in pocket.   [6] load.   [7] mere chance
that.   [8] tight.   [9] overwhelmed.   [10] we should be wise to make another agreement.   [11] taken as loot.   [12] vex.

3658. The expression apparently means, "I can take the case out of
your hands (and before Isope)." Cf. the proverbial phrases "wipe some
one's nose" (take by fraud) and "shave some one's beard" (defraud, do
out of); the line in the text may be a mixture of the two.

And ye blench[13] onys out of the hy-wey."
Thé proferid hym plegg and gage,[14] without more deley.　3660
　"Now ferthirmore," quod Geffrey, "vs ouȝt to procede,
For to the blynd mannys poynt we must answere nede:
That for to tel trowith, he lyvith al to long;
For his owne fawte and his owne wrong
On Beryn he hath surmysid,[15] as previth by his ple;　3665
And þat yee shulle opynlich knowe wele and se.
For as i vndirstod hym, he seyd þat fele ȝeris,
Beryn, þat here stondith, and he were pertyneris
Of wynnyng and of lesyng, as men it vse and doith;
And that þey chaungit eyen; and ȝit þis is sothe.　3670
But the cause of chaunging ȝit is to ȝewe onknow;[16]
Wherfor i wol declare it, both to hiȝe and lowe.
In that same tyme þat þis burgeys blynde
And my mastir Beryn, as fast as feith myȝt bynde,
Were marchaundis in comyn[16a] of al þat þey myȝt wyn,　3675
Saff[17] of lyffe and lyme and of dedely synne,
There fill in tho marchis[18] of al thing such a derth
That ioy, comfort, and solas, and al maner myrth
Was exilid cleen, saff oonly molestacioune,
That abood contenuell, and also dispiracioune.　3680
So when þat the pepill were in most myscheff,
God þat is above, þat al thing doith releve,
Sent hem such plenté of mony, fruyte, and corne,
Wich turned al to ioy hire mournyng al toforne.
Then gaff they hem to myrth, revel, pley, and song;　3685
And þankid God above, evir-more among,[19]
Of hire relevacioune[20] from woo into gladnes:
For aftir soure when swete is com, it is a plesant mes.[21]
So in the meen-while[22] of this prosperité,
There cam such a pleyer into þe same contré,　3690
That nevir theretofore was seyn such anothir;

---

[13] flinch, shy.　[14] surety and bond.　[15] blamed.　[16] unknown.　[16a] common.
[17] except.　[18] that region.　[19] continually.　[20] relief.　[21] course (at dinner).
[22] midst.

3661. On the impersonal verb, cf. Int. VII.A.1.
3676. I.e., neither shared the other's bodily organs or worst sins; an
important point in the case.

That wele was the creature þat born was of his modir
That myȝt se the mirthis²³ of this iogeloure;
For of the world wyde tho dayis he bare þe floure.²⁴
For there nas man ne vomman in þat regioune   3695
That set of hymselff the store of a boton²⁵
Yf he had nat sey his myrthis and his game.
So oppon a tyme, this pleyer did proclame
That alle maner of pepill [þat] his pleyis wold se
Shuld com oppon a certen day to þe grete ceté.   3700
Then among othir, my mastir here, Beryn,
And this same blynd, þat pledith now with hym,
Made a certen covenaunt þat þey wold see
The mervellis of this pleyer and his sotilté.
So what for hete of somyr, age and febilnes,   3705
And eke also þe long way, this blynde for werynes
Fil flat adowne to the erth: o foot ne myȝt he go;
Wherfor my mastir Beryn in hert was ful woo,
And seyd, 'My ffrend, how nowe? mowe ye no ferþer pas?'
'No,' he seyd, 'by Hym þat first made mas!²⁶   3710
And ȝit i had levir, as God my soule save,
Se these wondir pleyis þen al the good i have!'
'I can nat els,' quod Beryn, 'but yf it may nat be
But þat yee and i mut retourn aȝe,
Afftir yee be refresshid of yeur werynes;   3715
For to leve ȝewe in this plyte, it were no gentilnes.'
Then seyd this blynd, 'I am avisid bet:
Beryn, yee shull wend thidir without eny let,
And have myne eyen with ȝewe, þat they þe pley mowe se,
And i woll have yeurs tyll ye com aȝe.'   3720
Thus was hir covenaunt made, as i to ȝewe report,
For ese²⁷ of this blynd, and most for his comfort.
But wotith wele the hole science of al surgery
Was vnyd,²⁸ or the chaunge was made of both [hir] eye,
With many sotill enchauntours, and eke nygramancers,²⁹   3725
That sent were for the nonys, mastris and scoleris;

²³ entertainment.   ²⁴ bore the flower, was preëminent.   ²⁵ worth of a button.
²⁶ the service of the mass.   ²⁷ relief from trouble.   ²⁸ united.   ²⁹ magicians.

3713. Probably *but* is superfluous and anticipates the construction in
the next line.

So when al was complete, my mastir went his way
With this mannys eyen, and sawe al the pley,
And hastly retourned into that plase aye,
And fond this blynd seching, on hondis and on kne   3730
Grasping al aboute to fynd þat he had lore—
Beryn his both eyen,[30] þat he had tofore!
But as sone as Beryn had pleyne knowleche
That his eyen were ilost, vnneth he my3t areche[31]
O word, for pure anguyssh þat he toke sodenly,   3735
And from þat day till now3e ne my3t he nevir spy
This man in no plase there lawe was imevid;[32]
But nowe in his presence the soth is ful iprevid,
That he shall make amendis or he hen[ny]s pas,
Ri3te as the lawe wol deme, ethir more or les.   3740
For my mastris eyen were bettir and more clere
Then these þat he hath nowe, to se both fer and nere;
So wold he have his owne, þat propir[33] were of kynde;
For he is evir redy to take to the blynde
The eyen þat he had of hym, as covenaunt was,   3745
So he woll do the same. Nowe, soverens, in this cas
Ye mut take hede for to deme ri3te;
For it were no reson my mastir shuld lese his si3te
For his trew hert and his gentilnes."
      "Beryn," quod the blynd tho, "i woll the relese   3750
My quarell,[34] and my cause, and fal[35] fro my pleynt."
      "Thow mut nede," quod Geffrey, "for þow art atteynt![36]
So mut þow profir gage, and borowis[37] fynd also,
For to make amendis, as othir have ido.
Sire Steward, do vs lawe,[38] sith wee desire but ri3te!   3755
As wee been pese-marchandis, vs longith nat to fi3te,
But pleyn vs to the lawe, yf so wee be agrevid."
      Anoon oppon that Geffrey þese wordis had imevid,[39]
The blynd man fond borowis for al his maletalent,[40]
And were ientrid[41] in the court to byde þe iugement;   3760
For þou3e þat he blynd were, 3it had he good plenté,
And more wold have wonne, þurh his iniquité.

---

[30] Beryn's two eyes.   [31] command.   [32] pleaded.   [33] suitable.   [34] complaint.
[35] withdraw.   [36] convicted.   [37] sureties.   [38] give us justice.   [39] spoken as a plea.
[40] malevolence.   [41] (they) were entered (on the records)..

"Nowe herith, sirs," quod Geffrey, "th[r]e pleyntyfs been
    assurid:
And as anenst þe ferth this vomman hath arerid,[42]
That pleynyth here on Beryn, and seyith she is his wyff,   3765
And þat she hath many a day led a peynous[43] lyff,
And much sorowe endurid, his child to sustene;
And al is soth and trewe. Nowe riȝtfullich to deme,
Whethir of hem both shal othir obey,
And folow wil[44] and lustis, Sir Steward, ye mut sey."   3770
    And þerewith Geffrey lokid asyde on this vomman,
Howe she chaungit colours, pale, and eke wan:
"Al for nouȝt," quod Geffrey, "for yee mut with vs go,
And endur with yeur husbond both wele and woo;"
And wold have take hir by þe hond; but she awey did breyde,
And with a grete sighing, þese wordis she seyd: 3776
That ageyns Beryn she wold plede no more:
But gagid with too borowis,[45] as othir had do tofore.
    The Steward sat as still as who had shore his hede,
And specially the pleyntifs were in much drede: 3780
Geffrey set his wordis in such manere wise
That wele they wist þe[y] myȝt nat scape in no wise
Without los of goodis, for damage and for cost,
For such were hir lawis where pleyntis were ilost.
    Geffrey had ful perseyte of hire encombirment;[46]   3785
And eke he was in certen þat the iugement
Shuld pas[47] with his mastir; wherfor he anoon,
"Soveren sirs," he seyd, "ȝit must wee ferþer goon,
And answere to this Machyn, þat seith þe knyff is his
That found was on Beryn: thereof he seith nat amys.   3790
And for more pryve[48] he seith in this manere:

---

[42] as for the fourth (suit that) this woman has brought.   [43] troubled.   [44] i.e.,
which shall follow the other's will.   [45] gave bail through two sureties.   [46] per-
ception of their embarrassment.   [47] be given in favor of.   [48] proof.

3763. Vipan's emendation.
3771. MS. *aseyd.* "Geffrey noticed, with a sidelong glance. . . ."
3779. See *Oxford Dictionary, shave,* v., 5.c. A jocular way of saying,
"as if some one had cut off his head." After splitting an opponent's skull,
Ipomadon says (8087): *A monke ye may be when ye will, For ye be shavynne
wile þertill, And right wele be ye crownde . . . For ye be shavyne rounde.*
3791. MS. *pryvy.*

That here stondith present the same cotelere
That þe knyffe made, and þe precious stonys thre
Within the hafft been couchid, þat in Cristyanité,
Thouȝe men wold of purpose make serch and siche,[49]   3795
Men shuld nat fynd in al thing a knyff þat were it lich:
And more opyn pryue[50] þan mannys owne knowlech,
Men of lawe ne clerkis con nat tell ne teche.
Now sith wee be in this manere thus ferforth[1] ago,
Then were spedful[2] for to knowe howe Beryn cam first t[h]o 3800
To have possessioune of the knyff þat Machyn seith is his:
To ȝewe vnknowe, i shall enfourme þe trowith as it is.
    Nowe vii yeer be passid, oppon a Tuysday
In the Passion-Woke,[3] when men leven pley
And vse more devosioune, fastyng, and preyere   3805
Then in othir tyme or seson of þe ȝeer,
This Beryns ffadir erlich wold arise,
And barefote go to chirch, to [don] Goddis service,
And lay hymselff aloon, from his owne wyff,
In reverence of þe tyme and mending of his lyff.   3810
So on the same Tuysday þat i tofore nempt,[4]
This Beryn rose and rayd hym, and to þe chirch went,
And mervelid in his hert his ffadir was nat there,
And homward went ageyn, with drede and eke fere.
Into his ffadirs chambir sodenlich he rakid,[5]   3815
And fond hym ligg, stan-dede,[6] oppon the strawe al nakid,
And the clothis halyd[7] from the bed away.
'Out, alas!' quod Beryn, 'that evir i sawe this day!'
The meyné herd the noyse, how Beryn cried 'Allas!'
And cam into the chambir, al þat therin was.   3820
But the dole and the sorowe and anguyssh þat was there,
It vaylith nat at this tyme to declare it here;
But Beryne had most of all, have ye no doute.
And anoon they serchid the body al aboute,
And fond this same knyff, þe poynt riȝt at his hert   3825

---

[49] seek.   [50] proof.   [1] far.   [2] profitable.   [3] Holy Week.   [4] named, mentioned.
[5] rushed.   [6] stone-dead.   [7] dragged.

3797. MS. þat mannys.
3803. MS. vii yeer and passid.

Of Beryns ffadir, whose teris gan outstert
When he drow3 out the knyff of his ffadirs wound:
Then stan-dede[8] i sawe hym fal doun to þe ground,
In si3te of the most part þat beth with hym nowe here."
(And they affermyd it for sothe, as Geffrey did hem lere:)   3830
"And 3it had i nevir suspecioun, from þat day til noweth,[9]
Who did þat cursid dede, till Machyn with his mowith
Afore 3ewe hath knowlechid þat the knyff is his:
So mut he nedis answere for his deth, iwis."
    When Machyn had iherd al Geffreyis tale,   3835
He rose of bench sodynly, with coloure wan and pale,
And seyd onto Beryn, "Sir, ageyn the
I wolle plete no more; for it were gret peté
To combir 3ewe with accions,[10] þat beth of nobill kynde."
"Graunte mercy, sir!" quod Geffrey, "but 3it yee shulle fynde
Borowis, or yee pas, amendis for to make   3841
For our vndewe vexacioune, and gage also vs take
In signe of submissioun for yeur iniury,
As lawe woll and resone; for wee woll vttirly[11]
Procede, tyll wee have iugement finall.   3845
And therfor, Sir Steward, what þat evir fall,
Delay vs no lenger, but gyve us iugement!
For tristith ye noon othir but we be fullich bent[12]
To Isope for to wend, and in his hi3e presence
Reherce all oure plees, and have his sentence;[13]   3850
Then shul yee make[14] ffynys, and hi3lich be agrevid."
    And as sone as the Steward herd these wordis mevid,[15]
"Reson, ry3te, and lawe," seyd the Steward tho,
"Yee mut nedis have, where i woll or no.
And to preve my full will, or wee ferþer goon,"   3855
Quiklich he comaundit, and sparid nevir oon,
xxiiii burgeysis in lawe best ilerid,
Rehersyng hem the plees, and how Geffrey answerid;
And on lyffe and lym and forfetur of good,
And as they wold nat lese the ball within hire hood,[16]   3860
To drawe apart togidir, and by hire al assent,
Spare no man on lyve, to gyve trewe iugement.

---

[8] i.e., fainting.   [9] now.   [10] load you with lawsuits, who are.   [11] to the end.
[12] determined.   [13] opinion.   [14] pay.   [15] uttered.   [16] i.e., their heads.

And when these xxiiii burgeysis had iherd
The charge of the Steward, ri3t sore þey were aferd
To lese hire owne lyvis, but they demyd trowith;   3865
And eke of hire ney3bours þey had grete rowith,
For they perseyvid clerelich, in þe plee þurhoute,
Hire ffrendis had þe wors side; þerof þey had no doute:
"And yff wee deme trewly, þey wol be sore anoyid;
3it it is bettir then wee be shamyd and distroyed."   3870
And anoon þey were accordit, and seyd with[17] Beryn,
And demed euery pleyntyff to make a grete fyne
With Beryn, and hym submyt hoolich[18] to his grace
Body, good, and catell, for wrong and hire trespase,
So ferforth, till atte last it was so boute[19] ibore   3875
That Beryn had the dobill good[20] þat he had tofore,
And with ioy and myrth, with al his company,
He drou3e hym to his shippis ward,[21] with song and melody.
    The Steward and þe burgeyse from þe court bent[22]
Into hir owne placis; and evir as they went,   3880
They talkid of þe Romeyns, howe sotil thé were
To aray hym like a fole þat for hem shuld answere.
"What vaylith it," quod Hanybald, "to angir or to curs?
And 3it i am in certen i shall fare the wers
All the dayis of my lyff for þis dayis pleding.   3885
And so shall al the remnaunt, and hir hondis wryng,
Both Serophanus, and þe blynde, þe vomman, and Machayne,
And be bet avisid er they efftsonys pleyne;
And all othir personys within this ceté,
Mell[23] the les with Romeyns, whils þey here be.   3890
For such anothir fole was nevir 3it iborne,
For he did nau3t ellis but evir with vs scorne,
Tyl he had vs cau3t, even by the shyn,[24]
With his sotill wittis, in our owne gren."[25]

    The great Isope is so well pleased with Beryn's success in outwittmg
the Falsetowners that he induces him to live with him and marry his
daughter. "May we all find as good a friend in need!"

---

[17] judged in favor of. [18] entirely. [19] to such an extent . . . that it was brought
about. [20] twice the goods. [21] toward his ships. [22] went. [23] meddle. [24] shin,
leg. [25] snare.

3868. *þerof* is repeated in the MS.

3894. At the end of the tale is this note: *Nomen autoris presentis
cronica Rome, Et translatoris filius ecclesie Thome* (i.e., Canterbury).

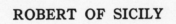

ROBERT OF SICILY

ROBERT OF SICILY

Strictly speaking, this is a pious legend, told to edify rather than to amuse. It is included in a vólume of romances as an example of a literature that borders on fiction and often uses its methods, but differs from it in being supposedly founded on fact. Its style is simple, severe, and reverent.

The writer's original is unknown, although many analogues have been discovered. For these, see Hibbard 58, and Wells 162. The poem was composed before 1370, probably in the south midlands. The scribe frequently writes *ou* for *you*, and uses -*u*- for -*i*- (*gult*, *guilt*).

Through the kindness of the authorities of the Bodleian Library, it has been possible to prepare the text from a rotograph of the Vernon Manuscript, MS. English Poetry A.1, fol. 300 ff. The divisions in the poem are as marked in the manuscript.

> Princes proude þat beþ in pres,[1]
> I wol ou telle þing not lees.[2]
> In Cisyle was a noble kyng,
> Fair and strong and sumdel ȝyng;
> He hedde a broþer in grete Roome,   5
> Pope of al Cristendome;
> Anoþer he hedde in Alemayne,[3]
> An emperour, þat Saraȝins wrouȝte payne.
> Þe kyng was hote Kyng Robert;
> Neuer mon ne wuste him fert.[4]   10
> He was kyng of gret honour,
> For þat he was conquerour;
> In al þe world nas his peer,
> Kyng ne prince, fer ne neer;
> And for he was of chiualrie flour,   15

---

[1] who are proud amid the throng. [2] false. [3] Germany. [4] afraid.

Heading. The MS. has, *Her is of Kyng Robert of Cicyle, Hou pride dude him begyle.*

His broþer was mad emperour;
His oþer broþer, Godes vikere,[5]
Pope of Rome, as i seide ere.
Þe pope was hote Pope Vrban:
He was good to God and man.   20
Þe emperour was hote Valemounde;
A strengur weorreour nas non founde
After his broþer of Cisyle,
Of whom þat i schal telle a while.
   Þe Kyng þhouȝte he hedde no peer   25
In al þe world, fer no neer,
And in his þouȝt he hedde pryde,
For he was nounpeer[6] in vch a syde.
   At midsomer, a[7] Seynt Iones Niht,[8]
Þe Kyng to churche com ful riht   30
For to heeren his euensong.
Hym þouhte he dwelled þer ful long:
He þouhte more in worldes honour
Þen in Crist, vr saueour.
   In *Magnificat* he herde a vers;   35
He made a clerk hit him rehers
In langage of his owne tonge;
In Latyn he nuste what heo songe.
Þe vers was þis, i telle þe:
"Deposuit potentes de sede,   40
Et exaltauit humiles."
Þis was þe vers, wiþouten les.
   Þe clerk seide anon riht,
"Sire, such is Godes miht
Þat he may make heyȝe lowe   45
And lowe heiȝe, in luytel þrowe;[9]
God may do, wiþoute lyȝe,
His wil, in twynklyng of an eiȝe."

---

[5] vicar.   [6] umpire, judge in disputes; hence a person of importance.   [7] on.
[8] June 24, St. John's Night.   [9] space.

35. The Magnificat (Luke 1:46) was a psalm sung by the Virgin Mary.
It is used in the vesper service.

41. "He hath put down the mighty from their seats, and exalted them
of low degree" (52). MS. *exultauit*.

þe Kyng seide, wiþ herte vnstable,[10]
"Al зor song is fals and fable;[11] 50
What mon haþ such pouwer
Me to bringe lowe in daunger?[12]
I am flour of chiualrye;
Myn enemys i may distruye;[13]
No mon lyueþ in no londe 55
þat me may wiþstonde;
þen is þis a song of nouht!"
þis errour he hedde in þouзt,
And in his þouht a sleep him tok
In his pulput,[14] as seiþ þe bok. 60
Whon þat euensong was al don,
A kyng ilyk[15] him out gan gon,
And alle men wiþ hym gan wende;
Kyng Robert lafte out of mynde.[16]
þe newe kyng was, as i ou telle, 65
Godes angel, his pruide to felle.
þe angel in halle ioye made,
And alle men of hym weore glade.
þe Kyng wakede þat lay in churche:
His men he þouhte wo to worche 70
For he was laft þer alon
And derk niht him fel vppon.
He gan crie after his men:
þer nas non þat spak aзen;
But þe sexteyn, atten eende,[17] 75
Of þe churche to him gan wende,
And seide, "What dost þou nouþe[18] her,
þou false þef, þou losenger?[19]
þou art her wiþ ffelenye,
Holy churche to robbye!"[20] 80
He seide, "Foule gadelyng,[21]
I am no þef; i am a kyng!

---

[10] inconstant. [11] a lie. [12] power. [13] destroy. [14] royal pew. [15] like. [16] was quite forgotten. [17] at last. [18] now. [19] lying knave. [20] rob. [21] rascal.

60. The book is unknown.

Opene þe churche-dore anon,
þat i mowe to my paleis gon!"
  þe sexteyn þouhte anon wiþ-þan[22]   85
þat he was sum wood man,
And wolde þe chirche dilyueret were
Of hym, for he hedde fere,
And openede þe chirche-dore in haste.
þe Kyng bygon to renne out faste,   90
As a mon þat was wood.
At his paleys ȝate he stood,
And heet þe porter gadelyng,
And bad hym come in hiȝing,[23]
Anon þe ȝates vp to do.   95
þe porter seide, "Ho clepeþ so?"
He onswerde anon þo,
"þou schalt witen ar i go:
þi kyng i am: þou schalt knowe!
In prison þou schalt ligge lowe,   100
And ben anhonged and todrawe
As a traytur bi þe lawe.
þou schalt wel witen i am kyng!
Open þe ȝates, gadelyng!"
  þe porter seide, "So mot i þe,   105
þe Kyng is mid his meyné!
Wel i wot, wiþoute doute,
þe Kyng nis not now wiþoute."
þe porter com into halle,
Bifore þe newe kyng aknes[24] gan falle,   110
And seide, "þer is atte ȝate
A nyce fool[25] icome late;[26]
He seiþ he is lord and kyng,
And clept me foule gadelyng.
Lord, what wol ȝe þat i do: 115
Leten him in, or leten him go?"
  þe angel seide in haste,
"Do him come in swiþe faste,
For my fol i wole him make

---

[22] thereupon. [23] haste. [24] on his knees. [25] silly fool. [26] just now.

Forte[27] he þe nome of kyng forsake."   120
Þe porter com to þe ȝate,
And him he called, in to late.[28]
He smot þe porter whon he com in
Þat blod barst out of mouþ and chyn.
Þe porter ȝeld him his trauayle:[29]   125
Him smot aȝeyn, wiþouten fayle,
Þat neose and mouþ barst a-blood;
Þenne he semed almost wod.

   Þe porter and his men in haste
Kyng Robert in a podel[30] caste;   130
Vnsemely heo maden his bodi þan,
Þat he nas lyk non oþer man,
And brouht him bifore þe newe kyng
And seide, "Lord, þis gadelyng
Me haþ smyte withoute decert:[31]   135
He seiþ he is vr kyng apert.[32]
Þis harlot[33] ouȝte, for his sawe,[34]
Ben ihonged and todrawe,
For he seiþ non oþer word
Bote þat he is boþe kyng and lord."   140
   Þe angel seide to Kyng Robert,
"Þou art a fol, þat art not ffert
Mi men to don such vilenye;
Þi gult þou most nede abuye.
What art þou?" seide þe angel.   145
Qwath Robert, "Þou schalt wite wel
Þat i am kyng, and kyng wol be!
Wiþ wronge þou hast my dignité.[35]
Þe Pope of Roome is my broþer,
And þe Emperour myn oþer: 150
Heo wol me wreke, for soþ to telle;
I wot heo nulle not longe dwelle!"
   "Þow art my fol," seide þe angel;
"Þou schal be schoren,[36] euerichdel,
Lych a fool, a fool to be.   155

---

[27] until. [28] let. [29] repaid him for his pains. [30] puddle. [31] deserving.
[32] openly. [33] vagabond. [34] speech, assertion. [35] dignity; i.e., usurp my state.
[36] shaved.

Wher is now þi dignité?
þi counseyler schal ben an ape,
And o cloþing ou worþ ischape:[37]
I schal him cloþen as þi broþer
Of o cloþing: hit is non oþer.[38]   160
He schal beo þin owne feere:
Sum wit of him þou miht lere!
Houndes, how so hit falle,
Schulen eten wiþ þe in halle;
þou schalt eten on þe ground;   165
þin assayour[39] schal ben an hound,
To assaye þi mete bifore þe.
Wher is now þi dignité?"
He heet a barbur him bifore,
þat as a fool he schulde be schore   170
Al around, lich a frere,
An honde-brede[40] boue eiþer ere,
And on his croune make a crois.
He gan crie and make nois:
He swor þei schulde alle abuye,   175
þat him dude such vileynye;
And euere he seide he was lord,
And vche mon scorned him for þat word,
And vche mon seide he was wod;
þat proued wel he couþe no good,[41]   180
For he wende in none wyse
þat God Almihti couþe deuyse
Him to bringe to lower stat;[42]—
Wiþ o drauht he was chekmat![43]
Wiþ houndes eueri niht he lay,   185
And ofte he criȝede weylaway
þat he euere was ibore,
For he was a mon forlore.
þer nas in court grom ne page

---

[37] the same sort of clothes shall be made for both of you.   [38] it shall not be otherwise.   [39] taster (to provide against poison or bad cooking).   [40] hand-breadth.   [41] had no wisdom.   [42] state.   [43] move he was checkmated.

166. An assayer was also one who placed the food before the diner. Probably both functions are included in the term here.

Þat of þe Kyng ne made rage,[44]   190
For no mon ne mihte him knowe:
He was defygured[45] in a þrowe.
So lowe er þat was neuer kyng;
Allas, her was a deolful[46] þing,
Þat him scholde for his pryde   195
Such hap among his men betyde!
Hunger and þurste he hedde grete,
For he ne moste no mete ete
But houndes eeten of his disch,
Wheþer hit weore fflesch or ffisch.   200
He was to deþe neiȝ ibrouht
For hunger, ar he miht eten ouht
Wiþ houndes þat beþ in halle;
How miȝt him hardore bifalle?
And whon hit nolde non oþur be,[47]   205
He eet wiþ houndes gret plenté.
    Þe angel was kyng, him þhouȝte long;[48]
In his tyme was neuer wrong,
Tricherie, ne falshede, ne no gyle
Idon in þe lond of Cisyle.   210
Alle goode þer was gret plenté:
Among men loue and charité;
In his tyme was neuer strif
Bitwene mon and his wyf;
Vche mon louede wel oþer: 215
Beter loue nas neuere of broþer.
Þenne was þat a ioyful þing
In londe to haue such a kyng;
Kyng he was þreo ȝeer and more.—
Robert ȝeode as mon forlore.   220
    Seþþe hit fel vppon a day
A luytel bifore þe moneþ of May,
Sire Valemound, þe Emperour,
Sende lettres of gret honour

---

[44] sport.   [45] altered in appearance.   [46] sorry.   [47] would not be otherwise.   [48] it
seemed long to him; cf. 407. He wishes to return to heaven.

195. MS. þat he.

To his broþer, of Cisyle Kyng,   225
And bad him come withouten lettyng,
Þat heo mihten beo boþe isome
Wiþ heore broþer, Pope of Rome.
Hym þhouȝte long heo weore atwinne;[49]
He bad him lette for no wynne,[50]   230
Þat he neore of good aray[1]
In Roome an Holy þoresday.[2]
    Þe angel welcomede þe messagers
And ȝaf hem cloþes riche of pers,[3]
Furred al wiþ ermyne;   235
In Cristendom is non so fyne;
And al was chouched mid perré.[4]
Better was non in Cristianté.
Such cloþ, and hit weore to dihte,
Al Cristendom hit make ne mihte.   240
Of þat wondrede al þat lond,
Hou þat cloþ was wrouȝt wiþ hond;
Wher such cloþ was to selle,
Ne ho hit maade, couþe no mon telle.
    Þe messagers wenten with þe Kyng   245
To grete Rome, wiþoute lettyng.
Þe ffool Robert also went,
Cloþed in lodly garnement,[5]
Wiþ ffoxes tayles mony aboute:
Men miht him knowen in þe route!   250
    Þe angel was cloþed al in whit;
Nas neuer seyȝe such samyt;[6]
And al was chouched[7] myd perles riche:
Neuer mon seiȝ none hem liche.
Al was whit, atyr and steede;   255
Þe steede was feir þer he ȝede;

---

[49] apart. [50] gain; i.e., consideration. [1] clothing; ie., festival attire. [2] Ascension Day, ten days before Whitsunday. It usually comes in May (cf. 222). [3] sky-blue material. [4] set with jewels. [5] hideous clothing. [6] rich silk. [7] adorned.

255. MS. *Al whit atyr was.* Horstmann's emendation.
256. Another MS. has *place* for *steede.*

So feir a steede as he on rod
Nas neuer mon þat euer bistrod.
  Þe angel com to Roome sone,
Real, as fel a kyng to done;[8] 260
So real kyng com neuere in Rome;
Alle men wondrede wheþen he come.
His men weore realliche[9] diht:
Heore richesse con seye no wiht.
Of cloþus, gurdeles, and oþer þing, 265
Eueriche sqyȝer þhouȝte a kyng,
And alle ride of riche aray
Bote Kyng Robert, as i ow say:
Alle men on him gon pyke,[10]
For he rod al oþer vnlyke: 270
An ape rod of his cloþing,[11]
In tokne þat he was vnderlyng.
Þe Pope and þe Emperour also
And oþer lordes mony mo
Welcomede þe angel as for kyng, 275
And made ioye of his comyng.
Þeose þreo breþeren made cumfort;[12]
Þe angel was broþer mad bi sort;[13]
Wel was þe Pope and Emperour
Þat hedden a broþur of such honour ! 280
  Forþ con sturte Kyng Robert
As ffol and mon þat nas not fert,
And criȝede wiþ ful egre speche
To his breþeren to don him wreche
Of him þat haþ with queynte gyle[14] 285
His coroune and lond of Cisyle.
Þe Pope ne þe Emperour nouþer
Þe ffol ne kneuȝ not for heor broþer.
Þo was he more fol iholde,
More þen er a þousend folde, 290
To cleyme such a breþerhede:

---

[8] royally as befitted a king.   [9] royally.   [10] peer.   [11] i.e., clad as he was.   [12] merriment.   [13] destiny.   [14] through a clever trick.

281. MS. *com.*

Hit was holde a foles dede.
Kyng Robert bigon to maken care,[15]
Muche more þen he dude are,
Whon his breþeren nolde him knowe;   295
"Allas," quaþ he, "nou am i lowe!"
For he hopede, bi eny þing,[16]
His breþeren wolde ha mad him kyng;
And whon his hope was al ago,
He seide allas and weilawo!   300
He seide allas þat he was bore,[17]
For he was a mon forlore:
He seide allas þat he was mad,
For of his lyf he was al sad.[18]
Allas! allas! was al his song: 305
His heer he tar,[19] his hondes wrong,
And euere he seide, "Allas, allas!"—
And þenne he þouȝte on his trespas:
He þouȝte on Nabugodonosore,[20]
A noble kyng was him bifore: 310
In al þe world nas his peer,
Forte acounte,[21] fer ne neer.
Wiþ him was Sire Olyferne,[22]
Prince of knihtes stout and steorne.
Olyferne swor euermor   315
By God Nabugodonosor,
And seide þer nas no God in londe
But Nabugodonosor, ich vnderstonde;
þerfore Nabugodonosor was glad
þat he þe name of God had,   320
And louede Olofern þe more;
And seþþe hit greued hem boþe sore.
Olofern dyȝede in dolour:
He was slaye in hard schòur.[23]
Nabugodonosor lyuede in desert;   325
Dorst he nouȝwher ben apert;[24]

---

[15] be sorrowful.   [16] in any event.   [17] born.   [18] weary.   [19] tore.   [20] Nebuchadnezzar.   [21] according to record.   [22] Holofernes.   [23] pain.   [24] openly.

315. See the Book of Judith, vi.

Fyftene ʒer he liuede þare,
With rootes, gras, and euel fare,
And al of mos[25] his cloþing was;
"Al com þat bi Godes gras: 330
He criʒede merci with delful chere:
God him restored as he was ere!
Nou am i in such caas,
And wel worse þen he was.
Whon God ʒaf me such honour   335
Þat i was clepet conquerour,
In eueri lond of Cristendome
Of me men speke wel ilome,[26]
And seiden nouʒwher was my peer
In al þe world, fer ne neer.   340
For þat name i hedde pride:
And angels þat gonne from ioye glyde,[27]
And in twynklyng of an eiʒe
God binom[28] heore maystrie,
So haþ he myn, for my gult;   345
Now am i wel lowe ipult,[29]
And þat is riht þat i so be!
Lord, on þi fool þow haue pité!
I hedde an errour in myn herte,
And þat errour doþ me smerte;   350
Lord, i leeued not on þe.
On þi fol þou haue pité!
Holy Writ i hedde in dispyt;
For þat[30] is reued my delyt—
For þat is riht a fool i be!   355
Lord, on þi fool þou haue pité!
Lord, i am þi creature;
Þis wo is riht þat i dure,[31]
And wel more, ʒif hit may be.[32]

---

[25] moss.   [26] often.   [27] i.e., angels who fell from heaven.   [28] took away.
[29] brought down.   [30] therefore.   [31] endure.   [32] i.e., greater suffering would be justified, if it were possible.

343. The construction is faulty, the sense clear. Nuck read *As in*.
354. In all MSS. the lines begin as here or with *Therefore;* the second *For þat* is hence correct.

Lord, on þi fool þou haue pité!   360
Lord, i haue igult[33] þe sore!
Merci, Lord: i nul no more;
Euere þi fol, Lord, wol i be.
Lord, on þi fol [þou] haue pité!
   "Blisful Marie, to þe i crie,   365
As þou art ful of cortesye;
Preye þi Sone, þat dyed for me;
On me, his fol, þow haue pité.
Blisful Marie, ful of graas,
To þe i knowe[34] my trespas;   370
Prey þi Sone, for loue of þe,
On me, his fool, he haue pité!"
He seide no more, "Allas, allas!"
But þonked Crist of his gras,
And þus he gon himself stille,[35]   375
And þonked Crist mid good wille.
Þen Pope, Emperour, and Kyng
Fyue wikes[36] made heore dwellyng.
Whon fyue wykes weore agon,
To heore owne lond heo wolden anon,   380
Boþe Emperour and þe Kyng;
Þer was a feir departyng.[37]
   Þe angel com to Cisyle,
He and his men in a while.[38]
Whon he com into halle,   385
Þe fool anon he bad forþ calle;
He seide, "Fool, art þow kyng?"
"Nay, sire," quaþ he, "wiþoute lesyng."
"What artou?" seide þe angel.
"Sire, a fol; þat wot i wel,   390
And more þen fol, ȝif hit may be;
Kep[39] i non oþer dignité."
Þe angel into chaumbre went,
And after þe fol anon he sent;
He bad his men out of chaumbre gon: 395
Þer lafte no mo but he alon

---

[33] sinned against. [34] acknowledge. [35] calm. [36] weeks. [37] leave-taking. [38] after a time. [39] assume.

And þe fol þat stod him bi.
To him he seide, "Þou hast merci:
Þenk, þou weore lowe ipult,[40]
And al was for þin owne gult.   400
A fool þou weore to Heuene-kyng;
Þerfore þou art an vnderlyng.
God haþ forȝiuen þi mysdede;
Euere herafter þou him drede!
I am an angel of renoun,   405
Isent to kepe þi regioun;
More ioye me schal falle
In heuene, among my feren alle,
In an houre of a day,
Þen in eorþe, i þe say,   410
In an hundred þousend ȝeer,
Þeiȝ al þe world fer and neer,
Weore myn at my lykyng!
I am an angel, þou art kyng."
He went in twynklyng of an eȝe;   415
No more of him þer nas seȝe.
    Kyng Robert com into halle;
His men he bad anon forþ calle.
And alle weore at his wille
As to heore lord, as hit was skille.[41]   420
He louede God and holi churche,
And euere he þouhte wel to worche.
He regned after two ȝer and more,
And louede God and his lore.
Þe angel ȝaf him in warnyng   425
Of þe tyme of his diȝing.
Whon tyme com to dyȝe son,
He let write hit riht anon—
Hou God myd his muchel miht
Made him lowe, as hit was riht.   430
Þis storie he sende eueridel
To his breþeren vnder his seel;[42]
And þe tyme whon he schulde dye

---

[40] brought down, thrust.   [41] i.e., as if he had been their (true) lord, as was right.
[42] seal.

Þat tyme he diȝede as he gon seye.
Al þis is writen, withouten lyȝe,   435
At Roome, to ben in memorie
At Seint Petres Chirche, i knowe;
And þus is Godes miht isowe,[43]
Þat heiȝe beoþ lowe, þeiȝ hit be ille,[44]
And lowe heiȝe, at Godes wille.   440
Crist, þat for vs gon dye,
In his kynereche let vs ben heiȝe,
Euermore to ben aboue,
Þer is ioye, cumfort, and loue.   AMEN.

---

[43] disseminated.   [44] though they dislike it.

435. The "Gesta Romanorum," which has a story like this, was long thought to have been compiled from Roman records. Probably this allusion is to the "Gesta," although it is not the immediate source. Cf. Miss Rickert's "Emaré" xviii, n.2.

439. MS. *ben.*

KING EDWARD AND THE SHEPHERD

KING EDWARD AND THE SHEPHERD

The poem is in the Cambridge University Library Manuscript Ff V 48 (fifteenth century), fols. 40b to 56b. Through the kindness of the authorities of the library, it has been possible to prepare the text from photographs of the manuscript, and to correct the numbering of the folios. In transcribing, *Ff* is printed *F* at the beginning of lines; *S* in the long form has been expanded at the ends of words to *-is* or *-ys;* the abbreviation for *-er*, *-ar*, and *-ur* has been expanded according to the customary spelling in the manuscript.

The poem has been printed only once before—by C. H. Hartshorne, in "Ancient Metrical Tales" (1829). It has never been carefully studied. For various information, other versions, and analogues, see Child V.67 ff; *FF Communications* No. 42.5, 17; Wells under "Rauf Coilȝear"; W. A. Clouston's "Group of Eastern Romances and Stories" 425, etc.; J. Bolte and G. Polivka, "Anmerkungen zu den Kinder- und Hausmärchen der Brüder Grimm" (1913) 15.18, III. 214–233. ; G. Liebau's "König Edward III in Lichte Europäischer Poesie" has summaries and material. The closest parallel is "The King and the Hermit" (W. C. Hazlitt's "Remains of the Early Popular Poetry of England" I.11). Cf. especially the details in 253 ff., 421 ff., and 436 ff.

Whatever the origin of the story, it found great favor in England, being told of four kings: Henry II (by Giraldus Cambrensis), Edward II, Edward III, and Edward IV. Analogous stories are attached to Henry IV and John.

Probably it was composed at about the end of the fourteenth century. The words in the vocabulary are suitable to that time; it occurs in a manuscript of antiquarian pieces; and its style is that of ordinary romance. The chronology is sufficiently inexact to prove that it was written long after the events it relates; but it must have been written for an audience that knew something of the life of Edward III, and could appreciate the humor of passages such as 43 ff. and 98 ff. From references to the Black Prince (928, 972) and Warenne, the very date of the fictitious adventure can be set as not long after 1340. Thomas Hoccleve knew a tradition that Ed-

949

ward III liked to go about in disguise ("Regement of Princes" 2556; cf. also Child V. 71. n.2); hence the tradition must have been persistent.

The dialect is northern, though it has been altered by the copyist (cf. rhymes such as *ȝong—knoyng, countenence—Fraunce*). Probably it was written down from recitation, because mistakes like those in ll. 340 and 350 seem to be a result of imperfect memory rather than of careless copying. Flourishes at the ends of words have been printed as -*e*, with the following exceptions: final -*ll*, which is crossed everywhere but in ll. 110 and 446, is not expanded; final -*ch* has a cross-stroke everywhere except in ll. 783, 862, and 916, and is not expanded; final -*g* sometimes has a tag, which has been disregarded.

The truth of the social conditions reflected in the poem is attested in many documents. Complaints about the prevalence of marauding bands and the corruptness of officials are often addressed to Parliament; the constant poaching is evident from the many statutes directed against it; outlaws were numerous in the forest. Cf. in this volume "Gamelyn" and "Havelok"; Furnivall's note on the bondman in "John de Reeve," Percy Folio Manuscript II.xxxiii; R. D. French's "Chaucer Handbook" 14, 30; W. H. Clawson's "Geste of Robin Hood" 102 ff.; and Jusserand. For facts about the forest laws, mostly of an earlier time, see Pollock and Maitland; *Publications of the Selden Society*, xiii, "Select Pleas of the Forest," especially the introduction; and John Manwood's "Treatise of the Forest Laws," especially the article on hunting.

> God, þat sittis in Trinité,
> Gyffe thaym grace wel to the
>   That listyns me a whyle!
> Alle þat louys of melody,
> Off heuon blisse God graunte þaim party:[1]   5
>   Theyre soules shelde fro peryle.
> At festis and at mangery,[2]
> To tell of kyngys, þat is worthy—
>   Talis þat byn not vyle.
> And ȝe wil listyn how hit ferd   10
> Betwene Kyng Edward and a scheperd,
>   ȝe shalle lawghe of gyle.[3]

---

[1] share. [2] banquets. [3] deceit (practised by Edward).

Oure Kyng went hym in a tyde
To pley hym be a ryver side[4]
  In a mornyng of May;   15
Kny3t ne squyer wold he non
But hym self and a grome,[5]
  To wende on þat iorney.
With a scheperde con he mete,
And gret hym with wordis swete,   20
  Without any delay.
Þe scheperde louyd his hatte so well,
He did hit of neuer a dele,
  But seid, "Sir, gud-day."

The Kyng to þe herde[6] seid þan,   25
"Off whens art þou, gode man,
  Also mot i the?"
"In Wynsaure was i borne;
Hit is a myle but here beforne;[7]
  Þe towne þen maist þou see.   30
I am so pylled[8] with þe Kyng
Þat i most fle fro my wonyng,
  And therfore woo is me.
I hade catell; now haue i non;
Thay take my bestis and don þaim slone,   35
  And payen but a stik of tre."

---

[4] i.e., hawking.   [5] groom.   [6] shepherd.   [7] only a mile ahead.   [8] robbed by.

16. Versions in which the king is unaccompanied are few. Usually a bishop or knight is with him.

22. This episode is also peculiar to this one version.

35. Cf. the letter written to Edward III about 1333: "The harbingers of your court and various grooms and servants take many goods by violence from their owners: bread, beer, eggs, poultry, beans, peas, oats, etc., for which scarcely any payment is made," D. A. Hughes, "Illustrations of Chaucer's England" 173. See also Simon Islip's "Speculum Regis Edwardi III" (ed. J. Moisant, 1891), a long complaint.

36. Wooden tally-sticks were exchanged between buyer and seller as memoranda of indebtedness in credit transactions. These could be mislaid or altered by the buyer; the practice caused much trouble. Cf. *Archæologia* 74.289.

The Kyng seid, "Hit is gret synne
Þat þei of sich werkis wil not blynne,
    And Edward wot hit noȝt;
But come to-morne when it is day: 40
Þou shal be seruyd of[9] þi pay;
    Therof haue þou no thoȝt.
For in your towne borne i was;
I haue dwellid in diuerse place
    Sithe i thens was broght;   45
In þe courte i haue sich a frende:
Þe treserer, or þen i wende,
    For þi luffe shalle be soght."

Þis gret lord þe herd con frayne,
"What wil men of your Kyng seyne?   50
    Wel litull gode, i trowe!"
The herd onsweryd hym riȝt noȝt,
But on his schepe was all his thoȝt,
    And seid agayn, "Char, how!"[10]
Þen loogh oure Kyng and smyled stille:[11]   55
"Þou onsweris me not at my will;
    I wolde þai were on a lowe![12]
I aske þe tythyngys of oure Kyng,
Off his men and his wyrkyng;
    For sum[13] i haue sorow.   60

I am a marchant and ride aboute,
And fele sithis i am in doute[14]
    For myn owne ware.
I tell it þe in priueté,
Þe Kyngys men oon[15] to me   65
    A M pounde and mare.
Owe he ouȝt mycull[16] in þis cuntré?

---

[9] presented with.   [10] stop, ho! A common cry of shepherds to their flocks.
[11] i.e., to himself.   [12] in the mire.   [13] i.e., some of his deeds.   [14] fear.   [15] owe.
[16] any great sum.

43. Edward III was born at Windsor November 13, 1312.
57. Possibly a proverbial trope; cf. "Leave a scold in a ley and let the devil get her out."

What siluer shall he pay the,
    For Goddis haly are?
Sith þou art neghtbur myne,   70
I wil my nedis do and thyne;
    Tharof haue þou no care."

"Sir," he seid, "be Seynt Edmonde,
Me is owand iiii pounde
    And odde[17] twa schillyng.   75
A stikke i haue to my witnesse—
Off hasill[18] i mene þat hit is;—
    I ne haue no noþer thyng.
And gif þou do as þou has me hote,
Then shall i gif þe a cote,[19]   80
    Withowt any lesyng;
Seuen schelyng to-morne at day
When i am siruyd of my pay."
    "Graunte,"[20] seid oure Kyng.

"Tel me, sir, what is þi name,   85
Þat i for þe haue no blame,
    And wher þi wonnyng is."
"Sir," he seid, "as mot i the,
Adam þe scheperde men callen me,
    For certan sothe iwysse."   90
Þe scheperde seid, "Whos son art þou of oure towne?
Hat not þi fadur Hochon,
    Also haue þou blisse?"
"No, for God," seid oure Kyng,
"I wene þou knowist me nothyng;   95
    Þou redis alle amysse."[21]

"My fadur was a Walsshe knyȝt;

---

[17] in addition. [18] hazel. [19] coat. [20] agreed. [21] guess all wrong.

73. Cf. preface to "Athelston."
91. The first three words are probably an insertion.
92. *Hochon* was a common name in the North; it is a form of *Hugh.*
97. Edward II was born at Carnarvon, Wales, and was said by tradition to have been presented to the Welsh as their king.

Dame Isabell my modur hyȝt,
For sothe as i tell the.
In þe castell was hir dwellyng,   100
Thorow commaundment of þe Kyng;
   Whene[22] she þar shuld be;
Now wayte[23] þou wher þat i was borne.
The toþer Edward here beforne,
   Full well he louyd me,   105
Sertanly withowte lye.
Sum tyme i live be marchandye,
   And passe well ofte þe see.

I haue a son is with þe Whene;
She louys hym well, as i wene;   110
   That dar i sauely say.
And he pray hir of a bone,
ȝif þat hit be for to done,[24]
   She will not onys say nay;
And in þe courte i haue sich a frende,   115
I shal be seruyd or i wende,
   Withowt any delay.
To-morne at vndern[25] speke with me:
þou shal be seruyd of þi moné[26]
   Er þan hye mydday."   120

"Sir, for Seynt Thomas of Ynde,
In what place shall i þe fynde,
   And what shalle i þe calle?"
"My name," he seid, "is Ioly Robyn;
Ilke man knowes hit well and fyne,   125
   Bothe in bowrs and halle.
Pray þe porter, as he is fre,
þat he let þe speke with me,
   Soo faire hym mot befalle.[27]

---

[22] queen.   [23] know.   [24] i.e., if it be possible.   [25] morning.   [26] money.   [27] as
he may prosper (with your blessing).

98. Isabella of France was the Queen of Edward II.

109. Edward III's queen was Philippa of Hainault.

121. The apostle Thomas was traditionally the founder of Christianity
in India.

For fer owtward[28] shall i not be;   130
Sumquer[29] i trow þou shall me see,
 Within þe castell wall.

For þou and oþer þat lene your thyng,[30]
Wel ofte sithes ye banne[31] þe Kyng,
 And ȝe are not to blame;   135
Hit er oþer[32] þat do þat dede;
Þei were worthy, so God me spede,
 Therfor to haue gret shame.
And if i wist whilke þei were,
Hit shulde come þe Kyng to ere,[33]   140
 Be God and be Seynt Iame.
Þen durst i swere þei shold abye
Þat dose oure Kyng þat vilanye,
 For he berys all þe fame."[34]

The herd onswerd to þe Kyng,   145
"Sir, be Seynt Iame, of þis tithyng
 Þou seist þerof right well:
Þei do but gode, þe Kyngus men;[35]
Þei ar worse þen sich ten,
 Þat bene with hym no dell.   150
Þei goo aboute be viii or nyne
And done þe husbondys mycull pyne,[36]
 Þat carfull is theire mele.[37]
Thai take geese, capons, and henne,
And alle þat euer þei may with renne,   155
 And reves vs oure catell.

---

[28] distant.   [29] somewhere.   [30] lend your property.   [31] curse.   [32] other persons;
stewards, etc.   [33] to the king's ear.   [34] infamy.   [35] the king's men do only good.
[36] do farmers much mischief.   [37] full of sadness is their speech.

141. The shrine of St. James at Compostella in Galicia, Northern
Spain, was an object of pilgrimage and very famous.

148. Statute of the twenty-fifth year of Edward III: "No forester nor
keeper of forest or chase, nor none other minister shall make or gather
sustenance, nor any other gathering of victuals nor other things by color
of his office . . . but what is due of ancient right." Possibly this explains
his popularity and that of his retainers among the people of Windsor
Forest, though the statute was not often enforced.

Sum of þeim was bonde sore,
And afturwarde hanget þerfore,
   For sothe, as i yow say.
ȝet ar þer of þeim nyne moo,   160
For at my hows þei were also
   Certis ȝisturday.
Þei toke my hennes and my geese
And my schepe with all þe fleese,
   And ladde þem forthe away.   165
Be my doȝtur þei lay alnyȝt;
To come agayne þei haue me hyȝt;
   Off helpe i wolde yow pray.

With me þei lefte alle þeire thyng,
Þat i am sicur of þeire comyng,   170
   And þat me rewes soore.
I haue fayre chamburs thre,
But non of þeim may be with me
   While þat þei be þore.
Into my carthaws[38] þei me dryfe;   175
Out at þe dur þei put my wyfe,
   For[39] she is olde gray hore.
Had i helpe of sum lordyng,
I shulde make with þeim recknyng;
   Þei shulde do so no more.   180

For oþer iii felowes and i,
We durst wel take party[40]
   These nyne for to mete.
I haue slyngus[41] smert and gode
To mete with þeim ȝif þei were wode, 185

---

[38] cart-house.   [39] on the ground that.   [40] take a side in a combat.   [41] slings.

157. Cf. "Havelok" 2440 ff.

160. No matter how severe the punishment of outlaws, their ranks were constantly recruited, partly from rogues, partly from men outlawed for trivial offenses, and partly from small landowners and nobles who improved their income by robbing travelers. See Pollock and Maitland I.476.

168. MS. *i y wolde.*

178. MS. *lordyngys.*

And reve hem her lyves swete.
þe best archer of ilkon,[42]
I durst mete hym with a stone,
  And gif hym leve to schete.[43]
þer is no bow þat shall laste   190
To draw[44] to my slynges caste,
  Nought be fele fete.

þer is non archer in þis lande,
And i haue my slyng in hande;
  For i dar lay with hym ale[45]   195
þat whoso sonyst hittys a bauke,
For to haue þe toþer haut
  To what thyng he will hale;[46]
þat whoso furst smytys a thyng
Off[47] his bow or my slyng—   200
  Vndirstande my tale—,
Be þe deth þat i shall dye,
þerto my hed þen dar i ley,
  Now sone in þis swale."[48]

With talis he made þe Kyng to dwell,   205
With mony moo þen i can tell,
  Till hit was halfe gan prime.
His hatte was bonde vndir his chyn;
He did hit nothyng of[49] to hym:
  He thoȝt hit was no tyme.[50]   210
"Robyn," he seid, "i pray the,
Hit is þi will, come hom with me,

---

[42] of them all.   [43] shoot.   [44] fly as far as.   [45] wager him a drink.   [46] drink.
[47] this depends on *whoso*.   [48] shade.   [49] did not remove it.   [50] i.e., there was no
occasion.

192. MS. *feel.*
196. Corrupt. The rhyme-words may have been *benke . . . shenke.*
An archery bank was a butt, a pyramidal mound of earth on which a
paper bull's-eye was fixed; and shots which hit the mound and missed
the bull's-eye counted as misses. The general sense may have been,
"I propose as terms that whoever first hits the bank (misses) is to order
poured out for the other whatever he will drink."
199. Present tense for future: "shall strike." The sense is "I am
ready to bet my head as to who will first hit a mark."

A morsell for to dyne."
The Kyng list of his bourdis lere;[1]
"Gladly," he seid, "my lefe fere,   215
I wil be on of thyne."[2]

As þei hamward can gon,
Þe Kyng saw conyngys[3] mony on;
Þerat he can smyle.
"Adam," he seid, "take vp a ston   220
And put hit in þi slyng anon;
Abyde we here a while.
Gret bourde it wold be
Off þeim to slee twoo or thre,
I swere þe be Seynt Gyle."[4]   225
"Do way!"[5] quod Adam, "let be þat!
Be God, i wolde not for my hat
Be takyn with sich a gyle.[6]

Hit is alle þe Kyngus waren;[7]
Ther is nouþer knyȝt ne sqwayne   230
Þat dar do sich a dede,
Any conyng here to sla
And with þe trespas awey to ga,
But his sidis shulde blede.
The warner[8] is hardy and fell;   235
Sirtanly, as i þe tell,
He will take no mede.
Whoso dose here sich maistrye,[9]
Be þou wel sicur he shall abye
And vnto prison lede.   240
Þer is no wilde foule þat will flyne
But i am sicur hym to hittyne;

---

[1] wished to hear his jokes. [2] one of your company. [3] rabbits. [4] Saint Giles.
[5] stop. [6] trick. [7] warren. [8] keeper of the warren. [9] evil deed.

229. Forest game was under the king's protection. Poaching was punishable by imprisonment, and poachers were often roughly handled. Illegally killing a rabbit remained a serious offense until late in the nineteenth century.
242. Cf. note 425.

Sich mete i dar þe hote.
ʒif hit be so my slyng will last,
ʒif i fayle of hym a caste,   245
    Brok[10] þan welle my cote.
When we come and sittes in same,
I shalle tech þe a gamme;
    I can hit wel be rote.
Þen shal þou se my slyng-slaght,[11]   250
And of þe best take vs a draght,
    And drynk well right be note."[12]

The scheperde hows ful mery stode
Vndir[13] a forest fayre and gode,
    Of hert and hynde gret mynde.[14]   255
Þe Kyng seid, "Be God Almyght,
In thy hert þou may be liʒt
    Hamward when þou shall wende;
I the swere, be Goddis grace,
And i had here sich a place,   260
    I shulde haue of þat kynde;[15]
Ouþer on euen or on morneng,
Sum of þeim shuld come to ryng,[16]
    Þerwith to make me a frende."[17]

Þe herd bade, "Let soch wordis be!   265
Sum man myʒt here the;
    Þe were bettir be still.
Wode has erys, fylde has siʒt;
Were þe forster here now right,
    Thy wordis shuld like þe ille.   270
He has with hym ʒong men thre;
Þei be archers of þis contré,
    Þe Kyng to serue at wille,[18]
To kepe þe dere boþe day and nyʒt,
And for þeire luf a loge[19] is diʒt   275
    Full hye vpon an hill.

---

[10] i.e., take my coat. [11] game taken by my sling. [12] i.e., with a song to guide us.
[13] close beside. [14] numbers. [15] sort (venison). [16] to hand. [17] i.e., with gifts. [18] at
his pleasure. [19] lodge.

I wolde haue here no standyng,
But ride now forthe in my blessy[ng],
    And make vs wel at ese.
I am glad þou come with me;   280
Goo sit now wher þi willes be,
    Right at þine owne ese;
Þoughe sumdel of my gode be lorne,
I shall haue more; and God beforne,[20]
    He may hit wel increse;   285
And i shall tech þe play—
When tyme comys, þou shalt asay—
    Whilke play be not lese.''[21]

A fayre cloth on þe borde he leyd;
Into þe boure he made abrayde,[22]   290
    Gode mete for to fette.
Brede of whete bultid[23] smalle,
ii peny ale he brouȝt with all:
    Therof wolde he not lett;
A ffesaunde[24] brid and þerwith a crane—   295
Oþer fowles were þer gode ane[25]—
    Before þe Kyng he sette.
''Adam,'' quod þe Kyng, ''blessed þou be:
Here is better þen þou heȝtist me,
    To-day when þat we mette.''   300

''Sir,'' he seid, ''do now gladly;
ȝet haue i mete þat were worthy
    A gret lord for to fech.''
He broȝt a heron with a poplere,[26]
Curlews, boturs,[27] boþe in fere,   305
    Þe maudlart[28] and hur mech;[29]
And a wylde swan was bake.
''Sich fowle con my slyng take;
    Þeroff am i no wrech;[30]
I bade felowes to my dynere;   310
And sithen þei wil not cum here,

---

[20] with God's guidance. [21] in vain. [22] incursion. [23] sifted. [24] pheasant. [25] number. [26] spoonbill. [27] bitterns. [28] mallard. [29] mate. [30] niggard.

A devoll haue who þat rech!

3if þou wilt ete, þou shall non waue;[31]
But gif þou will any drynk haue,
    þou most con thy play;   315
When þou seest þe cuppe anon,
But þou sei 'passilodion,'
    þou drynkis not þis day.
Sely Adam shall sitt þe hende,[32]
And onswere with 'berafrynde,'   320
    Leue vpon my ley."[33]
Þe Kyng seid þat he wold lere:
"Me þink it bourde for to here:
    Teche me, i þe pray."

"Passilodyon, þat is þis: 325
Whoso drynkys furst, iwys,
    Wesseyle þe mare dele![34]
Berafrynde also, i wene,
Hit is to make þe cup clene,
    And fylle hit ofte full wele.   330
Thus shal þe game go aboute,
And who so falys of þis route,[35]
    I swere be Seynt Mighell,
Get hym drynk wher he will,
He getys non here—þis is my skill[36]—   335
    No3t to a noþer sele."[37]

Þe Kyng seid, "Let se þat drynke;
I shall say ri3t þat i thynke:
    Me thirstis swythe sore."
The scheperde bade þe cup fill;   340
Þe Kyng to drynk hade gode will,
    With passilodion more. . . .

---

[31] hesitate.   [32] worthy Adam shall sit near thee.   [33] statement.   [34] the more
health to him!   [35] rote, formula.   [36] opinion.   [37] another occasion.

313. *Non* for *not?*

317. *Passilodion* and *berafrynde* are nonsense-words. On the custom,
see Brand, under "Pledging."

340. The scribe has inadvertently omitted most of this stanza, and has
replaced part of it with ll. 350–5, below.

"I can riȝt wel my lore."
"Berafrynde," iseid Adam,
"Iwysse þou art a wytty man;   345
  þou shalt wel drynk þerfore."

Thus þei sate withoute strife,
Þe Kyng with Adam and his wyfe,
  And made hym mery and glad.
The scheperde bade þe cuppe fill;   350
The Kyng to drynke hade gode will;
  His wife did as he bade.
When þe cuppe was come anon,
Þe Kyng seid "passylodion,"
  When he þe cuppe hade.   355
Hit was a game of gret solas;
Hit comford[38] all þat euer þer was;
  Therof þai were noght sade.

Þe scheperde ete till þat he swatte,[39]
And þan nou erst he drew[40] his hatt   360
  Into þe benke-ende.[41]
And when he feld[42] þe drynk was gode,
He wynkid and strokyd[43] vp his hode,
  And seid, "Berafrynde."
He was qwyte as any swan;   365
He was a wel begeten man,
  And comyn of holy kynde.[44]
He wold not ete his cromys drye:
He louyd nothyng but it were trie,[45]
  Neþer fer ne hende.[46]   370

Þen seid þe Kyng in his reson,[47]
"Whoso were in a gode town,
  Þis wold ha costed dere,

---

[38] comforted. [39] sweat. [40] removed. [41] end of the bench. [42] felt. [43] pushed.
[44] worthy parents. [45] choice. [46] near. [47] speech.

348. In some versions the wife is an important character; in others she
is entirely omitted.
365. A white skin was a mark of gentility.

In þis maner to be fed
With alkyn dentethe wel bested,[48]   375
As we haue had now here.
I shalle þe whyte,[49] be hode myne.
Now hade i leuer a conyne[50]
Diȝt in my manere;
But-ȝif hit were of buk or doo,   380
Þer is no mete i louyd soo,
And i come[1] þer hit were."

Þe scheperde seid, "So mot þou the,
Can þou heyle[2] a priueté?
And þou shalt se gode game."   385
"ȝe !" seid þe Kyng, "be my levté,[3]
And ellis haue i mycul maugré[4]
ȝif hit be for my frame.[5]
What man þat wrye[6] a gode frende,
Þouȝ he were riȝt sibbe of my kynde,[7]   390
He were worthy gret shame."
Þen seid Adam, "Þou seis sothe;
ȝet i haue a morsel for þi tothe,
And ellis i were to blame."

He went and fett conyngys thre,   395
Alle baken well in a pasty,[8]
With wel gode spicerye,[9]
And oþer baken mete alsoo,
Boþe of hert[10] and of roo;
Þe venyson was full trye.[11]   400
"Sir," he seid, "asay of this:
Þei were ȝisterday qwyk, iwysse,
Certan, withouten lye;
Hider þei come be mone-liȝt.
Eete þerof well apliȝt,[12]   405
And schewe no curtasye."

---

[48] dainties well set out.   [49] requite.   [50] rabbit.   [1] if I should come.   [2] conceal.
[3] honor.   [4] mischance.   [5] profit.   [6] betrays.   [7] blood-relative.   [8] pie.   [9] spices.
[10] hart.   [11] choice.   [12] straightway.

379. MS. *maners.*

To þe scheperd seid þe Kyng,
"þe forsters[13] luf þis ouer al thyng;
   þou art alle þaire felawe:
To þaire profett þou con foulis slyng,[14]   410
And þei will venyson to þe bryng:
   þerof stande þei non awe.[15]
Were þou as perfete in a bowe,[16]
þou shulde haue moo dere, i trowe,
   Sothe to say in sawe.[17]   415
Ʒet i rede þat þou fande[18]
þan any forster in þis land
   An arow for to drawe."

þen seid þe scheperde, "Noþing soo:
I con a game worthe þei twoo[19]   420
   To wynne me a brede:[20]
þer is no hert ne bucke so wode
þat i ne get without blode,
   And i of hym haue nede.
I haue a slyng for þe nones   425
þat is made for gret stonys;
   Therwith i con me fede.
What dere i take vnder þe side,[21]
Be þou siker he shall abide
   Til i hym home will lede.   430

Conyngus with my noþer slyng
I con slee and hame bryng,
   Sumtyme twoo or thre;
I ete þaim not my self alon:
I send presandes[22] mony on,   435
   And fryndes make i me,

---

[13] wardens. [14] kill with a sling. [15] they are not afraid. [16] with a bow. [17] as one remarks (a tag). [18] are readier. [19] two of that. [20] roast. [21] i.e., hit in the ribs. [22] presents.

421. MS. *bridde*, which fits neither the rhyme nor the sense.

425. Strutt (II.ii) devotes part of a chapter to the Saxon practice of hunting with a sling. Slings might be of two kinds: leather thongs, which were whirled about before the missile was released; and sticks over the ends of which stones could be flipped.

Til gentilmen and ȝemanry;
Thei haue þaim all þat ar worthy,—
   Those þat ar priué.
Whatso þai haue, it may be myne,   440
Corne and brede, ale and wyne,
   And alle þat may like me.

Do now gladly, Ioly Robyne:
ȝet shall þou drynk a drauȝt fyne
   Off gode drynk, as i wene;   445
Off Lanycoll þou shall proue:[23]
Þat is a cuppe to my behoue;[24]
   Off maser[25] it is ful clene.
Hit holdis a gode thryden dele[26]
Ful of wyne euery mele;   450
   Before me it is sene.
Fil þe cuppe," he seid anon,
"And play we passilodion,
   Sith no moo þat we bene."[27]

When þe drynk was filled,   455
Þe wife askid, "Who shuld begynne,
   Þe godeman, sir, or ȝe?"
"Take my geyst,"[28] seid Adam þan,
"Sithe he his gamme con;
   I wil þat it so be."   460
Þe Kyng toke þe cuppe anon
And seid, "Passilodion!"
   Hym thoȝt it was gode gle.
Þe sheperde seid certanly,
"Berafrynd shal be redy,   465
   Also mot i the."

He drank and made þe cuppe ful clene,
And sithe he spake wordis kene,

---

[23] taste, try.   [24] profit.   [25] maple-wood.   [26] i.e., enough for three.   [27] i.e., since there are but two of us.   [28] give to my guest.

438. MS. þei ar.
448. Glass vessels were uncommon at the tables of peasants.

þat gamme was to here:
"This cuppe hit hat Lonycoll; 470
I luf it wel, for it is holl;[29]
 It is me lefe and dere;
Fil it efte to Ioly Robyn;
Iwisse, he drank no better wyne
 Off alle þis seuen ȝere! 475
To alle þat wil my gamme play,
Fill it be þe ee,[30] i þe pray,
 My bourdis þat wil lere."

Then dranke oure Kyng and toke his leue;
Þe sheperd seid, "Sir, not þe greue, 480
 And it þi wille be:
I shalle þe schew, Ioly Robyn,
A litull chaumber þat is myne,
 Þat was made for me."
Þe Kyng þerof was ful glad, 485
And did as þe scheperde bad:
 Moo bourdis wold he se.
He lad hym into a priué place
Ther venyson plenté in was,
 And þe wyne so claré.[31] 490

Vnder þe erth it was diȝt;
Feire it was, and clene of syȝt,
 And clergially[32] was hit wroȝt.
The Kyng seid, "Here is feyre ese:
A man myȝt be here wel at ese, 495
 With gamme ȝif he were sauȝt."[33]
The Kyng seid, "Gramercy, and haue goday!"[34]
Þe scheperde onswerid and said, "Nay,
 Ȝet ne gose þou noughte;
Þou shalle preue[35] furst of a costrell tre[36] 500
Þat gode frendis send to me,

---

[29] hollow, capacious. [30] eye; i.e., full. [31] like claré. Probably *so* is a scribal error. [32] learnedly; i.e, cleverly. [33] contented. [34] farewell. [35] taste. [36] wooden bottle.

470. Probably the words are addressed to his wife. Cf. 348.

þe best þat myght be bouȝt.

Telle me now, whilke is þe best wyne
Off Lonycoll, cuppe myne,
   Als þou art gode and hynde?   505
Play onys passilodion,
And i shall onswer sone anon,
   Certes, 'berafrynde.'
This chamber hat Hakderne, my page;
He kepis my thyng and takis no wage,   510
   In worde[37] wher þat i wende.
þer is no man þis place con wrye
But thiself, ȝif þou will sey,[38]
   And þan art þou vnkynde.[39]

Ther is no man of þis contré   515
So mycull knowes of my priueté
   Als þou dose, Ioly Robyn;
Whil þat i liff, welcum to me;
Wyne and ale i dar hete þe,
   And gode flesshe for to dyne."   520
þe Kyng his stede he can stride,
And toke his leue for to ride;
   Hym þoȝt it was hye tyme.
þe scheperde seid, "I will with þe goo:
I dar þe hete a foule or twoo,   525
   Paraunter with a conyne."

þe Kyng rode softely on his way;
Adam folowyd, and wayted his pray;
   Conyngus saw he thre.
"Ioly Robyn, chese þou which þou wylt;[40]   530
Hym þat rennys er hym þat sitt,
   And i shall gif hym the."
"He þat sittis and wil not lepe:
Hit is þe best of alle þe hepe,
   For soth so thynkithe me."   535
þe scheperde hit hym with a stone

---

[37] world; i.e., wherever I go (a tag).   [38] if you should tattle.   [39] disloyal.   [40] want.

And breke in two his brest-bon;
Thus sone ded was he.

Þe Kyng seid, "Þou art to alow:[41]
Take hym als þat rennyth now,   540
    And þan con þou thy crafte."[42]
"Be God," quod Adam, "here is a ston
Þat shalle be his bane anon;"
    Thus sone his life was rafte.
What fowle þat sittis or flye,   545
Wheþer it were ferre or nye,
    Sone with hym it lafte.
"Sir," he seid, "for sothe i trowe
This is bettur þen any bowe,
    For alle þe fedurt schafte.[43]   550

Ioly Robyn, brok wel my pray
Þat i haue wone here to day:
    I vouchesafe wele more:
I pray þe telle it to no man
In what maner þat i hit wan: 555
    I myȝt haue blame therfore;
And gif þou do my errand of riȝt,[44]
Þou shalle haue þat i þe hyȝt,
    I swere be Goddis ore."
Þe Kyng seid, "Take me thy tayle;[45]   560
For my hors, i wolde not þe fayle,
    A peny þat þou lore."

The Kyng to court went anon,
And Adam to his schepe con gon;
    His dogge lay ther fulle stille.   565
Home er nyȝt come he noȝt;
New mete with hym he broȝt:
    For defaute wolde he not spill.[46]
"Wife," he seid, "be not sory:
I wil to courte certanly;   570

---

[41] be praised.   [42] (then I shall admit) you know your art.   [43] feathered
arrow.   [44] rightly.   [45] tally-stick.   [46] he would never die of want.

I shalle haue alle my will.
Ioly Robyn, þat dynet with me,
Hase behette me my moné,
    As he can lawe and skill.[47]

He is a marchande of gret powere: 575
Many man is his treserere;
    Men awe hym mony a pounde.
The best frend he had sith he was borne
Was þe toþer Edwart here beforne,
    Whil he was holl and sounde.   580
He hase a son is with þe Qwene;
He may do more þen oþer fyftene,[48]
    He swerys be Seynt Edmonde.
Thou3 he shuld gif of his càtell,
I shalle haue myne, euery dell,   585
    Off penys holl and rownde."

On morow when he shuld to court go,
In russet clothyng he tyret[49] hym þo,
    In kyrtil[50] and in curtebye,[1]
And a blak furred hode   590
Þat wel fast to his cheke stode,
    Þe typet[2] myght not wrye.[3]
Þe mytans clutt[4] forgate he no3t;
Þe slyng cumys not out of his tho3t,
    Wherwith he wrou3t maystrie.   595
Toward þe court he can goo;
His do3ter lemman met he thoo,
    And alle his cumpanye.

---

[47] means.   [48] than any other fifteen men.   [49] attired.   [50] tunic.   [1] short cloak
of coarse material.   [2] fur muffler.   [3] conceal.   [4] cloth mittens.

586. Coins were frequently clipped, so that whole and round pennies
were hard to obtain.

588. From the Rolls of Parliament for 1363: "Cowherds, shepherds
. . . and all manner of men engaged in husbandry, and other people who
have not goods and chattels worth forty shillings, shall wear no cloth save
blanket and russet [coarse brown material], twelve pence the yard,"
Hughes 165. The statute proved unenforceable, and was soon withdrawn.

589. MS. *surstbye.*

He thoȝt more þen he seyde;
Towarde þe court he gaf a brayde,[5]　　600
　　And ȝede a well gode pas,
And when he to þe ȝatis come,
He askid þe porter and his man
　　Wher Ioly Robyn was.
He was warned what he shuld sayn;　　605
Off his comyng he was fayne,
　　I swere be Goddis grace.
"Sir, i shall tel þe wher he is;"
And þan be[gan] þaire gammen, iwis,
　　When he come forthe in place.　　610

The Kyng seid to erles tweyne,
"Ȝe shall haue gode bourd,[6] in certayne,
　　Ȝif þat ȝe will be stille,
Off[7] a scheperde þat i see
Þat is hider come to me　　615
　　For to speke his wille.
I pray yow alle, and warne betyme,[8]
Þat ȝe me calle Ioly Robyne,
　　And ȝe shalle lawȝ your fille.
He wenys a marchand þat i be;　　620
Men owe hym siluer here for fe:[9]
　　I shalle hym helpe þertille.

But a wager i dar lay,
And ȝe will as i yow say,
　　A tune[10] of wyne, iwysse:　　625
Þer is no lorde þat is so gode,
Þouȝ he avayle[11] to hym his hode,
　　Þat he wil do of his.
Sir Raufe of Stafforde, i pray the,
Goo wete what his will be,　　630

---

[5] proceeded rapidly.　[6] fun.　[7] at the expense of.　[8] betimes.　[9] in payment.
[10] large measure.　[11] lower, remove.

629. Ralph de Stafford (d. 1372) was a well-known courtier, who distinguished himself in war and was made earl in 1351. This gives an early limit for the composition of the piece. (Cf. 644.)

And telle me how hit is."
"Gladly, lord, so mot i the,
Sich bourdis i wolde ful fayne se,
Off thyngus þat fallis amysse."

And whan he to þe herde came,   635
He seid, "Al hayle, godeman:
Whider wiltow goo?"
He onsweryd as he thouȝt gode,
But he did not of his hode
To hym neuer þe moo: 640
"Ioly Robyn, þat i yonder see,
Bid hym speke a worde with me,
For he is not my foo."
Þen onswerid þat Erle balde,
"Take þe porter þi staffe to halde,   645
And þi mytens also."

"Nay, felow," he seid, "so mot i the,
My staffe ne shal not goo fro me:
I wil hit kepe in my hande;
Ne my mytans getis no man   650
Whil þat i þaim kepe can,
Be Goddis Sone alweldand;[12]
Ioly Robyn, þat i yonder see,
Goo bidde hym speke a worde with me,
I pray the, for Goddis sande: 655
I wolde wete how hit is:
I am aferd my schepe go mysse[13]
On oþer mennys lande."

And when he to þe Kyng came,
Þen seid þe Kyng, "Welcum, Adam,   660

----

[12] almighty. [13] astray.

631. In the MS. line 633 follows here. But probably the whole passage is corrupt, and ll. 657-8 are echoed.
633. MS. *whilke bourdis.*
645. It was customary for guests to surrender all their weapons to the attendants. The shepherd's failure to do so is a sign of his unfamiliarity with court etiquette.

As to my powere !"[14]
"Ioly Robyn," he seid, "wel mot þou be!
Be God, so shuld þou to me
  On oþer stede þan here.[15]
I am commyn, þou wat wherfore;   665
Þi trauayle shal not be forlore:
  Þou knowis wel my manere."
"For God," seid þe Kyng þo,
"Þou shal be seruyd er þou goo;
  Forthy make glad chere."[16]   670

"Ioly Robyn," he seid, "i pray the
Speke with me a worde in priueté."
  "For God," quod þe Kyng, "gladly!"
He freyned þe Kyng in his ere
What lordis þat þei were   675
  "Þat stondis here þe bye?"
"The Erle of Lancaster is þe ton,
And þe Erle of Waryn, Sir Iohn,
  Bolde and as hardy;
Þei mow do mycull with þe Kyng: 680
I haue tolde hem of þi thyng."
  Þen seid he, "Gremercy!"

Þe scheperde seid, "Sir[s], God blesse ȝew!
I know yow not, be swete Ihesu!"
  And swere a wel gret oth.   685
"Felaw," they seid, "i leve þe well:
Þou haşe sene Robyn or þis sell;[17]
  Ȝe ne ar nothyng wrothe."[18]
"No, sirs," he seid, "so mot i the,
We ar neghtburs, i and he;   690
  We were neuer lothe."
As gret lordis as þei ware,

---

[14] as far as is in my power. [15] i.e., anywhere. [16] i.e., look happy. [17] time, moment. [18] i.e., are friendly.

677. See introduction to this poem. All the persons named were important noblemen. Lancaster (d. 1361) was the king's chief adviser. Warenne was the earl of Surrey. Since he died in 1347, the poet is in error in representing Ralph de Stafford as an earl at this time (cf. l. 629).

He toke of his hode neuer þe mare,
But seid, "God saue yow bothe."

þe lordis seid to hym anon,   695
"Ioly Robyn, let hym noȝt gon
    Till þat he haue etyn.
Hym semys a felow[19] for to be;
Moo bourdis ȝet mow we se
    Er his errand be gettyn."   700
þe Kyng to þis scheperde con say,
"Fro me ne gost þou not away
    Tille we togeder haue spokyn;
An errande i hyȝt þe for to done;
I wolde þat þou were seruyd sone,   705
    þat hit be not forgetyn.

Goo we togeder to þe marshalle,
And i myself shall tel þe tale—
    The better may þou spede."
"Robyn," he seid, "þou art trwe;   710
Iwis, it shalle þe neuer rew:
    þou shalt haue thy mede."
To þe hall he went, a ful gode pase,
To seke wher þe stuarde was;
    þe scheperde with hym ȝede.   715
Long hym thouȝt, til mydday
þat he ne were seruyd of his pay;
    He wolde haue done his dede.[20]

When he into þe hall came,
þer fande he no maner of man;   720
    þe Kyng hym bade abyde:
"I wil go aboute þi nede,
For to loke gif i may spede,
    For þing þat may betide."[21]
"Robyn, dwel not long fro me: 725
I know no man here but the;

---

[19] eccentric, "character."   [20] finished the business. Cf. 657.   [21] happen what may.

This court is noȝt but pride;[22]
I ne can of no sich fare:
These hye halles, þei ar so bare!
   Why ar þei made so wyde?"   730

Then lowȝ þe Kyng, and began to go,
And with his marsshale met he tho;
   He commaundit hym aȝeyne;
"Felaw," he seid, "herkyn a liȝt,
And on myne errand go þou tyte,   735
   Also mot þou thynne:
A scheperde abides me in hall:
Off hym shall we laȝ alle,
   At þe meyte when þat we bene.
He is cum to aske iiii pounde;   740
Goo and fech it in a stounde,
   Þe sothe þat i may sene.

Twey schelyng þer is more:[23]
Forgete hem not, be Goddis ore,
   Þat he ne haue alle his pay.   745
I wolde not for my best stede
But he were seruyd er he ȝede,
   Er þen hye mydday.
He wenys a marchande þat i be;
Ioly Robyn he callis me,   750
   For sertan soþe to say.
Now sone to mete when i shall goo,
Loke he be noȝt fer me fro."
   "Lorde," he seid þen, "nay."

Forþe þe marshale can gon,   755
And brouȝt þe stuard sone anon,
   And did adowne his hode.
"Herstow, felow, hast þou do

---

[22] ostentation.   [23] in addition.

742. The king means to see that the steward withholds none of the money; cf. "Sir Cleges."
758. These lines are spoken by the king.

þe thyng þat i seid þe to,
　　For þe gode rode?"   760
"Sir," he seid, "it is redy;
I know hym not, be oure Lady,
　　Before me þoʒ he stode."
"Goo, take ʒond man and pay betyme,[24]
And bidde hym thonke Ioly Robyne;   765
　　We shall sone haue gamme gode."

Forþe þei went all thre,
To pay þe scheperde his moné
　　þer he stode in þe halle.
þe stiward at hym frayned tho,   770
"What askis þou, felaw, er þou goo?
　　Telle me, among vs alle."
"Sir," he seid, "so mot i the,
Foure pounde ʒe owe to me,
　　So fayre mot me befalle !"[25]   775
Twey schillyngis is þer odde:
I haue wytnesse þerof, be God,
　　With in þis castell wall.

Hit is skorid here on a tayle;[26]
Haue; brok[27] hit wel withowt fayle: 780
　　I haue kepte hit lang enoʒ !"
þe stiwarde: "þerof i ne rech:
Iwisse, i haue þerto no mech !"[28]
　　At hym ful fast þei looʒ;
"Ne were[29] Ioly Robyn, þat i here se,   785
To-day [ʒe] gate no moné of me,
　　Made þou it neuer so towʒ;[30]
But for his luf, go tel[31] it here."
þen made þe scheperde right glad chere,
　　When he þe siluer drowʒ.[32]   790

---

[24] at once.   [25] as I hope for good luck.   [26] tally-stick.   [27] here: enjoy.   [28] mate.
[29] were it not for.   [30] tough; i.e., no matter how much you complained.   [31] count
it out.   [32] reckoned.

785. Said by the steward. Destroying the mate to a tally-stick was an
easy way of evading payment.
786. MS. illegible.

He did it vp, þe sothe to say,
But sum þerof he toke away
　　In his hand ful rathe.
"Ioly Robyn," he seid, "herkyn to me:
A worde or tweyne in preueté　　　　　　　　795
　　Togedir betwene vs bathe:
I hiȝt þe ȝistirday seuen shyllyng;
Haue: brok it wel to þi clothyng:
　　Hit wil do þe no skathe.
And for þou hast holpyn me now,　　　　　　800
Euermore felowes i and thow,
　　And mycull þanke, sir, now haue ȝe."

"Graunt mercy, sir," seid þan he,
"But siluer shalt þou non gif me,
　　I swere be Seynt Martyne!"　　　　　　　805
"Be God," seid þe scheperde, "ȝys!"
"Nay," seid oure Kyng, "iwys,
　　Noȝt for a tune³³ of wyne;
For þi luf, i wolde do more
Then speke a worde or ii þe fore;³⁴　　　　　810
　　þou may preue sum tyme.³⁵
ȝif þou be fastyng, cum with me
And take a morsell in preueté;
　　Togedir þen shalle we dyne."

"Nay, sir," he seid, "so God me spede!　　　815
To þe Kyngis meyte haue i no nede:
　　I wil þerof no dele.
þer is non of his proud meny
þat hase alway so gode plenté
　　[As] i haue euery sele."³⁶　　　　　　　820
þe Kyng bare wittnesse, and seid, "ȝa!
But þou myȝt onys, er þou ga,
　　Etyn with me a mele!
þe grettist lordis of þis lande

---

³³ cask. ³⁴ for you. ³⁵ test my friendship some time. ³⁶ at every season.

802. This line begins a page, and seems to be a copyist's error.
820. MS. (apparently) *ha ne.*

Haue bidde þe tary, i vndirstonde,   825
And þerfore bere þe well."

"For þi luff, Robyn, i wil gladly;
Today þen mett i myne enmye,
For sothe as i the tell—
He þat be my doȝtir lay;   830
I tolde þe of hym ȝistirday—
I wolde he were in hell!
At my howse is alle þe rowte;
They wil do harme whil i am owte;
Full yuel þen dar i dwell.   835
Wold þou speke for me to þe Kyng,
He wolde avow[37] me my slyngyng;
Thaire pride þen shulde i fell!"

Kyng Edwart onswerid agayne,
"I wil go to these erles twane   840
þat stode lang ore be me;
þai ar aperte,[38] of my knowyng;
þei shall speke for þe to þe Kyng,
þat wrokyn shal þou be.
In þis courte þai ar twenty   845
At my biddyng to bidde redy[39]
To do a gode iornay;
When þou comys home, make no bost:
þei shal be takyn er þou it wost,
þouȝ þai were sech thre."[40]   850

Thus þe Kyng held hym with tale,
þat alle þat euer was in þe sale[41]
Off hym hade gret ferly.
Togedir þei ȝede vp and downe
As men þat seid þaire orison,   855
But no man wist why.
þe scheperde keppid his staf ful warme,
And happid[42] it euer vndir his harme[43]

---

[37] sanction. [38] bold. [39] ready to be commanded at my order. [40] i.e., three times as many. [41] hall. [42] wrapped. [43] arm.

As he romyd hym by;
He wold no man toke it hym fro　　　　860
Til þat he shulde to meyte goo;
　Sich was his curtasy!

The Kyng commaundit al his[44]
Þat no man speke to hym amysse,
　As þei wolde be his frynde.　　　　865
When tablys were layd and cloþes sprad,
Þe scheperde into þe hall was lad
　To begynne a bordis ende.[45]
His mytans hang be his spayre,[46]
And alway hodit[47] like a frere,　　　　870
　To meyte when he shulde wende;
And when þe waytis blew lowde hym be,
Þe scheperde þo3t, "What may þis be?"
　He wende he hade herd a fende.[48]

And alle þat hym aboute stode　　　　875
Wende þat man hade bene wode,
　And low3 hym to hethyng[49]
For he so nycely[50] 3ede in halle,
And bare a staffe among þaim alle,
　And wolde take[1] it nothyng.　　　　880
Þe stwarde seid to Ioly Robyn,
"Goo wesshe, sir, for it is tyme,
　At þe furst begynyng;
And for þat odir Edwart loue,
Þou shalt sitte here aboue,　　　　885
　Instidde alle of þe Kyng."

When he had wasshen and fayre isett,
Þe Qwene anon to hym was fett,
　For sche was best worthy.
At euery ende of the deyse　　　　890

---

[44] his company.　　[45] sit at the head of a table.　　[46] slit in clothing near the waist.　　[47] hooded.　　[48] devil.　Devils made hideous sounds.　　[49] scorn.　　[50] foolishly.　　[1] yield.

872. Waits were minstrels who blew trumpets or pipes at stated hours. Their signal here is for the bringing on of the first course.

Sate an erle, withowt lese,
And a fayre lady.
Þe Kyng commandet þe stuard þo
To þe scheperde for to goo
And pray hym specially 895
A tabul dormant² þat he begynne;
"Þen shal we lawȝ, þat be hereine,
Off his rybaudy."³

"Adam," he seid, "sit here downe,
For Ioly Robyn of þis towne, 900
He gifis þe gode worde.⁴
And for þou art of his knoyng,⁵
We vouchsafe, olde and ȝong,
Þat þou begynne þe borde."
"Perdy," seid þe scheperde "nowe !⁶ 905
What shal be þouȝt, if þat i mow,
Hit is wel kept in horde !⁷
But-if i do Robyn a gode iorné,
Ellis mot i hangyt be
With a hempyn corde !" 910

And when þe hall was rayed out,⁸
Þe scheperde lokid al aboute,
How þat hit myȝt bene.
Surketis⁹ oueral he con holde;¹⁰
Off knyȝtis and of persons bolde, 915
Sich hade he non sene.
Þe Prince was feched to þe borde
To speke with þe Kyng a worde,
And also with þe Qwene.
Then he frayned hym in his ere 920
If he wolde 'passilodion' lere,

---

² table fixed to the floor. ³ uncouth blunders. ⁴ speaks well of you. ⁵ acquaintance. ⁶ no. ⁷ secret; i.e., better left unsaid. ⁸ decked out. ⁹ outer coats. ¹⁰ behold.

896. The *Oxford Dictionary* cites Chaucer's use of *tabul dormant* in 1386 as the earliest.

906. MS. *Hit shal.*

911. MS. *rayed oȝt.*

And 'berafrende' bedene.

"Lorde," he seid, "what may þat be?
I know it not, be Goddis tre!
　　It is a new language."　　　　　　　　　925
"I leue þe well," seid þe Kyng,
"Þou may not know al thyng:
　　Þou þerto ne has non age.
Þer is a mon in þis towne
Þat will it preue gode reson[11]　　　　　930
　　To kyng, squyer, and page;
And gif þou wille gif any mede,
I shal do þe to hym lede,
　　Vnto his scole a stage.[12]

Hit is a scheperde þat i of mene;　　　　935
At his howse þen haue i bene
　　Within þis seuen-ny3t;
A dosan[13] kny3tis, and þai had cum with me,
Þei shulde haue had mete plenté
　　Off þat i fonde redy dy3t."　　　　　940
Then he tolde hym alle þe case,
Off 'passilodion,' what it was,
　　And 'berafrynde' ipli3t.[14]
"He sittis yonde, in a furred hode;
Goo, bere hym here a golde ryng gode,　　945
　　And þat anon right,

And þank hym mycul for Ioly Robyn:
He wenys þat it be name myne,
　　For soth as i þe say.
He wot i haue a son here,　　　　　　　950
Þat is þe Quene lefe and dere:
　　I tolde hym so 3isterday.
As ofte as þou wilt to hym gan,
Name 'passilodian,'

---

[11] sense.　　[12] (to pùrsue) a study in his school.　　[13] dozen.　　[14] as well.

934. *Stage* in this sense is given in the *Oxford Dictionary* as first occurring in "The Pearl."

And wete what he will say."   955
"Lorde," he said, "i wil gladly:
I can hit wel and parfitely;[15]
Now haue i lornyd a play."[16]

When he to þe scheperde came,
He seid, "Do[17] gladly, gode Adam,   960
And mycull gode hit þe doo!
Micul þanke for Ioly Robyn,
Þat þou did[18] my lorde to dyne;
And oþer[19] þer is also:
Whi playes þou not 'passilodion,'   965
As þou did ȝisterday at home?
I wil onswer þerto:
I know þi gamme to þe ende,
For to say 'berafrynde,'
As haue i rest and roo."[20]   970

Þen looȝ þe herd, and liked ille,
And seid, "Lefe childe, be stille,
For Goddis swete tre!
Go sei þi fadir he is to blame
Þat he for[21] gode dose me schame!   975
Why has he wryed me?
Haue i maugré[22] for my god dede,
Shall i neuer more marchand fede,
Ne telle my pryueté!"
He stroked vp his hud for tene,   980
And toke a cuppe and mad it clene;
A gret drauȝt þen drank he.

Þe Prynce seid, "Þat was wel done:
Hit shal be filled aȝeyne ful sone,
Alle of the best wyne.   985
Play 'passilodion,' and ha no drede,
And haue a gold ryng to þi mede,

---

[15] perfectly. [16] diversion. [17] eat. [18] caused, invited. [19] another matter. [20] peace.
[21] in return for. [22] bad treatment.

972. The Black Prince was born in 1330.
986. MS. *drade*.

And were[23] it for luf myne."
"I wil it not, for sothe to sey:
Hit shulde not laste me halfe a day,   990
  Be Goddis swete pyne![24]
When it were brokyne, farewell he![25]
An hatte were bettir þen sech thre
  For reyne and sonneschyne."

When þe Prince hade hym beholde,   995
He ȝede and sate hym where he wolde,
  As skille and reson is;
And alle þe lordyngis in þe halle
On þe herd þei lowgen alle
  When any cuppe ȝede amys.   1000
When þei hade etyne and cloþis draw,
And wasshen, as hit is landis lawe,
  Certan sothe iwysse,
Þan dranke þai aftir sone anon,
And played passilodion   1005
  Tille ilke man hade his.

Þe lordis anon to chawmber went;
Þe Kyng after þe scheperde sent;
  He was broȝt forth full sone.
He clawed his hed, his hare he rent,   1010
He wende wel to haue be schent:
  He ne wyst what was to done.
When he French and Latyn herde,
He hade mervell how it ferde,[26]
  And drow hym euer alone.   1015
"Ihesu," he seid, "for þi gret grace,
Bryng me fayre out of þis place!
  Lady, now here my bone!

---

[23] wear.   [24] suffering (on the cross).   [25] farewell to it!   [26] what was happening.

990. Possibly a reference to the robbers.
1007. The chamber was a room adjoining the banquet-hall where the men gathered. The women went to their apartments, usually on another floor.
1015. MS. *alove.*

"What eyled[27] me? Why was i wode,
þat i cowth so litell gode
   Myseluen for to wrye?
A, Lord God! þat i was vnslye![28]
Alasse, þat euer he come so nye,
   þe sothe þat i shulde seye!
Wolde God, for His Modirs luf,   1025
Bryng me onys at myne abofe[29]—
   I were out of þeire eye,—
Shuld i neuer, for no faire spech,
Marchande of my cowncell teche,
   Soo aferde i am to dye!"   1030

The Kyng saw he was sory;
He had þer of gret myrth forþi,
   And seid, "Come nere, Adam;
Take þe spices and drynk þe wyne
As homely[30] as i did of thyne,   1035
   So God þe gif þe dame!"[31]
Fulle carfully in he ȝede;
"Haue i þis for my gode dede?
   Me rewes þat i here came!"
He toke þe wyne and laft þe spice;   1040
Then wist þei wel þat he was nyce;
   Wel carfull was þat man.

He ete þe spyce, the wyne he drank;
Oure Kyng on þe scheperde wanke[32]
   Priuely with his eye.   1045
"Ioly Robyn," he þoȝt, "wo þou[33] be
þat tyme þat i euer met with þe,
   Er euer þat i þe seye!
Be God," he þouȝt, "had i þe nowe
þer were ȝisturday i and þow,   1050
   Paynes þen shulde þou drye![34]
I shulde chastis þe so with my slyng,

---

[27] ailed. [28] guileless. [29] into a better state. [30] familiarly. [31] judgment. [32] winked.
[33] i.e., may the time be evil to you. [34] suffer.

1026. On *abofe*, see Koelbing's note, "Ipomadon" 5.

þou shulde no moo tythyngis bryng,
On horse þouȝ þou were hye !"

The Kyng commaundit a squyer tere,[35]　　　1055
"Goo telle þe scheperde in his ere
　þat i am þe Kyng,
And þou shall se sich cowntenence
þat hym had leuer be in Fraunce,
　When [he] heris of þat tythyng !　　　1060
He has me schewid his priueté:
He wil wene ded to be,
　And make þerfore mornyng.
Hit shalle hym mene al to gode:
I wolde not ellis, be þe rode,　　　1065
　Nouȝt for my best gold ryng !"

The squyer pryuely toke his leue
And plucked þe scheperde be þe sleue
　For to speke hym with:
"Man," he said, "þou art wode !　　　1070
Why dose þou not down þi hode?
　þou art all out of kithe ![36]
Hit is þe Kyng þat spekis to þe,
May do þe what his willis be,
　Berefe þe lym and lithe;[37]　　　1075
And gif þou haue do any trespas,
Fall on knees and aske grace,
　And he will gif þe grithe."

þen was þat herd a carful man,
And neuer so sory as he was þan,　　　1080
　When he herd þat sawe;
He wist not what hym was gode,
But þen he putte doune his hode;
　On knees he fel downe lawe.
"Lorde," he seid, "i crye þe mercy !　　　1085

---

[35] fine.　[36] company; i.e., your conduct is inappropriate.　[37] a tag, both words meaning limb.

1060. MS. not clear.

I knew þe not, be oure Lady,
When i come into þis sale,[38]
For had i wist of þis sorowe
When þat we met ȝister-morowe,
I had not bene in þis bale."   1090
NON FINIS SED PUNCTUS.

In other versions of the story, the king makes his host a knight and
rewards him well.

---

[38] hall.

1086. MS. *know.*

THE TOURNAMENT OF TOTTENHAM

THE TOURNAMENT OF TOTTENHAM

This burlesque, in the dialect of the north of about 1400–1440, is less famous than Chaucer's "Sir Thopas," but shows the same familiarity with the machinery of chivalry and the same unwillingness to take it seriously. It survives in two MSS., Harleian 5306 (H.), dated 1456, and Cambridge University Library MS. Ff. II 38 (C.), after 1431. C. was first printed in 1631 by William Bedwell, rector of Tottenham, who published a text with modernized spellings. Several antiquaries reprinted this version, evidently subscribing to Bedwell's opinion that it had historical value. Percy printed it in the first and second editions of his "Reliques of Ancient English Poetry" (1765, 1767); but was then informed by Tyrwhitt of the existence of H.; and, perceiving its superiority to Bedwell's text, he used it in subsequent editions, with a few of Bedwell's readings where H. was obscure. In "Ancient Songs and Ballads" (1790), Joseph Ritson attacked Percy venomously for tampering with the texts in the "Reliques," and, as a part of the rebuke, edited this poem from H.; but his work contains several inaccuracies and unwarrantable emendations. In 1836, Thomas Wright edited the text from C.; this was reprinted by Hazlitt in "Remains of the Early Popular Poetry of England," vol. iii, with readings from H. and Bedwell's edition. No critical text has been attempted.

The stanza is a variation of a type common in the north; but, because of the state in which this poem has survived, it is nearly impossible to tell whether the normal line was iambic or doggerel. In either event, variations are numerous.

Through the kindness of the authorities of the Department of Manuscripts of the British Museum and of the Library of Cambridge University, it has been possible to prepare the text from rotographs of both manuscripts. Since H., which has the better version, is wretchedly copied and in many places almost illegible, the readings of C. furnish many valuable clues.

The incidents in the piece are very like those in other pieces involving boasts. Especially close is the parallel with "The Avowis of Alexander" (*STS.* 21): they boast in the presence of a lady; they threaten to capture each other's horses and swords (5440); two of them dispute as to their prowess; the prize is a peacock (not a hen);

989

and one boast is generally granted to be better than all the rest.
Some of the words in the Scotch poem also occur in this.

Why a poem written in the northern dialect should deal so familiarly with the topography of the district about London that
Tottenham antiquaries have included it in their histories of the
parish is something of a puzzle.   Long -*a* is frequently retained where
the midland form had -*o* (*ga*, go); the plurals of verbs and nouns are
often in -*ys*, and so are the third singulars of many verbs (*stonys*,
getis).   For a discussion of the language, see *PMLA*. 43. 124.

Of all þes kene conquerours to carpe it were kynde:
Of fele feȝtyng-folk ferly we fynde;
The Turnament of Totenham haue we in mynde:
It were harme[1] sych hardynes were holden byhynde,[2]
   In story as we rede—   5
   Of Hawkyn, of Herry,
   Of Tomkyn, of Terry,
   Of þem þat were dughty
    And stalworth in dede.

It befel in Totenham, on a dere[3] day,   10
Þer was mad a schurtyng[4] be þe hyway.
Þeder com al þe men of þe contray—
Of Hyssyltoun, of Hygate, and of Hakenay,[5]
   And all þe swete swynke[rs].[6]
   Þer hopped Hawkyn,   15
   Þer davnsed Dawkyn,
   Þer trumped Tomkyn;
    And all were trewe drynkers,

Tyl þe day was gon, and euyn-song past,
Þat þay schuld rekyn þer scot and þer contes cast;[7]   20
Perkyn þe potter in to þe press past,
And sayd, "Rondol þe refe,[8] a doȝter þou hast,

---

[1] would be evil.   [2] concealed.   [3] i.e., memorable.   [4] festival.   [5] Islington, High-
gate, Hackney.   [6] blessed workmen.   [7] reckon their bill and cast up their
accounts.   [8] reeve, bailiff.

Title.   Tottenham and the other towns mentioned were at this time
separate parishes just north of London.

8. MS. *dughyt.*

21. MS. *prest*, probably a miscopying of long double -*s*.

Tyb, þe dere:
þer-for wyt wold i
Whych of all þys bachelery⁹   25
Were best worthy
    To wed hur to hys fere."

Vp styrt þes gadelyngys¹⁰ with þer long staues,
And sayd, "Randal þe refe, lo! þis lad raues!
Baldely amang us þy duȝter he craues,   30
And we er rycher men þe[n] he, and more god haues,
    Of catell and corn."
þen sayd Perkyn, "To Tybbe i haue hyȝt
þat i schal be alway redy in my ryȝt,¹¹
If þat it schuld be þys day seuenyȝt,¹²   35
    Or ell[is] ȝet to-morn."

þen sayd Randolfe þe refe, "Euer be he waryed¹³
þat about þys carpyng lenger wold be taryed!
I wold not þat my doȝter þat scho were myscaryed,¹⁴
But at hur most worschyp¹⁵ i wold scho were maryed.   40
    þer-for a turnament schal begin
    þys day seuenyȝt,
    With a flayl for to fyȝt,
    And [he] þat ys of most myght
        Schall brouke hur with wynne.   45

"Whoso berys hym best in þe turnament,
Hym schall be granted þe gre, be þe comon assent,
For to wynne my doȝter with dughty[nes] of dent,
And Coppeld, my brode¹⁶-henne, was broȝt out of Kent,
    And my donnyd¹⁷ kowe.   50

---

⁹ company of young men. ¹⁰ rogues. ¹¹ to defend my rights. ¹² week. ¹³ cursed.
¹⁴ should do badly. ¹⁵ to her greatest honor. ¹⁶ brood. ¹⁷ brown.

23. In the MS., *dere* has been altered in other ink to *devoll*.
38. MS. *atryed*.
39. *þat* is carelessly doubled.
47. MS *camon*.
49. Copple, meaning "crested," seems to have been a common name
for a hen. Cf. "Townley Mysteries" p. 99. A bird is often the prize
of such a contest.

F[or] no spens[18] wyl i spare,
For no catell wyl i care:
He schal haue my gray mare,
    And my spottyd sowe !''

Þer was many bold lad þer bodyes to bede;[19]   55
Þan þay toke þayr leue, and homward þay ȝede,
And all þe woke[20] afterward þay grayþed þer wede,
Tyll it come to þe day þat þay suld do þer dede.
    Þay armed ham in mattis:[21]
    Þay set on þer nollys,[22]   60
    For to kepe þer pollys,[23]
    Gode blake bollys,
      For[24] batryng of battis.

Þay sowed þam in schepe-skynnes, for[25] þay suld not brest;
Ilkon toke a blak hat insted of a crest,   65
A harow brod as a fanne[26] aboune on þer brest,
And a flayle in þer hande, for to fyght prest.
    Furth gon þay fare !
    Þer was kyd mekyl fors[27]
    Who schuld best fend his cors;[28]   70
    He þat had no gode hors,
      He gat hým a mare.

Sych anoþer gadryng haue i not sene oft !
When all þe gret cumpany com rydand to þe croft,[29]
Tyb on a gray mare was set upon loft,   75
On a sek ful of sedys, for scho schuld syt soft,
    And led hur to þe gap.[30]

---

[18] expenditure. [19] i.e., undertake it. [20] week. [21] mattings. [22] heads. [23] crowns.
[24] to prevent. [25] so that. [26] an arrow broad as a fan. [27] much might shown.
[28] defend his body. [29] field. [30] opening in the hedge.

62. MS. *bellys.*
64. I.e., sewed themselves in securely.
67. MS. *syght.*
72. By preference, knights used chargers. Cf. Perceval's early adventures.
76. C. has *senvye,* mustard seed.
77. MS. *cap.*

For cryeng of al þe men,
Forþer wold not Tyb þen
Tyl sche had hur gode brode-hen   80
    Set in hur lap.

A gay gyrdyl Tyb had on, borwed for þe nonys,
And a garland on hur hed, ful of rounde bonys,
And a broche on hur brest, ful of safer[31] stonys—
With þe holy rode tokenyng was wrethyn[32] for þe nonys: 85
    No catel was þer spared!
When ioly Gyb saw hure þare,
He gyrd[33] so hys gray mere
Þat sche lete a faucon-fare[34]
    At þe rereward.   90

"I wow to God," quod Herry, "i schal not lefe behende!
May i mete with Bernard, on Bayard þe blynde,
Ich man kepe hym out of my wynde;[35]
For whatsoeuer þat he be befor[36] me i fynde,
    I wot i schal hym greue!"   95
"Wele sayd!" quod Hawkyn;
"And i avow," quod Dawkyn,
"May i mete with Tomkyn,
    His flayl hym refe."

"I vow to God," quod Hud, "Tyb, sone schal þou se   100
Whych of all þis bachelery grant is þe gre!
I schal scomfet[37] þaym all, for þe loue of þi;
In what place so i come, þay schal haue dout of me,
    Myn armes ar so clere:[38]

---

[31] sapphire. [32] it was worked with the sign of the cross. [33] struck. [34] broke
wind. [35] course. [36] be (whom) before, etc. [37] discomfit. [38] shining (!).

85. MS. *wrotyn*. The inscription gave the jewel its power.
89. MS. *þe sche.*
92. Bayard was a common name for a horse; the original Bayard was
the marvelous steed of the four sons of Aymon, and was popularly reputed to have been blind.
104. Possibly a reference to the light-giving power of the arms of heroes.
See Wimberly 92.

I bere a reddyl[39] and a rake,   105
Poudred with a brenand drake,[40]
And iii cantell[41] of a cake
   In ycha cornare."

"I vow to God," quod Hawkyn, "yf i haue þe gowt,[42]
Al þat i fynde in þe felde presand[43] here aboute,   110
Haue i twyes or thryes redyn þurgh þe route,[44]
In ycha stede þer þay me se, of me þay schal haue doute
   When i begyn to play.
I make a vow þat i ne schall,
But-yf Tybbe wyl me call,   115
Or i be thryes doun fall,
   Ry3t onys com away."

þen sayd Terry, and swore be hys crede,
"Saw þou neuer 3ong boy forþi hys body bede,
For when þay fy3t fastest, and most ar in drede,   120
I schal take Tyb by þe hand and hur away lede.
   I am armed at þe full:
In myn armys[45] i bere wele
A do3 trogh and a pele,[46]
A sadyll withouten a panell,[47]   125
   With a fles of woll."

"I vow to God," quod Dudman, "and swor be þe stra,[48]
Whyls me ys left my mere, þou getis hur not swa;
For scho ys wele schapen, and ly3t as þe ro:[49]
þer ys no capul[50] in þys myle befor hur schal ga;   130
   Sche wil me no3t begyle.

---

[39] gardener's hedging-stick.   [40] with figures of a fiery dragon sprinkled over it.
[41] sections.   [42] although I have the gout.   [43] rushing.   [44] throng.   [45] coat of arms.
[46] dough-trough and baker's-shovel.   [47] saddle-cloth.   [48] straw.   [49] roe.   [50] horse.

105 ff. The items enumerated are all painted on his coat of arms; they
are not weapons.
   109. MS. *yf he.*
   110. MS. *felte.*
   119. *For þi* may be a mistake for *forþer*, i.e., more recklessly.
   128. MS. *sws; has* is written over *ys.*
   131. Nearly illegible. *Wil ne?*

She wyl me bere, i dar wele say,
On a lang somerys day,
Fro Hyssyltoun to Hakenay,
Noȝt oþer half myle!"[1]   135

"I vow to God," quod Perkyn, "þou spekis of cold rost![2]
I schal wyrch wyselyer, withouten any bost:
V of þe best capullys[3] þat ar in þys ost,[4]
I wot i schal þaym wynne, and bryng þaym to my cost;[5]
    And here i graunt þam Tybbe.   140
Wele, boyes, here ys he
Þat wyl fyȝt and not fle,
For i am in my iolyté,[6]
    With io forth, Gybbe!"[7]

When þay had þer vowes [made], furth [g]an þey hye,   145
With flayles and hornes and trumpes mad of tre.
Þer were all þe bachelerys of þat contré:
Þay were dyȝt i[n] aray as þamselfe wold be.
    Þayr baners were ful bryȝt,
    Of an old roten fell;[8]   150
Þe cheuerone, of a plow-mell[9]
And þe schadow[10] of a bell,
    Poudred with mone-lyȝt.[11]

I wot it ys no chylder-game whan þay togedyr met!

---

[1] i.e., no more and no less.   [2] roast; i.e., your news is late.   [3] horses.   [4] host.
[5] side.   [6] in good spirits.   [7] keep on, Gilbert! i.e., let's be doing something.
[8] rotten hide.   [9] the chevron (pointed ornament) is in the likeness of a mallet
carried by plowmen for breaking clods.   [10] silhouette.   [11] moons being sprinkled
over the field.

133. MS. *sonerys.*
134. The distance is some three miles.
137. MS. *swyselyer.*
138. MS. *of þo.*
146. Wooden horns and trumpets were common in the Middle Ages,
and were still sometimes used in England as late as the eighteenth century.   Though their tone was satisfactory, they were discarded because of
their clumsiness.
150 ff. The heraldic terms were confusing both to this scribe and to the
scribe of MS. C. Hence the exact meaning of some of the phrases is con-
jectural. MS. *raton.*

When icha freke in þa feld on hys felay be[t],   155
And layd o[n] styfly; for noþyng wold þay let!
And faght ferly fast, tyll þer horses swet,
    And fewe wordys spoken.
Þer were flayles al to-slatred,[12]
Þer were scheldys al to-clatred,[13]   160
Bollys and dysches al to-schatred,
    And many hedys brokyn.

Þer was clynkyng of cart-sadellys and clattiryng of cannes;[14]
Of fele frekis in þe feld, brokyn were þer fannes;[15]
Of sum were þe hedys brokyn, of sum þe brayn-panes;[16]   165
And yll ware i[t] be sum or þay went þens,
    With swyppyng of swepyllys.[17]
Þe boyes were so wery for-fught[18]
Þat þay myȝt not fyȝt mare oloft,[19]
But creped þen about in þe [c]roft   170
    As þey were croked crepyls.[20]

Perkyn was so wery þat he began to loute;[21]
"Help, Hud! i am ded in þys ylk rowte![22]
A hors for xl pens, a gode and a stoute,
Þat i may lyȝtly come of my noye out![23]   175
    For no cost wyl i spare."
He styrt up as a snayle
And hent a capul be þe tayle,
And raȝt[24] Dawkyn hys flayle,
    And wan þer a mare.   180

Perkyn wan v and Hud wan twa;
Glad and blyþe þay ware þat þay had don sa:

---

[12] split. [13] smashed. [14] metal pots. [15] winnowing shovels. [16] skulls. [17] blows from the leather of flails. [18] fought out. [19] i.e., on horseback. [20] broken cripples. [21] sink. [22] throng. [23] easily come out of my vexation. [24] seized from.

159 ff. MS. *flatred . . . flatred.* The emendation is suggested by the readings of C.
163. MS. *chaltitryng.*
166. MS. illegible in part.
172. MS. *louter.*
173. MS. *rowet.*
178. MS. *be þo.*

Þay wold haue²⁵ þam to Tyb and present hur with þa.
Þe capull were so wery þat þay myȝt not ga,
   But styl gon þay stand.   185
"Allas!" quod Hudde, "my ioye i lese!
Me had leuer þen a ston²⁶ of chese
Þat dere Tyb had al þese,
   And wyst it were my sand."²⁷

Perkyn turnyd hym about in þat ych thrange;   190
Among þes wery boyes he wrest and he wrang:²⁸
He threw þam doun to þe erth, and þrast þaim amang,²⁹
When he saw Tyrry away with Tyb fang,³⁰
   And after hym ran.
Of hys hors he hym drogh,   195
And gaf hym of hys flayl inogh.
"We, te-he!" quod Tyb, and lugh,³¹
   "Ȝe er a dughty man."

Þus þay tugged and rugged³² tyl yt was nere nyȝt.
All þe wyues of Totenham come to se þat syȝt,   200
With wyspes and kexis and ryschys³³ þer lyȝt,
To fech hom þer husbandes, þat were þam trouth-plyȝt;
   And sum broȝt gret harwes,³⁴
Þer husbandes hom for to fech;
Sum on dores and sum on hech,³⁵   205
Sum on hyrdyllys and sum on crech,³⁶
   And sum on welebaraws.

Þay gaderyd Perkyn about, euerych syde,
And graunt hym þer [þe gre]; þe more was hys p[r]ide.
Tyb and he, with gret merthe homward con þay ryde,   210
And were al nyȝt togedyr, tyl þe morn-tyde;
   And þay in fere assent:³⁷
So wele hys nedys he has sped³⁸

---

²⁵ bring. ²⁶ stone, fourteen pounds. ²⁷ sent by me. ²⁸ twisted and jerked. ²⁹ i.e.,
jabbed with his flail. ³⁰ start. ³¹ laughed. ³² scuffled. ³³ twists of straw
and flax and rushes. ³⁴ sledges, hurdles. ³⁵ gratings. ³⁶ lattices. ³⁷ agree with
one another. ³⁸ brought to a successful issue.

210. MS. *mothe.*

Þat dere Tyb he has wed;
Þe pryse folk þat hur led   215
   Were of þe turnament.

To þat ylk fest com many, for þe nones:
Some come hyp-halt,[39] and sum tryppand[40] on þe stonys;
Sum a staf in hys hand, and sum two at onys:[41]
Of sum were þe hedys to-broken, and sum þe schulder-bonys: 220
   With sorow com þay þedyr!
  Wo was Hawkyn, wo was Herry;
  Wo was Tomkyn, wo was Terry;
  And so was al þe bachelary,
   When þay met togedyr.   225

At þat fest þay were seruyd with a ryche aray:
Euery v and v had a cokenay;[42]
And so þay sat in iolyté al þe lang day,
And at þe last þay went to bed, with ful gret deray.[43]
   Mekyl myrth was þem amang: 230
  In euery corner of þe hous
  Was melody delycyous,
  For to here precyus,
   Of vi menys sang.[44]

                 EXPLICIT.

---

[39] limping. [40] stumbling. [41] i.e., staves in both hands. [42] cf. note. [43] unsteadiness. [44] contrapuntal song for six voices.

214. MS. *had.*
215. MS. *prayse.*
219. MS. *þys þay.*
227. The *Oxford Dictionary* cites this passage as an illustration of the word *cockney* in the sense of "small egg"; but that sense is obviously unsatisfactory. The word seems to mean "cook." See "King Lear" II. iv. 120.

VOCABULARY

INTRODUCTION

Only common words are included, and only a few references for each. Words neither glossed nor included here have the sense of their phonetic equivalents in Modern English. Compounds (e.g., *aslaghe, dore-barr*) are hastily dealt with; for spellings and derivations, see the root-form of the words (*slaghe, dore,* etc.).

The following conventions in spelling have been observed:

When *y-* is equivalent to *i-*, the word is listed under *i*, regardless which letter is used (*ynne* under *in*). But participles in *i-* are listed under the letter immediately following the *i-*.

Æ is listed as if it were *a*, not *æ*.

The character *þ* is not used, and is replaced with *th*.

C and *k*, which were used interchangeably in Middle English for the hard sound of *c*, are listed according to the modern spellings of the words, so far as possible (*karpe* under *c*). For *cw-, kw-*, see *qu-*.

For Old English and Old French *-u-*, see *-ou-*. Scribes used *u* and *v* interchangeably; here all are listed under *u*, except a few initial *v's*. They also did not discriminate between *ȝ* and *z*; and their practice has been followed here.

F, which between vowels was often voiced, has been replaced with *u*.

Forms of a word that differ only by the addition of final *e* have usually not been distinguished, except when the *-e* is a case ending.

For *ȝ*, see *y-* or *g-*.

Cases and modes are not always noted unless their forms have peculiarities. Verbs are in the indicative mode unless otherwise noted. The persons of pronouns and verbs are indicated by the figures, 1, 2, 3, etc.

The following abbreviations for grammatical terms are used:

a., accusative	OF, Old French
adj., adjective	ON, Old Norse
adv., adverb	plu., plural
comp., compound	pp., past participle
conj., conjunction	pr., present tense
cp., comparative	prep., preposition
d., dative	pro., pronoun
f., feminine gender	prp., present participle
g., genitive	pt., preterite
imp., imperative	rel., relative
inf., infinitive	sb., adjective as noun
int., interrogative	sg., singular
interj., interjection	sj., subjunctive
m., masculine and neuter genders	sup., superlative
n., { noun / nominative case }	vbl., verbal
	vs., strong verb
OE, Old English	vw., weak verb

In the vocabulary, entries are followed by a reference to poem and line. Titles of poems are abbreviated as follows:

Al, "Alexander"
At, "Athelston"
Av, "The Avowing of Arthur"
B, "The Tale of Beryn"
CA, "Chevelere Assigne"
Cl, "Sir Cleges"
D, "Sir Degaré"
EG, "Eger and Grime"
Em, "Emaré"
ET, "The Earl of Toulouse"
FB, "Floris and Blancheflour"
G, "Gamelyn"
Hr, "King Horn"
Hv, "Havelok the Dane"
Ip, "Ipomadon"

K, "King Edward and the Shepherd"
Lv, "Sir Launfal"
Ly, Laymon's "Brut"
O, "Sir Orfeo"
P, "Sir Perceval of Galles"
R, "Robert of Sicily"
Sd, "The Sultan of Babylon"
Sq, "The Squire of Low Degree"
SS, "The Seven Sages of Rome"
Tr, "The Destruction of Troy"
TT, "The Tournament of Totten ham"
Yw, "Ywain and Gawain"

VOCABULARY

A

a, cf. an, on, ai, at.
abide, vs., (OE abīdan), (1) dwell, remain. inf., abyde, G 742, D 479; pt.`sg., abood, B 3680; abeod, Ly 28381; habade, P 1731; pp., abide, G 337.
(2) await. inf., G 24; pr., habyddis, P 1278; pt., abood, At 753.
(3) wait, delay, stop. pt., abood, D 48; imp. sg., habide, SS 2991.
(4) endure. inf., EG 418; abide, Hr 1048; habyde, P 72.
abie, abegge, vs., (OE abycgan), pay for, atone for. G 816; aby, SS 4288; haby, P 1903; abugge, Hr 75; abeie, Hr 110; abygge, Al 4199; pt. sg., abought, G 76; aboht, Ly 27638. Used absolutely, Yw 413, Sd 1793.
aboute, prep. and adv., (OE onbutan), about, around, near. aboute, Tr 83; abute, Hr 1081; abuten, Ly 27567; abouʒt, Cl 43.

ac, conj., (OE ac, ah), but. Hr 523; D 29; Ly 27734.
adight, cf. dight.
admiral, n., (OF amiral), Saracen viceroy or officer. Ly 27680; admirail, Ly 27668; admirad, Hr 89; g. sg., admirale, Ly 27689; amerayle, Em 109.
adoun, adv., (OE of dūne), down. Hr 428; adun, Ly 27459; Hr 1488.
adred, adj., (OE ofdrædd), afraid, terrified. SS 502; Hr 291; adrad, G 562; adradde, Ly 27962.
afered, adj., (OE afæran), frightened. ET 661; D 101.
afore, aforn, prep. and adv., before. G 656, 806; auornon, Ly 28313.
after, (OE æfter), (1) prep., next in order. Hv 171.
(2) (sent) for. G 17; aftur, CA 129.
(3) (name) for. Ly 27921.
(4) in accordance with, according to. Ly 27529; EG 517; efter, SS 2816.

(5) in pursuit of. Hr 880.

(6) *adv.*, afterwards. Tr 81; Sd 1877; SS 310; aftir, P 1808.

(7) *conj.*, according as. Hv 2810.

again, (OE ongēn, ongegn), (1) *adv.*, back, in return. ET 52; aȝen, D 267; ayein, D 931; agen, Hr 582, aye, B 3276.

(2) once more. ogayn, SS 468; aȝeyn, CA 316; aȝe, B 3720.

(3) *prep.*, against. aȝaynns, Av 219; aȝaynus, Av 315.

(4) toward, nearing (*of place and time*). aȝeyn, Em 203; P 1129; D 967.

(5) until. Ip 3067.

(6) in anticipation of. Ip 3217; Hv 1106.

(7) before, in the face of. Em 206; aȝein, Ly 27980; ayen, Lv 989.

(8) *conj.*, in preparation for the time when. P 198.

comp. as *adv.*, ageynward, in return. B 3314.

agast, *adj.*, (OE agæstan), afraid, in awe of. D 900; G 7; ET 451.

aȝe, back; *cf.* again.

ah, *cf.* ac, but; awe, owe, own.

ahon, *v.*, hang. Ly 28407.

ai, ay, (OE ā, ō), (1) *adv.*, always, ever. SS 2816; Tr 18; æi, Ly 27729; a, Ly 28090.

(2) *adj.*, eternal. Av 434.

comp., for ay, forever, SS 855; Ip 1162.

air, *cf.* heir.

aither, *cf.* either.

al, alle, (OE eall, all), (1) *adj. and adj.-pro.*, all. Hr 756; Hv 35. *old g.*, aller, of us all, G 321; our alther, of us all, G 256; alther best, best of all, Hv 182; althir best, P 1883; alther leste, least of all, Hv 1978; alre, of all. Ly 27807; alder, FB 551.

(2) *adv.*, wholly, entirely. Ly 27840.

comp., alkyn, all sorts of, Yw 1073; algate, any way, G 115; always, yet, O 229 .

ælc, *cf.* ilk.

alighte, alighted; *cf.* light.

als, also, *cf.* as.

alsone, *adv.*, (OE al swa sōna), (1) straightway. P 1011; alssone, SS 518.

(2) as soon (as). Yw 233.

amis, *adv. and adj.*, wrong, wrongly. D 60.

amorwe, a-marȝen, to-morrow; *cf.* morne.

an, *adj.*, (OE ān), one. Hv 114; a, Cl 521; on, Sd 1582; *d.f.*, are, Ly 27992; *d.m.*, ane, Ly 27947; *a.m.*, enne, Ly 27667; ænne, Ly 27549.

an, *cf.* on, one, and.

and, an, *conj.*, (OE ond), (1) and. Hr 699; Hv 4; an, Ly 27556; D 153.

(2) if. At 403; Av 443.

ani, *adj. and pro.*, (OE ænig), any. Hv 10; anny, Ip 1086; eni, G 260.

anon, *adv.*, (OE on ān), at once, quickly. D 79; anone, ET 253; anan, Ly 27508; onane, SS 819. *comp.*, anon right, straightway, G 734; anæn swa, as soon as, Ly 28242.

another, (OE ān oðer), (1) *adj. and pro.*, another. Hr 578.

(2) *adv.*, otherwise. B 3538.

anowȝ, enough; *cf.* inogh.

answer, *vw.*, (OE ondswerian), answer. *pt.*, answarede, Hr 42; andswarede, Ly 28094; vnsquarut, Av 129; *pt. pl.*, ansuereden, Hv 176.

aplight, *adv.*, (OE on pliht), (1) at once. D 1048.

(2) indeed. D 775.

are, (OE ær), (1) *conj.*, before. G 605; or, Ip 3041; are, P 653; er, G 568; ar, Hr 546.

(2) *adv.*, earlier, formerly. Lv

1019; ær, Ly 27491; ære, Ly 27959; ayre, Ip 1064; *sup.*, arst, first, formerly, G 538; ærst, Ly 27456.
(3) sooner, rather, SS 3023, 4253.
(4) *prep.*, before, earlier than. SS 4303.
comp., er thane, before the time when. Hr 1435.
aright, *adv.*, (OE on riht), (1) rightly. G 29.
(2) straightway (*often used merely to intensify*). Hr 457.
arise, *vs.*, (OE arīsan), arise, get up. *pt.*, aros, Hr 1313; aræs, Ly 28006; *imp. plu.*, ariseth, G 643.
armed, *pp.*, *adj.*, armed. iarmed, Hr 803; armut, Av 77; yarmed, O 134.
as, als, also, (OE alswa), (1) *conj.* as, as if. P 2263; ase, D 272; os, ET 613.
(2) as (*correlative*). D 1039; ET 409; alswa (. . swa), Ly 27458.
(3) when. Hv 2120.
(4) in such manner. Hr 538; Ly 27648; alse, Ly 28413.
(5) as surely as (*followed by subj.*). Hr 775.
(6) however, in whatever manner. Hr 543.
(7) *adv.*, thus, so, likewise. Yw 839.
(8) also. CA 91; Ly 27884.
(9) very (*in phrases, such as:* also swithe, *etc.*). D 746; Hr 471.
(10) *prep.*, like. Hv 319.
(11) *expletive, untranslatable.* Av 896; Tr 8668.
aslaghe, slain. asla3en Hr 897, 1491.
astonied, stunned. Sd 2057.
aswoue, aswowe, swooning. D 903; Lv 755.
at, *prep.*, (OE æt), (1) in (a place). Hr 253; a, Ly 27505.

(2) with. O 138; Hr 1033.
(3) of, from. P 179; Em 185; atte, Av 1081.
(4) according to (*in the phrase:* at will). Av 3.
(5) to. B 3481.
comp., atte, at the. B 3002; ate, D 576.
aueden, had; *cf.* haue.
auenture, aunter, (OF aventure), (1) *n.*, adventure. G 777; antur, Av 1015.
(2) fate, chance, luck. auentoure, D 624; Tr 67.
(3) occurrence, happening. auntris, B 3436; aventowres, Em 754.
(4) *vw.*, take a risk. auntre, G 217; aventure, ET 927.
(5) happen. *pt.*, auntrid, Tr 8632.
aught, (OE āwiht, āuht, āht), (1) *pro.*, anything. awght, Ip 476; aw3te, CA 204; oght, Sd 2713; o3te, Av 431; ou3t, B 3611.
(2) *adv.*, at all. Hr 976; P 1157.
auter, awter, altar.
awe, owen, *vs.*, (OE āgan), (1) own, have. Hv 1292; a3en, Ly 27989; *1 sg. pr.*, ah, Ly 28022; *3 sg. pr.*, oweth, Ip 477; *pr. sj.*, a3e, Ly 28423; *pt.*, aute, Hv 743; awcte, Hv 207; ahte, Ly 27729; au3t, D 710 *pr. sj.*, hawe, Hv 1188.
(2) ought, should. *pt. as pr.*, aughte, P 2175; aucte, Hv 2787; auhte, Hv 2800; *pr.*, owth, Em 667.
(3) owe. K 577; *pr. sg.*, aw, Yw 92; *pr. plu.*, owe, K 621; *pt.*, aughte, P 1490.
awe, *n.,* fear. aw3e, FB 909.
awen, awin, a3en, *cf.* own.
awreke, avenge; *cf.* wreke.
axe, axid, ask, asked. B 2941, 3372.
ayen, aye, a3e, *cf.* again.

B

bac, back, *n.*, (OE bæc), back. Hv 47; bake, P 2235; Tr 8599; bakke, CA 291.

bald, bold, *adj.*, (OE beald, bald), (1) bold. Hr 90; *g. plu.*, baldere, Ly 27510.
(2) fine, spirited. D 394; *d.f.sg.*, baldere, Ly 27873.
comp., baldelike, boldly. Hv 53; boldelych, G 717.

bale, *n.*, (OE bealu), (1) sorrow, evil, trouble. P 1411; Ip 3101; *pl.*, balys, Lv 971; *often in the following phrases:* bale bett, repair an injury, rescue from trouble, ET 515; balys bete, Lv 971; boteles bale, irreparable injury, ET 607.
(2) destruction. balu, Ly 27478.

band, bond, *pt. of* bind. Ip 388; G 818.

bane, *n.*, (OE bana), (1) ruin, death. Yw 709; EG 137; P 568.
(2) murderer, slayer. P 1926.

barnage, group of barons. SS 273; barronage, the lands of a baron, EG 1452.

bath, see both.

be-. *For all forms with the prefix* be-, *cf.* bi-.

be, ben, *vs.*, (OE bēon, wesan), *inf.*, EG 545; Hr 8; bee, Av 66; beo, Hr 1285; bene, Em 626; beon, Ly 27641. *pr. 1 sg.*, am, D 98; ame, P 1501; *2 sg.*, art, B 2926; ert, SS 503; ært, Ly 28098; *(with enclitic pronoun)* ertou, SS 2916. *3 sg.*, is, D 78; his, Hv 279; es, P 205, SS 245; beth, B 3315. *As future*, bese, P 2077; beth, Hv 1261; biʒ, D 127. *1 plu.*, aren, Hv 619; ben, G 162; beʒ, D 104. *2 plu.*, ar, Av 643; beoth, Ly 27610. *3 plu.*, arne, Av 1130;

be, D 980; beth, O 57; ben, Hv 2599; sunden, Ly 28224; er, SS 363; bethe, B 3313; byn, K 9; buth, Al 3959. *subj. 1 sg. pr.*, be, Ip 3101. *3 sg.*, beo, Ly 28148; *(with nunnation)* beon, Ly 28637; be, D 811. *pt. 1 sg.*, was, D 873; wos, Av 921. *2 sg.*, were, Av 846; P 544; wore, Hv 684. *3 sg.*, wasse, Av 638; was, D 302. wes, Ly 27478. *plu.*, war, SS 218; wore, Em 410; ware, Av 400; was, Av 865; weoren, Ly 27432; werun, Av 242; wern, Cl 17; weryn, O 18; wheryn, Lv 261. *sj. sg.*, were, CA 180; ware, P 150; weer, B 3566; weore, Ly 27643; wore, Hv 1938. *imp. sg.*, beo, Hr 541; be, Hv 683. *plu.*, bes, Hv 2246. *pp.*, be, Sd 2440; bene, P 2231; ybeon, Al 3921; byn, Ip 3189; iben, D 232; ibe, B 3040. *Used for auxiliary of intransitive v. in pt.*, is wente, Av 538; er went, SS 304.
Negative forms, nas (ne was), G 29, D 11; nam (ne am), O 428; nis (ne is), O 129; nes, (ne wes), D 708; neoren, neoruen (ne weoren), Ly 27533, 27654.

bede, *vs.*, (OE bēodan), (1) offer, present *(sometimes of blows)*. TT 119; *pr. 1 sg.*, bede, Av 296; *(with enclitic pronoun)* biddi, Hv 484.
(2) command, summon, invite. *pr. 2 sg.*, bedes, Hv 2392; *pt.*, bede, Av 744; bedʒ, Hr 504; *pp.* ybede, FB 859.
The forms were gradually superseded by forms of bidde *(q.v.),* pray, beg. *They were often confused in M.E. times.*

beie, bye, *vs.*, (OE bycgan), (1) buy, redeem. Hv 53. *pt. 3 sg.*, boʒte, Av 646; bowʒt, Cl 335.
(2) pay for, atone for, suffer for. boʒte, Hr 1388; bouthe, Hv

875. *pp.*, **boght**, SS 546; **bouth**, Hv 883.

bere, *vs.*, (OE **beran**), (1) carry, bear. D 771; **beor**, Al 4170; **iberen**, Ly 27850. *pt. 3 sg.*, **bar**, D 247. *pp.*, **borne**, Em 258; **yboren**, Hv 2557.
(2) comport oneself. *pr. 3 sg.*, **berys**, TT 46.
(3) ride down, strike down. *pr. 3 sg.*, **berythe**, Ip 3179; *pt. 3 sg.*, **bare**, Av 422; **bore**, EG 130.
(4) give birth to. *pt. 1 sg.*, **bere**, CA 196; **bare**, CA 211; *pp.*, **bore**, Sd 2195; **ibore**, D 181, Hr 138; *pt. sj.*, **bere**, Hv 974.
(5) *in idiomatic senses:* wear, Hr 1286; have, Em 924; weigh down, CA 297.

berst, brest, *vs.*, (OE **berstan**), burst, break. *inf.*, CA 317; Ly 27683. *sj. 2 sg. pr.*, **berste**, Hr 1192. *pt.*, **brast**, Yw 814; Av 1027.

beste, beeste, *n.*, (OE **beste**), beast. Hv 279; CA 214, 218; *plu.*, **beste3**, P 176.

bet, bette, better; *cf.* **gode**.

bete, *vs.*, (OE **bēatan**), beat, strike. D 348; *pr. 3 sg.*, **betus**, Av 58; *pt. 3 sg.*, **bet**, TT 155; *plu.*, **beten**, Hv 1876; *imp. plu.*, **beteth**, G 111; *pp.*, **beten**, G 115.

bethe, *cf.* **both**.

be3st, best; *cf.* **gode**.

bi, by, be, (OE **be, bī**), (1) *prep.*, beside. Hr 35; D 1025.
(2) by means of. Tr 23; Hr 436.
(3) in the name of. B 3105; Ip 471.
(4) to the extent of. D 909.
(5) concerning. B 3598; CA 5.
(6) during. G 65.
(7) about (*of time*). Hr 1431.
(8) in groups of. D 895.
(9) *adv.*, near. CA 109.

(10) *conj.*, by the time that. Av 689; SS 845.
comp., **be that**, then, when. Cl 58; D 273; **by that**, CA 248, At 496.

bicome, *vs.*, (OE **bicuman**), (1) become, happen. *pt. plu.*, **bicomen**, Hv 2257. *imp. plu.*, **bicomes**, Hv 2303.
(2) betake oneself, go. *pr. 3 sg.*, **bicome3**, D 178; *pt. 3 sg.*, **bycome**, Yw 438; *pp.*, **bicumen**, Ly 28057; **bicome**, O 192.

bidde, *vs.*, (OE **biddan**), (1) ask, beg, pray, invite. Hr 457; D 490. *pr. 1 sg.*, **bidde**, G 744; **biddus**, Av 66; *pt. 3 sg.*, **bade**, Av 549; **bad**, G 238, Hr 1069.
(2) command. *pr. 3 sg.*, **byddyth**, CA 262. *pt. sg.*, **bad**, Hr 273, Cl 398; **badde**, CA 155; *imp. plu.*, **bidde3**, D 212.

bide, *vs.*, (OE **bīdan**), (1) remain, delay. Av 409; *pt.*, **bod**, At 405; **bade**, P 569; *pp.*, **biddn**, EG 79.
(2) await. *pr. 3 sg.*, **bidus**, Av 244.

bidene, bedene, *adv.*, (OE ?), (*usually following* **al**), at once, at the same time, together. Lv 907; Yw 50; SS 231.

bifore, biforn, (OE **biforan**), (1) *prep.*, in the presence of. **biuore**, Hr 233; **biuoren**, Ly 28417.
(2) in front of. Cl 399; Ly 28024.
(3) earlier than. Hv 246.
(4) *adv.*, earlier, in front of, *etc.* P 107; **beforne**, Ip 458; Ly 27555.

biginne, *vs.*, (OE **biginnan**), begin, do. *inf.*, Hr 1277. *pt. plu.*, **bigunnen**, Ly 28315, Hr 1433; *sg.*, **byganne**, CA 183. *The preterit is frequently equivalent to the past tense of the following verb:* **bigan**, to flow, flowed, Hr 117.

bihald, biheld, *vs.*, (OE **bihaldan, bihealdan**), look at, look about.

Hr 1147. *pr. sg.*, **behylde**, Ip 419; **byholde3**, P 534; **byhaldes**, P 673; *pt. sg.*, **biheld**, D 756, FB 262; *plu.*, **byhelde**, P 66.

bihate, **bihete**, *vs.*, (OE **behātan**), promise. *pr. 1 sg.*, **bihete**, Yw 158; *pt.*, **bihet**, Hr 470; **behight**, Cl 468; **byhey3te**, Al 3926; **behe3te**, Av 532; **byheet**, G 418; **byhette**, Al 3988; *pp.*, **bihoten**, Hv 564; **behette**, K 573; *vb.n.*, **byhotyng**, Al 4000.

bihoue, *vw.*, (OE **bihōfian**), behoove (*always impersonal*), befit. *pr.*, **bihoueth**, Hr 178; **behovys**, Ip 1163; **behouus**, Av 300; *pt.*, **byhoued**, P 2228.

bileue, *vw.*, (OE **belǣfan**), (1) remain, survive. Hr 363; *pr. 3 plu.*, **bilauen**, Ly 28119; *pt. 3 sg.*, **belafte**, Em 472; **bilefte**, Hv 2963.

(2) leave, relinquish. **bileofuen**, Ly 28184; **bilæfuen**, Ly 28189. *pt. sg.*, **bilæfden** (*with nunnation*), Ly 27899; *pp.*, **bylefte**, CA 240; **bileued**, G 98.

bileue, *vw.*, (OE **gelyfan**), believe. Hr 1321; *etc.*

bilinne, *vs.*, hesitate. G 552.

biliue, quickly; *cf.* **bliue**.

bireue, *vs. and w.*, (OE **bereafian**), deprive of, take away. *pt.*, **byrafte**, CA 199; *pp.*, **byreeued**, G 85; **byreued**, G 97; **biræued**, Ly 27907.

biswike, *vs.*, (OE **biswīcan**), beguile, cheat, betray. *inf.*, H*r* 290; **biswiken**, Ly 28126; *pt. sg.*, **biswac**, Ly 28416; *pp.*, **biswike**, Hv 1249.

biteche, **bitake**, *vs.*, (OE **betǣcan**), commit, entrust, give. *pr. 1 sg.*, **beteche**, CA 312; **bitache**, Ly 28602; *3 sg.*, **bytaketh**, CA 151; *pt. 2 sg.*, **bitahtest**, Ly 28108; *3 sg.*, **bitaughte**, P 2156; **betoke**, Ip 449; **bitaucte**, Hv 206; **bitawt**,

D 331. *pp.*, **bytaken**, CA 163. *Very common in the phrase:* to Gode bitechen, farewell; CA 312, G 338.

biwreie, *vw.*, (OE **-wregan**), reveal, betray. Sd 1580; *pr. sj.*, Hr 362.

ble, **blee**, *n.*, (OE **blēo**), complexion, hue. Lv 849; ET 198; Em 270.

blethelye, *cf.* **blithe**.

blinne, *vs.*, (OE **blinnan**), stop, cease, put an end to. Sd 2442; **bylynne**, G 557; **blin**, EG 641; *pt.*, **blan**, Av 919; **blanne**, ET 241; **blunne**, Hv 2670.

blithe, *adj. and adv.*, (OE **blīðe**), happy, happily. Hr 274; **blethelye**, CA 278; **bli3e**, D 171; **blethelyche**, FB 148.

bliue, *adj. and adv.*, (OE **bi līfe**), quick, quickly. ET 1066; **belyffe**, P 878; **biliue**, SS 3013; Ly 28346.

blow, *vs.*, (OE **blāwan**), blow. Hv 587; **blauwen**, Ly 27815; *pt. plu.*, **bleou**, Ly 27813; **bleowen**, Ly 27442; *imp. sg.*, **blou**, Hv 585; *prp.*, **blawand**, Yw 340.

bone, *n.*, (OE **bān**), bone. D 16; **bonus**, Av 184.

bone, *n.*, (ON **bōn**), request, a request granted, reward. At 731; G 153; Yw 1075.

bord, *n.*, (OE **bord**), (1) board. Hv 2106; **burde**, Yw 186.

(2) table. P 438; ET 609; *d. sg.*, **borde**, Ly 28573; **burdes**, Av 751.

boru, **borow**, *n.*, (OE **burh**, **burg**), city, town. **burh**, Ly 28380; **burh3e**, Ly 28389; **borw**, Hv 847; **borowes**, P 1762; **burwes**, Hv 55.

bote, *n.*, (OE **bōt**), remedy, help, welfare. P 223; **boote**, EG 1050, 899; Lv 894.

bote, *n.*, (OE **bāt**), boat. Hr 202; **boot**, Em 268; **botis**, B 2971.

both, (ON **bāðir**), (1) *adj. and pro.*, both. Hr 1523; **bothen**, G 625; **bethe**, Hv 1680. *In the phrase:*

both two, both of them, Em 935, Cl 185.

(2) *adv.,* as well. G 843.

(3) *correlative,* **bath,** SS 361; Tr 56.

bouhte, bouthe, bought, *cf.* **beie.**

boun, bowne, *adj.,* (ON būinn), ready, prepared. ET 66; Av 254; **bownn,** P 1066. *In the phrase:* made him boun, hewent, SS 2894.

braid, breid, *vs.,* (OE bregdan), **(1)** draw (a sword). *pt. sg.,* **braid,** Ly 27626; Av 214; *plu.,* Sd 1795.

(2) start, jump, rush. **braid,** Tr 8644; Av 607; **bræid,** Ly 27674; **breyde,** B 3775.

brand, brond, *n.,* (OE brand, brond), sword. P 1185; D 947; Av 214; *d. plu.,* **bronden,** Ly 27519.

breke, *vs.,* (OE brecan), break. *pt. sg.,* **brake,** Ip 3132; **breke,** CA 165; **brakk,** ET 1118; **brak,** Hr 681; *plu.,* **breken,** Ly 27506.

brenne, berne, *vw.,* (ON brenna), burn. CA 68; ET 36; **bren,** SS 585; *pt. 3 sg.,* **brent,** P 773; **brente,** CA 344; *plu.,* **brenden,** Hv 594; *pp.,* **brent,** Tr 4777; ET 572; **brend,** SS 4253; *prp.,* **brynnande,** P 440; SS 2827; **brennyng,** Av 866.

briȝt, bright, *adj. and adv.,* (OE bryht), bright, shining (*often of beauty*). B 2928; CA 8; **brythe,** Em 697.

bringe, *vs.,* (OE bringan), bring. Hr 338; **brenge,** D 43; *pt. 3 sg.,* **browght,** Em 82; **broȝte,** Hr 466; **browȝte,** CA 59; **brouth,** Hv 336; (*by nunnation*) **brohten,** Ly 28472; *plu.,* **brohten,** Ly 28309; **brouthen,** Hv 2791; *pp.,* **browȝtt,** Cl 274; **ibrout,** D 102; **ybrowght,** Em 224.

brinie, corslet; *cf.* **brunie.**

brode, *adj.,* (OE brād), broad. **broode,** CA 297; **brade,** P 126; *a.m.,* **bradne,** Ly 27675.

brouht, brouth, brouct, *cf.* **bringe.**

brouke, *vs.,* (OE brūcan), enjoy, use (*word used mostly in emphatic sentences, in subjunctive*). TT 45; **brook,** EG 82; **bruke,** Ly 28263; *sj.,* **brouk,** G 273; **brok,** Av 1011; **browke,** P 1630; *imp.,* **brok,** K 551.

brunie, burnie, *n.,* (OE byrne), corslet. Hr 841; **brinie,** Hv 1775; **burne,** Ly 27748; *plu.,* **burnen,** Ly 27466.

brygge, bridge. ET 439.

bure, bur, apartment, room. Hr 269.

burgeis, *n.,* (OF burgeis), burgess, townsman. Sd 1748; *plu.,* **burgeys,** B 3188; **burgeysis,** B 3149; **burias,** SS 2789; **buriays,** O 502.

burh, burȝe, town; *cf.* **boru.**

burn, *cf.* **brenne.**

buske, *vw.,* (ON būask), **(1)** adorn, prepare, get ready. ET 819; *pt.,* **busked,** P 1030; **buskyd,** ET 232; **buskute,** Av 146.

(2) hasten, go. *pt.,* **buskit,** Tr 4705.

bute, (OE būtan), **(1)** *conj.,* but, yet. Hr 193; Ly 27840; **buten,** Ly 27874; **bot,** P 2213.

(2) unless. D 214; **butte,** Av 1039.

(3) *prep.,* except. **bote,** D 74; **butte,** Av 1077.

(4) without. **buten,** Ly 28150.

(5) *adv.,* only. Hr 198; **ne but,** B 3331.

comp., **butte,** but the. B 3250; **bot-if,** unless, P 383; **butte-giffe,** Av 111; **but-ȝif,** D 31; **but-on,** except that, provided that, if, Hv 505; EG 1049; Hv 962; **but-that,** unless, Lv 679.

C

can, *vs.*, (OE cunnan, conne), (1) know, know how, be able. *pr. 1 sg.*, kane, P 318; kan, CA 313; *2 sg.*, kane, P 1268; (*with enclitic pronoun*) canstu, Hr 1206; *3 sg.*, can, ET 252; cunne, Ly 28644; *plu.*, kan, P 1135; conne, G 63; con, B 3408; kunne, Hv 435; *pt. sg.*, kan, D 510; can, D 508; cowthe, Cl 208; coude, B 3611, G 4; cowdist, B 3336; couthe, Av 257; *plu.*, couthen, D 58; couth, Av 471; *pr. sj. sg.*, cone, Hv 622; cunne, Hv 568; *pt.*, couthest, D 595.
(2) did (*used with infinitive to make the equivalent of a preterit, a result of confusion with* gan, *q.v.*), EG 123; con, Av 84; conne, Av 92; cold, EG 122, 634; con, D 45.
In the phrases: als he can, as best he can, in his best manner, P 967; that wele kan, who know their business, P 1135.

carbuncle, *cf.* Hv 2145.

care, *n.*, (OE cearu), grief, sorrow, distress. Hr 1244; Ly 28634; kare, Em 627. carefull, wretched, Em 328.

carpe, *vw.*, (ON karpa), speak, say. TT 1; ET 587; *pr. 3 sg.*, carpys, P 1469; carpus, Av 574; *sj. plu.*, carpe, Av 158; *pt.*, carputte, Av 170; karped, Yw 498; *prp.*, carpand, Sd 538.

cas, case, *n.*, (OF cas). *Used loosely for any* matter, chance, case, *or* condition of affairs. O 173; B 2956; Tr 25.

caste, *vs.*, (ON kasta), cast, throw. *pt. sg.*, caste, G 237; kist, B 2955; keste, P 1710; *plu.*, kest, Av 637; *pp.*, kest, SS 882; casten, SS 892.

catel, (OF catel, chatel), (1) goods, property. TT 32; Hv 225.
(2) cattle, beasts. K 156.

certes, surely; *cf.* sertes.

charbocle, *cf.* Hv 2145.

chaunce, *n.*, (OF cheance), circumstance, fortune (good or bad). CA 123; Em 684.

chere, (OF chere), (1) *n.*, countenance. B 3525; Av 658.
(2) expression of face. cheere, G 319; *in the phrases:* make heavy chere and make ill chere, lament. SS 515; Em 300.
(3) mood, state of mind. Sd 2032.
(4) kind act, friendliness. Sd 2023; EG 111; Sd 2781.
(5) *adj.*, happy. Sd 3030.

cherl, *n.*, (OE ceorl), churl, rustic (*a term of reproach*), bumpkin. D 478; chorle, Cl 296; cherel, Yw 612; carl, Hv 1789.

chese, *vs.*, (OE cēosan), choose. Cl 427; *pr.*, Sd 2934; cheose, Hr 664; *pt.*, chese, P 1207; chase, ET 568; ches, At 110; chose, EG 938; *pp.*, icoren, Ly 28643; *as adj.*, chosen, choice; ycore, O 103.

child, *n.*, (OE cild), (1) child, youth. Ip 3079; *plu.*, chyldyrn, Cl 160; *g. plu.*, children, Hv 499.
(2) aspirant to knighthood. Hr 25; Ip 391.

claré, wine mixed with honey and spices, and then strained clear (*not* claret). Lv 344.

clene, clane, *adj. and adv.*, (OE clæne). (1) clean. Av 611.
(2) correct, true. Tr 53, 57.
(3) thoroughly, entirely. Av 598; Ly 27943; cleane, EG 130; cleen, B 3326.

clepe, *vw.*, (OE cleopian, clypian), cry, call, summon. cleopien, Ly 28418; *pr. 2 sg.*, clepeist, B 3024; *3 sg.*, clepeth, G 106; *pt. sg.*,

clepede, D 49; clupede, Hr 225;
clepid, B 2922; cleopede, Ly
27602; *pp.*, clepid, B 2945;
ycleped, O 50; clepet, R 336.
clere, *adj.*, (OF cler), of attractive
appearance, shining. Cl 374;
cleare, EG 917.
clerk, scholar, student. D 285;
Tr 53.
clippe, *vw.*, (OE clyppan), embrace.
pt., clipped, Sd 1935; Em 212;
clepte, D 673; klippt, FB 806.
cniht, knight. Ly 28563.
come, *vs.*, (OE cuman), (1) come.
At 305; cume, Ly 28262; cumme,
Av 656; *pr. 2 sg.*, comste, Cl 284;
3 sg., cummys, Av 30; Ip 353;
comth, G 602; *pt. sg.*, come, CA
110, 113; com, Hr 1365; kam,
Hv 766; *plu.*, comen, G 23;
comyn, Tr 4737; icom, Hr 1318;
comun, Av 480; keme, Hv 1208;
pr. sj. 1 sg., come, P 681; *2 sg.*,
(*by nunnation*) cumen, Ly 28143;
3 sg., come, Ly 28507; *imp. plu.*,
cumeth, Ly 27611; comes, Hv
1798; *pp.*, comen, D 207; comyn,
ET 263; icome, D 63, Hr 176;
icomen, Hr 202; icume, Ly
27595; *prp.*, comande, Av 246;
cumand, SS 592.
conne, *cf.* can.
corune, crowne, *n.*, (OF corōne,
ON krūna), (1) king's crown.
corune, Hv 1319; crune, Hr 475;
corowne, At 270.
(2) top of the head. crowne, ET
72; Hr 1487.
counsail, *n.*, (OF cunseil), (1) advice. SS 582; counseil, Sd 1772.
(2) secret, secrets. ET 1037; SS
328.
couthe, knew; *cf.* can.
couthe, known, Av 745; *cp.* uncouthe.
crepe, *vs. and w.*, (OE crēopan),
creep. Hv 68; *pr. 3 sg.*, crepis,

SS 822; *pt. sg.*, crope, EG 188;
Av 1021; creped, TT 170.
croise, *n.*, cross. Hv 1263; CA
328; Hr 1309; croyce, Yw 826.
cume, *cf.* come.
cunne, cunde, *cf.* kin, kind.
curteis, *adj.*, (OF courtois), well-
mannered, courteous. D 92;
curtays, Em 64; curtase, Av 743;
cp., corteysear, Cl 13.
curteisye, courtesy. Hv 194; corteci, Cl 455.

D

dai, *n.*, (OE dæg), day, lifetime.
G 12; dawes, Lv 1; daȝes, Ly
27863; *d. pl.*, daȝen, Ly 28439.
dais, *n.*, (OF deis), a raised plat-
form at the end of a hall. D 765;
dese, Yw 1207; P 968; dece, Av
741; deys, Lv 899; deyse, K 890.
dalt, dealt; *cf.* dele.
dece, *cf.* dais.
ded, *adj. and sb.*, (OE dēad), dead,
the dead. P 155; deed, Em 267.
dede, *n.*, (OE dǣd), deed. Em 456;
Ly 27585; *plu.*, dedes, Hr 537;
dede, Ip 1139; dedus, Em 4;
dedys, Tr 50; deden, Ly 27795.
dede, *cf.* dethe, ded, do.
defaut, defawte, lack. Lv 202.
degre, prize; *cf.* gre.
deie, *vw.*, (ON deyja), die. Hr 109;
dey, Av 855; dye, Ip 1191;
dyȝe, R 427; dee, Av 698; degh,
Tr 8648; *pt. sg.*, deyde, G 68;
dyȝede, R 323; deghit, Tr 8617;
plu., deid, Tr 4723; *pp.*, dyyd,
At 32; *vb.n.*, diȝing, R 426.
dele, *n.*, (OE dǣl), part, share, bit.
ET 671; Sd 2024; deel, G 635;
deyle, Ip 1071; deale, EG 447;
in the phrases: ilka del, Sd 2016;
some deale, somewhat, EG 447;
neuer a dele, no dell, not at all,
K 150.

dele, *vw.*, (OE dǽlan), share, associate with, divide, give (*of blows*). D 653; G 18; *pt. sg.*, delt, SS 2829; dalte, P 458; *plu.*, dalten, G 45; *imp. plu.*, deleth, G 37; *pp.*, deled, G 49.

dele, sorrow; *cf.* dole.

deme, *vw.*, (OE dēman), judge, pass sentence on, adjudge. Yw 1186; *pr. plu.*, deme, B 3437.

dent, blow; *cf.* dint.

dere, *n.*, (OE dēor), beast, animal. *plu.*, dere, Ip 3066; *g. plu.*, deoren, Ly 28066.

dere, *adj., sb., and adv.*, (OE dēore), (1) beloved, dear. Av 6; deore, Ly 28051; *sup.*, derrist, Tr 39. (2) expensive, precious. Sd 1902; *sup.*, derreste, P 1555.

dere, *n.*, (OE daru), injury, harm, grief. Yw 744; EG 810; deere, EG 320; deyre, Ip 1120; der, D 1005.

dere, *vw.*, (OE derian), injure, afflict, harm. P 1171; derie, Hr 786; deyre, Ip 1115; deire, Tr 8648; *pr. plu.*, deris, P 1370.

dethe, *n.*, (OE dēað, O Frisian dād) death. Tr 4757; dæthe, Ly 27922; dede, P 390; Yw 906; At 180; dead, EG 753; deȝ, D 463.

dighte, *vs. and w.*, (OE dihtan), (1) arrange, prepare, ordain, get ready, put (*a word of vague meaning, roughly equivalent to the various senses of* "set"). Sd 2763; *pt. sg.*, diȝte, D 718; *plu.*, dyȝte, Em 193; dihten, Ly 27437; idihten, Ly 27481; *pp.*, dyght, Em 133; dightede, P 1556; adight, G 731. (2) dress, accouter. diȝte, Av 813; *pt. sg.*, dight, P 787; *pp.*, idiȝte, B 2970; idihte, Ly 28627; ydyȝth, Em 395. *In the following special phrases and compounds:* to dethe dyght, kill. ET 492; yuel

dight, badly treated, G 87; to yrthe dyght, fall, Em 285.

dint, *n.*, (OE dynt), blow, stroke. CA 138; D 338; dent, TT 48; dunte, Hr 609, Ly 27681; *plu.*, dynttys, P 72; dintus, Av 43.

disese, *n.*, (OF desaise), discomfort, annoyance. Sd 2318; B 3552.

do, don, *vs.*, (OE dōn), (1) cause to happen (*followed by an active infinitive in the passive sense*). D 558; *pt.*, dede, G 866; *plu.*, dyd, Ip 1053; deden, Hv 242; *imp. plu.*, doth, Hv 2037; *pp.*, do, G 144. (2) act, perform, do. doon, G 207; done, D 244; *pr. 2 sg.*, doost, Lv 364; *pr. 3 sg.*, dose, D 53; dos, Hv 2390; *pt. 3 sg.*, dude, Hr 1247, Ly 27864; dedde, CA 172; *imp.*, do, CA 138; doyth, ET 893; *pp.*, ido, Ly 28110; *pt. sj.*, dudde, ET 636; doon, G 211. (3) put, place, put on, take off. *pt. 3 sg.*, dede, D 664; *imp. sg.*, do, G 269; *pp.*, EG 849. (4) complete, finish. *pp.*, idoon, G 270. (5) *in emphatic conjugations, used for other verbs: pr. 3 sg.*, deth, Ly 28500; doith, B 3005. (6) *in the following special phrases:* don of liue, kill, Hr 180; idon of lif-dæȝen, killed, Ly 27847; do to ded, kill, SS 4310.

dole, *n.*, (OF doel), (1) sorrow, sorrowful sight. B 3269; diol, O 196; deole, Hr 1050; dool, At 367; dele, ET 876; doll, Tr 4776; *comp.*, delful, pitiful, R 331. (2) compassion, pity. CA 134; Em 356. (3) lamenting. SS 2928; Em 613.

dome, *n.*, (OE dōm), judgment, doom, verdict. At 562; SS 2790; dom, Hv 2473; *plu.*, domus, CA 91.

doughter, *n.*, (OE dohtor), daughter. D 47; dowȝter, Em 109; doghter, Hr 994; dowter, D 440; douwter, D 601; thowȝtur, Em 226.

doughti, dughti, *adj.*, (OE dyhtig), powerful, brave. D 364; TT 8; doghty, P 203; doȝty, Lv 724; duȝti, Av 6; duhti, Ly 27862; *cp.*, dowtyar, Cl 8.

doun, *adv.*, (OE a dūne), down. Hv 901; dowun, Av 801.

dout, *n.*, (OF doute), (1) doubt. douthe, Hv 1331; douȝtt, Cl 44. (2) fear. Av 1019; SS 3012; TT 103.

doute, *vw.*, (OF douter), doubt, fear. *pr. 1 sg.*, dute, Hr 344; *pt. sg.*, doutede, Hv 708; *plu.,* doutiden, G 78; *imp. sg.*, dowt, G 517.

drawe, *vs.*, (OE dragan), (1) draw, drag, pull. *pt. 3 sg.*, drogh, SS 844; TT 195; drouȝ, D 830; drowe, ET 94; *pp.*, drawe, ET 575; drawen, P 850.
(2) withdraw, go, come. Av 92; draȝe, Hr 1289; *pt.*, droȝe, Hr 1006; droghe, Tr 88; *pt. sg.*, drowȝ, CA 33.
(3) disembowel (*usually in connection with hanging*).
(4) remove (*of a table-cloth*). *pt.*, drouȝ, D 830; *pp.*, draw, K 1001.
(5) portray. *pp.*, ydrawe, Hr 1303.

drede, *n.*, (OE ondrǣdan, *vb.*), fear, dread. Av 860; ET 233; dread, EG 718; *especially in the phrase:* wythoute drede, beyond doubt. ET 512.

drede, *vw.*, (OE ondrǣdan), dread, fear. Av 143; *pr. 3 sg.*, dredus, Av 632; *pt.*, dred, SS 2946; dradde, Hr 120; dredden, Hv 2289; *prp.*, dredand, SS 2888.

driue, *vs.*, (OE drīfan), (1) push along, drive, force. *pt. sg.*, drof, Tr 8639; G 124; *plu.*, droffe, Cl 158; *pr. sj.*, driue, Hr 1333.
(2) rush, ride. D 929; dryfe, P 2008; driuen, Ly 28073; *prp.*, driuende, Hv 2702.

dubbe, *vw.*, (OE dubbian), dub, confer knighthood (*a ceremony which could be performed by a knight or head of a monastery*). Hr 458; *pt.*, doubbede, P 1638; dubd, EG 1416. *In the phrase:* dub to knight, D 414; *vb.n.*, dubbyng, At 233.

dune, doune, meadow, down. Ly 28065.

dwelle, *vw.*, (OE dwellan), (1) live in a place. *pr. 3 sg.*, dwelles, Em 721.
(2) tarry, linger, remain for a short time. Hr 374; *pt. 3 sg.*, duellut, Av 749.

E

eche, *adj. and pro.*, (OE ǣlc, ylc), (1) every, each. Hr 1087; D 403; ich, TT 93; vche, Av 951. *comp.* echone, each one, B 3387; ychon, Sd 2778; icha, TT 155.
(2) same, very; ich, O 538.

een, eghne, *cf.* eie.

eft, *adv.*, (OE eft, æft), afterwards, again. D 527; æft, Ly 28114. *comp.*, efftsonys, sooɳ again, B 3888.

efter, *cf.* after.

eie, *n.*, (OE ēage), eye. *sg.*, Hv 2545; iȝe, Hr 755; *plu.*, eyen, Lv 570; yen, CA 135; een, Tr 57; eghne, P 537; yȝen, Em 298; egȝe, D 504; eyȝen, O 109; eeyn, Lv 810; eyȝnen, Al 6740.

eir, *cf.* heir.

either, other, (OE ǣgðer), (1) *adj. pro.*, either, each. aither, Tr 65;

Ip 3132; **euther,** Tr 57; **aythur,** CA 220; **eythir,** Av 382.

(2) *conj.,* or. **owther,** SS 243; **outher,** K 262; **other,** CA 324; *correlative,* **other . . . other,** Ly 28496.

eke, ok, *adv.,* (OE ēac; ON auk), also. D 26; **eeke,** G 480; **hec,** Hv 2348; **æc,** Ly 27630.

elde, *n.,* (OE eldo), age. SS 4273; G 649.

elles, *adv.,* (OE elles), else, otherwise. Hr 246; D 253; CA 215; **ellis,** TT 36.

eme, *n.,* (OE ēam), uncle. ET 994; **eemes,** At 29; **æm,** Ly 27599.

eni, any. Hr 316, G 318.

enoghe, *cf.* **inoghe.**

enuye, *n., commonly* hatred, wrath; *rarely* envy.

eode, went; *cf.* **yede.**

eow, you; *cf.* **thou.**

er, ere, before; *cf.* **are.**

erst, first; *cf.* **are.**

ethe, *adj. and adv.,* (OE ēaðe), easy, easily. Hr 835.

euer, *adv.,* (OE ǣfre), ever. Hr 79; **aure,** Av 662; **auere,** Ly 27483; *in the phrase:* **euyr among,** continually, ET 748.

eueri, *adj. and pro.,* (OE ǣfre ǣlc), every. Em 14; **eurech,** Hr 216; **euerilk,** Hv 2258; **euereche,** Hr 934; *comp.,* **euerichon,** every one, B 3068; D 138; **euerilkane,** SS 252; P 1163.

F

fai, faith, *n.,* (OF fei, feid), faith, word. Em 296. *Usually in the phrases:* **par fay,** SS 242; **in faye,** Sd 1970.

faile, *vw.,* (OF faillir), **(1)** fail (in an undertaking). *pt. 3 sg.,* **faylyd,** ET 1119.

(2) be lacking, disappoint (*usu-*

ally impersonal). Hr 638; *pr. 3 sg.,* **faylis,** Av 51; SS 2977.

fain, *adj. and adv.,* (OE fægn), glad, gladly. ET 723; Yw 1346; **feyn,** B 3334.

fair, *adj., sb., and adv.,* (OE fæger), **(1)** comely. CA 217; **veire,** Ly 27770; **uæir,** Ly 28010; *cp.,* **fairer,** Hr 10; **fayre,** ET 980; *sup.,* **fayrist,** Av 1136; **færȝest,** Ly 28459.

(2) justly, well. Tr 82; CA 266.

(3) readily. D 144.

falle, *vs.,* (OE feallan). (*The forms are often substituted, through confusion, for those of* **felle,** knock down.) **(1)** fall. **uallen,** Ly 27455; *pt. sg.,* **fell,** Em 551; **fil,** D 375; **feol,** Hr 428; **ffil,** B 3707; *plu.,* **fillen,** D 73; **fellyn,** Tr 4748; **feollen,** Ly 27469; **uellen,** Ly 27465; *pp.,* **fallun,** Av 200; **falin,** Tr 94; **ifallen,** D 534.

(2) occur, befall, happen. **fal,** SS 341; *pt. sg.,* **fil,** D 624, B 2956.

(3) befit, appertain to (*usually impersonal*). **falle,** Av 966; *pt. sg.,* **fell,** Em 383; SS 2872; *pt. plu.,* **fillen,** O 15. *In the phrase:* **felle to,** P 1104.

fare, *n.,* (OE faru), **(1)** behavior. G 199.

(2) journey. Hv 1337; **uore,** Ly 28248.

(3) encounter, adventure. P 1431, Yw 462.

fare, *vw. and s.,* (OE faran; *by confusion,* fēran), **(1)** go, march. At 330; **fore,** Av 151; *pr. 2 sg.,* **farst,** Hr 793; *pt. sg.,* **ferde,** Hr 649; *plu.,* **ferd,** Av 796; **fore,** P 1425; *pp.,* **faren,** Tr 29.

(2) prosper, get on, behave. D 648; *pp.,* **ifare,** Hr 468; **fare,** Hr 1355; **farren,** EG 1165; **farn,** Yw 911; **iuaren,** Ly 28011.

(3) happen, befall. *pt. 3 sg.*, Tr 94; *pp.*, ifaren, Ly 28369.

fast, *adj. and adv.*, (OE **fæste**), (1) rapid, rapidly. Em 659.
(2) firmly, fixedly, attentively. feste, Av 1026; SS 2989; Hv 2148.

faute, fault, lack, Av 736, B 3664.

fe, *n.*, (OE **feoh**), property, wealth, fief. Sd 1749; fee, Cl 437.

fecche, *vw.*, (OE **feccan**), fetch, bring. TT 204, Hr 351; *pt. sg.*, feched, K 917; *pt. plu.*, fett, ET 1145; fochet, Av 565; *pp.*, fette, CA 274; fet, Sd 3188; yfet, O 168; *imp. plu.*, fetteth, G 643.

fei, **feith**, *cf.* **fai**.

feire, *cf.*, **fair**.

fel, *adj. and adv.*, (OE **fel**), fierce, cruel, savage. G 151; SS 931; fele, TT 2; felle, Tr 8663; feolle, Al 4121.

felawe, *n.*, (ON **fēlagi**), (1) companion, comrade. fellow, Av 934; felaȝe, Hr 996; felay, TT 155; *plu.*, felawis, Av 1119.
(2) servant (*often a term of reproach*). G 227, Av 798.

feld, *n.*, (OE **feald**, **feld**), field (*often* battlefield). D 10; fild, Av 507; ffylde, Tr 94; *plu.*, ueldes, Ly 27468.

fele, *adj. and adv.*, (OE **fela**, **feolu**, *etc.*) many, frequent. Em 823; Hr 1329; ET 170; feole, Ly 27830; fale, Lv 496; fell, Ip 414.

felede, followed; *cf.* **folwe**.

felle, *vw.*, (OE **fellan**), knock down, cause to fall. *pr. 3 sg.*, feollen, Ly 27617; *pt. sg.*, felde, Ip 3161; fulde, Hr 1488; G 593; *plu.*, fælden, Ly 27508; *pp.*, fellyd, Cl 96; *by confusion with* **falle**: *inf.*, auallen, Ly 28405; afallene, Ly 27811; *pt.*, felle, Av 331, 667; feollen, Ly 27754; *pp.*, falleth, CA 310; fall, TT 116.

fend, *n.*, (OE **fēond**), (1) enemy. feond, Ly 28116; ueond, Ly 27667; *plu.*, feonden, Ly 27649.
(2) devil, fiend, the Devil. **fende**, Em 540; *in the phrase:* the fende mote hym haue, CA 120; **fynde**, Av 104..

fer, *adj. and adv.*, (OE **feorr**), far, distant. D 77; ffarre, Ip 405; fere, Ip 1171; ferre, ET 485; feor, Hr 769; ueor, Ly 27539; *cp.*, fer, Tr 78; ferre, Tr 96; furre, CA 311; (*by confusion with* forth) forthir, Av 790; ferther, CA 127.

fere, *n.*, (OE **gefēra**), fellow, comrade, wife. TT 27; feere, R 161; *plu.*, feris, B 3201; feiren, Hr 237; ferin, Hr 1242; ifere, Hr 102; iueren, Ly 27449. *In the phrase:* in fere, together, TT 212; ifere, D 67; in feere, G 667.

fere, go, fare; *cf.* **fare**.

fereden, uereden, carried, conveyed. Ly 28079, 28629.

ferli, **ferlik**, *adj.*, *sb.*, *and adv.*, (OE **færlīc**), marvel, marvelous, marvelously; amazement. SS 896; TT 2; Em 351; *plu.*, ferlies, Tr 96; SS 404.

ferthe, fourth. B 3764, Hv 1810.

fest, *cf.* **fast**.

feste, *n. and v.*, (OF **feste**), feast. Hr 477, Cl 61.

ff-. *For words beginning with* **ff**, *see* **f**.

fighte, *vs.*, (OE **feohtan**), fight. Hr 514; fehten, Ly 27711; feȝte, Av 52; fyȝte, CA 200; *pt. sg.*, faght, Tr 8608; faugt, D 122; faht, Ly 28554; *plu.*, foghten, Tr 4738; faght, Yw 655; fuhten, Ly 27491; faȝte, Av 361; *prp. sb.*, feȝting, Av 38.

fiht, **uiht**, *n.* fight; *d.s.*, feohten, Ly 27821.

finde, *vs.*, (OE **findan**), find. O 257;

fynd, Yw 1051; *pr. 3 sg.,* fint, O
237; *pt.,* fond, O 424; ifunde,
Ly 27777; fande, K 720; favnd,
Ip 1119; fonde, P 1611; *pp.,*
yfounde, Lv 35; fonden, P 519;
ifunde, Hr 955; fownden, CA 239.

fir, fur, fyer, fire. CA 159; Ly
27788; ffeer, At 631.

fle, *vs.,* (OE flēon), flee (*forms
confused with* fleie). fleon, Ly
28354; *pt. 3 sg.,* fley, G 127;
flah, Ly 28462; *plu.,* floghen, Tr
4732; fluȝen, Ly 27824; *pp.,*
flowe, G 133.

fleie, *vs.,* (OE flēogan), fly. fleon,
Ly 27456; flyne, K 241; *pt. sg.,*
fleye, CA 319; flegh, Lv 473;
fleh, Ly 27788; *plu.,* flowenn, CA
148; *pp.,* flowe, B 3616; *prp.,*
fliand, Av 1023.

florine, *n.,* (OF florin), florin (*a
coin containing 55 grains of gold,
issued at Florence and much used
in trade. In 1343, an English
coin of the same name, worth six
shillings, was struck.*) D 295;
floranse, ET 389; florences, EG
1232.

fo, *n.,* (OE fāh), foe, enemy. Fa,
SS 4245; *plu.,* fos, Tr 4715; foon,
ET 462, G 541; ifan, Ly 27617.
comp., foomen, G 682; famen,
SS 454.

fole, *n.,* (OF fol), fool, eccentric.
B 2937; SS 2927; foule, Ip 1061;
plu., folis, B 2988.

folwe, *vw.,* (OE folgian), follow,
pursue. fulien, Ly 27733; *pt.
sg.,* felede, Hv 67; folut, Av 167;
plu., folutte, Av 90.

fonde, *vw.,* (OE fundian), seek,
search, try, go. D 2; funde,
Hr 133; founde, At 702; *pt.,* fond,
Lv 962; fonded, Al 3993.

fonge, *vs.,* (OE fōn, ON fangen),
seize, receive, catch. Hr 327;
fang, Yw 299; *pt. sg.,* iueng,

Ly 28069; *pp.,* ifon, Ly 28137.

for, *prep. and conj.,* (OE for),
*Only the unusual senses are here
given:* (1) *prep.,* by reason of.
Hr 1104; Tr 13.

(2) by the agency of. Ip 435.

(3) on account of. Em 618; Hr
69.

(4) *as sign of infinitive.* Hr 280;
Hv 38.

(5) in spite of. Sd 1686; P 356.

(6) *conj.* because, for. Cl 489;
Sd 2008.

(7) in order that, lest (*with neg-
atives*). SS 4267; B 3002.

(8) on condition that. Ly 28275.

for-, *prefix,* (OE for-). *Indicates a
destructive sense or the intensify-
ing of a bad sense in the verb
which follows it:* forwunded, Ly
27908; forwurthe, perish, Ly
28425; forloren, D 84; forsworn,
CA 199; fordon, kill, Ly 28168;
forfare, perish, G 74; destroy,
SS 2931; forfarn, Yw 976.

forȝ, forht, forth. D 56; D 227.

forthan, uorthæn, because of this,
for this reason, Ly 28159.

forthi, *adv. and conj.,* (OE for þī,
because, therefore, provided that.
P 647; Av 985; CA 218; Hv 2043.

forward, *n.,* (OE foreweard), agreement. ET 220; forthward, G
747; foreward, Hr 452.

fot, *n.,* (OE fōt), foot. Hr 758;
fout, Hr 134; *plu.,* fete, Av 595;
fote, Av 191; Ip 3134.

foule, foȝel, *n.,* (OE fugel), bird.
D 732; Hr 1398; *plu.,* fuȝeles,
Ly 28063; foȝeles, Hr 129.

foule, *adj. and adv.,* (OE fūl), foul,
vicious, ugly. CA 239; G 485;
fule, Ly 27634.

fraine, *vw.,* (OE fregnan), ask, in-
quire, question. ET 941; Yw
579; Tr 98; *pt.,* 94. *Often used
with the prepositions* to *and* at.

fre, *adj. and sb.*, (OE frēo), (1) free. Hv 262; freo, Ly 28393.

(2) generous, noble (*a term of general commendation*). ET 382; Sd 1615; fri, Hv 1072.

freli, *adv. and adj.*, (OE frēolīc), goodly, worthy, worthily (*sometimes used in the sense of* freely). CA 218; Em 507; P 38.

frend, *n.*, (OE frēond), friend. frynde, Av 642; *plu.*, frindus, Av 211; freond, Ly 28420; frende, Ip 346.

fro, from, *prep. and conj.*, (OE fra, fram). (1) *prep.*, from. CA 159; Hr 72.

(2) *conj.*, from the time when. SS 306; Av 869.

ful, *adj. and adv.*, (OE full), quite, very, very greatly. (*Often used as a metrical filler, not to be taken seriously in translation.*) Hr 429; D 372.

fur, fire; *cf.* fir.

G

galow-tre, gallows. SS 2866.

game, *n.*, (OE gamen), sport, enjoyment, playfulness, contentment, jest. ET 164; B 3263; Hr 198; gamyn, SS 808; *plu.*, gamus, Ip 1134; gamyns, SS 388; gammen, K 609.

gange, *vs.*, (OE gangan), go, walk. Ip 1150; EG 457; ʒeongen, Ly 28070; *prp.*, gangande, Hv 2283. (*The preterit is usually supplied from* yede, *q.v.*)

gate, *n.*, (OE geat, ON gatt), (1) road, path. P 258; Em 828.

(2) gate, wicket. ʒate, CA 22; ʒæte, Ly 27932; yate, EG 65.

(3) means. P 1675. *Especially in the phrases:* so-gates, thus-gates, in this wise, P 877; 1839.

gent, *adj.*, (OF gent), of good ancestry, well bred. ET 695; Ip 3171.

gere, gare, *vw.*, (OE gearwian), prepare, cause. At 477; SS 412; gerre, P 832; yaren, Hv 1350; *pt.*, gerutte, Av 176; gerut, Av 330; gert, Yw 1102; garte, At 251; (*with metathesis*) gret, Ip 3060; *imp. sg.*, gers, SS 556.

gere, *n.*, (OE gearwe), equipment of any sort, things, clothes, armor. P 189; Av 324; gayre, EG 428.

gete, *vs.*, (OE -gietan), (1) get, obtain. *pt. sg.*, gate, Tr 76; gatt, EG 456; *pp.*, gotten, Ip 1131; ygete, O 14.

(2) beget. *pr.for fut. sg. 2*, gettes, SS 342; *pt.*, gette, CA 34; *pp.*, geten, D 688.

gethurt, gedrit, gadred, gathered.

gif, *cf.* if *and* give.

ginne, *vs.*, (OE ginnan), (1) begin, start. Hr 546; *pr. 3 sg.*, gynnyth, CA 66; *pt. sg.*, agon, Ly 28060; gun, Ly 28070; *plu.*, gonnen, Ly 28552.

(2) *in preterit, frequently means* "did." gan, Hr 1047; goon, G 236; gun, P 740; *plu.*, gon, G 236; gonne, D 628.

giue, ʒiue, *vs.*, (OE giefan), give. giffe, Av 283; Ip 445; gif, K 932; *pr. 1 sg.*, gyff, Ip 468; *3 sg.*, ʒiffes, P 85; *plu.*, gyffen, Tr 4741; giffus, Av 977; gifis, K 901; *pt. sg.*, ʒaf, D 326; ʒæf, Ly 27918; ʒefe, P 2086; ʒeef, FB 184; yaf, Hv 1635; *plu.*, gafe, Av 1083; *imp. sg.*, yif, Hv 674; giffe, Av 5; *pp.*, gifen, SS 2818; yʒeue, G 870; gevyne, Ip 480; yoven, Hv 1643; *in the phrase:* ʒaf him ylle, lamented. Em 778.

gle, glewe, *n.*, (OE glēow), mirth, amusement, singing. O 381; Em 132; gleu, Hv 2333.

go, *vs.*, (OE gān), go, walk. D 720;
goo, ET 280; gon, D 80; gone,
Em 741; ga, SS 354; *pr. 3 sg.*,
gooth, CA 157; gos, Ip 1177;
goose, Ip 3026; gase, SS 888;
goht, D 77; goȝ, D 82; geth, O
236; *imp.*, gowe, G 661; *plu.*,
goth, G 36; *pp.*, agoo, B 3033;
agan, Ly 28089; igoon, G 347;
go, Sd 2760; gane, SS 251; ago,
R 299; gon, D 682; *prp.*, gan-
ninde, Ly 28524. (*The preterit
is supplied from* yede, *q.v.*)
gode, *adj. and adv.*, (OE gōd), (1)
good. gude, Yw 83; *a. m.*, god-
ne, Hr 720; *cp.*, bet, betere, Lv
698; Hr 567; bette, Sd 1716; *sup.*,
beste, Hr 174; Av 958; beȝst, Ly
27613.
(2) *sb.*, property, goods; profit,
advantage. Hr 770; gudeȝ,
P 185; best warriors, *d. plu.*,
beȝsten, Ly 27661.
grace, *n.*, (OF grace), grace, heav-
enly favor; *hence* chance, fortune,
luck, destiny. Tr 76; Em 944;
Yw 548; graas, R 369; gras, R
374.
graithe, *vw.*, (ON greiða), prepare,
make ready. graiȝ, D 849;
pt., graythed, TT 57; graithet,
Tr 4749; *imp.*, graiȝ, D 849;
greytheth, Al 4156.
gramarcy, great thanks! Cl 421;
gramercy, Ip 474; grant merci,
D 976.
graunte, *vw.*, (OF granter), (1) agree,
accede, admit. *pr. 2 sg.*, grantes,
SS 4293; *3 sg.*, grawuntus, Av
461; *pt.*, grauntede, Lv 259; Av
128.
(2) grant, give. *pr 3 sg.*, graunteth, CA 278; *pr. sj. 2 sg.*, graunte,
Cl 286; *pp.*, grant, TT 101.
gre, degre, *n.*, (OF gre), (1) victor's title, prize. TT 47; EG
478; Tr 4780.

(2) excellence, rank. EG 562;
Sq 1.
gret, *cf.* gere, prepare.
grete, *vs.*, (OE grǣtan), weep, wail.
pt. sg., gret, SS 2914; grette,
Em 556.
grette, greeted. D 468; G 668;
gret, D 810.
greue, *vs.*, (OF grever), grieve, injure. TT 95; *pt.*, greuyt, Tr
4726.
gripe, *vw. and vs.*, (OE grīpan),
grasp, seize. *pr. 3 sg.*, gripus,
Av 382; *pt. 3 sg.*, grippit, Tr
8656; igrap, Ly 27676.
grisli, grisliche, *adv. and adj.*, (OE
grīslic), fearful, horrible. Lv
600; Ly 28063; Av 192.
grith, *n.*, (OE grið), peace, security.
Sd 2850, P 1648; greth, Cl 299.

H

H-. *For the following words spelled
with* h- *in the text, cf. the second
letter:* hec, heke, also; heie, eye;
helde, heldest, old; his, is; hun-
till, hentill, to, until; habydes,
awaits; her, before; herl, earl;
hete, eat; heuere, ever; hi, hic,
I; hold, old; hure, our; hore,
grace; haby, atone for; hoc, also;
hawe, awe.
ha, han, *cf.* haue. ha, *cf.* he.
halp, helped. G 60.
haluendel, half. G 272.
hap, *n.*, (ON happ), chance, fate,
luck. Yw 229; happe, Av 434;
Em 651.
harrow Helle, to despoil Hell.
(*According to the late Gospel of
Nicodemus, Christ, between his
crucifixion and resurrection, descended into Hell and liberated
the souls of patriarchs, prophets,
and saints.*) At 422; Sq 148.
haue, *vw.*, (OE habban), have, own.

hauen, D 27; ha, K 373; han, Lv
406; *pr. 1 sg.*, habbe, Ly 28086;
hafe, P 1961; has, EG 142; *2
sg.*, hase, Av 267; hathe, Ip 1066;
hafst, Ly 27638; haste, P 1664;
3 sg., hafeth, Ly 28136; haues,
SS 551; *plu.*, habbeȝ, D 64;
haues, TT 31; habbeoth, Ly
28607; *pt. sg.*, hauede, Hr 48;
hafde, Ly 27597; hefde, Ly
27708; hade, Tr 54; *plu.*, hadden,
EG 194; *pt. sj.*, hadde, CA 181;
pp., hadde, Hr 9; ihad, G 357;
negative forms, nabbe, Ly 28092;
nade, O 390; nadde, Hr 863.
With enclitic pro., hadestow, hadst
thou, O 531; hasto, hast thou,
Yw 911; *negative with enclitic
pro.*, nastu, Hr 1193.
he, heo, hem, hit, *pro.*, (OE he,
etc.), (1) he, he. *n.*, Hr 127; *g.*,
his, Sq 4; is, Ly 27900; hes, Ip
425; *d. and a.*, him, D 170; hine,
D 913, Hr 1028; *reflexive*, him;
often used after intransitive verb:
Ly 27563.
(2) heo, she. *n.*, Hr 69; he, Hr
71; hye, O 79; ha, Ly 28219; ho,
Av 281; hi, D 80; *g.*, her, Sq 585;
here, Em 830; hyr, Em 803; hire,
D 49; hure, Hr 1121; *d. and a.*,
here, Em 164; hure, Hr 1103;
hyr, Cl 146.
(3) hit, it, there. *n. and a.*, Hr 6;
hitte, Av 471; *g. and d. as masculine*, him, Hr 570. *Used to post-
pone the true subject*, Em 716;
*also superfluously in apposition
with the object*, Ly 27650.
(4) they. *n.*, Hv 54; hi, Hr 22;
hye, O 89; hii, D 48; heo, Ly
27454; *g.*, her, Em 211; hir, B
3343; hare, Lv 59; hore, Hr 854;
hor, Tr 4715; hur, FB 564;
heore, Ly 27518; *d. and a.*, hem,
CA 52; hom, Tr 24; heom, Ly
27885; ham, Lv 20; hym, B 3425.

hed, heued, *n.*, (OE hēafod), head.
Av 110; ET 113; hafd, Ly 28048;
hafued, Ly 28148; hedde, CA
27; heed, G 430.
heie, heghe, *adj., adv., and sb.*,
(OE hēah), high, noble, tall,
great. D 925; P 683; hiȝe, B
3165; heiȝe, O 203; hye, CA 217;
cp., hæhȝer, Ly 27445; heȝer,
Av 49; *sup.*, hexte, Hv 1080;
heghhest, Av 1036. *Especially
in the phrases: on* hyȝe, aloud,
CA 25, 64; *on* heghȝ, on high, up,
D 533; *cf. also* hight *and* hie.
heir, *n.*, (OF heir), heir. G 365;
air, D 873; SS 333; *plu.*, aire,
SS 2844; heyre, EG 731.
hem, them; *cf.* he.
hende, *adj., sb., and adv.*, (OE
gehende), (1) lovely, gracious.
At 224; hinde, Yw 700; heende,
G 663.
(2) well trained, proficient. Tr
8610; heynde, Av 82.
adv., *also* hendeliche, hendly, D
999, SS 237.
hende, hands.
henne, *adv.*, (OE heonan), hence.
D 130; Hr 46; hennys, Sd 1922.
hente, *vw.*, (OE -hentan), seize,
grasp, receive. Av 203; *pr. sg.*,
hint, P 754; *pt.*, hent, SS 849;
hente, CA 85; *pp.*, hynt, P 1666;
hente, CA 3.
heo, she; *cf.* he.
herte, *n.*, (OE heorte), heart. D
543; hartt, Cl 190; heort, Ly
27673; heorte, Hr 263.
hest, *n.*, command. Al 4073.
hethen, *adv.*, (ON heðan), hence.
P 1905; hethinn, Av 1102.
hethennes, heathendom. Em 109;
hethenisse, O 511.
hexte, tallest; *cf.* heie.
hider, *adv.*, (OE hider), hither. D
470; hedur, Av 396.

hie, *vw.*, (OE **higean**), hasten, hie.
Av 1102; **hiȝe**, Hr 880; **hy**, Yw
1073; *pr. 3 sg.*, **hiees**, Av 816;
pt., **hiet**, Av 490; *sj. pr.*, **hyȝe**,
CA 139; *vbl.n.*, **hyȝynge**, Em 511;
esp. in the phrase: **on heying**, in
haste, D 753.
hie, *n.* (*from the verb*), haste. P
1550; **hyȝ**, At 716. *Especially
in the phrases:* **on** *or* **in hie**, in
haste; **on hy**, CA 326, P 534; **on
high**, Cl 266. *Cf. also* **hight** *and*
heie.
hie, she, they; *cf.* **he**.
hight, *n.*, (OE **hēahðo**), height. *Especially in the phrase:* **on hight**,
meaning: (1) on high, up. SS
226; **opon hiȝte**, Av 215.
(2) aloud; **opon hiȝte**, Av 513;
opon heȝte, Av 633.
(3) in haste (*by confusion with*
hie, *q.v.*); **in hiȝte**, D 136.
highte, *vs. and w.*, (OE **hātan**), (1)
command, issue commands. *pr.
1 sg.*, P 403; *3 sg.*, **hoteth**, Al
4069; *pt. sg.*, **hehte**, Ly 28308;
hete, Ly 28519.
(2) promise. *pr. 1 sg.*, **heȝte**, Av
350; **hete**, SS 935; **heete**, CA 18;
pt. 2 sg., **heȝtist**, K 299; *3 sg.*,
heȝte, Av 604; **highte**, Ip 3147;
hette, Av 965; *plu.*, **heȝte**, Av
147.
(3) call, be called, named (*originally from a different stem, but
confused with this verb*). *pr. 1 sg.*,
hote, Hr 767; *3 sg.*, **hehte**, Ly
27916; **hat**, Yw 1053; *pt.*, **hatte**,
Ly 28534; **heet**, R 93; **het**, Hr 25; *pp.*, **ihaten**, Ly
27593; **ihote**, Hr 201; **hoten**, Al
4166.
hinge, hang. SS 2788.
ho, *cf.* **he** *and* **who**.
holde, *vs.*, (OE **healdan**), (1) keep
in one's possession. D 390;
by assimilation, **halt**, FB 546;

helde, Hr 902; **halden**, D 30;
pt. 3 sg., **heeld**, CA 152; **hylde**,
Ip 3170.
(2) repute, account, consider.
pr. 1 sg., **hold**, Ip 3158; *pt. plu.*,
heelden, G 553; *pp.*, **holde**, CA
70; **holdyn**, Ip 402; **yholde**, Lv
521.
(3) keep to (a road, course of
conduct, *etc.*) *pt. sg.*, **heold**, Ly
28430; *plu.*, **held**, Av 949; **halden**,
Ly 28547; *pr. sj.*, **holde**, Hr 452;
pp., **holdunn**, Av 1143.
(4) go, advance. *pt. sg.*, **halde**,
Ly 27702; *plu.*, **hælden**, Ly
27523.
holpen, helped, EG 1050; **holpyn**,
K 800.
holt, *n.*, (OE **holt**), wood, forest.
Av 288. *Especially in the phrase:*
holtis hore, grey woods. O 212;
Lv 171.
honde, hand, hands. Ly 28037.
honge, hang. EG 122.
hope, *vw.*, (OE **hopian**), believe,
expect, fear. **houppe**, P 731;
pt., **hopid**, SS 820.
hors, horse. *plu.*, **hors**, At 628;
horsen, Ly 27473.
hu, how. Hr 468; **heou**, Ly 28247.
hw-. *See* **wh-**.
hwat, *cf.* **quath** *and* **what**.
hwor, *cf.* **whether**.

I

I, ich, *pro.*, (OE **ic**), I. *n.*, **y**, Hr 344;
ich, D 6; **ihc**, Hr 149; **iich**, D 98.
g., **min**, Hr 1281; **my**, CA 27.
d. and a., me, SS 343; *frequently
attached to a verb:* **ichave**, I have;
ichil, I will; **icham**, I am; **ichim**,
I *plus* him, O 426. *In older pieces,
the genitive* **min** *is inflected like
an adjective.* **mire**, *d.f.*, Ly
28047; **minne**, *a.m.*, Ly 28186
plu. n., we. **wee**, CA 302. *g.*

owre, Av 1037; ure, Hr 132; vre, Hr 516. d. and a., us. Hr 682; ous, D 922.

ientyll, gentle.

if, *conj.*, (OE gif), if, whether, although. CA 192; yff, Ip 413; giffe, Av 68; 3if, D 203; yef, B 2981; 3hif, D 312.

ifan, foes; *cf.* fo.

ifere, *adj.*, together; *sb.*, comrade; *cf.* fere.

ilke, *adj. and pro.*, (OE ylca, ælc), each, same. P 340; ilka, SS 450; vlke, Hr 1199; ælchere, *d.f.*, Ly 28498. *In the phrases:* ilkone, each one, Ip 3124; thilke, *for* that ilke, Lv 542.

in, *prep. and adv.*, (OE innan), in, within, into, on, among, *etc.* Em 257; Hr 17; i, Ly 27623; ynne, ET 243.

inogh, inowe, *adj. and adv.*, (OE genōh), enough. TT 196; Ip 438; inow3e, B 2963; inowgh, Ip 2998; inoh, Ly 28443; ino3e, Hr 1228; anou3, O 60; eno3, K 781.

intil, *prep.*, to, into.

ioie, *n.*, (OF joie), joy. Ip 2998; ioy, B 2966; yoye, ET 1144.

iorné, iurnai, *n.*, (OF jornée), (1) trip. D 425, 724; yurney, ET 967.
(2) day's work. iornay, SS 4322.

is, *cf.* be, he.

isome, isame, together; *cf.* samen.

isunde, *cf.* sound.

iswoue, iswo3e, swoon; *cf.* sowne, *n.*

iwis, *adv.*, (OE gewis), certainly. ET 1065; D 77; iwisse, Av 64.

i3e, eye; *cf.* eie.

K

kene, *adj.*, *sb.*, *and adv.*, (OE cēne), (1) spirited, brave, fierce. TT 1; P 1980.

(2) sharp (*of a weapon*). Tr 8640.

kenne, *vw.*, (OE cennan), recognize, discern, know, make known, instruct. D 129; ken, SS 913; ikenne, Ly 28559; *pt.*, kend, Yw 931; *pp.*, kende, P 1676; kennet, Av 619.

kepe, *vw.*, (OE cēpan), (1) guard, restrain, watch, care for. Yw 1024; *pt.* kepte, Hv 879; keped, SS 494.
(2) pay attention to. P 576; *sg.*, keptest, D 853.
(3) intend. *pr. sg.*, kepe, Ip 3011; Av 582.

kin, *n.*, (OE cynn), (1) kindred. Hv 393; kunne, Hr 865; kynne, ET 246; kenne, Lv 153; ken, D 319.
(2) kind, sort. cunne, Ly 28165. *In the phrase:* none kines, Hv 861, 2691.

kinde, *n.*, (OE cynd), (1) nature, disposition. B 3196; Sd 2228.
(2) family, race, rank. cunde, Hr 421.
(3) sort, variety. B 3615.

kinde, *adj. and adv.*, (OE cynde), (1) natural, real. Tr 70; kindeliche, Av 162; *adv.*, kyndely, Av 258.
(2) proper, fitting. TT 1; Tr 70.
(3) kind.

kineriche, kingeriche, kinerike, *n.*, kingdom.

kithe, *vw.*, (OE cȳðan), show, make known, display. P 366; *imp. plu.*, kithe, Sd 1947; *pt.*, kedde, Lv 368; kyd, Yw 647; *pp.*, kid, Hv 1060; kyde, Ip 1142.

knaue, *n.*, (OE cnapa), servant, boy, fellow. B 3207; Av 737; cnaue, Ly 28590.

knowe, *vs.*, (OE gecnāwan), (1) know. knawe, Hv 2785; *pr. 2 sg.*, knoes, Av 788; *pt.*, icneou,

icneouwen, Ly 27488; kneuȝ, R 288; kneow, Al 4231.
(2) acknowledge. R 295.

L

laie, to lay; *cf.* lege.

laine, *vw.*, (OE lēgnian), conceal. P 143; Av 306; *pr. 3 sg.*, laynes, Av 1113; *pp.*, lained, EG 361.

large, *adj.*, (OF large), (1) liberal, generous. Hv 97.
(2) at liberty. B 3136; 3362.
(3) of great size.

las, lasse, less. Av 768.

lauȝh, lagh, *vs. and vw.*, (OE hlehhan), smile, laugh. B 3006; ET 718; laȝ, K 738; *pt.*, loughe, Sd 2602; louȝgh, Ip 2997; loghe, Av 510; lawȝe, B 3335; lowe, Cl 517; lugh, TT 197; lowgȝ, D 793; lawuȝid, B 3161; louȝ, O 312; loogh, K 55.

leche, *n.*, (OE lǣce), physician. G 614; *plu.*, leeches, EG 224.

lede, *vw.*, (OE lǣdan), (1) lead, govern. Hr 908; *pt.*, ladde, CA; *prp.*, ledande, Av 279; *pp.*, iledde, Ly 27713.
(2) carry, take. Hr 1393; *pp.*, ilad, G 528.

lede, *n.*, (OE leod), people, subjects. Yw 865; leede, Em 702; G 61; leode, Ly 27503.

lefe, *adj., adv., and sb.*, (OE lēof), (1) beloved, dear. Av 603; leue, D 695; lef, P 1; lyfe, ET 565; leof, Hr 708; leef, Ip 1118; liif, O 404.
(2) willing, willingly. leeue, EG 514; Hv 261.
(3) pleasing. leffe, Ip 1052; leofen, *d.s.*, Ly 28151.
(4) *cp.*, rather. leuer, SS 4257; levir, B 3038. *sup.*, leueste, ET 396; leofeste, Ly 27604.

lege, *vw.*, (OE lecgan). (*Forms confused with those of* lie.)

(1) to lay, put. legge, Hr 1057; *pt. plu.*, layn, Tr 4751; leien, D 71; laid, D 185.
(2) strike (with a sword, *etc.*) *pt.*, leid, D 357; *plu.*, leiden, Ly 28549.

leie, to lay; *cf.* lege.

lemman, *n.*, (OE lēofman), lover (of either sex). Hr 433; ET 798.

lene, *vw.*, (OE lǣnan), (1) lend. At 4; CA 277; *pt.*, lente, CA 239.
(2) give, bestow. *pp.*, lent, Em 404.

lengore, *cp. adv.*, longer. D 226; leng, longer, O 82.

lep, leaped. D 421; leop, Al 4239.

lere, *n.*, (OE hlēor), face, countenance. Sd 2289; leyre, Lv 936; lyre, Cl 153; *plu.*, leris, B 3202.

lere, *vw.*, (OE lǣran), teach, instruct; learn. SS 332; At 707; *pp.*, lered, SS 362; ilerid, B 3857.

lese, lesing, *adj. and sb.*, (OE lēas, lēasung), false, falsehood. lees, ET 472; lesynges, G 385; At 83; leasing, EG 1006. *Especially in the phrase:* withoute lese, *or* lesing, truly, D 517.

lese, *vs.*, (OE lēosan), lose. Sd 1683; leose, Hr 663; *pr. 1 sg.*, lese, TT 186; losse (*as future*), Ip 3197; *pt.*, les, D 23; *pp.*, lore, G 202; ilore, G 301; lorn, Yw 958; loren, D 669; lest, Cl 70; ylore, O 543.

lete, *vs.*, (OE lǣtan), (1) allow, permit, let fall. Av 402; late, G 722; *pt.*, Hr 1222; *imp.*, lates, Yw 507; *in imperative and hortatory phrases:* lat we be, SS 257; *with inf.*, bewiten hine lette, let him be guarded, Ly 27854.
(2) leave, relinquish, lose. Sd 1510; *pt.*, lett, EG 334; *imp. plu.*, lattes, SS 577; *pp.*, laten, Hv 240.

(3) remain. *pt.*, **lat**, D 1035.
(4) cause, put. *pt.*, **let**, Hr 1381;
G 311.
lete, *vw.*, (OE **lettan**), (1) delay,
hinder. **lette,** Sd 2610; **leten,**
Hr 929; EG 151; *pp.*, **letted,**
EG 464; *vbl. n.*, **letting,** Av 10;
Cl 291.
(2) deprive. Sd 1510.
(3) cease. TT 156; **lett,** Cl 61.
(4) forbear. *pr. sj.*, **let,** Yw 131.
lete, *n.* (*from the verb*), hindrance,
delay. *Usually in the phrase:*
withouten lette, P 45; Av 187.
leue, *vw.*, (OE **lǽfan**), (1) stay
behind, remain. *pt.*, **leued,** Yw
1270; **lefte,** Hr 647; **lefde,** Hr
1378; Sd 2734; **lafte,** K 547.
(2) forsake, give up. **lefe,** Sd
1896; *pr. plu.*, **leuen,** CA 87;
pt., **leuyt,** Tr 4732; *pp.*, **leued,**
Hv 225.
leue, *cf.* **lefe,** dear.
leue, *vw.*, (OE **lēfan**), believe, trust.
CA 28; *pr. plu.*, **ileueth,** Ly
28636; *pt.*, **levid,** B 3380; *imp.*,
leeve, Sd 2636; CA 242.
leuedi, lefdi, lady. D 229, Hr 335.
lewed, *adj.*, (OE **lǽwede**), un-
learned, unlettered, common. G
505.
libbe, *cf.* **liue.**
lich, like, similar. B 3796. *Also
used as a suffix, meaning* "in
like manner, like."
lie, *n.*, falsehood. **lyȝe,** R 47.
lie, *vs.*, (OE **licgan**). (*Forms confused with those of* **lege.**) (1)
recline. **lien,** G 598; **ligge,** Hr
1275; At 527; **liȝe,** Hr 1158;
lig, SS 4256; *pr. 3 sg.*, **lise,** Av
937; **lyce,** Av 1139; **lis,** D 209;
liggeth, Hv 330; **lyethe,** Ip 351;
lygges, P 64; **lith,** O 241. *plu.*,
liggeoth, Ly 27943; *pt.*, **lay,** Hr
1303; **læi,** Ly 28015; **ley,** CA 98;
leyen, Hv 475; **laien,** Al 3965;

prp., **liggande,** EG 334; **liggeand,**
O 386.
(2) dwell, remain. *pt.*, **lay,** SS
804; **læi,** Ly 28427.
lie, *vw.*, (OE **lēogan**), tell a falsehood. *pr. 2 sg.*, **lixte,** G 297;
pr. sj., **leye,** Hv 2010.
life, *in the idioms:* **on liue,** alive,
P 541; **of the lyve,** dead, B 3393;
have the lyve, live, B 3488.
lighte, *vw.*, (OE **līhtan**), alight, get
down. **alihten,** Ly 27740; *pr.*,
lyghte, Ip 1196; **liȝte,** Hr 519;
pp., **lyȝth,** Lv 308.
liking, *n.*, (OE **līcung**), pleasure,
comfort, ease. Tr 71, CA 13.
liste, *vs.*, (OE **lystan**), (1) wish,
desire. *pt.*, **lust,** B 3504; **lyst,**
Ip 3078.
(2) please (*usually impersonal*).
pt., **liste,** P 2111; **luste,** Hr 406;
pr. sj., **leste,** Hr 862.
lite, little. Hv 276; **lyȝt,** Cl 69.
liue, *vw.*, (OE **libban**), live.
Sd 3031; **libbe,** Hr 63; **lyfe,** CA
54; *pr. as f.*, **lif,** Av 356; *pt.*,
leuyd, P 1774; **leuede,** P 253;
liffede, P 1779; *prp.*, **leuand,**
Av 1050; **lyfand,** Yw 670; **leueande,** P 46.
longe, *vw.*, (OE **langian**), befit, appertain to (*usually impersonal*).
pr., **longith,** B 2990; **longis,** Ip
407.
lore, *n.*, (OE **lār**), counsel, wisdom,
training. P 231; Em 412.
lore, loren, *cf.* **lese,** lose.
loth, *adj.*, (OE **lāð**), (1) reluctant,
unwilling. CA 48; *often in the
tag:* **looth and leffe,** unwilling
and willing; *i.e.*, every one, B 3566.
(2) hateful, hated, displeasing,
hostile. **lath,** Yw 135; **loth,** CA
249.
loue, *vw.*, love, praise. Ip 458.
louerd, *n.*, (OE **hlāford**), lord,
feudal superior. D 470; **lauerd,**

Ly 27665; **lardes**, SS 4270; **lordys**, Ip 354; **lordyng**, gentleman, Em 965.

lufsome, *adj. and sb.*, lovely; **lofsom**, Lv 942.

M

ma, *cf.* make, more.

Mahoun, *lit.*, Mahomet, *but supposed to be a Saracen god and idol.*

mai, *vs.*, (OE magan), may, can. *pr. 1 sg.*, Hr 562; *2 sg.*, **mayt**, Hv 845; (*with enclitic pro.*) **maistow**, Sd 1826, B 3021; **mowe**, B 3316; *3 sg.*, **mowe**, Hv 175; *plu.*, **mowe**, G 675; **mowne**, ET 909; **mone**, Av 43; (*confused in form with* mun, *q.v.*); *pt.*, **miȝte**, D 521; **movghte**, Ip 3110; **mahte**, Ly 28385; **maght**, Hv 1348; **moucthe**, Hv 376; *plu.*, **micten**, Hv 516; **mouthen**, Hv 1183; (*with enclitic pro.*) **miȝtou**, D 319.

maie, maiden. Ip 3113.

main, *n.*, (OE mægen), strength, power, might. EG 141; **imaine**, Ly 27679; **mein**, D 579.

make, *vw.*, (OE macian), make, force, display. Hr 358; **ma**, P 1728; **maa**, P 520; *pr. 2 sg.* (*with enclitic pro.*), **makestow**, G 199; *3 sg.*, **mekes**, Av 241; **mase**, ET 996; *pt. sg.*, **maked**, D 384; *plu.*, **makede**, Hr 1234; **madun**, Av 1134; *pp.*, **mad**, TT 11; **maad**, At 778; *pr. sj.*, **moo**, Ip 1152.

manere, *in the phrases:* some maner thing, some sort of thing; all maner thyng, every sort of thing, B 3021, Em 466; on al manere, by all means; in this maner wise, thus, SS 2805; B 2959.

maugré, *prep.*, (OF maugré), de-

spite (*usually in phrases of anger or contempt*). Yw 783; D 562.

me, men (*often used impersonally*). Hr 366; Ly 27933.

mede, *n.*, (OE mēd), (1) reward, deserts. Hr 470; EG 746; *in the phrase:* God do thee mede, God reward you, Yw 728. (2) bribe, gratuity. Hv 1635.

meiné, *n.*, (OF maisonnée), household, troop, retinue, company. Sd 1981; **mayne**, Sd 2022; **menye**, Tr 37; **menȝe**, SS 905; **mene**, Av 71; **meny**, K 818; **meyny**, Ip 352; **maigne**, Al 4141.

mekill, *cf.* muchel, much.

mene, mone, *vw.*, (OE mǣnan), (1) signify, intend. *pr sg.*, **manes**, Yw 93; **menes**, Hv 597; *plu.*, **menes**, SS 428; *pp.*, **mynt**, P 1667; **iment**, D 511; **mente**, Av 201; **imint**, D 1032. (2) speak, tell. K 935; *pt.*, **menede**, CA 124; **ment**, Cl 126. (3) moan, complain, lament. (*Same stem as preceding in* OE, *though senses have always been different.*) **mone**, EG 126; **moone**, Ip 1069.

mete, *n.*, (OE mete), food, meal. Av 720; CA 88; **meyte**, K 739; **met**, D 822.

mete, *vw.*, (OE mǣtan), dream. Hr 1408; **imætte**, Ly 28016.

mete, *vw.*, (OE mētan), meet, encounter. *pr.*, **mette**, Hr 1027; **imette**, Ly 27715.

miche, **mech**, much.

mid, *prep.*, (OE mid), with. Hr 220; Ly 27661; **mide**, D 217; **myde**, Al 4111.

misfare, *vw.*, do amiss, go astray. CA 238.

moche, much.

mochel, much; *cf.* muchel.

mode, *n.*, (OE mōd), mind, state of mind, pride, courage. ET

619; Ip 1031; **moode,** Sd 2077.
mone, *n.* (*from the vb.*), moan,
lament. Av 1087; **mane,** P
1063; **moon,** B 3190.
mone, moon. Em 2.
monnen, men. Ly 27830.
moo, *cf.* **more, make.**
more, *cp. adj., adv., and sb.,* (OE
mára, mã), more, greater. Hr
554; **mo,** Hr 808; **moo,** ET 156;
mære, Ly 27864; **ma,** SS 264.
morne, morwen, *n.,* (OE morgen),
morrow. **morun,** Av 794; *often
in the following phrases, meaning
"*to-morrow"*: **amorewe,** D 481;
to-morn, Ip 3006; **a marȝen,** Ly
28004; **a moreȝe,** Hr 645.
moste, *sup. adj., sb., and adv.,* (OE
mæst, mest), most, greatest.
P 899; **mest,** Hr 250; **maste,** SS
448; **mæste,** Ly 27482.
mote, moste, *vs.,* (OE *pr.,* mõte,
pt., mõste) may, shall, must.
pr. and pt., G 233; **mut,** B 2932;
moot, G 577; **moste,** CA 50;
plu., **mot,** G 131; **moten,** Hv 18.
muchel, *adj., sb., and adv.,* (OE
mycel), much, great. Hr 83;
mochel, D 10; **mycull,** Av 35;
mucle, Ly 27732; **mekill,** Av 335.
cp., **more,** *q.v.; sup.,* **moste.**
mun, mon, *vs.,* (OE mon; ON
mun), must, shall (*forms confused with* **mai,** *q.v.*) Av 367,
SS 465; **mon,** Ip 1198, P 567.

N

N-. *For the following negative
compounds, see the word indicated:* **nas, nis, nes, nam, neoren,
næs,** *cf.* **be;** *not,* **note, niste,** *cf.*
**wite; nabben, nastu, nafte, nade,
nauede,** *cf.* **haue; nalde, nulde,
nolde, nil, null, nel,** *cf.* **wille.**
nauthir, neither.
ne, *adv. and conj.,* (OE ne), **(1)** not,

nor (*correlative,* **ne . . . ne**). Hr
46; D 253; **ny,** Em 320.
(2) only (*correlative,* **ne . . . but**).
Hr 198.
nede, *n.,* (OE nēad), need, necessity. Hr 48; **neoden,** *d.s.,*
Ly 28395; **neodde,** Ly 28437;
d. as adv., **nede,** necessarily, B
3102; *g. as adv.,* **nedys,** Ip 1163.
negh, *adj., adv., and prep.,* (OE
nēah), nigh, near, almost. **negȝ,**
D 255; **neghȝ,** D 534; **ny,** ET
150; **neȝ,** Hr 252; **nyȝe,** B 3564·
neh, Ly 28353; **neyh,** G 626;
aneh, Ly 27651; **neiȝ,** R 201.
neghe, *vw.,* (OE nēhwan), approach,
draw near. **nyȝhe,** Sd 2100;
newhen, Hv 1866; *pr.,* **neghes,**
P 808; **neh,** Ly 27735; **neȝe,** Av
827; *pt.,* **neȝhit,** Av 1003;
neghed, Tr 4731; *imp.,* **neghe,**
Av 854; *prp.,* **nyȝyng,** Lv 829.
nemnede, named. D 252; **nempned,**
O 598.
nere, *adj., adv., and prep.,* (OE
nēah), near. SS 520; **neerr,** EG
276. *cp.,* **nerre,** P 2072; **ner,**
G 109; **neer,** G 138. *comp.,*
nerhand, nearly, Cl 70, At 327;
nerehonde, Sd 2998; **neerehand,**
EG 158.
netheles, *adv.,* nevertheless. Hv
1658; **neotheles,** Ly 27974; **nethirles,** B 3368.
nice, *adj.,* foolish. B 3416.
nime, *vs.,* (OE niman), **(1)** take,
seize. *pt.,* **nam,** Hr 585; **nome,**
Hr 1173; **inom,** Ly 27726; **neme,**
Hr 60; *pp.,* **inome,** G 119;
nomen, EG 255.
(2) go, take the road. *pr. sj.,*
nimen, Hv 1336; *pt.,* **nom,** D
368; **ynome,** Lv 94.
nith, nicth, niht, night. Hv 575.
no, *adv., adj., and conj.,* (OE nã, nõ),
(1) no (*opposite of* "yes"). **(2)**
not any, not. Hr 11; **na,** Hr 1193.

(3) nor. SS 2969, Av 1010.
In the phrase: **withouten no;**
beyond denial, O 48. *comp.,* **nouȝ-**
wher, nowhere. R 326.

none, *pro. and adj.,* (OE **nān**),
none, no one, not any. **non,**
Hr 8; CA 250; **nane,** SS 485;
a.m., **nenne,** Ly 27977; *d.f.,*
nare, Ly 27838.

none, nones, *n.,* (OE **nōn**), nones
(*originally the sixth* canonical
hour, *coming about three p.m.*
But, when the Church required
fasting until nones *on fast-days,*
which were increasingly numerous
in the later Middle Ages, the time
drifted toward midday. In the
romances, the time can be deter-
mined only from the context, if at
all.) SS 4303; **novn,** Cl 88.

nonis, *in the phrase:* **for the nonis,**
a tag of slight meaning; lit., for
that occasion, just then; *often*
best translated "indeed." TT 82;
nones, D 1014.

nought, *pro., adj., and adv.,* (OE
nāwiht, naht), **(1)** naught, nothing. Ip 1052; **nowȝt,** Cl 110;
nott, Cl 352; **nowt,** D 253; **noȝt,**
Hr 937; **noȝth,** CA 290.
(2) not, not at all. **nat,** G 158;
note, Ip 426; **noȝt,** CA 236;
nougt, D 1005.

nowther, nother, noither, nouther,
neither.

nowȝe, noweȝ, now. B 3213, 3736.

O

O, written for **a, on, one, or, of.**

of, off, *prep.,* (OE **of**). *Only the*
more unfamiliar senses are noted:
(1) by (*agency*). Av 693.
(2) from, out of. CA 287.
(3) from, at the hands of. Hr
365.

of, *a common spelling for* **off.** Tr
4755.

olde, *adj. and sb.,* (OE **eald**), old.
K 177; G 79; **eld,** D 210; **alde,**
Ly 28444; *sup.,* **heldeste,** Hv
1396.

on, an, one.

on, *prep. and adv.,* (OE **on**), on (*in*
most of the senses of Modern
English). **one,** P 60; **o,** Hv 1251;
an, D 411; **a,** Ly 27744.

one, *pro., adj., and adv.,* (OE **ān**),
(1) one. **oon,** ET 778; **o,** B 3076;
on, CA 143; **tone** (*by assimilation*
from that one), P 708; **ton,** K 677.
(2) *Used to complete a comparison:*
A kinder knight then Grime was
one (*i.e.,* than G. was), EG 499.
(3) alone. CA 15; **ane,** P 2043.

ones, *adv.,* (OE **ānes**), once. **onys,**
B 2993; **onus,** Av 868; **anes,** Yw
292; **ones,** CA 196.

or, *conj.* (*contraction of* **other;** *cf.*
either), or. CA 30; **ar,** Cl 35;
our, Cl 418; **er,** Sd 2732.

or, before; *cf.* **are.**

ore, *n.,* (OE **ār**), mercy, favor,
grace. ET 226; **are,** K 69.

orn, ourn, ran; *cf.* **runne.**

os, *cf.* **as.**

other, *pro., adj., and adv.,* (OE
ōðer), **(1)** other, the other. Hr
238; **vther,** Yw 634; **odur,** ET
610; **odir,** K 884.
(2) next, second. D 228; EG
625; Hr 187.
(3) otherwise. **othyr,** ET 117;
Ly 27898.
Assimilations: **no nodur,** no other,
ET 459; **my nothir,** mine other,
Av 42; **tother,** the other, Av 297;
todirs, other's, B 3094.

other, or; *cf.* **either.**

ouer, *prep. and adv.,* (OE **ofer**),
over. Hv 293; **ouur,** CA 175;
aure, Av 623.
comp., **oueral,** everywhere, Ly
27471, O 206.

our, *cf.* **I** and **or.**

owe, ought, *cf.* awe.

own, *pro. and adj.*, (OE āgen), own. awin, SS 284; awne, Av 315; oȝene, Hr 249; *d.f.*, aȝere, Ly 28107; owyn, Cl 534; owhen, O 161; oȝe, Hr 984.

P

paie, *n.*, pleasure. Cl 144.

paie, *vw.*, (OF paier), (1) pay. K 36. (2) please. pay, SS 396; *pp.*, payde, ET 157; paid, Yw 1057.

palefrai, *n.*, (OF palefrei), saddle-horse (*as distinguished from steed, or war-horse*). Cl 250; Hv 2060.

par (*in oaths*), in the name of, by. par charité, in the name of charity; pardy, perdé, by God, Ip 1085; parauenture, by chance, D 127; par fai, by my faith, D 761; par ma foy, by my faith, G 367.

paramour, *n.*, (OF par amour), lover. Lv 303; *as adv.*, fervently. Lv 106.

pas, *n.*, pace; *especially in the phrase:* ful gode pase, rapidly. K 713; gude pase, Yw 619.

passe, *vw.*, (OF passer), (1) pass, go. pas, SS 2848. (2) escape, go away. B 3062; SS 487.

pere, *n.*, (OF per), (1) peer, noble. Hv 989. (2) an equal. At 33; per, D 1010.

piment, spiced wine. Sq 758; pyement, Lv 344.

pine, *n.*, (OE pīn), pain, suffering. CA 92; EG 692; Sd 2030.

pine, *vw.*, (OE pīnian), torment, cause pain. Hr 635; *pp.*, pyned, CA 26.

plight, *vw.*, (OE plihtan), pledge, assure. pliȝte, Hr 305; *pr.*, Av 428; plyght, ET 210.

pouer, poor, power; pouerlich, poorly.

prese, *n.*, (*fr.* OF presser), throng, tumult. Em 464; press, TT 21; prece, Av 742.

prest, priest.

prest, *adj. and adv.*, (OF prest), ready, quick. At 745; TT 67; Av 19.

preue, *cf.* proue.

price, prise, *n.*, (OF pris), (1) worth, esteem, excellence. Em 92; Av 20; priis, O 49. (2) judgment of superiority, prize. D 582; Av 529; Ip 1099. (3) *as adj.*, worthy, noble. TT 215, CA 279.

prike, *vw.*, (OE prician), spur, ride rapidly. Em 737; preke, Av 1116; *pt.*, prikit, Tr 8657; prekut, Av 289; *prp.*, prekand, Av 623.

prime, *n.*, beginning of the day (*strictly, the canonical hour after sunrise; extended to cover the period between six and nine a.m.*) SS 359.

priué, *adj.*, (OF privé), secret. prevée, P 154; priuyé, EG 1341.

priueli, *adv.*, secretly. B 3632; preuely, Av 853; Ip 1126.

priueté, *n.*, (OF priveté), secret counsels, secrecy. preueté, SS 284; Av 947; Ip 488.

proue, *vw.*, (OF prover), (1) prove. preue, CA 252; *pr.*, preues, P 55; *pp.*, preuyt, Tr 47. (2) make trial of. proue, Hr 545.

Q

Qu-, Qw-. *For northern words beginning with this combination, see* Wh-.

quath, quod, *vs.*, (OE cweðan). *Only in preterit:* said, quoth. Hr 127; quod, CA 99; quad, D 175; hwat, Hv 1650; quoth, Al 3984.

quik, *adj., sb., and adv.*, (OE cwic),

(1) alive, living. D 164; SS 895; quic, Hr 86; qwyk, K 402.

(2) quick. D 832.

quite, *vw.*, (OF quiter), (1) repay, requite. B 3519; *pt.*, qwyte, P 1491; *pp.*, quytte, Ip 478; *in the phrase:* quite him his mede, give him his deserts, ET 693; Sd 1921.

(2) acquit, redeem, clear. quyȝtt, Cl 63; *pp.*, quyte, B 3534.

R

rape, *adj. and adv.*, quick. G 101.

ras, rase, roos, rose.

rathe, *adj. and adv.*, (OE hræð, hrædlīce), quick, impatient. P 98; Av 248; radylye, EG 1236; radly, Tr 4714.

rawghte, *cf.* recchen, reach.

reche, rekke, *vs.*, (OE rēcan), care, take heed. *pr. 1 sg.*, recche, Hr 366; *2 sg.*, rekke, CA 306; *3 sg.*, reche, Av 808; *pt.*, rowȝte, CA 177; roght, Sd 1878; *pt. sj.*, roght, Yw 969.

recche, *vw.*, (OE ræccan), (1) reach, grasp. *pt.*, rawȝt, Cl 196. (2) hand over, deal (a blow). *pr. sg.*, recheth, CA 176; rawȝte, CA 177; raught, EG 978; *plu.*, rawȝten, CA 316.

rede, *n.*, (OE ræd), advice, counsel, plan. SS 910; Av 964; G 432; ræd, Ly 27977; redd, ET 430; *in the phrase:* couthe no rede, was uncertain what to do, P 153.

rede, *vs. and w.*, (OE rædan), read. *pt.*, radde, D 243.

rede, *vs.*, (OE rædan), advise, counsel, direct. *pr. 1 sg.*, CA 169; Ip 1150; read, EG 605; *pt.*, radde, Lv 39; rathe, Hv 1335.

reson, *n.*, (OF raison), good sense, due cause, justice. ET 902.

reue, *vw.*, (OE rēafian), take away, deprive of. SS 875; refe, TT 99; *pt.*, rafte, Av 100; *pp.*, rafte, ET 1206; reued, G 704.

rewe, *vs. and w.*, (OE hrēowan), (1) regret (*often impersonal*). Hr 378; Cl 269; *pt.*, rewed, CA 55; rew, Lv 177.

(2) pity. rewythe, Lv 102; *pt.* (*with prep.*), rued on, Sd 1561.

rewthe, *n.*, (OE hrēowð), pity, sorrow. O 112; ruthe, Hr 673; routhe, G 677.

riall, *adj.*, splendid, royal.

riche, *adj. and sb.*, (OF riche), wealthy, powerful, well born; sumptuous, expensive. Em 416; Hr 314; B 2963.

riche, rike, *n.*, (OE rīce), kingdom, realm. SS 3001; Yw 142; Ly 28273.

ride, *vs.*, (OE rīdan), ride. Hr 34; rith, Hv 2690; *pt.*, rade, Av 146; rid, EG 336; rood, G 190; rod, Hr 32; ritte, D 537; *pp.*, redyn, TT 111; ride, G 191; iriden, D 56; *prp.*, rydand, TT 74; ridinde, Ly 28524.

rife, *adj.*, (OE rīf), thick, numerous, crowded, frequent. P 560; Tr 4770; ryue, G 783.

rigge, *n.*, (OE hrycg), back. Hr 1058; rig, SS 885; rug, Ly 27821; rigg, D 526.

right, *n.*, (OE riht), that which is fitting, proper, or just. Cl 36; riȝte, D 52; *g. as adv.*, rightis, Sd 2278; *in the phrase:* on ryght, aright, ET 516.

right, *adj. and adv.*, (1) right, proper, just, immediate, direct. Cl 254; rith, Hv 2235; *adv., often a mere filler, meaning* "indeed": right, Cl 9; ryȝth, CA 352; reght, P 227.

(2) right (*as opposed to left*). rith, Hv 604.

rode, *n.,* (OE rōd), the cross of Christ. Hr 328; **roode,** G 639; **rod,** ET 1044.

rode, *n.,* (OE rudu), complexion. D 813; **rud,** EG 217; **ruddy,** Sq 713.

rowte, *n.,* (OF route), throng, crowd, turmoil. G 285; Tr 4701; **rowt,** Yw 1024; **rowȝt,** Cl 267; **rout,** O 281.

runne, *vs.,* (OE irnan), run. **rynn,** P 1662; **vrn,** Hr 878; *pr. sg.,* **rinnes,** Av 59; *pt. sg.,* **orn,** Ly 28068; **ourn,** O 83; *pt. plu.,* **runnun,** Av 384; **vrn,** O 87; **ronnen,** CA 314; *pp.,* **iorne,** Hr 1146; *prp.,* **rinyng,** SS 881; **rennynge,** CA 113; **rinand,** Yw 1067.

S

sagh, saw; *cf.* **se.**

sai, say, *cf.* **seie.**

samen, *adj. and adv.,* (ON saman), together, in company. **samyn,** SS 338; **samin,** Yw 24; **somyn,** Tr 66; **somun,** Av 385; in **same,** At 754; Sd 1938; **isome,** R 227.

sand, sond, *n.,* (OE sand), shore, strand (*especially in the phrase:* **see and sonde,** sea and land). Em 18, Hv 708.

Saresyns, *n.,* Saracens, Turks. Sd 3103; **Sarazins,** Hr 1319; **Sarezyne,** Em 482; **Sarsynys,** Lv 266.

saunfail, without fail. Yw 1004; D 1016; **sanȝ fail,** SS 913.

sawe, *n.,* (OE sagu), (1) speech, talk, remark, proverb. ET 574; Ip 3018.

(2) story, tale. Em 319; CA 162.

sayne, seen, say; *cf.* **se** *and* **seie.**

sc-, sch-, *cf.* **sh-.**

scl-, *cf.* **sl-.**

scape, *vw.,* (OF escaper), escape.

skape, G 576; *pt.,* **scapyd,** ET 115.

sceldes, shields. Ly 27463; **scelden,** Ly 27784.

scipen, ships, Ly 28234; *g. plu.,* **scipen,** Ly 28437.

se, *vs.,* (OE sēon), see, look upon. **seen,** Sd 1588; **seon,** Hr 1345; **yseo,** Al 3882; **ise,** Ly 28470; **yse,** O 528; *pr. 1 sg.,* **see,** ET 538; *2 sg.,* **sese,** SS 426; **sest,** Hv 534; *3 sg.,* **sese,** SS 822; **seese,** P 422; **seth,** O 249. *plu.,* **sen,** Hv 168; **sayne,** P 114; *pt. sg.,* **saȝ,** Hr 777; **sagh,** Yw 152; **segh,** D 87; **sye,** ET 1001; **seȝ,** D 335; **saugh,** Sd 2985; **isiȝe,** Hr 1157; **seigh,** G 120; **seghȝ,** D 731; **siȝe,** O 353; **saye,** Sd 1998; **sey,** G 330; **se,** Av 776; **seyȝ,** CA 22; **seiȝe,** O 295; **isæh,** Ly 28382; *plu.,* **seghen,** D 139; **yseiȝe,** O 326; **see,** Tr 57; **syȝen,** Em 299; **sy,** Em 869; **iseȝe,** D 503; **sowen,** Hv 1055; **isehȝen,** Ly 27518; *pt. sj.,* **isiȝe,** Hr 976; *imp. plu.,* **seith,** B 3159; *pp.,* **seyn,** B 3574; **sen,** D 586; **sey,** B 3697; **sene,** CA 53; **sayne,** Ip 378; **seȝe,** R 416. *In the phrase:* **God you see,** God be gracious to you, Sd 2707; Lv 253.

seche, seken, *vw.,* (OE sēcan), (1) seek, look for. **sech,** B 3298; **seke,** Ip 1065; **siche,** B 3795; *pr. with enclitic pro.,* **sechestu,** Hr 942; *pt.,* **sowȝt,** Em 307; **soght,** Tr 8624.

(2) come, go. *pt.,* **sowghtte,** Ip 366; **sowȝte,** CA 60; **soghten,** Tr 8671; *imp.,* **seche,** CA 53; *pp.,* **sought,** Ip 404; **sowȝt,** Cl 207.

(3) attempt. *pp.,* **soght,** ET 618.

segh, saw; *cf.* **se.**

seie, *vw.,* (OE secgan), say, speak, tell (*often used absolutely*). CA 311; **sigge,** Al 4198; **sayne,** Sd

1736; sugen, Ly 27837; sai, D
166; *pr. 1 sg.*, sigge, Al 4023;
pr. 2 sg., seyst, Hv 2008; *3 sg.*,
saise, P 1953; seyt, O 554; *plu.*,
seyn, CA 217; suggeth, Ly 27480;
says, Av 936; *pt.*, seide, D 431;
Hr 271; sede, Hr 531; iseid, K
344; *pp.*, seyd, Hv 1281.

self, selue, *pro. and adj.*, (OE self),
self, same. seluun, Av 70;
seoluen, Ly 28146. *Often used
without preceding personal pronoun.*

semblaunt, *n.*, (OF semblant),
(1) expression of countenance.
Yw 631; sembelant, Em 220;
sembland, Yw 631.
(2) show, display. Ip 2995.

semeli, *adj. and adv.*, (ON sœm-
iligr), (1) handsome, pleasant,
attractive. CA 42; P 543;
semyle, Lv 285.
(2) fitting, proper. *cp.*, semelyer,
ET 348.

sen, since, see; *cf.* sithen, se.

sertes, *adv.*, (OF certes), surely.
SS 339; sertis, Ip 1127; certys,
Em 647.

shaft, *n.*, (OE sceaft), shaft, (*by
metonymy*) spear, arrow. SS
801; schafte, P 52; scaftes, Ly
28553.

shal, *vs.*, (OE sceal), shall, will, be
expected to, be supposed to.
pr. 1 sg., schal, Hr 544; sal, Yw
465; chal, D 652; *2 sg.*, shalst,
EG 1308; *3 sg.*, sall, P 91; sale,
SS 901; sschal, D 30; *plu.*, shole,
Hv 562; schuln, G 842; schulle,
Hr 847; schul, G 587; scullen,
Ly 28198; *pt. sg.*, sholde, CA 94;
sold, SS 274; schust, O 418;
sulde, P 738; schud, Lv 803;
plu., schuld, Av 780; sholden,
Hv 1020; sculden, Ly 27980;
schild, Av 930; *pr. sj.*, sschulle,
D 86; *with enclitic pro.*, shaltow,

schaltu, D 318.

shape, *vs. and w.*, (OE scieppan),
form, create, give shape to. Em
242; *pt.*, shope, Tr 72; ET 948;
shoope, Em 2; shaped, Hv 424.

she, *pro. (origin uncertain)*, she.
For oblique cases, see he. ssche,
D 54; ʒhe, D 23; ʒe, D 78; sho,
SS 519.

shende, *vw.*, (OE scendan), (1)
injure, disgrace. Sd 1682;
scende, Ly 27793; *pp.*, schente,
Av 692; ishente, Sd 2286.
(2) abuse, reprove. *pp.*, schente,
ET 302; G 704.

shene, *adj.*, (OE scēne), shining,
lovely, beautiful. Em 150;
schene, Av 454; schine, O 356;
sheene, CA 298; *in the phrase:*
schene vndur schild (*tag for a
warrior*), Av 622.

shewe, *vw.*, (OE scēawian), (1)
show, reveal. shauwe, Hv 2206;
Hr 1311; *pr. sg.*, schewes, P
1072; *pp.*, shewed, Hv 2056;
schewid, K 1060.
(2) declare. sheue, Hv 1401.
(3) look at, gaze upon. shewe,
Hv 2136.

shir, bright, shining. Hv 1253.

shitte, *cf.* shut.

shole, should; *cf.* shal.

shon, shoon, *plu. of* sho, shoe. G 212.

showe, *cf.* shewe.

shul, *cf.* shal.

shut, *vw.*, (OE scyttan), shut.
schitte, G 286; *pt.*, shet, Sd
2960; *pp.*, ischet, G 292; shit,
Sd 2963.

sibbe, *n. and adj.*, (OE sibb), kin,
blood-relation. D 618; sib, Ip
3086; EG 45.

sike, *vw.*, (OE sīcan), sigh, lament.
Hv 291; siʒe, B 3270; syche,
Lv 249; *pt.*, siʒte, D 866; siʒhid,
B 3017; sykede, CA 25; *prp.*,
sikend, D 133; syʒthyng, Cl 98;

syghynge, Cl 108; *vbl. n.,* **sykynge,** Ip 1051; Em 328.

siker, *adj. and adv.,* (OE **siker**), sure. D 115; B 3634; **seker,** Yw 601; **sicur,** K 170; *adv.,* **securly,** P 202; Ip 440; Cl 219; **sekerlike,** ET 952.

sin, since; *cf.* **sithen.**

sithe, *n.,* (OE **sīð**), time, occasion. Hr 356; P 985; *plu.,* **sithe,** EG 1164; At 585; **sythis,** At 783.

sithen, *adv., conj., and prep.,* (OE **seoððan,** **siððan**), (1) since, after (*of time*), afterwards. CA 25; **sethin,** SS 453; **sethun,** Av 157; **sythinn,** Av 1107; **sith,** B 3175; **sen,** P 296; **seoththen,** Ly 27803; **syn,** Cl 213; **sethn,** SS 4326; **suththe,** Hr 1078.

(2) because, since (*of cause*). **sithin,** Av 937; **sith,** B 3288; **sen,** SS 339.

sitte, *vs.,* (OE **sittan**), sit. *pr. sg.,* **sitte,** G 749; *pt. sg.,* **seet,** G 790; **set,** D 157; *plu.,* **seten,** Em 218; **sete,** G 681; *pp.,* **sette,** G 805; **iset,** B 3055.

sle, slo, sla, *vs.,* (OE **slēan**), (1) slay, kill. **slee,** G 822; **sla,** P 293; **sloo,** ET 150; **sclo,** Lv 837; **sloe,** Av 940; **slean,** Ly 28180; **slone,** K 35; **slen,** D 922; *pr. sg.,* **slos,** Hv 2706; *pt. sg.,* **sluȝe,** Av 1029; **slogh,** SS 843; **slouȝ,** O 312; **slowgh,** D 890; *plu.,* **slogh,** Tr 4766; *pr. sj.,* **slaey,** Av 111; **slos,** Hv 2596; *pp.,* **slane,** P 1774; **sloe,** EG 433; **slawe,** At 705; **islæȝen,** Ly 27926; **aslæȝe,** 28330; **sclayn,** Lv 610; **sclawe,** Lv 723; **slone,** P 2154; **slawene,** Sd 2802.

(2) strike, beat on. **slæn,** Ly 27486; *pt. plu.,* **slowe,** Sd 2565.

slike, such; *cf.* **swilk.**

slo, slay, strike; *cf.* **sle.**

slogh, slew, struck; *cf.* **sle.**

snell, *adj., sb., and adv.,* (OE **snell**),

quick, active. Em 309; Lv 441.

so, *cf.* **swa.**

soghte, sowȝte, sought; *cf.* **seche.**

solas, *n.,* (OF **solaz**), enjoyment, comfort. Lv 407, G 328; **solace,** SS 253.

sonde, *n.,* (OE **sond**), (1) message. Hr 271.

(2) providence, mercy. CA 36, Em 332; **sande,** K 655.

(3) messenger. Hr 933; *plu.,* **sonde,** Ly 27966.

sone, *adv.,* (OE **sona**), at once, straightway, speedily. Hr 42; Em 230; **soune,** Ip 3045.

sone, sune, *n.,* (OE **sunu**), son. Ip 3081, D 592; *g. sg.,* **sune,** Av 268; **son,** SS 4296; *plu.,* **sonnes,** CA 42.

sonne, sunne, sone, sun.

sore, (OE **sār, sāre**), (1) *n.,* sorrow, pain. Hv 152, EG 318.

(2) *adj. and adv.,* sad, wretched, painful. EG 847; **sare,** SS 563, ET 1012; **sor,** D 578; **soure,** SS 546; *cp.,* **sorrere,** At 565; **sarlic,** Ly 28457.

sori, *adj. and adv.,* (OE **sārig**), (1) sad, wretched. Hv 151; **særi,** Ly 28333; **sorye,** Ip 1065; **særȝ-est,** Ly 28459.

(2) regretful. **sary,** SS 852.

sorwe, sorghe, *n.,* (OE **sorg**), sorrow. Hv 57; **sorow,** SS 3027; *plu.,* **soreȝe,** Hr 261; **sorȝen,** Ly 28443; **sorhful,** sorrowful, Ly 28335.

soth, *adj. and sb.,* true, the truth. SS 4263, ET 158; **south,** Sd 1689; *cp.,* **soththere,** Ly 28461. *In the phrases:* **forsothe, to sothe, be sothe,** in truth, CA 18, Ly 28142, Cl 485.

soun, *n.,* sound, noise.

sound, *adj.,* (OE **gesund**), sound, unhurt, in good health. EG 789; **sund,** Hr 1341; **sowunde,** Av

1034; **isunde,** Ly 28615.

sowdan, sultan. P 977; **sawdan,** Av 917; **sowdon,** Sd 2095.

sowne, swoone, *n.* (*from the verb*), swoon, daze. EG 60; **swown,** SS 863; **swoue,** D 1064; **iswoue,** D 1061; **swogh,** Yw 824.

sowne, swone, *vw.*, swoon, be dazed. *inf.*, **swony,** D 1063; *pt.*, **sooned,** EG 1347; **sowened,** Em 780; **squonut,** Av 390; **swoned,** O 195; **swownyd,** At 604; *pp.*, **iswoʒe,** Hr 428; *prp. as noun,* **sowenynge,** Em 284; **svounnyng,** Cl 89; **swownyng,** Yw 868.

spede, *vw.*, (OE spēdan), (1) hasten, speed. D 749, Ip 3005; *pr. plu.*, **spede,** Sd 2842.

(2) prosper, progress, succeed. Sd 2433; *pr. sg.*, **spette,** G 806; *pt.*, **spedde,** P 934. *Especially in the phrase:* God us spede, God give us success, Ip 486.

spede, *n,* (OE spēd), (1) speed, P 759; *d. as adv.,* **gode spede,** fast, Av 628.

(2) success, Sd 1737.

spell, *n.*, (OE spell), (1) tale, news. Yw 149, Hr 1030; *pl.*, **spelles,** Ly 28175.

(2) language. *pl.*, **spellen,** Ly 28165.

spille, *vw.*, (OE spillan), (1) destroy, kill, spill blood. Av 314, ET 1132; *pp.*, **spild,** Av 216; **spilt,** SS 4290.

(2) perish. Hr 194, Hv 2422.

squ-, sqw-, *cf.* sw-.

squete, sweet; Av 833.

stande, *vs.*, (OE standan), (1) stand, stand up, stand still. **stonde,** Hr 399; *pr. sg.*, **stant,** G 814; **stont,** B 3173; *pt.*, **stod** Hr 529.

(2) stop, delay. **stande,** P 960.

(3) *in various idiomatic senses:* issue out (*of light*). *pt,* **stod,**

Hv 591; blow (*of wind*); *pt.*, **stod,** Ly 28305, Em 833.

staleworth, *adj.* (*origin uncertain*), stalwart, valiant, strong. D 288; **stalworthi,** Hv 24; **staloworth,** CA 326.

stede, *n.*, (OE stēda), horse, steed (*generally used of a war-horse*). D 408; *d. sg.*, (*by nunnation*) **steden,** Ly 27741.

stede, *n.*, (OE stede, styde), place, location. P 154; **stid,** Av 1091, Tr 8627; **stude,** Ly 28534; *in the phrase:* stand in stedde, be an aid to, Ip 3083.

sterte, *vs.*, (ON sterta), jump, rush. **sturte,** R 281; *pr. sg.*, **stertis,** P 2229; **stirttes,** P 430; *pt.*, **sterte,** G 219, Sd 1606; **styrte,** CA 326; **stirt,** D 923.

sterue, *vs.*, (OE steorfan), die, perish. *pr.*, **sterue,** Hr 910; *pp.*, **isterue,** Hr 1167.

steuen, *n.*, (OE stefn), voice. Sd 2258; **steuyn,** ET 74; **steuenne,** CA 106.

sti, *n.*, (OE stīg), path. Ip 3088, Hv 2618.

stiffe, *adj. and adv.,* (OE stif), valiant, stubborn, strong. P 1472, EG 643; **stif,** D 9; **stef,** D 531; **stifly,** Av 326, TT 156.

stiward, *n.*, (OE stigweard), steward. (*This official was seldom popular with minstrels, as he discouraged prodigality toward wayfarers.*) Hr 227; **stuard,** Av 1070; **stward,** Em 496.

stounde, *n.*, (OE stund), time, period of time, occasion. SS 2991; **stonde,** EG 611; **stunde,** Hr 739; **stowunde,** Av 409; *d. as adv.,* this stownde, on this occasion, now, SS 781.

stowre, *n.*, (OF estour), tumult, uproar, combat. Yw 1221, P 138; **stoure,** Tr 8652. *Especially*

in the phrase: **stiffe in stowre,**
valiant in battle.
sturien, stir. Ly 27440; *pt.,* **stu-
rede,** Ly 27424.
sugge, say; *cf.* **seie.**
sumdel, *adj. and adv.,* somewhat.
K 283.
sunden, be; *cf.* **be.**
suthe, very; *cf.* **swithe.**
suththe, afterwards; *cf.* **sithen.**
swa, so, *adv., and conj.,* (OE **swa**).
*The senses are as in Modern Eng-
lish except:* (**1**) since, because, as.
Ip 1136; Hr 590.
(**2**) as if, provided that. B 3746;
Hr 718.
swein, swain, *n.,* (ON **sveinn**),
(**1**) peasant, servant (*often an
epithet*). P 700, G 527, Em 384;
sqwayne, K 230.
(**2**) retainer, soldier. Ly 28339.
swerd, *n.,* (OE **sweord**), sword.
sweord, Ly 27626; **squrd,** Av
247.
swere, *vs.,* (OE **swerian**), swear,
take oath. **squere,** Av 320; *pr.,*
suereth, Hv 647; *pt.,* **swor,** Hv
398; **squere,** Av 466; **sworen,**
Hr 1249; *pp.,* **swore,** G 302.
swilk, swich, slike, (OE **swylc,** ON
slīkr), (**1**) *pro., adj., and sb.,*
such. CA 49; SS 404; Yw 820;
seche, Av 34; **swihc,** Hr 166;
sich, P 159; *comp.,* **swilkane,**
SS 2994.
(**2**) *conj. and prep.,* as if, like.
Hv 2123; **swulc,** Ly 27455.
swire, swere, *n.,* (OE **swîra**), neck.
CA 44, D 1018; **sweere,** G 273.
swithe, *adv.,* (OE **swīð, swȳð**),
(**1**) quickly. Hr 273; **swyde,**
CA 158, Em 219; (*by nunnation*)
swithen, Ly 27527; **squith,** Av
218; **sqwithely,** Av 320; **swiȝe,**
D 305.
(**2**) very, very much. Hr 174;
suthe, Hr 178; **squytheli,** Av 732.

swone, swoone, swoue, swoon; *cf.*
sowne.

T

taa, tan, *cf.* **take.**
take, *vs.,* (ON **taka**), (**1**) take, seize,
receive, lift. Hv 409; too, P
1022; **tan,** At 495; **taa,** P 498;
pr. sg., **tase,** P 790; *pt. sg.,* **tok,**
D 1036; **tuke,** P 186; *pt. plu.,*
token, CA 226; *pp.,* **itake,** G
350; **token,** Hv 1194; **tone,** P
2155; **take,** Ip 1162; **tane,** Ip
1049; *prp.,* **takeand,** EG 1237.
(**2**) entrust, give. B 3608; *pr.,
1 sg.,* **take,** G 747; *3 sg.,* **taketh,**
CA 104; *pt.,* **tok,** D 295; **toke,**
Em 547; **tuke,** P 195; *imp. sg.,*
tak, SS 3003.
(**3**) *in various idiomatic senses:*
take no keep, have no regard for,
ET 746; **toke hem bitwene,** decided between them, Em 799,
Hv 1833; **take, tane,** take oneself, go, P 1060; **the ded to take,**
receive the death-penalty, SS
4295.
tale, *n.,* (OE **tæl**), (**1**) speech, tale,
story. Hv 3, Hr 311.
(**2**) number, count. Hv 2026,
Ly 27606.
teche, *vs.,* (OE **tǽcan, tǽcean**), teach.
pt., **tauȝt,** D 285; **taȝte,** Hr 244;
tauhte, Hv 2214; **thawȝth,** Em
58; **thawȝte,** Em 973; *pp.,*
tawȝte, CA 312; **taght,** SS 797.
telle, *vs.,* (OE **tellan**), (**1**) talk, tell,
relate. B 2966; *pt.,* **tolde,** Hr
467; **talde,** Ly 28254.
(**2**) enumerate, count. Hr 617;
pp., **italde,** Ly 27432.
(**3**) count out (money), pay.
ET 968.
tene, *n.,* (OE **tēona**), (**1**) injury,
sorrow. Sd 2896, Ip 1082, Av
902.

(2) wrath, anger. P 1986, Tr 4724; *as adj.*, angry, P 301, 1972, Ip 2996.

tha, those, then, when; *cf.* **tho.**

thanne, thenne, *adv. and conj.*, (OE þanne), (1) then. Ip 451, Hr 439; **than,** Tr 8608; **thon,** P 2249.

(2) than, than if. Hv 944; **thane,** Hr 13; **thene,** Ly 27450; **then,** B 3027.

(3) when, the time when. CA 330, Sd 2527.

(4) *correlative.* **thanne** . . . **thanne,** then . . . when, Hv 1203.

that, (OE þæt). *Only uses fairly uncommon in Modern English are given:* (1) *rel. adj.*, that which, who, whoever, what. Sd 2489; D 244; that of which, B 3482.

(2) *conj.*, that, so that, in order that. ET 780; **thet,** Ly 28119.

(3) *conj.*, until, when. Av 870, Ly 27746.

(4) because. Hv 161.

(5) *used with other conjunctives; not to be translated:* **whenne that,** when; **yif that,** if; **what that,** what, *etc.* Em 617; *(with enclitic pro.)* **thatow,** that thou, O 452.

thaw3th, thaw3te, taught; *cf.* **teche.**

the, *adj.*, (OE þe), (1) the *(definite article).* Hr 27; **theo,** Al 3946; *n.f.,* **tha,** Ly 28068; *d.f.,* **there,** Ly 27931; *d.m.,* **than,** Ly 27932; *a.f.,* **tha,** Ly 28022; *a.m.,* **thane,** Ly 27628; **thene,** Ly 27506; **then,** Ly 28183; *plu., n. and a.,* **thæ,** Ly 28072; **tha,** Ly 27806; *d.,* **than,** Ly 27490.

(2) *relative pro. (indeclinable),* who, which. **the,** Ly 28169; **tha,** Ly 27613; **thæ,** Ly 27481.

thee, *vs.,* (OE þeon), prosper, thrive. ET 417; **the,** K 2;

then, Sd 1593; **thynne,** K 736; *especially in the oath:* **so mote i thee,** as I hope to prosper, Av 812, Cl 538.

thei, thai, *pro.,* (ON þeir), they. D 65, Hv 414; **the,** Em 202, EG 270; *g.,* **there,** Hv 1350; **thayre,** Av 145; *d. and a.,* **tham,** SS 230; **theim,** K 160; **thaym,** Av 630; *cf.* **he.**

thei, although; *cf.* **thouh.**

thein, thain, *n.,* (OE þegn), thane *(a land-holding freeman, not noble).* Hv 1327; *plu.,* **theines,** Ly 28325; **theinen,** Ly 27510.

thenche, thenke, thinke, *vs.,* (OE þencan, þyncan, *which became confused in Middle English*), (1) think, be mindful of, believe, intend. D 455; *pr. 2 sg., (with enclitic pro.)* **thenkestu,** Hv 578; *pt.,* **thow3te,** CA 250; **tho3te,** Hr 1274; **thoucte,** Hv 691; **thhou3te,** R 25; **thow3th,** Em 227; *pp.,* **thouth,** Hv 312; **ithoht,** Ly 28087; *prp.,* **thinkand,** SS 233.

(2) seem *(impersonal).* Hr 1151; **thenke,** CA 30; *pr.,* **think,** SS 449; *pt.,* **thu3te,** Hr 278; **thouthe,** Hv 1286; **thught,** Tr 4717; **thuhte,** Ly 28297; *pt. sj.,* **thouwte,** D 597.

thenne, *cf.* **thanne,** then, when; *and* **thethin,** thence.

theo, *cf.* **the** *and* **tho.**

there, thore, *adv. and conj.,* (OE þær, þār), (1) there, in that place. Hr 298; **thore,** Av 90; **thar,** Hr 505; **thare,** Av 749; **thær,** Ly 27825.

(2) where, wherever. Hv 142; to the place where, **ther,** Ly 27777; Hr 936.

(3) *comp.,* **ther-at,** thereat, Ip 2996; **ther-as,** where, Em 545; **ther-uore,** for which, Ly 28017;

there-on, in this, Ip 1105; ther-tille, concerning that, Av 518; there-to, in addition, D 596, SS 796, Sd 2193; to or concerning this, B 2952, 3328; therwhile, while, D 156; ther-whiles, while, D 653.

thethen, adv., (OE þeþan, þanan), thence. Hv 2498; thethin, Yw 382; thenne, CA 248; thennes, G 545.

thider, adv. and conj., (OE þider), (1) thither. Hr 699; theder, CA 265; thedur, Ip 3058; thether, Cl 166; thuder, Hr 1424.
(2) to the place from which. thedyr, Ip 411.

thilke, this same, that same; cf. ilk.

thinge, plu., things, creatures. Av 830, Em 333.

this, pro. and adj., (OE þys, þes), this. thes, Hr 804; g.m.sg., theos, Ly 27689; g. and d.f.sg., thissere, Ly 28211; d.m.sg., this-sen, Ly 28189; a.m.sg., thisne, Ly 28145; plu., this, D 655; thes, Tr 50; theos, Ly 27730; theis, P 909; g., theos, Ly 27689; a., thas, Ly 28202.

tho, tha, pro., (OE þā), those. tho, Av 977; tha, TT 183; thoo, P 219; thaa, P 516.

tho, adv. and conj., (OE þā), (1) then, when. Cl 145; thoo, Em 51; thaa, P 497; tha, Ly 28446; theo, Ly 27489.
(2) although. thoo, Ip 1076; cf. thouh.

thonked, 3onked, pt., thanked, D 246, 384.

thore, cf. there.

thou, pro., (OE þu, ge, ēow), thou, you. n. sg., thou, G 145; thu, Hr 91; tu, Hv 2903; tow, O 450; thw, Hv 1316; g., thy, G 142; thine, G 241; thi, Av 268; g.

and d.f., thire, Ly 28104; a., the, G 140; te, O 100; de, Em 450; pl. (used also as polite form of the singular), n. and a., ye, Sd 2478; 3e, G 170; 3o, Av 111; 3aw, Av 106; 3ew, B 2962; eou, Ly 28174; g., yeur, B 2982; 3owre, SS 449; 3oure, Hr 814; 3or, R 50; ou, R 65.

thouh, thei, adv. and conj., (OE þēah, þēh, ON þō), although, though. thou3e, B 3167; thow3e, Ip 1078; thoghe, P 1622; thofe, P 616; thowe, Cl 70; thah, Ly 28543; thei, D 461; thai, D 560; thou, Hv 124; the3, Hr 317; dou3, Lv 204; thau3, Al 4226; thei3, R 412; thogfe, P 1453.

thow3tur, daughter; cf. doughter.

thridde, adj. and pro., (OE þridda), third. D 489, ET 614; thrid, SS 793, Av 1047.

thurgh, thorow, prep. and adv., (OE þurh), through (with senses as in Modern English). Em 332, Tr 8652; thorrowe, EG 340; thurh, B 3502; thro3he, Av 1040; thure3, Hr 875; thorw, Hv 264; thuruth, Hv 52; thoruth, Hv 1065; thoru3, Lv 484; thourgh, D 334; thurght, Tr 8641; thurch, O 534; comp., thorw3out, At 611; thurhout, B 3201.

tide, n., time, hour. Hr 849, Cl 188; d. as adverb, tʰat tyde, then, Ip 1161; this tyde, now, SS 421. Especially in the phrase: in are tiden, once on a time, Ly 27992.

tide, v., betide. pt., tide, Tr 81.

til, prep. and conj., (ON til), (1) to, towards. Hr 938; tille, Sd 1640; tylle, ET 523.
(2) for. til, Hv 761.
(3) until. Hr 124; thyll, Em 502.

tite, adv., (ON tīðr), speedily. Yw 409, Ip 3060; tit, Tr 4758; tytlye, CA 84.

tithande, tidinge, *n.*, (ON tīðindi), news, tidings. Av 748; tithandes, Yw 140; **tydynge,** CA 59; **tithing,** Av 679.

to, (OE tō), **(1)** *adv.*, too. G 398. **(2)** *adv.*, to, towards. Ly 27456; tow, Ip 406.

(3) *prep.*, to. *Examples of senses unusual in Modern English:* te, to, Yw 207; to, during, Ly 28090; to, until, Av 1061; to name, by name, CA 204; to, as, Ly 27546, Hv 575; to, according to, Ly 28437; to, in consideration of, Hv 486.

(4) *conj.*, until. Ip 3146, SS 307.

to, two; *cf.* tweie.

to-. *A prefix, with the force of* "violently" *or* "apart": **tobarst,** burst to pieces, G 537; **tobreste,** Lv 482; **toborsten,** D 1043; **tofallen,** fallen to ruins, Ly 27893; **torent,** torn to pieces, D 353; **togrinde,** grind to pieces, D 85; **todrawe,** torn apart, Lv 606; **tobreke,** broke in two, D 936; **tobrent,** burned up, Al 3982.

tofore, toforn, *adj., adv., and prep.,* former, formerly, before. B 3018, 3684.

to3eines, towards. Ly 28529.

tone, *cf.* one, take.

tosomne, together. Ly 27424.

tothir, todir, *cf.* other.

toune, *n.*, (OE tūn), town. Hv 2911; **tun,** Ly 27918; **tune,** Hr 153.

tour, *n.*, (OF tour), tower. D 871; **tur,** Hr 1453.

toward, *commonly separated in Middle English:* to himward, toward him.

tre, *n.*, (OE trēo), **(1)** wood. Yw 187, Av 1074.

(2) beam, plank. Em 656.

(3) tree. D 72; *plu.,* **treoes,** Al 4074; **trene,** FB 634.

(4) the Cross. ET 387.

treuthe, trowthe, *n.*, (OE trēowð), truth, troth, pledged word. Hr 672, At 155; **trowith**, B 3105; **trauthe,** Av 428; **trowthe,** ET 276; **truthe,** Hr 674.

trone, throne. Em 1.

trowe, *vw.*, (OE trēowian), believe, trust. P 1107; **tro,** Hv 2862; **trowes,** Yw 981; *pt.,* **trowed,** P 586; *imp. sg.,* **trowes,** SS 938; *especially in the phrase:* for to trowe, surely, Ip 3155.

tryste, trust, reliance. ET 553.

tuke, *cf.* take.

tweie, twa, *adj. and pro.*, (OE twā, twegen), two. G 202; **twa,** SS 263; **twei3e,** Ly 28473; **tway,** ET 900; **too,** B 3179; **to,** B 3169; **tow,** EG 491; **toe,** Av 932; **tvo,** O 81.

U

uncouthe, *adj.*, (OE uncūð), strange, unfamiliar, unknown. P 1047; **vncowthe,** Av 618; **vncuthe,** Hr 729; **vncoth,** EG 405.

under3ete, *vs.*, understand, perceive. D 165.

unethe, *adj. and adv.*, (OE unēaðe), **(1)** *adj. as sb.*, discomfort. Ly 27673.

(2) *adv.*, scarcely, with difficulty. onnethe, Sd 3000; **vnnethes,** Yw 372.

unkinde, *adj. and adv.*, (OE uncynde), unnatural. SS 3008; **unkindelike,** Hv 1250.

until, *prep., adv., and conj.*, (OE un + till), to, unto, until. Hv 2913; **hentill,** Av 124.

unto, to, unto, until. Yw 930.

upon, (OE up on), upon. *Only senses unusual in Modern English are:* **(1)** *prep.*, in the course of, during. Hr 1097, Hv 468;

against, Hv 2689; **uppen**, above, Ly 28019.

(**2**) *adv.*, above, from above. Hr 11.

ure, vre, our; *cf.* **I.**

urn, vrn, ran; *cf.* **runne.**

V

venesun, *n.*, (OF veneisun), meat of any game-animal. Av 262; **venesoun**, D 773; **ueneysun**, Hv 1726.

verrament, *adv.*, (OF veraiment), truly. ET 862; **varraiment**, D 11; **veramend**, Cl 189; **werament**, Cl 237; **verement**, Lv 485.

vnsquarut, answered; *cf.* **answer.**

vomen, *cf.* **wimman.**

W

w-. *The following words are spelled in* w- *for* wh-: **wo**, who; **wich**, which; **were**, where; **wan**, when; **wat**, what; **wether**, whether; **wilke, whilk**, which.

wa, wai, walawa, *cf.* **wo.**

wan, *cf.* **when** *and* **winne.**

ware, *adj.*, (OE wær), (**1**) aware, conscious. CA 122, Ip 3130; **warre**, P 881.

(**2**) wary, resourceful. **war**, Av 13, Yw 1241.

wasche, *vs. and vw.*, (OE wascan, wescan), wash. **washen**, Hv 1233; *pt. plu.*, **wasschyd**, Cl 154; **wessh**, Sd 1871; **wyshe**, Em 866; **wesh**, Em 218; **wessche**, D 831; **wisschen**, G 542; **whesshen**, Em 890; *pp.*, **waisschen**, G 439; **wasshen**, K 887.

wat, *cf.* **what** *and* **wite.**

waxe, wexe, *vs.*, (OE weaxan), grow, become. Cl 151; **wex**, B 2940; *pr.*, **wexeth**, CA 158; *pt.*, **wax**, Ip 364; **wexe**, P 212; **waxe**,

ET 400; *pp.*, **woxe**, G 232; **woxen**, Em 950; **wax**, Em 365; **waxen**, Yw 1212.

we, *cf.* **I** *and* **wo.**

wede, *n.*, (OE wæde), garment, clothing, armor. ET 245, SS 799; **weed**, EG 98; *especially in the complimentary rhyme-tag:* **wordy vnthur wede**, worthy under weeds, Em 250.

wei, weilawei, *cf.* **wo.**

wel, welle, *adv.*, (OE wel), (**1**) well, excellently. Hr 484, CA 352.

(**2**) quite, fully; very, very much (*often used as a metrical filler*). Hr 808; **wele**, SS 230; **will**, Cl 127; **vel**, Hr 445.

welde, *vw.*, (OE geweldan), wield, manage, have power over, govern, protect. SS 4274; **walden**, Ly 27652; **awelden**, Ly 27894; *pr. sg.*, **weldythe**, Ip 3138.

wele, wealth, prosperity. *Especially in the phrase:* **yn wo and wele**, in ill and good, Em 573.

wende, *vw.*, (OE wendan), go, turn. Ip 1198; **weynde**, Av 641; *pr. sg.*, **weyndes**, Ip 3102; *pt. sg.*, **wente**, ET 1190; **wende**, Sd 2958; **iwende**, Ly 27619; *pt. plu.*, **wenten**, G 609; **wenden**, Ly 27512; **wenton**, Tr 4716; **wenden**, CA 364; **weynde**, Av 81; *pp.*, **went,** Ip 3076; **iwent**, Hr 440; **wente**, Av 538; *vb.n.*, **wending**, Yw 538; *imp.*, **went**, Hr 325.

wene, *vw.*, (OE wēnan), think, expect, believe. *pr.*, **wene**, Av 756; **ween**, B 3479; (*with enclitic pro.*) **wenestu**, Hv 1787; *pr. as future*, **wene**, Ly 28123; *pt.*, **wende**, D 81; **wente**, CA 67; **wend**, B 3479.

wepe, *vw. and vs.*, (OE wēpan), weep. *pr.*, (*with enclitic pro.*) **wepestu**, Hr 656; *pt. sg.*, **wep**, D

108; **weop,** Hr 69; **wepputte,** Av 280; *plu.,* **wepen,** D 987; *prp.,* **wepeand,** SS 890; **wepende,** D 132.

wepen, wepne, *n.,* (OE **wǣpen**) weapon. Hv 89; *plu.,* **weppun,** Av 609; **weppon,** Tr 4752; **wapynes,** P 20; **iwepnen,** Ly 28388.

wer, were, werre, war, combat. Av 332, Tr 88.

werche, *cf.* **wirche.**

werd, world; *cf.* **werld.**

werk, *n.,* (OE **weorc**), (1) deed, work. Tr 8625, Av 941.

(2) construction, fortification. Hr 1432; **werc,** Ly 27857.

werld, world, *n.,* (OE **weorold,** *etc.*), world. **weorld,** Ly 28131; **werd,** Hv 1290; **worl,** At 136; *g.,* **wordes,** Em 824.

what, (OE **hwæt**), (1) *adj. and pro.;* what, which. **wat,** D 6, Hr 942.

(2) *relative and interrogative pro.;* what, whatever. Hr 765; **wat,** SS 2962; **wæt,** Ly 28385; **hwat,** Hv 596; **qwatt,** Av 962. why, what, D 676, B 2978.

(3) *interjection,* what! lo! **hwat,** Hv 2547.

comp., **what-so,** whatsoever, P 1257.

what, *cf.* **wite.**

whennes, *adv. and conj.,* (OE **hwanan**), whence. **whenns,** Em 418; **whannes,** Hr 161.

when, whan, *adv. and conj.,* (OE **hwanne**), when. **whan,** Cl 49; **whanne,** Hr 915; **quen,** Av 52; **qwen,** Av 424; **hwan,** Hv 408; **wan,** D 629; **wanne,** Hr 913.

where, *adv. and conj.,* (OE **hwǣr, hwār**), where. **whar,** Ly 28057; **quere,** Av 304; **were,** Av 1117; **hwere,** Hv 1083; **hware,** Hv 1881; **war,** Ly 28479; **wer,** D 462.

comp., **whereto,** why, Em 929;

wharesom, wheresoever, SS 2999; **hworeso,** Hv 1349.

where, *cf.* **whether** *and* **be.**

whesshen, washed; *cf.* **wasche.**

whethen, *adv. and conj.,* (ON **hvaðan**), whence. Yw 1044; **quethun,** Av 301.

whether, (OE **hwæðer**), (1) *conj.,* whether, whether or not. **whedur,** Ip 410; **quether,** Av 963; **wher,** B 3034; **hwere,** Hv 549; **wether,** D 862.

(2) *adj. and pro.,* which, whichever. **whether,** G 249; Yw 1002.

(3) *untranslatable expletive, sign of a question.* **whethir,** P 1691; **wher,** G 430; **whethur,** Em 794; **hwor,** Hv 1119; **wether,** Hv 292.

whether, wheder, whither, FB 96.

whi, qui, qwi, hwi, why.

while, (OE **hwīl**), (1) *n.,* space of time. Hr 1317; **hwile,** Hv 722; **quile,** B 3616.

(2) *d. as adv.,* formerly. **whilen,** Ly 28633; **while,** Ly 27979.

(3) *oblique cases as conj.,* while, during the time that. **the while the,** Ly 27652; **tha wile,** Ly 28219; **hwile,** Hv 301; **whils,** B 2969; **whyles,** CA 145; **quille,** Av 286; **qwiles,** Tr 39.

whilk, which, who, P 1979; **wilke,** P 281.

white, *adj.,* (OE **hwīt**), white. **why₃te,** Ip 3095; **whyght,** Ip 3091; **qwyte,** K 365; **quyte,** Av 1090; **whythe,** Em 66; **hwit,** Hv 1729; **with,** Hv 48.

who, *rel. and int. pro.,* (OE **hwa**), who, whoever. D 311; **hwo,** Hv 296; **wo,** D 1053; *d. and a.,* **wham,** Hr 352; **whæm,** Ly 27486; **quo,** Av 108; **ho,** Cl 329.

comp., **wha-swa,** whosoever, Ly 28518; **quo-so,** Av 135.

wife, *n.,* (OE **wīf**), (1) woman.

SS 409.

(2) wife. wif, Hr 553; whif, SS
932; *g.sg.*, whife, SS 2803; wiif,
O 496.

wight, *adj. and adv.*, (ON vīgt),
valiant, powerful, active, quick.
Sd 2077, ET 96; wicth, Hv 344;
with, Hv 1008; wiȝte, Av 15;
wightly, Sd 2682, Tr 4716.

wight, *n.*, (OE wiht), (1) whit,
particle, bit. wicth, Hv 97;
with, Hv 1763, wiȝt, Hr 503, D
776.
(2) person, creature. wiȝte, Hr
671, Av 304; wihȝte, D 97; wyȝth,
Lv 307.

wille, *n.*, (OE willa), pleasure, wish,
will. Hr 288; will, P 843; iwulle,
Av 315; *plu.*, iwillen, Ly 27529;
in wille, desirous, Ip 1183.

wille, *vs.*, (OE willan), will, wish,
desire, be willing. *pr. 1 sg.*,
wille, D 6; wole, Sd 1910; wulle,
Ly 27888; woll, Em 248; *2*, wolt,
G 182; *(with enclitic pro.)* wiltu,
Hv 681; wilte, Hv 528; *3*, wile,
Hr 811; wulle, Av 523; wol, B
2961; wole, Sd 1906; *pr. plu.*,
wille, D 742; wulleȝ, Hr 603;
wol, B 3423; wele, Sd 2633; *pt.*,
wolde, Hv 367; wald, SS 262;
weolde, Ly 28390; wolden, D 57;
pr. sj., wile, D 714. *Negative
forms compounded with* ne: *pr.*,
nel, D 525; nulleth, Ly 28130;
nyl, B 3110; null, Hr 1144; nyll,
Av 1060; *pt.*, nolde, D 194;
nold, O 138; nulde, Ly 28002;
nalden, Ly 27732.

wimman, woman, *n.*, (OE wīfman),
woman. wimman, Hv 1720;
vomman, B 3204; wommon, Em
245; *plu.*, wymmanne, Hr 67;
wemen, Av 559; vommen, B 3205;
g. plu., wimmonne, Ly 28459;
wimmonnen, Ly 28035.

winde, *vs.*, (OE windan), go, turn,

roll. Ip 411, Av 72; *pt. sg.*, wond,
Ly 28049; *plu.*, wunden, Ly
27785.

winne, *n.*, (OE wynn), joy. TT
45, ET 840; wunne, Ly 28621.

winne, *vs.*, (OE winnan), (1) attain,
win, conquer. Hr 1357; wen,
Ip 1129; wyn, B 3255; *pt. sg.*,
wan, TT 181; wonn, P 1735;
wann, Ip 1099; *pt. plu.*, wonen,
Tr 4780; *pp.*, wonnen, CA 170;
wonen, Tr 8607; wonun, Av 542;
woon, EG 684; ywon, O 559.
(2) make one's way, go, get up.
Sd 2969; wyn, P 2199; *pt. sg.*,
wan, Av 210; wane, P 1270;
wann, Ip 3175; *pt. plu.*, wan,
ET 242; wonnen, Tr 4751;
wonyn, Tr 4761.

wirche, *vw.*, (OE wyrcan), (1) do,
work, perform. werch, Cl 164;
wirke, P 1718; worch, B 3342;
worche, G 500; *pr. plu.*, wurchun,
Av 939; *pp.*, iwrouȝt, B 3009;
wrouth, Hv 1352.
(2) cause, make, build, create.
wurchen, Ly 27856; werke, CA
78; wirchen, Hv 510; *pt.*, wrowȝte,
CA 119; wroghte, P 284; *pp.*,
wroght, ET 312; rought, EG 559;
iwrout, D 607; wrouth, Lv 265.
In the phrase: syn he was man
wrowȝt, since he was born, Cl
213.

wise, *adj. and adv.*, (OE wīs), wise,
sage. Hr 989; wyce, Ip 348;
whise, SS 2799; *sup.*, wiseste;
cp. adv., wyselyer, more wisely,
TT 137.

wise, *n.*, (OE wīse), manner, means,
way. Yw 1073, Hr 360; *d. sg.*,
wisen, Ly 27835.

wisse, *vw.*, (OE wissian), direct,
guide, advise. Hv 104, At 661;
wise, D 267; *pr. sg.*, wys, Yw
1046; *imp.*, wysshe, Tr 4.

wite, *vs.*, (OE witan *and* wītan; *the*

forms become confused in Middle English), (**1**) know, learn. Lv 653; **wit,** SS 3040; **iwite,** D 201; **witte,** Ip 1172; **wete,** B 3544; **witen,** Hr 288; *pr. plu.*, **wetith,** B 3539; **wite,** Hv 2808; **witen,** Hv 2208; *pt. with the force of pr.*, **wott,** Ip 1073; **wate,** At 108; **woot,** B 3116; **wost,** Hv 527; **wot,** D 84; **watte,** Ip 1112; *as future,* **watte,** Ip 435; *pt.*, **wot,** D 78; **what,** Ly 28088; **wiste,** Tr 23; **wisste,** CA 35; **wuste,** Ly 28298; *pp.*, **wist,** EG 751; *imp. sg. and plu.*, **witte,** Av 327; CA 195; *pt. sj.*, **wyst,** TT 189. *Negative forms compounded with ne; pr.*, **note,** B 3049; **not,** D 254; *pt.*, **nist,** D 69; **nuste,** Ly 27604.

(**2**) guard, guard against, decree. **wite,** CA 136; *imp.*, **wite,** Hv 1316, Ly 28604.

with, *prep.*, (OE wiδ), with. **wiჳ,** D 44. *Senses unusual in Modern English are:* (**1**) against. Ly 27581, Hr 830.

(**2**) by. P 836, Tr 53.

(**3**) *in the phrase:* with wronge, unjustly. Hr 905.

(**4**) *comp.*, **with-thi,** if, on condition, P 584; **with-than,** provided that, Hv 532.

with, *cf.* **wight,** courageous; white; and **wight,** person, particle.

withoute, *prep. and adv.*, (OE wiδūtan), (**1**) without, lacking. **withute,** Hr 188; **withouten,** Ip 375; **withowtun,** Av 10; **wiჳouten,** D 320.

(**2**) except. **withuten,** Hv 425.

(**3**) outside, outside of. **withoute,** Av 1095; **withouten,** SS 366.

(**4**) *in the following rhyme-tags meaning* "surely": **withouten les,** without lies; **withouten wene,** beyond doubt; **withouten faile,** without fail; **withouten let(ting),** without hindrance; **withouten drede,** beyond doubt; **withouten othe,** beyond the necessity of taking oath.

witterly, *adv.*, (ON vitrliga), surely. At 80; **witturly,** Av 86; **weterly,** SS 4255; **wyttyrly,** ET 1069.

wo, wa, wei, *adj., n., and interj.*, (OE wā, wēa; ON vei), (**1**) alas, woe, sorrow. **wa,** Yw 432; **way,** O 232; **wo,** Hr 115; **woo,** Tr 8592; **we,** Ip 1118; **wæ,** Ly 28329; **wowჳ,** Al 4026.

(**2**) sad, sorrowful, wretched. **wa,** SS 2850; **woo,** Em 324; **At** 81.

(**3**) *comp.*, **walawai,** alas! woe is me! Hr 956; **walawa,** Ly 27532; **wale,** Ly 28092; **wellaway,** EG 748; **weilawei,** Hv 462.

wod, *adj.*, (OE wōd), (**1**) mad, insane. Lv 470; **wood,** At 250; **woode,** EG 986.

(**2**) fierce, raging. **wode,** Ly 27895, ET 108.

wode, *n.*, (OE wudu), (**1**) wood, fuel. Hv 940.

(**2**) a wood, woods. **wude,** Hr 361; **wode,** D 59.

wolde, *cf.* **wille.**

won, *n. and adj.*, (OE gewuna), (**1**) accustomed. SS 230; **wone,** Hv 2151.

(**2**) dwelling, place. **woon,** ET 459; **wone,** At 238; **won,** Tr 4780; **wane,** P 1347.

won, *n.*, (OE wēn, ON vān), plenty, quantity. Sd 2093; **woon,** Sd 2478; **wane,** SS 265. *Especially in the phrases:* ful god wone, plenty, plentiful, plentifully, G 125; Hv 1024; well good won, repeatedly, Lv 360.

wonder, wunder, *n.*, (OE wundor), (**1**) marvel, wonderful or terrible occurrence. Hr 1247.

(2) *as adj.*, strange, wonderful. Yw 267; **wondir**, Sd 1697.
(3) *as adv.*, very, wonderfully. ET 162; **wondir**, B 3017; **wonthere**, Lv 511.
wone, *vw.*, (OW **wunian**), (1) dwell, inhabit. P 165; **wune**, Hr 731; **wunien**, Ly 28620; *pr.*, **wonnes**, P 1769; **wuneth**, Ly 28101; *pt. sg.*, **wond**, SS 288; **wonede**, Hr 917; **wunede**, Ly 27947; (*by nunnation*) **wuneden**, Ly 27959; *prp.*, **wonnande**, P 2138; *prp. as noun.*, **wonnyng**, dwelling, ET 1223; **woniyng**, D 223.
(2) be accustomed. *pp.*, **woned**, Hr 34; **wonte**, Cl 112.
(3) delay, remain. At 716; *pp.*, **woned**, Yw 212.
worche, **wurche**, **wroʒte**, *cf.* **wirche**.
word, *n.*, (OE **word**), word, fame, report. **weorde**, Ly 28535; *plu.*, **word**, Ly 28202; **worden**, Ly 28461; **wurdus**, Av 441; **worthes**, CA 32.
word, world; *cf.* **werld**.
worschip, *vw. and n.*, honor, praise. ET 840, EG 456.
worthe, *vs.*, (OE **weorðan**, **wyrðan**), be, become (*often as auxiliary for passive*). G 491; *pr. as future*, **worst**, O 168; **wurth**, Hr 684; **wurthest**, Ly 28452; (*with enclitic pro.*) **wurstu**, Hr 324; **worht**, D 115; *pt.*, **wurthen**, Ly 27468; **iwurthen**, Ly 27520; *pp.*, **iwurthen**, Ly 28207; *sj.*, *especially in the exclamations and oaths:* **worthe them woo!** woe be to them, ET 760; **særi wurthe his saule!** wretched be his soul, Ly 28333; **wo worth dedes wronge!** woe come to wrong deeds, Em 648.
wrathe, *vw.*, (OE **gewrāðian**), grow angry, make angry, vex. **wraththe**, G 80; **wreth**, Yw 995; *pr.*, **wrathis**, Av 906; *pt.*, **wraththed**,

G 91; **iwrathede**, Ly 27698; *pp. as adj.*, **wroʒt**, Lv 700.
wrathe, wrath; *d. sg.*, (*by nunnation*) **wraththen**, Ly 27773; **wreththe**, Lv 470.
wreie, *vw.*, (OE **wrēgan**), betray. *pr.*, **wrye**, K 389; *pt.*, **wryed**, K 976; *pr. sj.*, **wrye**, ET 527.
wreke, *vs.*, (OE **wrecan**), avenge. D 913, Yw 587; **wreche**, Hr 1284; **awreken**, Ly 28112; **wrecke**, EG 673; *pr.*, **wreke**, Ly 27612; *pt.*, **wrak**, G 303; *pp.*, **wreke**, G 346; **iwroken**, G 541; **awræken**, Ly 28221; **wrocken**, EG 137; **awreke**, Lv 706; **wrokyn**, K 844.
writ, *n.*, (OE **writ**), writing, letter. Hr 930; *plu.*, **writes**, Hv 2275; **writen**, Ly 27480.
write, *vs.*, write. *pp.*, **wryte**, FB 213; **ywrete**, FB 132.
wrong. *Especially in the phrase:* **with wronge**, unjustly, wrongfully.
wroth, *adj. and adv.*, (OE **wrāð**), angry. B 2940; **wroʒth**, Lv 450; **wroʒt**, Lv 700; **wrothe**, Hr 348; **wroth**, EG 719; *sup.*, **wrathest**, Ly 28503.
wunde, *n.*, (OE **wund**), wound. Hr 640; **wonde**, SS 2992; *plu.*, **wowundes**, Av 44; **woundeʒ**, P 151; *g.*, **wunden**, Ly 28579.
wunien, **wunede**, dwell, dwelt; *cf.* **wone**.

Y

yare, *adj. and adv.*, (OE **gearu**, **geare**, **gearwe**), ready, fast, quick. Sd 1720; **ʒare**, P 1537; **ʒaru**, Ly 28397; **ʒarewe**, Ly 28224.
ye, **ya**, *adv.*, (OE **gēa**, ON **jā**), yes (*usually confirmatory; cf.* **yis**). Hr 100; **ʒe**, CA 302; **ya**, Hv 2607; **ʒoe**, Av 378; **ʒa**, SS 566; **ʒoo**, Em 888.

yede, yode, *v. defective,* (OE ēode),
went (*in preterit only; cf.* go).
sg., 3eode, Hr 381; yede, Ip 3025;
3ode, ET 620; youde, Ip 456;
eode, Ly 27805; (*by nunnation*)
eoden, Ly 27961; *plu.,* 3eeden,
G 510; 3ode, Av 421; yeede, EG
280; 3ede, TT 56.

yeftes, yiftes, gifts. Cl 50.

yelde, *vs.,* (OE geldan), (**1**) yield,
give up. Hv 2712; 3ild, Av
1058; 3ulde, Al 4149; 3ylde, ET
1126; *pr. sg.,* 3eldeth, CA 335;
eldythe, Ip 3137; *pt.,* yald, Tr
8660; 3olde, P 2104.
(**2**) repay, requite. 3elde, CA
336; *pt.,* 3ald, Lv 420; *pp.,*
i3olde, Hr 460.

yeme, *vw.,* (OE gēman), govern,
guard, protect. SS 789; *pr.,*
3eme3, D 151; *pt.,* yemede, G
267; *pp.,* yemed, Hv 305; *prp.,*
3emande, P 1136.

yen, eyes; *cf.* eie.

yere, *n.,* (OE gēar), year. 3er,
D 103; *plu.,* 3er, Em 733; 3ere,
P 228; 3eris, B 3177.

yerne, yorne, *adv.,* (OE georne),
(**1**) eagerly, earnestly, violently.
3erne, Hr 1085; 3orne, ET 449.
(**2**) speedily. 3erne, D 82.

yerne, *vw.,* (OE gyrnan), yearn for,
desire. 3erne, Hr 915; 3irnen,
Ly 27886; *pr.,* 3ernes, Yw 1242;
pt., 3irnden, Ly 27969.

yet, *adv.,* (OE giet, gyt, *etc.*), yet,
nevertheless. 3ete, D 541; 3et,
G 272; 3it, B 2961; 3ute, Hr 70;
3ette, Av 347; 3yt, ET 81; 3hit,
D 187.

yeue, yaf, *cf.* giue.

yghen, y3en, eyes; *cf.* eie.

yif, *cf.* if and giue.

yis, *adv.,* (OE gise), yes (*usually
contradictory; cf.* ye). 3is, SS
2973; 3ys, CA 309; 3isse, Av
589.

yon, yond, *adj., adv., and prep.,*
(OE geon, geond), (**1**) yonder.
3one, P 330, Av 120; **yound,** Ip
445; younde, Ip 3178.
(**2**) through, throughout. 3eond,
Ly 27470.

yong, ying, *adj. and sb.,* (OE geong,
iung), young. 3ong, B 3235;
3ing, SS 2846; yenge, Cl 517;
3eonge, Ly 28001; yongh, Lv 186.

yore, yare, *adv.,* (OE gēara), (**1**)
long ago. 3ore, D 882; 3are,
Hr 1356.
(**2**) for a long time. 3ore, O 557.

you, 3owre, ye, *cf.* thou.